THE WRITING ON THE WALL

THE WRITING ON THE WALL

Britain in the Seventies

Phillip Whitehead

MICHAEL JOSEPH
in association with Channel Four Television Company Ltd

First published in Great Britain by Michael Joseph Limited
44 Bedford Square, London WC1
1985

© Brook Productions Limited 1985

British Library Cataloguing in Publication Data

Whitehead, Phillip
The writing on the wall: Britain in the
seventies.
1. Great Britain – Politics and government –
1966–1981   2. Great Britain – Politics and
government – 1966–1981
I. Title
320.941   JN231

ISBN 0 7181 2471 5

The lines from Philip Larkin's poem
'Going, Going' on page 243 are reproduced
by permission of Faber and Faber Ltd

Typeset by Rowland Phototypesetting Limited
Bury St Edmunds, Suffolk
Printed and bound in Great Britain by
Billings and Son Limited, Worcester

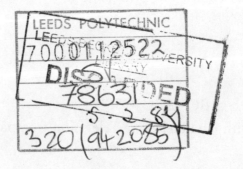

In memory of
Ian Weinberg
1937–69

Scholar of Exeter College, Oxford
Professor of Sociology, University of Toronto

Contents

LIST OF ILLUSTRATIONS

CBI leaders arrive in Downing Street to talk with incoming Prime Minister Wilson. *(Central Press)*
Enoch Powell campaigns on an anti-market platform. *(Popperfoto)*
Helmut Schmidt pleads with the Labour party conference to keep Britain in the Common Market, November 1974. *(Central Press)*
Cartoon by Jak
Margaret Thatcher helps to clear up after a Conservative rally in 1973. *(Keystone)*
A streaker at Twickenham. *(Daily Mirror)*
Cartoon by Garland

Between pages 222 and 223:
Harold Wilson ennobles his secretary after the row about land re-clamation. *(Private Eye)*
Keith Joseph sees his leadership bid collapse after an unwise speech in Birmingham. *(Private Eye)*
Cartoon by Garland
Energy Secretary Tony Benn in 1976. *(Camera Press)*
Denis Healey tells the Labour Party conference that Britain must negotiate with the IMF. *(Keystone)*
A powerful slogan for the SNP. *(Camera Press)*
Malcolm Muggeridge addresses 80,000 demonstrators at an anti-abortion rally in Hyde Park. *(Keystone)*
Women say no to the Corrie Anti-abortion Bill in 1979. *(Network)*
The Queen with her husband, four children, Princess Margaret, Captain Mark Phillips and Lord Mountbatten on the balcony of Buckingham Palace. *(Keystone)*
Jubilee street party, Whitechapel. *(Keystone)*
Graffiti comments on sexist advertisements, 1979. *(Jill Posener)*
James Callaghan puts his balancing skills to good use in the skateboard craze of 1977. *(Press Association)*

Between pages 318 and 319:
Lewisham teenagers in 1979. *(Camera Press)*
Police defend National Front marchers against counter-demonstrators in Lewisham, 1979. *(Camera Press)*
The winter of discontent: the strike by refuse collectors. *(Keystone)*

INTRODUCTION AND ACKNOWLEDGEMENTS

This book has its origins in the idea for a television series first proposed in 1981, provoked by the state of British politics at that time. We had come through a decade of gloom and fitful despair. The pattern of the seventies had become one of pessimism, with concern on the right about fallen standards, on the left about betrayed ideals. The economic background was of retrenchment, comparative failure and perceived decline. In that year of party upheaval, urban riot and hunger strikes, the United Kingdom appeared bitterly polarised. Fifteen years earlier Labour had won such a convincing electoral victory that it had seemed established for a generation as an agent for political change. Now it was split, while its trade union allies, so recently in possession of both power and responsibility, were treated with cold disdain by a government which offered them neither. That government, the product of what one of its wittier dissidents called 'the longest hijack in history', was the testament to a real shift in Conservative views both of what Westminster could do and what previous Tory administrations had done. Many still invoked Disraeli and Churchill; few praised Edward Heath. There were no U-turns on this highway, even when the crash barriers came in sight. It was one of the most determined governments Britain has had this century, and it set out to change the whole political agenda. The beneficiaries of the new polarity, the Manicheism of both Margaret Thatcher on the one hand and Tony Benn on the other, then appeared to be the Liberal Party, which had been slowly hauling itself away from the bottom rung of the political ladder and now found others — the breakaway Social Democrats — on the same rung, though whether to push them up or shove them sideways was not clear.

To understand how British politics developed in this way needed at least a fifteen-year perspective. I was encouraged to think in terms of the seventies alone; television is enamoured of the neatly packaged decade. But what we think of as the politics of the seventies began in the sixties, in the opportunity and the failure of 1966, and its climax came in 1981. The road to 1981, in some respects, began still further back. The signs were there to read. But in that dark defile from 1966, when three successive administrations found themselves ambushed by events, it became possible to count the reasons as well as the bodies. Britain drew in upon itself. Whereas a Labour Prime Minister had proclaimed that 'our frontier is on the Himalayas', many of the British were uneasy when they turned back to Europe, less sure than Edward Heath was that Brussels could be the new frontier. It was entirely possible that the United Kingdom itself might break up, with the line of the Cheviots marking a separate Scotland, and the six counties of Northern Ireland going their own way, under whichever of their two rival nationalisms prevailed. The latter possibility remained in 1981 as the IRA, having failed to move London by destruction of life and property, employed their ultimate weapon by destroying themselves for political reincarnation. I have tried to concentrate the terrible onrush of events in Northern Ireland largely in one chapter and a 1981 postscript, because this painful dilemma of the two Irelands and their unreconciled priorities stands set in its own time sequence, apart from the main.

In the sixties there had been a raffish optimism, a feeling that things were on an upswing of talent and opportunity, if only everyone over forty would somehow get out of the way. From that came gains and transformations, as the young generation of the sixties moved into their early middle age; less deference to authority, greater freedom of sexual preference, a radicalisation of politics which made the torpid majority aware of the problems – if unwilling to concede the solutions. In a book which has drawn heavily on sources in national politics, the movements which sprang from these changes, involving groups which have even now barely broken into the conventional white male middle-class domination of politics, have been covered in less detail than they deserve. But the impact of such movements in the seventies can be measured by their tenacious continuance in the eighties, even under a government which has made the majority on the sunny side of the threshold of disadvantage its main concern.

As dictated by the length and the shape of the television series, there are areas which have been excluded. The series and the book cover the broad sweep of British domestic politics; foreign affairs, with the exception of entry into Europe, are not included. (Through the vicissitudes of the European Commission and the eccentricities of the Common Agricultural Policy, membership of the Common Market became a domestic concern – affecting issues from the colour and shape of our fields to the balance and direction of our trade.) Thus there is no mention except in passing of our general foreign policy, from the posturing of the sixties through the real if limited detente of the seventies, from the four-power agreement on Berlin to the Helsinki accords of 1975. Nor is there space for our patchy post-colonial record, the sad betrayal of the Greek Cypriots and the endless fumbled attempts to settle, or at least escape from, the Rhodesian imbroglio.

We have tried to explain the flow of politics in these fifteen years, 1966–81, up to the watershed when Margaret Thatcher successfully purged the 'wets', and the mutual antipathies of the Labour left and the breakaway Social Democrats fragmented the opposition. Consensual politics – the two-party system in which each party tried to keep a purchase on half the available political ground by remaining a large internal coalition – seemed then to be at a discount. Today, the new style of 'conviction politics' associated with Thatcher and Benn seems to be past the crest of the wave, but for the period examined here it had the unique advantage that it had not been tried before, while everything else had, in the days of crisis avoidance. The seventies will be remembered for their reactive pessimism as well as for their sharper conflicts, and to this the new style of politics seemed an antidote. But the travails of Wilson, Heath and Callaghan, whose administrations now seem more of a continuum than partisan rhetoric would then have admitted, have to be set against the knowledge and power they actually had at the time. We can all be wise after the event about the oil crisis, or resolute when not looking down the barrel of the IMF gun. Most of the men and women whose stories are told here hoped to do the state some service. Most of them ended in failure and frustration. The advantage of even limited hindsight is that the failures, as well as the triumphs, can be seen to be relative.

As MP for Derby North for eleven of the fifteen years described in this book, I watched all four Prime Ministers and their administrations from the backbenches. The democratic politician should aspire to resemble Günter Grass's description of Willy Brandt:[1]

'. . . a man who in the course of his rise has collected defeats at every turn, bundled them up and carried them with him. (But even after victories, which were never more than partial victories, he was never willing to unload, to drop ballast.)'

This book has its share of partial victories as well as its burden of defeats. They speak for themselves. I am a member of the Labour Party, and it would be disingenuous to claim detachment about the period, though some of my friends may claim that such detachment as this book achieves is a fault and not a virtue. Like the television series on which it has drawn, it is an attempt to marshal the evidence, in the accounts of the principal witnesses, as dispassionately as possible. It is their story not mine. That can wait, for a lighter hour.

Many people helped in the making of the television series *The Writing on the Wall*. At Channel 4 I had the wise counsel of Jeremy Isaacs, himself without peer in this kind of television history, and his commissioning editor Carol Haslam. At Brook Productions, a small company living dangerously as all who are dependent on their last contract from Channel 4 must do, I benefited greatly from the help of my colleagues David Elstein, Udi Eichler and Anne Lapping. The series itself was fortunate to have the advice of a number of busy people, who found more time in crowded lives to be our consultants. I would like to thank especially our principal advisers, Dr Bernard (now Lord) Donoughue, and Dr Keith Middlemas. They led a number of spirited discussions before production began with our panel of consultants, the latter being Professor Stuart Hall, Sarah Hogg, Sir John Hoskyns, Peter Kellner, David Lipsey and Professor Robert Skidelsky. The programme team sat at their feet, and occasionally trod on them, in the getting of wisdom. Any failures of interpretation are our fault not that of the consultants, and mine most of all. I owe a particular debt of gratitude to the production team, who proved that small is bountiful, if not always beautiful, in their output over a short time span. Robert Kee wrote and delivered a deft and elegant commentary, to remind me once again that good words need the spaces in between if they are to have force and clarity. Professor Adrian Thomas found a modern guise for an old folk song of hard times for our title music. Morag Buchan, Christopher Cook, Tony Daniels, Cate Haste, Rosaleen Hughes, Jean Kerr, John Kerry, Jeremy Mayhew, Hamish Robertson, Ben Shephard and Mark Wakefield all worked desperately hard in difficult conditions. We were also helped when we needed reinforcements by Elly Beintema, Vivienne Hurley and Roger Miles.

In the same year the directors and researchers added to their burden by preparing drafts of some of the chapters of this book. I am grateful in this regard to Cate Haste for work on chapters 1, 2, and 15; Rosaleen Hughes for chapters 6, 7, 8, 11, 15, and 18; Jeremy Mayhew for chapters 3, 4, 5, 9, 17 and 19; Ben Shephard for parts of chapters 3 and 4; and Mark Wakefield for chapters 12, 13, 18 and parts of 4 and 14. Again, all errors and failures of interpretation are mine. A book of twenty chapters is a vastly different undertaking from a television series of seven programmes. The method we have followed is to let those who spoke to us on the record speak for themselves, as far as possible, in this account. Such contributions are reproduced, without other attribution, as they were made during the interviews for the series. Shaping all this into a book called for a combination of professional scrutiny and saintly patience which I had not thought common in publishing – or anywhere else. I am particularly grateful to Sarah Jane Evans for her help and comments on the manuscript, to Anne McDermid of Curtis Brown, and to Henrietta Heald of Michael Joseph, who turned endurance into an art form as she watched me burst through one deadline after another.

Thanks are due to the large number of people who gave up their time to talk to us and to be interviewed, on or off the record. I list them alphabetically on pages 423–5, with a mention also for a number of other individuals who were prepared to help us, but did not want acknowledgement.

It remains to record a personal debt. I am grateful to the many people both in London and Derbyshire who have borne with my outbursts and absences in the months during which this book was written. They know the cost. I hope the finished work makes it understandable, perhaps even worthwhile. I owe my family a special appreciation for their help. My children believed that their long run as political orphans was over when I was defeated at the 1983 election and came home o'nights. My wife thought that in future we would hear the chimes of midnight together. The cottage industry I brought home was not what they expected. So, many thanks to them: to Joshua on the photocopier, Robert at the printer, and Lucy, who set the alarm. And to my wife Christine, who heard it go off, and bore the chimes at 3.00 a.m. with fortitude.

PHILLIP WHITEHEAD
August 1985

THE END OF SOME ILLUSIONS

On 16 June 1970 Prime Minister Harold Wilson's motorcade pulled into Oldham on the last stage of his election tour. A breathless television commentator recorded for posterity that Wilson was 'supremely confident that he would pull off a hat-trick of victories'. He had every reason to be. Four days earlier, the NOP poll had put Labour 12% ahead. When given the figures in Manchester, the harassed opposition leader, Edward Heath, had turned away like a wounded animal. Marplan on the eve of poll was to show a Labour lead of 8%. Almost every political commentator echoed the television reporter: it would be three in a row. The bookies thought the same: Ladbrokes made Labour 12 to 1 on to win; they had stopped taking bets. For a few hot days in June the troubles of the past few years, as one Labour illusion after another had been shed, seemed to have faded into a different universe. But in those closing days of the campaign, support was moving away from Wilson – not because a change of goalkeepers had cost England a semi-final place in the World Cup, nor because of a temporary break in the weather. In the end, there were just not enough voters prepared to keep him in Downing Street. What Wilson called the 'natural party of government' had moved well across the political spectrum, pushing the Conservatives before it into a territory on the right that had been vacant for twenty-five years. Now Labour was isolated. Its supporters stayed at home.

Six years earlier, it had all been so different. Harold Wilson had come into office with a narrow majority but a boundless opportunity – to provide an alternative government in the tradition of European social democracy, committed to planning for economic growth and the equitable division of the social product in a welfare society. Britain had paid a high price for winning the war in ancient practices and ossified institutions. The whole ethos of the sixties, in which 'classless' was the favourite adjective, and a young population thrilled to the cult of the new, was one to which Wilson could adapt. The new Prime Minister's PPS, Peter Shore, remembers his phenomenal capacity for work, and his style:

'What Harold Wilson offered was not just an image but to some extent also the reality of a modern man, a competent man – none of the old Labour business of lumbering along . . . There was no touch of the carthorse about him. He was on the move. He knew what the modern world was all about.'

Wilson's bustling style was a deliberate contrast to the gentlemanly amateurism of his predecessor in the premiership, Sir Alec Douglas-Home. The message of socialism was transmuted into that of modernity, the class war into the replacement of an incompetent elite by technologists in white coats. Wilson first articulated this theme, around which a divided party was happy to unite, in 1963 during his first conference speech as party leader, in Scarborough:

'If we try to abstract from the automotive age, the only result will be that Britain will become a stagnant backwater, pitied and held in contempt by the rest of the world. The danger, as things are, is that an unregulated private-enterprise economy in this country will promote just enough automation to create serious unemployment but not enough to create a breakthrough in the production barrier . . . Only if technological progress becomes part of our national planning can that progress be directed to national ends.'

These words spoke of the white heat of the technological revolution, and Wilson was later to be mocked for them. He was desperately serious. Tony Benn, then the youthful Ganymede of the Ministry of Posts and Telecommunications, acknowledges the importance of Wilson's Scarborough speech, despite the two men's later differences:

'He was saying that rapid technological change will destroy people's lives unless there is planning. He was not saying he would go round with a blow-lamp, as it were, building a new society.'

Wilson placed the responsibility for planning in the hands of his deputy leader, George Brown. The mercurial Brown, whose intellectual freshness was coupled to an unstable temperament, set up the Department of Economic Affairs (DEA), which was intended 'to relegate the Treasury to the role of bookkeeper', and take over the long-term strategy for the planned growth of the British economy. The response was predictable, as Lord Kearton* remembers:

'The Treasury was not amused, and to put it mildly the Treasury

---

* Frank Kearton was the first director of the Industrial Reorganisation Corporation, established in 1966.

was not exactly disposed to accept the new DEA as an equal, let alone as a rival, let alone as a superior . . . Their attitude was one of gentle mockery and derision, sometimes not so gentle.'

Nonetheless Brown soon appeared in public flourishing a joint Declaration of Intent, signed by both employers' and union representatives, for a voluntary accord on prices, productivity and incomes. The first element of his new strategy, the precursor of the 1965 Prices and Incomes Board, was in place. 'Here on one sheet of paper,' he declaimed, 'are stated the aims of a modern society which has put the class war behind it.'

Elsewhere, however, the class war was being continued by other means. As soon as it became clear that the new Chancellor, James Callaghan, would raise pensions and sickness benefits in his first budget, to be paid for by tax increases, the Wilson government faced a sterling crisis. On coming into office, Labour had inherited a balance of payments deficit at the then unprecedented level of £800 million. The leading professional economist in the government, Tony Crosland, who was Brown's junior at the DEA, favoured an immediate devaluation of the pound to restore Britain's competitive position. So did the economic advisers Nicholas Kaldor and Robert Neild. If it were done swiftly, the outgoing Tories could be blamed. Wilson would have none of it. 'You're talking nonsense,' he told his cabinet colleague Richard Crossman, who raised the matter.[1] 'Devaluation would sweep us away. We would have to go to the country defeated. We can't have it. No, I have my lines of Torres Vedras which I am retreating to . . .' The retreat was a long one. Unlike the Duke of Wellington, having got to his Torres Vedras, Wilson had to try to maintain permanent residence there. The temporary case against devaluation – that Labour had a precarious majority, that import surcharges and an effective prices and incomes policy might restore Britain's competitive position and allow a breakout from 'stop-go' economic policies – became a permanent one. Wilson saw sterling, says his Defence Secretary Denis Healey, 'as a sort of virility symbol; if sterling went, you had somehow failed the exam'.

In the Prime Minister's mind the position of sterling was linked with Britain's influence abroad. He assured the doubters that he had not come into office to preside over the destruction of Britain's world role. To a glittering City audience at the Mansion House in November 1964 the white-tied Labour leader proclaimed:

'. . . our faith but also our determination to keep sterling strong and to see it riding high. It is basic to all our plans for preserving values at home . . . and for all we hope to do in world affairs.'

He went on to make a sweeping claim: 'If there is one nation which cannot afford to chalk on the wall "World Go Home" it is Britain. We are a world power and a world influence or we are nothing.'

So Britain's grossly overextended and costly foreign commitments remained – although some defence projects, the TSR2 aircraft and a fifth Polaris submarine, were cancelled. Britain kept its bomb, increased its reliance on American defence hardware, and stayed on East of Suez, sharing there the burden of the United States, now totally enmeshed in the conflict in Vietnam. American support for sterling was a quid pro quo for the British government's remaining in line. As long as this posture was maintained, President Johnson was happy to tell the visiting Wilson, in the slogan of a short-lived publicity stunt of the time, 'I'm backing Britain'. The cost of backing *him*, in widespread disillusion within the Labour Party, would be counted later.

For eighteen months the Labour government survived precariously, and with some skill. It had achievements to its credit: the repeal of the hated Rent Act to give greater security to the tenant, and a modest Race Relations Act to tackle overt discrimination against coloured immigrants. Obvious signs of weakness at home and abroad were shrugged off. The attempt to renationalise steel was foiled by two right-wing Labour MPs. The Rhodesian UDI left the government talking tough – planes sent to Zambia, progressively tightened sanctions to bring about the end of the rebellion in 'weeks not months' – but doing little. The sanctions flopped. The planes could not take to the air without clearance from ground control in Salisbury. Wilson came through it all with remarkable ease. He was new, and he was news, on the national scene. His flair for stunts distracted the public. His mastery of the House of Commons delighted his backbenchers. The opposition were preoccupied by the election and installation of a successor to the hapless Douglas-Home, who had taken early hints after the election defeat that he should stand down. Edward Heath's approach, dogged, factual, made no early impression on the Prime Minister's standing.

The election of 1966 was no contest, therefore. Everything favoured Labour when Wilson timed his fresh appeal to the country in March, to win an overall majority. A paper edifice of proposals was erected, built upon the 'National Plan', which had been unveiled by George Brown's DEA in September 1965. This list of objectives outlined the planned growth of the economy at 3.8% per annum, and the improved export performance which was to follow greater competitiveness and efficiency. It was assumed that the voluntary cooperation between unions and employers in prices and incomes restraint would continue. In fact, the Plan itself had been thrown together as part of the election preparations. Both sides of industry had deep reservations about it. A last-minute dash up the motorway by Brown to meet doubting industrialists over Frank Kearton's dinner table secured their assent. The unions welcomed the benefits but not the costs of the proposals. Frank Cousins, the TGWU General Secretary who then sat somewhat unhappily in the cabinet as Minister of Technology, warned Brown that the unions would not accept the 3% pay norm laid down by the new Prices and Incomes Board. 'The trade unions really hate your policy,' Crossman records him saying in cabinet.[2] 'I myself disagree with it so utterly that I can no longer make a political speech.' The policy was not statutory, although the government tried to persuade the TUC to accept a statutory early-warning system.

The cabinet accepted the National Plan with what Barbara Castle describes as 'perfunctory' critical comment. What they would do with it if the balance of payments went further into deficit, or the prices and incomes policy broke down, was left for the morrow. The Plan stood well with the election pledges unveiled for the spring of 1966: 500,000 houses to be built each year, an Industrial Reorganisation Corporation to finance mergers and new investment, increased spending on education and the arts, a Parliamentary Commissioner (the name of the Scandinavian model – the Ombudsman – has stuck). The emphasis was on a remodelled capitalism. The renationalistion of steel, in the context of improved planning, was all that remained of socialism's designs on the commanding heights of the economy. Wilson won the election with the most emphatic victory for his party since 1945, gaining 48% of the votes cast, on the slogan 'You Know Labour Government Works'.

For a brief interlude it appeared to be fulfilling the slogan's promise. But the new enlarged parliamentary party had plenty to be restive about. Wilson found himself under fire from both left and right for his East of Suez posture, and from the left over the continuing support for the USA in Vietnam. In the next three months the course of his government up to 1970 – and, in reaction to it, of his party for much longer – was to be determined. With the balance of payments still showing no sign of improvement, the traditionally moderate National

Union of Seamen struck for what was in effect a 17% pay claim – well in excess of the government targets. The Prime Minister's rough response, dubbing the strike leaders a 'tightly knit group of politically motivated men', and suggesting deep Communist influence (to which he devoted three pages of justification in his memoirs), paid off at one level. The seamen went back to work. But the hyperbolic language used during the dispute both imperilled trade union support for further prices and incomes legislation and worsened the doom-laden picture of Britain from abroad, which in turn accentuated the pressure on sterling. When the Prices and Incomes Bill came before Parliament with its statutory powers to delay wage increases (average earnings rose in the year from May 1965 to 8%), Frank Cousins resigned from the government, joining the members of his union in their opposition to pay policy.

The worst crisis of the Labour government followed. There were further raids on sterling in the international currency markets. After the announcement of a fall in the gold and dollar reserves on 4 July, the pound fell to $2.78 despite all attempts to maintain the $2.80 exchange rate. Rumours that the British were seeking entry to the Common Market, but had been rebuffed by President Pompidou, were rife. While making leisurely progress round a Moscow trade fair, Wilson was called back to Britain. 'Seminars,' he recalls in his memoirs, 'were taking place all over Westminster.'[3] Their purpose was to argue the case for a devaluation of the pound, casting aside the cherished sterling parity. George Brown was the leading devaluationist. At various times Richard Crossman, Anthony Crosland, Roy Jenkins, Barbara Castle and Tony Benn all took the same view. Brown, who used to make a 'D' sign in the air as he passed backbench allies in the corridors, was convinced that Wilson's opposition to a devaluation was linked to support from the USA. Barbara Castle recorded Brown's frantic remarks while Wilson was flying back from Moscow:[4]

'He won't budge. He can't budge. Why? Because he is too deeply committed to Johnson . . . What did he pledge? I don't know; that we wouldn't devalue and full support in the Far East? But both of these have got to go.'

It was Brown who went. Wilson backed the Treasury line. The devaluationists unwisely let Crossman lead for them. Instead of devaluation, there was a massive deflationary package. There was to be a six-month prices and wages freeze, stiff increases in purchase tax and hire-purchase repayment terms, and cuts in both public expenditure and in overseas commitments. Brown tried to resign, was taken back, but was allowed to move to the Foreign Office in the following month. At the end of his life he looked back with undiminished bitterness at the defeat over devaluation:

'We had assured the TUC that the prices and incomes policy which they were required to accept would not be a restraint, would be a policy of controlled growth . . . The moment we decided to make the value of the pound take precedence over that objective we killed the prices and incomes policy. The moment we did that we also rang the bells as far as private enterprise was concerned – they wouldn't get the resources they needed . . . We killed all that in the interests of the pound, and that finished the DEA . . . It was undoubtedly the turning point; the point at which the Labour Party's attitude to life changed.'

This knock-on effect, more than the severity of the measures themselves, made July 1966 a watershed. Distance has lent increased disenchantment, in Labour eyes, to the July measures.

The cuts stunned the party; left and right, from Stuart Holland to Joel Barnett, agree on this point, whatever their views on the efficacy of devaluation itself. Why did Wilson opt for deflation? Those close to him believe, with Peter Shore, that he was 'emotionally committed' to sterling, 'as though it were a necessary ingredient of discipline, somehow, in national affairs, and his own credibility was involved, so that he couldn't bring himself really even to discuss the matter after a certain time'. There were serious arguments too. Devaluation would raise import prices at once. That would mean inflationary pressures, and a tougher battle still over incomes. It was not known how soon lower export prices would filter through the web of the great multinational companies to help Britain's balance of payments. In cabinet Wilson argued that a devaluation or floating of the pound would shake the dollar. The Americans too had a massive balance of payments deficit, as the American economy sucked in imports to finance the Vietnam war. As Brown suspected, Wilson regarded the relationship with the US President as crucial. Cecil King records in his diary a lunch with the British Treasury's man in Washington, John Stevens, during the crisis. Stevens told him:[5]

'Johnson made quite clear to Wilson that the pound was not to be devalued and no drastic action taken East of Suez until after the American election in November. In return the pound would be supported to any extent necessary.'

Ironically, Wilson was doubly stricken by Vietnam, although not a single British soldier ever fought there. He attempted to avoid public criticism of the Johnson administration. After the Americans bombed Hanoi and Haiphong in late June 1966, he was forced to denounce the action; but by then he had fatally alienated many of the young and the left in his own party. Simultaneously, world inflationary pressures were building up through the excessive American monetary demand in servicing the war, which threatened the real income of British workers, and increased their desire to hold onto what they had, regardless of whatever government policy, pay norm or union official stood in the way. The Vietnam war struck British Labour in its ideals and in its wage packet, and Wilson was the each-way loser.

The Prime Minister's resilience amazed observers. He went on television to make a broadcast of sub-Churchillian rhetoric, saying that the nation had been 'blown off course' by the seamen's strike:

'One thing this crisis has done, it has focussed the eyes of the world on us. This is a chance to show what we are made of. We'll show them that a time of crisis is a time for greatness.'

After surviving the parliamentary debate on the cuts, he flew to the United States, to receive the encomium of Lyndon Johnson that he was 'a man of mettle'. The man of mettle was back in London in time for the World Cup final at Wembley, and basked in England's victory. At the celebration dinner that night, watching a euphoric Brown call for yet another chorus of 'I'm Forever Blowing Bubbles', his hopes still seemed intact.

The time was fast approaching, though, when a reappraisal of Britain's overseas posture was inevitable. The 1966 Defence White Paper proposed naval cuts severe enough to provoke the resignation of the First Sea Lord and his Minister, Christopher Mayhew, and the eventual British withdrawal from Aden. After the July cuts, a gradual withdrawal from Singapore and Malaysia was planned, while the Labour Party in Parliament pressed for disengagement at once. Britain, they pointed out, was still spending almost 6% of GNP on defence, entangled as she was in a worldwide network of bases and treaty obligations. The Prime Minister remained 'determined to keep our military presence in the Far East', Crossman noted in December 1966,[6] 'even if it involves keeping penny-packets of British troops scattered over the world'. In February 1967 the discontent spilled over into widespread abstention by Labour MPs on the Defence White Paper, causing Wilson to round on his critics with the remark:

'Every dog is allowed one bite, but a different view is taken of a dog that goes on biting the whole time . . . He may not get his licence renewed.'

The Prime Minister began to pay the price for his exceptional dexterity. His initiatives led to too many failures, aroused too many suspicions. There had been a rough reception for the British at the Commonwealth conference for their supine attitude to Rhodesia. Wilson then made a determined attempt to get a settlement with the illegal Rhodesian regime by direct talks. He was baulked by the bovine folly of Ian Smith's hardliners, who did not know, or did not care, how much had been conceded to them. When the talks on HMS *Tiger* failed, and left him forced to publish his proposed concessions, Wilson bounced back to attack the Conservative opposition, under the eye of the admiring Crossman:[7]

'. . . rallying his troops against Heath, the criminal collaborationist, and completely burning his bridges by swinging from a mood of extreme appeasement to a mood of no concession to treason'.

Another mission was afoot which Wilson had to take seriously. From 1966 onwards he came to share the view that Britain ought to re-apply for membership of the Common Market. George Brown, as Foreign Secretary, was a long-time committed pro-European. He recalls that:

'Tremendous pressure had to be exerted on Wilson not merely to make him change his attitude into a more positive one, but to get him to persuade enough members of the cabinet to move over.'

The cabinet agreed in October 1966 to exploratory talks, although the party conference voted against entry. Wilson and Brown were authorised to go round the European capitals in tandem, because, according to Brown, 'other members of the cabinet didn't trust me, and were willing to trust him'. In Brown's uncharitable view:

'Wilson by now began to see this as another political coup, [though] I don't think he ever became a European in the sense I was . . .'

The political coup would have been threefold. Entry was popular in the country – in 1966, opinion polls showed 71% in favour, 12% against – and not especially unpopular in the party. A wide body of opinion in the cabinet was prepared to go through with it for the economic advantages which they believed Britain, especially if it floated the pound, would have in the huge and booming European market. Second, the Community offered a new theatre in which to operate, in concert with the European socialists who were pressing Britain to join them. Wilson saw it, Barbara Castle thinks, as 'a second-best world stage', if the East of Suez posture had to be abandoned. Third, entry into Europe would dish the Tories; above all else, this was the issue with which the Conservative leader Edward Heath was most closely identified. Wilson's view of his own change of heart is laconic:

'We were being starved out of markets and the Commonwealth wasn't providing enough of an alternative . . . and we were under a lot of pressure from friendly countries that we should go in and stand up to this costly French self-regard.'

French self-regard sank the application when it was eventually made in 1967. The British Parliament voted by 488 to 62 in favour of the application, with Heath imposing a three-line whip on the Tories to vote with the government. (34 Labour MPs voted against and 51 abstained.) Two weeks later the British were snubbed by General De Gaulle, who feared that the British would come in as the Americans' Trojan horse, and would delay or prevent the provisions of the Rome Treaty becoming permanent.

At once, Wilson said that the British government would not take no for an answer. After De Gaulle's resignation in 1969, he was able to reactivate the British application. His party's formal position remained to approve entry if terms could be negotiated, although by 1969 the Common Agricultural Policy with its high food prices had become a permanent feature of the EEC. The significance of the 1967 sortie, therefore, was that it left both major British political parties in favour of entry if the opportune moment arrived. This not merely made the acceptance of entry easier in Britain, but had profound consequences for the Labour Party when its rank and file began to swing back to a hostile position. For four years, Europe was not to be an issue dividing the parties; the divisions were internal.

Richard Crossman has left an intriguing picture of the enigma of Wilson in the middle of his administration. He wrote:[8]

'What are Harold's long-term economic objectives for this country? Does he really want to go into Europe or doesn't he? I don't think he knows himself. Does he want to devalue? He certainly doesn't want to but is he going to after all? He knew the answer a few months ago; he's not so sure of it now. And what about the long-term future of the Labour Party? Does he see it as a real socialist party or does he, like the Gaitskellites, aim to turn it into an American Democratic Party or a German SPD? He certainly doesn't confide in me any profound thoughts about the future of the Labour Party and I'm prepared to say as of today that I don't think he has them . . . His main aim is to stay in office. That's the real thing and for that purpose he will use almost any trick or gimmick.'

A Prime Minister with a majority of 97 usually does not have to struggle very hard to stay in office. It was a measure of Wilson's plight that in the twelve months from mid-1967 his survival itself sometimes seemed in doubt, as his administration plunged from one crisis to another, outraging many of its own supporters. On the economic front there had seemed to be signs of improvement. Better trade figures in the first part of 1967 were followed by the end of the pay freeze in July and its replacement by a voluntary policy with residual government powers to delay wage settlements. Then the familiar cycle began again: falling gold and dollar reserves, bad trade figures, and the worst unemployment figures since the war – almost half a million. The Chancellor loudly proclaimed his faith in the $2.80 exchange rate. Wilson took personal charge of the DEA to suggest a new spirit of dynamism. It was later revealed by the Chancellor's son-in-law that papers arguing for the devaluation option had been suppressed by the Prime Minister.[9] By early November, however, devaluation looked like the least disastrous option. It was hastened after the Labour backbencher Robert Sheldon put down a parliamentary question aimed to point up the deflationary consequences of an overseas loan – the alternative to devaluation. The opportunity was seized on by others to cross-examine the unhappy Chancellor about devaluation. (Barbara Castle records Callaghan as saying before his interrogation,[10] 'This is the unhappiest day of my life.') He was forced to stall. The following day £300 million pounds were lost in speculative selling of sterling. On 18 November the pound was devalued by 14.3%. Peter Shore witnessed the Prime Minister's private response:

'That was terribly damaging to him personally. He felt it, and it was damaging to him politically as well, and to the whole coherent reputation and authority of the Labour government.'

The political damage was intensified by Wilson's public insouciance. He said on television:

'This does not mean, of course, that the pound here in Britain, in your pocket or purse, or in your bank, has been devalued.'

Given the inflationary effect, it meant exactly that. By contrast, the Chancellor submitted himself to television interrogation by George ffitch with gloomy dignity. Did he feel he had broken his word? 'Yes,' he replied. Had the previous years been wasted? He thought not:

'I think it has been a period of stripping away illusions, and the need to adapt Britain more quickly to Europe and to the world generally.'

Callaghan left the Treasury, at first intent upon resignation but then swapping offices with the Home Secretary, Roy Jenkins. Because devaluation had been delayed through a long run on the pound, an international loan also had to be negotiated, on the understanding that £750 million would be cut out of home consumption. So there was a fresh deflationary package. Wilson, who had resigned from the Attlee cabinet in 1951 over proposed prescription charges, now had the humiliation of re-introducing them. The raising of the school-leaving age was postponed, the housing programme slashed. All British forces in the Far East apart from Hong Kong and the Gulf were to be pulled out. The order for American F-111 fighters was cancelled. In a broadcast the new Chancellor told the nation sombrely, 'We are recognising that we are no longer a superpower.'

Labour had already had a bad year in by-elections and local government. It had lost seats to the Welsh and Scottish Nationalists, emergent forces in territory over which Labour claimed proprietorial rights. Seats as dispersed as Glasgow Pollock, Leicester South-west, Walthamstow West and Cambridge fell to the Tories. The unfortunate Labour candidate in West Derbyshire, watching the Wilson devaluation broadcast during the by-election, was only with difficulty dissuaded from packing his bags and heading south. Wilson thought more and more about his own position. According to Edmund Dell,* Wilson's lunches with the DEA team in the three months before devaluation were dominated not by the coming economic crisis but by 'what he saw as threats to his position. I don't think they were real but he was very concerned with them.' These worries help to explain the extraordinary succession of leaks and counter-leaks about possible British arms sales to South Africa in December 1967. Wilson was reaching for what residual left-wing support he had in his party by exposing and isolating the advocates of arms sales in the cabinet.

He was in little doubt about the extent of left-wing disillusion. The horrors of Vietnam appeared nightly on television. It was a war with which Labour was associated, through support for Lyndon Johnson. Wilson recollects that at this time:

'The party behind me in the House, sitting behind me, were very worried about Vietnam, and wanted me to denounce it openly. And

---

* Dell was joint Parliamentary Under Secretary at the DEA 1967–8.

there was some pressure from some of the Conservatives. So . . . I got through on the phone to the President and I said, "Look, could I come over? I'm under terrible pressure," and so on. I'd chosen the wrong night – "I'm not having you flying across the Atlantic with your shirt tails flying off your —" and he mentioned the portion of my anatomy from which my shirt tails would be flying . . .'

LBJ had worries of his own. Wilson was asked to visit Washington in February 1968. Johnson remained friendly 'but he didn't change his policy'. And, because of his association with that policy, Wilson knew that he was at odds not just with his parliamentary left but with the whole grain of radical opinion in the country, for whom America's role in Vietnam was an obscenity, and the National Liberation Front heroes. Through 1967–8 a series of demonstrations, culminating in one outside the American embassy in Grosvenor Square, voiced loathing of American policy and British complicity.

The left was further outraged by the lamentable story of the 1968 Commonwealth Immigrants Bill. Labour had already decreased the quota of work permits for Commonwealth immigrants wishing to enter Britain, arguing that such action had been taken to protect immigrants already in Britain. As it became clear that the open door was closed as firmly under Labour as it had been under the Conservatives, party activists grew increasingly dismayed. But there was a large number of people abroad who had a guaranteed right of entry – the East African Asians who had been offered and had taken up British citizenship as a consequence of the independence arrangements for Kenya, Uganda, Tanzania and Malawi.

When Roy Jenkins left the Home Office work on a new Race Relations Bill was well advanced. Discrimination on the streets had already been outlawed. Now there were to be wider powers to tackle it in employment, housing and the provision of services – wherever the dishonest and insulting formulation 'Sorry, No Coloureds' was still to be found. Legislation was also drafted, however, to deal with the entry of East African Asians, if it became a 'flood'. Jenkins vehemently denies that he would have brought in such legislation:

'I can't say that it is inconceivable that I would have done it, because I did say that a draft bill could be prepared. But I certainly gave no approval in principle to a bill being brought in, and I do not think I would have taken the view that the influx or the threat of influx was such as to justify this highly divisive legislation.'

But it was introduced with indecent haste, during his successor's first months in office. As the Kenya government pushed ahead with its post-colonial Africanisation policy, there was some panic among the Kenyan Asians. For families whose members had, as an insurance policy, different citizenships, this seemed to be the moment for those holding British passports to go to Britain. Under pressure from right-wingers and the press, Home Secretary Callaghan announced that over 12,000 Kenyan Asians had entered Britain. Over 100,000 had the right to enter – but not for long. As soon as it appeared that the Labour government would remove that right of entry, the Asians panicked. Briefly, numbers swelled to the 'flood' about which the alarmists had warned, thus making restrictive action even more likely. With infamous haste, a Commonwealth Immigrants Bill was brought out, dusted down, and became law within a week of its publication. 35 Labour MPs, with 10 Liberals and 15 Tories, voted against. One of the Labour dissenters was Joan Lestor. Her disillusion was shared by many in the party:

'We'd gone in with such high hopes, such enthusiasm and with so much support from progressive people. I think that Vietnam was the first big disappointment that many of us on the young, enthusiastic left had had . . . Then the 1968 Act, which removed the rights of British citizens to whom we had given citizenship to come to Britain freely, disappointed me enormously . . . Many young people became disillusioned with politics completely. Some of them went into organisations that are now referred to as the "hard left". They saw, or believed, that the Labour Party would never meet their ideals and was always going to let them down.'

The precipitate action to exclude the Kenyan Asians, which cost the Labour Party dear among its own activists, did not calm internal tensions in Britain. Instead, it poisoned the atmosphere in which the Race Relations Bill was being debated. There was a new hardness in the discussion of race issues. Those Conservative politicians who had campaigned for the new immigration controls, such as Duncan Sandys and Enoch Powell, were not appeased. Powell's 1968 speeches (see chapter 2) not only convulsed his own party. It was clear that the fears he voiced, and the language he used, had a direct appeal to part of Labour's natural constituency. When the London dockers marched in his support on the House of Commons, they encountered their MP, Ian Mikardo:

'They didn't just boo me. They kicked me – actually kicked me in the Central Lobby . . . Yes, it was a very great shock indeed, and it made me rethink the need for a tremendous internal educational attitude within our own party.'

Immigrant workers found a painful contrast between Labour's past rhetoric and the way in which their white fellow workers now behaved. Ranjit Sondhi, then a student in Birmingham, remembers that:

'People who worked in factories . . . were absolutely appalled at the way in which white workers, with whom they'd worked side by side, suddenly found it possible to go and march on the streets asking for blacks to leave the country.'

On race Labour seemed to have forfeited the sympathy of its most committed as well as its most traditional supporters, whilst alienating potential new ones in the immigrant communities.

At the mid-point of its electoral voyage the Labour government was riding very low in the water. A tough budget from Roy Jenkins was not popular; nor was the government's incomes policy, increasingly beset by strikes. The opinion polls indicated a drastic fall in support and the 1968 local elections confirmed this. Labour lost three by-elections on the same day in March, and in the May local elections the party had its worst result since before the war. The Prime Minister became vulnerable. He had reshuffled his government when George Brown, 'tired and emotional' once too often, had finally been taken at his word when he offered to resign. The new cabinet had an entirely different balance. Instead of Callaghan and Brown, as rivals, there were now a number of possible leadership contenders. Wilson spun around himself a protective cocoon of insiders, an inner cabinet which included the rising stars Jenkins and Castle, but excluded Callaghan, wounded but still formidable. Another who was kept out, Tony Crosland, took the matter more philosophically, his wife reports:[11]

'His expulsion was not a great grievance – there being no sign that the inner cabinet was grappling with strategy – but he thought Harold an ass to keep him out.'

Throughout the year the Prime Minister's nerve was tested by open dissent and murmurs of palace revolutions. He was always nervous that dissidents in the cabinet would brief the press in their interest more effectively than he did in his own. 'Cabinets,' recollects Tony Benn, 'used to spend sometimes as long on discussing the leak after the last cabinet as they did on the business on the agenda for that day.'

On one occasion the cabinet went on past lunchtime because of one of these interminable inquests so that:

'When we left lunch, there in the *Evening Standard* was a statement of what Wilson had said to the cabinet: "Wilson Warns the Cabinet". Well, as nobody had left the room it was absolutely clear, so we all came back in with our *Evening Standard*s and said, "How did that get out . . .?"'

Wilson's suspicion of individual colleagues, sometimes encouraged by his resident bloodhound George Wigg, extended beyond their relations with the press. He was highly nervous of their relations with each other. Could they be arranging which one should wield the knife?

In fact, the only knife unsheathed came from a press proprietor with delusions of grandeur not uncommon in his family. Cecil Harmsworth King, chairman of IPC, publishers of the *Daily Mirror*, had been touting in amateurish fashion for a grand coalition. On 8 May he had made a vain attempt to recruit Lord Mountbatten to lead a new government if there was 'blood in the streets'. Mountbatten, warned by Sir Solly Zuckerman, whom he had asked to be present, that this was 'rank treachery', showed King the door.[12] Two days later King launched a signed onslaught in the *Daily Mirror* on a government which he claimed had 'lost all credibility, all authority' after the local election disasters. This greatly helped the Prime Minister. 'Enough is Enough' – King's headline – became his epitaph when he was dismissed from the chairmanship of IPC by his fellow directors.

The fall of King was a balm for the Prime Minister, but his wounds were still open. 'I know what's going on. I'm going on,' was to be his public response to chatter of plots. Privately he was much in need of reassurance. Denis Healey remembers that he was:

'. . . obsessed by the risk of a palace coup. He used to have a different daemon every few months. For a long time it was me, though I never had the slightest intention of doing so.'

Suspicion fell most heavily on Roy Jenkins, who enjoyed the approbation of the press. Jenkins had been a successful reforming Home Secretary; now he fitted the media's view of what an iron Chancellor should be. His assiduous press secretary, John Harris, kept Fleet Street well briefed. Younger MPs enjoyed his polished set-piece performances. With hindsight Jenkins says:

'I think it's possible, looking back, that if I'd been determinedly devoted to organising an intrigue, I could quite likely have pushed

Wilson out in 1968. But to be honest I was much too concerned with trying to hold the economic position together.'

Absorbing as cabinet intrigues might be to the participants, the real discontent was not at the top but at the bottom. Crossman records a dinner in his constituency in April 1968:[13]

'They were still terribly uncertain and unhappy . . . They just felt we had totally failed as a government, and nothing I said would alter their view that there had been no real improvement in their standard of living, only a series of crises which showed we weren't in control.'

Labour's ambitious social and industrial programmes failed because of the government's inability to stimulate either adequate economic growth or appropriate redistribution of what national resources were available. Harold Lever* says:

'The Labour Party leadership sincerely believed they had the secret of reversing the relative decline of Britain's performance compared with other European countries. It came as a shock to them to find that they hadn't . . . The people sensed that the leadership themselves no longer believed in the evangel they [had] honestly and confidently preached since 1964.'

Without growth, with the balance of payments now elevated to the status previously enjoyed by the pound sterling, the Wilson government put its trust in regeneration through merger. The Industrial Reorganisation Corporation (IRC) had been set up under Sir Frank Kearton in 1966 to tackle the problem of Britain's international uncompetitiveness. It came to act as a financial backer for the thrusting and the successful. Kearton's bright young men had no difficulty diagnosing a problem. The country suffered from persistent under-investment, obsolescent machinery, low productivity and deep hostility to innovation by both managements and workforce. Britain was paying the price of having won the war. Her institutions had not been overhauled; her outdated factories had not been flattened. Ancient custom and practice prevailed. (The Hudson Report demonstrated later that, in 1969, productivity per worker/hour was 3.45 times greater in the United States than in Britain, and 1.46 times greater in Germany.) As working methods fell further behind those of Britain's old foes and of her most powerful ally, profits shrank and a strong trade-union movement acted forcefully to preserve its own share of the take.

* Lever was Financial Secretary to the Treasury 1967–9, and Paymaster General 1969–70.

In the public mind the man most associated with the IRC strategy
was the youthful head of the Ministry of Technology, or Mintech as it
was trendily known. Tony Benn looks back now on his enthusiasm of
the time with scepticism:

'Wilson thought that by micro investment you could offset the
major act of deflation. There would be secret reflation by concentrating on certain industries, like computers, for example . . . Now I think
that was useful. It was within the framework of saving the system,
which I now think was doomed to failure, but it had merit.'

The ministry preached the gospel of bigness. One merger followed
another. £25 million went to assist the merger of the ailing British
Motor Corporation, itself an amalgam of Austin, Morris and much
else, with Leyland. Donald Stokes* was the much publicised symbol
of the new belief in fitness through weight gain. In fact, the efficient
elements in the merged company were rapidly dragged down by internal overlaps and chaos. Had they been willing, the new British
Leyland could also have had Britain's other collapsing car empire,
the Rootes Group, thrust upon them, to keep it out of the hands
of the US Chrysler Corporation. More successful, for a time, was the
merged computer company ICL. The merger which caused greatest
controversy, because of the number of redundancies which followed,
was that between the engineering giants GEC and AEI, in which GEC
received IRC financial support and avoided any reference to the
Monopolies Commission.

One of the first ailing industries with which Benn had to deal was
shipbuilding. There he found that:

'The old shipbuilders' idea of marketing in the early days was to go
to the club and see if there were any letters asking them to build ships.
And when things were going well, the shipbuilders used to say, "We
don't have to invest, we're making a profit." When things were going
badly, they couldn't afford to invest. So the result was they didn't
invest.'

Before Benn went to the Ministry of Technology the Geddes Report
had recommended grouping the largest yards by estuary. When he
defended the Geddes merger proposals to the workforce on the Upper
Clyde as their best option, Benn had received a rough response. In
1969 he was back. Of the newly grouped yards the merged group

---

* Stokes was chairman of British Leyland Motor Corporation 1968–75, and a
member of the IRC 1966–71.

called Upper Clyde Shipbuilders was in deepest trouble. The problems of nervous management and suspicious workforce had not vanished with the merger; they had intensified. Orders were not met on time. The yards were threatened with closure. The workforce argued for a further loan. 'The government has invested in farming, it's invested in the aircraft industry. Why not in shipbuilding?' they asked. After innumerable crisis meetings with management and unions (which convinced Benn that the latter had more to contribute if involved), there were changes at the top and 3500 redundancies in the workforce, in return for further loans. No one believed that the crisis at UCS was over.

Judgement was also suspended on the daring decision to invest £47 million in launch aid to Rolls-Royce to back its fixed-price contract with Lockheed to supply the new RB-211 engine. Rolls-Royce had merged with Bristol to maintain its position as a world-scale aero-engine firm. Its 1968 breakthrough with the RB 211 looked like a triumphant vindication of the strategy of selective investment. No one wanted to ask the awkward question: could the engineers untangle the immense technical problems in time to deliver? The other aircraft project dear to Benn's heart – and to that of his Bristol constituency – was the Anglo–French supersonic airliner, Concorde. The problems were known, the costs alarming; but the international and employment consequences of cancellation always carried more political weight than the doubts.

In spite of the occasional glittering success, the IRC did not bring about the industrial renaissance the government had been seeking. After three years in which the economy grew by not more than 1.5% per annum, the worst culprit seemed to be poor industrial relations – and not just poor, but worsening fast. From 1964 to 1967 the number of working days lost through strikes had hovered between two and three million. In 1968 it went up to 4.7 million, and in 1969 to 6.8 million. The proportion of the population who were trade union members began to rise after 1967, and the power of the shop steward at factory or branch level rose too. The government, and especially Barbara Castle, its new Secretary of State for Employment and Productivity, came to see the unofficial strike as the true British malaise.

The government's pay policy was deeply unpopular with the trade unions at grassroots level. It seemed, in Ian Mikardo's words, that:

'Everyone who wasn't a wage earner was getting away with it. It was only wage and salary earners who were being made to bear the burden of economic sacrifice in order to get over all the difficulties. There was so much conspicuously Lucullan expenditure, people doing so well out of capital gains . . . and everybody said, "I'm just being made the sucker, because I pay my taxes out of a wage packet."'

The more the trade union leaders were drawn into negotiations and deals with government for restraint, the more their members turned instead to the shop stewards' movement, itself influenced by the radicalism of the age. In the largest union, the TGWU, the incoming General Secretary, Jack Jones, had made a deliberate policy of devolving power downwards. In the second largest, the AEF, the shift to the left was marked by the election of Hugh Scanlon as President. At the 1968 TUC conference, the vote against pay policy was carried by a majority of 7 to 1. Labour's own conference followed suit.

The government already had before it proposals for trade union reform. The Donovan Commission, one of the first of the batch of Royal Commissions set up by Labour in 1965, proposed long-term voluntary reform of collective bargaining, with a new body to arbitrate in inter-union disputes. A majority of the commission thought that trade union immunities should apply only to registered trade unions. An influential minority of one, Andrew Shonfield, queried the commission report's general philosophy of non-intervention, and argued for sanctions against those who broke collective agreements. In November Barbara Castle took her officials, ministerial colleagues and assorted employers and trade unionists for a long weekend at Sunningdale. Much in her mind was an unofficial strike at the Girling Brakes factory, where 22 machine setters had brought 5000 car workers to a standstill. Castle described it in her diary as:[14]

'A classic case of an inter-union dispute where AEF craftsmen refuse to work under an ASTMS foreman, and where the men ought to be forced to go through a cooling-off period.'

At Sunningdale the idea emerged that, while Donovan was right to reject the legal enforcement of collective agreements, or the banning of the closed shop, the power to order ballots before strikes and to have a cooling-off period should be enforced. The theory had its attractions for the Prime Minister, although Denis Healey, reflecting on Wilson's views in cabinet, sees another motive:

'Harold Wilson came to the conclusion that his pay policy wasn't working, and didn't have public support, and therefore he'd go about it another way, and he made a cold-blooded calculation that he'd get more public support for a direct attack on union power through "In Place of Strife".'

There was another factor. The Conservatives had recently adopted their own proposals for trade union reform, 'Fair Deal at Work'. Here was a classic opportunity to steal some vital Tory clothes and make off towards the political centre. Sir Denis Barnes, Castle's permanent secretary, was happy to oblige. He got the message that, as he recollects:

'Many Labour politicians considered the trade unions a liability rather than an asset.'

The unhappily named white paper 'In Place of Strife' was published by the DEP on 17 January 1979. To Mrs Castle it was 'a charter of trade union rights', of membership, and of appeal against dismissal, incorporating much of the Donovan philosophy. But it also proposed penal sanctions if its proposals for strike ballots and conciliation pauses were disregarded, and fines went unpaid. Castle felt she could do nothing less. Rights implied obligations:

'"In Place of Strife" repeated that the right to strike is an essential freedom in a democracy, and this I profoundly believed. But what I also believed was that the arbitrary abuse of the right to strike that was taking place up and down the country in unofficial disputes was weakening a crucial weapon for the trade unions. And I warned them; I said – unless some of this anarchy is removed, then one day we are going to have a right-wing government in this country that is going to take away these basic rights from you which I am trying to strengthen.'

Castle had tried out her proposals on the TUC General Secretary, George Woodcock, in confidence:

'He said, "Barbara, you have let the trade union movement off very lightly. I don't think the Donovan proposals went far enough, and your proposals are better than Donovan."'

Woodcock had been a member of the Donovan Commission. The initial public reaction to the proposals was almost equally muted. Then things began to go wrong.

'In Place of Strife' was not the only controversial reform proposal of 1969. The disastrous failure of Crossman's parliamentary reforms came to a climax with the slow death of the Parliament (No. 2) Bill, intended to reform the House of Lords. A curious coalition of Labour abolitionists and Tory traditionalists combined to destroy it. Robert Sheldon, who led the filibuster, believes that the bill had to be stopped:

'It was going to give [the Lords] more power, and give the Prime Minister much more patronage . . . because he would have peerages that really meant something at his command. It would be another version of the aldermanic bench.'

The withdrawal of the bill had two fateful consequences: it left a hole in the parliamentary timetable into which the short Industrial Relations Bill could be slotted, and it made the defeat of that bill more likely. The backbenchers had tasted blood. They now knew that a major piece of legislation could be stopped in its tracks. They were encouraged to threaten the same fate for trade union reform, and the government had proof that they could deliver.

The powerful duo of Jack Jones and Hugh Scanlon were deeply hostile to 'In Place of Strife', reflecting the views of their active membership. They felt that they were being made scapegoats for failures elsewhere. As Scanlon puts it:

'Jack Jones and myself were almost thrust to the forefront as being enemies of the economic miracle that we thought would take place in Britain . . . We saw our destiny, our destiny I emphasise, in collaboration not in confrontation, and the idea that anyone could propose such laws should go on the statue book without the agreement of the trade unions . . . was against all that we'd believed in when we fought for the return of the Labour government.'

That government, however, proceeded apace to attempt to put the laws on the statute book. A short bill containing the power to impose settlements in inter-union disputes and to enforce twenty-eight-day conciliation pauses was announced by Roy Jenkins during his April budget speech. The bill's unveiling was linked to the announcement that statutory wage control would not be renewed – in the hope that foreign confidence, if shaken by the end of pay policy, would be reassured by this tough line with organised labour. Ministers, who had just seen their House of Lords reform bill mangled to death, urged haste. The longer the proposals and the White Paper remained around, Jenkins thought, the more likely that 'the rats would get at it'.

Through the spring of 1969 opposition to the Industrial Relations Bill mounted. The backbenches rumbled. Further losses in the May local elections reawakened the Prime Minister's old fears about coups. And James Callaghan, smarting under his exclusion from the inner circle, newly rehabilitated by his handling of the Northern Ireland crisis (see chapter 8), came to the aid of the unions. He and like-minded MPs were powerful allies within as the trade union battalions moved in on Westminster. 'They realised,' says Jones, 'that if they went along with Harold Wilson . . . whatever they had in terms of a trade-union base would be lost for ever.' The voice of the TUC was now no longer that of the whimsical philosopher-king George Wood-cock. Stricken by a heart attack, he had made way for Victor Feather, who told a special TUC conference in June that 'while we might like a lick at the lollipop, we're not going to swallow the stick'. Counter-proposals by the TUC, a 'Programme for Action', were voted through at the conference. Publicly, Wilson insisted that any alternative to the bill must be enshrined in a formal change of the TUC's own rules. But his negotiating position was weak. The Chief Whip was full of gloomy predictions that he could not get the bill through. Mrs Castle found her cabinet supporters melting away. Some who had been hot for action now lectured her, as Crossman did in the incongruous setting of Charles Forte's luxury yacht in the Mediterranean, that there would be 'disaster facing the party as a result of the IR Bill; the PLP in revolt and the party smashed in the election'.[15] On 17 June she saw her last supporters peel away in cabinet, beginning with Peter Shore, who had been at the original Sunningdale meeting, and ending with Jenkins, who reflects that he was 'almost the last on the burning deck'.

With no cards left to play, Wilson had to get what he could from the TUC: a 'solemn and binding' assurance that the unions would accept the TUC's own guidelines on unofficial strikes. (Solomon Binding became the nickname for any agreement that was a face-saving formula and no more.) The Prime Minister's failure was the more complete because of the almost reckless optimism he had shown in challenging the received wisdom of every section of the Labour movement. Defence of trade union rights and immunities had been a cardinal aim of the Labour Party since its foundation. The Industrial Relations Bill was too much for it to swallow. Its defeat kept trade union reform high on the political agenda, but its passage into law would not have taken the issue out of politics. Britain was too weak economically, and the trade unions apparently too strong, for union involvement in every industrial diagnosis to be avoided. The defeat of the bill seemed to ensure that trade union reform would be a taboo sub-ject for the Labour Party in future. The government had lost both trade union support for being too tough, and some public support by appearing in the last analysis to be too weak. Incomes policy had been thrown overboard too. The trade unions, for their part, could go into the seventies believing that the processes of collective bargaining and industrial relations were once more their exclusive preserve.

Only in one area was Barbara Castle marginally successful in altering some entrenched attitudes. In 1968 a strike by women sewing-machinists at Ford's Dagenham plant for equal skilled grading with men brought the factory to a standstill. The attitudes of the male-dominated union hierarchies, and the complex manoeuvres whereby the women's claims always seemed to get left over until the regrading issues had taken up most of the time and money, alerted her to the difficulties. Despite some doubts about whether to tackle the problem as one of low pay and a guaranteed minimum wage, or as one of equality, Castle's personal commitment to redressing these wrongs was the major factor in getting the 1970 Equal Pay Act on to the statute book. The act was a first step – paradoxically, because of the delays and obstructions placed in its way – to the campaign for anti-discrimination legislation in the seventies.

If the notional floating voter was left with a poor impression of Labour's ability to unwrap and deliver its reform packages, what of the effect of the government's social policies? Here too the record was patchy. Public expenditure on housing, education and social services had increased until 1968. So had expectations; they were unfulfilled. The 1968 cuts nullified Wilson's pledge to build 500,000 homes a year by 1970. Public housing programmes, with their dedication to the rapid elimination of slums and the use of system-built towers and 'streets in the sky' to speed up the process, brought disillusion even before the financial cutbacks. Crossman was Labour's first Housing Minister. Brian Abel-Smith, later one of his advisers, recollects that:

'[Crossman] believed deeply that system-building was the answer ... There had been a research study done in the fifties about what it was like living in high-rise flats, and this had been very negative, but that was all thrown away. You were in a hurry, and this was the cheapest way to do it.'

The collapse of Ronan Point in 1968 was a grim warning that the environment ambitiously planned by ministers of housing such as Crossman (who divided his time between a house in Vincent Square and a farm at Prescote) had heavy social costs. The initial genuine enthusiasm for the new flats, with their views and central heating, evaporated as tenants mourned broken lifts, vanished caretakers and lost community. By 1970 such people felt that, while they might now be better off, once more everyone else was better off still. That some were in fact much worse off was persistently highlighted by Shelter, one of the most successful of the new single-issue pressure groups into which the radical young were moving. There remained a housing shortage. As high interest rates cut into local authorities' ability to build, so the sense that the housing programme had been a failure became pervasive.

At the same time, the social-security system was failing to work effectively towards its stated aim of the redistribution of wealth. Those in greatest need were inevitably hit by successive deflations, despite attempts to protect them with increases in pensions and social-security benefits. Again, single-issue pressure groups were at hand to call attention to the shortfall. By 1969 it was estimated that over 5 million people were living below the poverty line. Abel-Smith became a forceful critic of the government he served:

'I think many of us in the Child Poverty Action Group thought that, once you exposed a problem – that there was a substantial number of children in poverty – inevitably a Labour government would react. And it reacted only in a very small way, which caused a great disappointment.'

The achievements of the government in its first four years, under severe financial constraint from lack of economic growth, were in areas that principally won middle-class approval. The 'liberal hour' in social reform initiated by Roy Jenkins at the Home Office allowed family-planning provision and abortion through the National Health Service – thanks to Private Members who had the courage of the Home Secretary's convictions. These removed some of the shame and guilt which unwanted pregnancy had brought to those for whom previously contraception had been unavailable and abortion illegal. The wretched persecution of homosexuals was abated by a reform in the law permitting adults over twenty-one to form homosexual relationships. In the backlash of the seventies all these reforms came under fire from chief constables, religious pressure groups, self-appointed moralists and small-town Grundies. But enough of them survived to be remembered as – incongruously, given his personal lack of enthusiasm for them – the last achievements of Wilson's administration.

In the field of education there were other gains. The government wanted to be on the side of youth. It gave eighteen-year-olds the vote. It maintained the expansion of higher education initiated by the Tories in the early 1960s, following the Robbins Report, whereby the institutions doubled in number. More children stayed on at school, although the raising of the school-leaving age was postponed. The middle classes chiefly benefited. Even the one university that was different, Wilson's promised University of the Air, the Open University – which became, along with Jennie Lee's work in the arts, one of the life-enhancing landmarks of his administration – began by giving middle-class non-graduates graduate qualifications. A fresh class structure was painstakingly constructed as a divide opened up between the universities and the new polytechnics, the source of much later anxiety about status and 'academic drift'. The social composition of the school sixth form hardly changed, and in vocational education there was regress. Whereas the Robbins Report had been enthusiastically accepted and carried through, the Henniker-Heaton Report on day-release vocational training was left to gather dust. There was little attempt to emulate the standards of Britain's industrial competitors in a modern and comprehensive system of apprentice training. Girls won almost no advantage from what day-release courses there were. Further, there was a failure of will over the social divide in the schools. The 1965 circular calling on local authorities to submit plans for comprehensive reorganisation left the onus on the authorities. The circular was perhaps a compromise between a Prime Minister who said publicly that the old grammar schools would be abolished over his dead body and a Secretary of State who said privately to his wife, 'I'm going to destroy every fucking grammar school in England.'[16] This Tony Crosland was unable to do; but by 1970 there had been a fourfold increase of comprehensive schools under the Labour administration, to 1150. Nor could he destroy a single private school; they were delivered to the scrutiny of another Royal Commission. By the time the commission's divided counsels had been reported to the government, Crosland, who might have realised the egalitarian injustice of leaving the private sector alone while the public sector carried through a partial comprehensivisation, had long been reshuffled away from education. Nothing was done about the public schools. Orwell's 'curse of class difference' remained to haunt the Labour Party's egalitarian expectations.

By a final irony, the government was to find that the recruiting ground for its critics on the left was that very sector of higher education which it had expanded. Students saw themselves as a new proletariat, the campus as an open experiment in constructive social protest. New heroes appeared: Tariq Ali, Vanessa Redgrave, Robin Blackburn – all well connected, glamorous, committed. The University of Essex was brought to the brink of closure by demonstrations. There were violent clashes at the LSE over the Rhodesian connections of a new director, Dr Walter Adams. At Hornsey Art College an occupation protested against the anti-democratic nature of the teaching. Abroad, heady examples beckoned – from the US anti-war and civil-rights movements, from Paris, from Prague, from Britain itself with the awakening of Northern Ireland (see chapter 8). The streets seemed the place to protest, by means of vivid agitprop theatre, factory-gate meetings (occasionally wrecked by a super-abundance of left factions armed with rival microphones), by demonstrations. At the greatest of these, in opposition to the Vietnam war outside the American embassy in Grosvenor Square, the complicity of the British government was excoriated. The cameras of Granada television followed one student protester, Dave Clark, throughout the day. He was, he said, 'flexing his muscles' for the struggle ahead, in which he saw no room for the Labour Party. Looking back on those days he sums up the mood:

'I think we wanted change and we wanted it now . . . If you could get out and show people what was wrong and how it should be changed – it was very idealistic – there would be a complete overthrow of the corrupt and rotten society as we saw it . . . There was the feeling that you couldn't do anything with the Labour Party. It was in the hands of evil or at least corrupt and incompetent people.'

The young quit the Labour Party in large numbers for the Marxist left (and some for the Young Liberals, which old Liberals thought was much the same thing). The International Socialists, the International Marxist Group, the Revolutionary Workers Party, all gained recruits. So did the single-issue pressure groups. Some of the class of '68 became teachers in their turn, in higher and secondary education. Half a generation of potential new recruits decamped from Labour. Eventually, in different names and guises, they were to come back. When they did so, they brought with them a suspicion of party platitudes, an expectation of betrayal, not just inculcated by the sects where they had sojourned, but from their case-hardened youth. The Labour Party had been the poorer without them; it was to be much changed by their return. In 1968 their movement was away from a party which by now seemed to them hopelessly far to the right – doomed at the polls. Yet the next year brought about a remarkable change in fortunes. It also answered the question: when the left-wing party moves centre-right, what happens to those who are on the true right all along?

2

A MAN WITH A PIPE AND A MAN WITH A BOAT

Conservatives do not like opposition. Government comes more naturally to them. One of the reasons they were so disoriented by, and came so to detest, Harold Wilson was his uninhibited zest in reversing the natural order of things, as they had come to see it after thirteen years. In their usual unsentimental way they soon came to the conclusion that Alec Douglas-Home, who could have emerged as leader only from a party long in government but unsure of its power, was unsuited to lead the opposition. He had been chosen to keep them in government, not to win it back. In July 1965, coming to believe the *Sunday Times* article which said it was 'The Right Moment to Change', Home stood down. He says now that:

'One of the reasons why I resigned was just that I'd been on the scene a long time, and I thought that the Tory Party needed somebody else who would have a slightly more modern outlook, perhaps, or be *thought* to have a more modern outlook.'

The new leader would be the first elected by the parliamentary party. The class of 1950 had now come through to the forefront of the party – Heath, Maudling, Macleod and Powell. The latter two had disadvantaged themselves by their refusal to serve in Home's government. Maudling, who had served, as Chancellor, had not only left the balance of payments deficit to which Harold Wilson so often referred, but also appeared too indolent, too fond of money, to be effective in opposition. That left Heath, the shadow Chancellor. His supporters saw him as the man most likely to pull the party together. Sara Morrison, later vice chairman of the party under Heath, explains why:

'The Tory Party had a nasty habit . . . of appearing as though it thought that people were fairly easy-going and relaxed and broadly apolitical, but also rather foolish . . . we thought there was a chance that Ted would put a lot of that right.'

The Conservative MPs thought so too. Heath was elected with 150 votes, against 133 for Maudling and only 15 for Powell. There was no provision in the new rules which Home had introduced for re-election. Election was novelty enough. The new leader was a calculated gamble by his party, a competent man who in background and style might trump what in 1965 looked like the Wilson ace. He swiftly brought forward men of his own stamp. Brendan Sewill, at thirty-five, became head of the Conservative Research Department. Sewill's predecessor, Michael Fraser, moved over to be vice chairman of the party. Heath was nothing if not well briefed, as his defeated rival, Enoch Powell, recalls:

'I remember the excitement which attended upon his first disastrous duel with Harold Wilson in the House of Commons, when he had so factual a brief, so exhaustively worked out, that the House was almost dead by the time he got through it. It was a crystallisation of what he was expected to do, to have all the answers, to have them accurately marshalled and therefore be able to destroy a political opponent. Unfortunately, it was only a demonstration to me of his most distressing characteristics – his characteristic of dealing, or attempting to deal, factually with things which are not matters of fact.'

Although Wilson had announced that there would be no election in 1965, another contest could not be long delayed. There were many matters of fact which the new leader wished to establish. Under Home, he had been chairman of the advisory committee on policy. Now he could increase its production. Sewill says that the Tories had noted the Labour government's failure to translate policy into practice as a result of insufficient preparation in opposition for civil-service objections:

'So we had thirty-six policy groups, and they all worked away . . . the detail was all right; what was wrong was that it was worked out too soon, because curiously all the main lines were laid down in 1965 . . . By the time we got to 1970 it was a little bit too set in concrete and couldn't change to meet the changing circumstances.'

The central theme was: '. . . efficiency, about creating a more perhaps American- or German-style economy, with get-up-and-go, encouragement of the young efficient executives, getting away from the old staid and hidebound routines.'

At Westminster the new men and new measures were not particularly popular among those who feared that they themselves might be dismissed as staid and hidebound. The historian and future Conservative MP Robert Rhodes James, then observing Westminster from afar, catches the mood as the party watched Heath surround himself with men who appeared to be managerial technocrats, such as Robert Carr, James Prior and Peter Walker:[1]

'Older Conservatives viewed them with the warm enthusiasm of a company that is suddenly invaded by icy time-and-motion experts . . . The hostility to the new men was not merely one of personality; there were Conservatives who considered that politics – and particularly Conservative politics – were much more complex than management techniques could fathom.'

Matters were not improved for Heath by the 1966 election. In October 1965, the thirty-six Conservative policy groups had produced the document 'Putting Britain Right Ahead'. (The word 'Ahead' was added, according to John Ramsden,[2] when Maudling pointed out that the original title begged the question of who had let the country go wrong.) The document placed heavy emphasis on entry into Europe, trade union reform, overhaul of the tax system to increase incentives and lower public expenditure, but left out incomes policy. As a basis for an election manifesto it was too detailed, too cumbersome, and was denied the extra impact of having any real socialist iniquities to bite upon. Iain Macleod, then shadow Chancellor, commented that the 131 proposals in the manifesto 'Action Not Words' were indigestible:

'This was far too much to put across to the electorate, and the net result was that everybody thought we had no policy.'

But Heath could not be blamed for the 1966 defeat, the second heaviest his party had ever suffered at the hands of Labour. Wilson had skilfully occupied the middle ground, and the electorate were disposed to give him a proper opportunity.

Wilson's ability to score at will off Heath at Westminster combined with the sour taste of electoral defeat to make the Conservative leader more prickly, less certain of himself. Heath's 'abrasive' qualities were no longer to be admired. There was, Sara Morrison remembers:

'. . . a sort of crackable quality in the relationship between Ted, the party organisation, the people out there in the sticks . . . and those who wished the new order of things in the Tory Party well.'

Some cracks appeared early. Even before the 1966 election, Heath had required Angus Maude to leave the front bench after he had written in the *Spectator* that 'for Tories simply to talk like technocrats will get them nowhere'. In 1967 the rising City businessman Edward du Cann was displaced with some acrimony as party chairman. His successor, Anthony Barber, was another congenial member of Heath's circle. Tory grumbling at Westminster that the opposition still thought like a government, that spokesmen such as Maudling and Edward Boyle were insufficiently acerbic in their criticisms of the administration, was muted by Wilson's plummeting popularity. Might it not be enough to wait for the inheritance?

One who thought otherwise was Enoch Powell. Powell had shadow responsibilities for defence, but he did not allow them to inhibit him. He had welcomed the emphatic nature of the election defeat as an opportunity for unbridled opposition, telling the City of London Young Conservatives in April 1966:

'"Words not action" describes with precision the role of the Conservative Party as this new phase opens . . . Some of our words will be harsh, fierce, destructive words, aimed in defiance and contempt at men and policies we detest.'

Powell was an awkward colleague. In 1965 he had put himself at odds with the official Tory position by advocating the abandonment of Britain's East of Suez role. His disenchantment with the Commonwealth led him to criticise sanctions against Rhodesia, an issue where Heath was always in difficulty with the right of his party. He shared with Tony Benn the knack of contriving to reshape party policy whilst apparently merely restating it – to the delight of those who preferred the fundamental verities. In Powell's case, these were a deep sense of the continuity of the English nation, and an abhorrence of state intervention. He once wrote:[3]

'The Conservative in principle denies, in practice minimises, government intervention in the economic field.'

Heath's emphasis on managerial efficiency, his inability to rouse the House of Commons with traditional Toryism, distressed Powell:

'[Ted] didn't really think, I believe, that the House of Commons has a heart, let alone the British people. At least, he's never shown any signs of being able to locate either.'

He feared that the Heath approach, embracing modernity for its own sake, would leave the Conservatives thinking in accordance with the premises of their opponents. A good example of the mutual incomprehension between the two men is contained in Powell's account of the row that broke out in the shadow cabinet over the unlikely subject of Black Rod. That functionary had been subjected to some ribald heckling when he arrived to summon the Commons to hear the Royal Assent declared by the Lords Commissioner in the absence of the sovereign, as was then the custom. The Wilson government proposed that this interruption should henceforth be abolished. The opposition were consulted. Powell remembers:

'At the end of a shadow cabinet, Ted said, "Of course we would all agree with that" . . . And I remember bursting out and saying, "Ted, but we can't do this. You can't destroy a thing like that. Do you realise that the formula which is used in the Royal Commission is that which was used in 1306 when Edward I was ill at the time of a Parliament of Carlisle, and it was probably two hundred years old at that time. You simply cannot destroy a thing like that." And Ted flushed with anger. He said, "This is exactly the sort of thing that does us so much harm. People simply do not understand that mumbo-jumbo." '

To Heath, Powell was a tiresome nuisance, the more so since he gave the hard-pressed Labour government an opportunity to exploit a situation in which, in Richard Crossman's words:

'. . . the titular leader sits nervously strumming on his piano in Albany, while our latter-day Savonarola rampages around the country summoning devout congregations of the faithful to reject as heretics those Conservative leaders [who] in his view, have departed from the straight and narrow path of nineteenth-century laissez-faire.'

The issue which caused the break, however, was not economics but race.

Race had not been a major issue in the 1966 election. Labour had not repealed the Tories' 1962 Commonwealth Immigrants Act. Indeed, they had reduced the number of vouchers for entry from 20,800 to 8500. In 1966 the two parties seemed united on controls, though not on assimilation, where, Rhodes James notes:[4]

'It can fairly be claimed that the Labour policy did at least contain some positive aspects; that of the Conservatives, none at all.'

At Westminster, Home Secretary Roy Jenkins and Conservative leaders such as Maudling, Hogg and Boyle succeeded for a while in keeping the race issue away from inter-party controversy. Tory MPs such as Harold Gurden and Cyril Osborne who persistently harped on immigration statistics were not entirely given their head. Powell, although he represented a Wolverhampton constituency affected by increasing immigrant numbers, rarely mentioned the subject before 1967. While he had drawn attention to immigrant numbers, he had also written, in 1964, that:

'The immigrants who have come already or who are admitted in the future, are part of the community. Their most rapid and effective integration is in the interests of all.'

In 1967 the arrival in Britain of the Kenyan Asians and Labour's Race Relations Bill both aroused Powell. On the Kenyan Asians, the running was made by Duncan Sandys, who saw no irony in the fact that he had been Commonwealth Secretary when they had been allowed to opt for United Kingdom citizenship. Powell joined in with a well-publicised speech during (but not at) the 1967 Conservative conference, in which he said:

'It is quite monstrous that an unforseen loophole in legislation should be able to add another quarter of a million [immigrants] without any control or limit whatsoever.'

By February 1968 at Walsall he was talking of '200,000 Indians in Kenya alone' with an absolute right of entry. The alarmist talk of Sandys and Powell helped to bring about the situation against which they warned, as nervous Asians tried to get in ahead of discriminating controls. The legislation to keep them out was rushed through. Iain Macleod was among the 15 Conservatives who voted against it, arguing that the pledge to the Kenyan Asians was inescapable. He wrote in the *Spectator*:

'We did it. We meant to do it, and in any case we had no alternative.'

Powell's Walsall speech aroused much comment. Its exaggeration of the numbers with a right of entry (120,000 at most) and its lurid language – he talked of 'a constituent whose little daughter was the only white child in her class at school' (later found to be true for the day when the other white children had all been absent ill) – attracted Tory grassroots support. Heath was obliged to say, rather heavily, 'Of course, Mr Powell has nothing to do with racialism.' When the shadow cabinet came to discuss what attitude it should take to the government's compensatory Race Relations Bill, and opted for a 'reasoned amendment' opposing the content rather than the principle, Powell was one of the three men set to draft it. He says now that he was filled with 'a sense of relief . . . that the Conservative Party was at last going to oppose a Race Relations Bill', and therefore proposed to set out his reasons. The 'rivers of blood' speech he made on Saturday, 20 April, in Birmingham, which was not shown to Central Office or to his shadow cabinet colleagues beforehand, reverberated around the party and the country. The shock waves were felt for years to come. The speech both made Powell a politician of the first rank and ensured that he would never attain the fruits of that position. Overnight, real fears and atavistic terrors found a voice and a name.

Powell, white, tense, his hands shaking more than their wont, made his hearers' flesh creep. He quoted a constituent who believed that:

'In this country in fifteen or twenty years the black man will have the whip-hand over the white man.'

He added information sent to him about a little old lady, never found, allegedly terrorised by a Negro landlord:

'Windows are broken. She finds excreta pushed through her letter-box. When she goes to the shops, she is followed by children, charming, wide-grinning piccaninnies. They cannot speak English, but one word they do know. "Racialist," they chant.'

Nothing better exemplifies Powell's use of language than the passage in the speech which was about the Race Relations Bill to be debated three days later, and its effect on the existing population:

'For reasons which they could not comprehend, and in pursuance of a decision by default, on which they were never consulted, they found themselves made strangers in their own country. They found their wives unable to obtain hospital beds in childbirth, their children unable to obtain school places, their homes and neighbourhoods changed beyond recognition, their plans and prospects for the future defeated . . . On top of this, they now learn that a one-way privilege is to be established by Act of Parliament: a law which cannot, and is not intended, to operate to protect them or redress their grievances, is to be enacted to give the stranger, the disgruntled, and the agent pro-vocateur the power to pillory them for their private actions.'

This extraordinary speech had an equally extraordinary reaction. Heath at once denounced it as racialist. He dismissed Powell from the shadow cabinet on the Sunday – and would have done so on the Saturday if he could have got through on the telephone to Wol-verhampton. Powell sees the dismissal as a tactical manoeuvre from a leader who was unwilling to accept his view of party policy:

'It didn't chime with the relationship which Ted Heath thought necessary for electoral success to maintain with what he called "the heavies", the respectable newspapers, or respectable opinion or liberal opinion in the country. So the lesser evil was to dispose of the Member of Parliament who had so accurately hit off the mood of the country, as the unprecedented exhibition of public opinion which followed proved.'

The 'heavies' indeed denounced the speech, analysing Powell's use of fact, myth and anecdote. It was also true that there was a massive expression of support for him after his sacking – some 110,000 letters, marches on the House of Commons by London dockers and meat porters, intent upon showing, as one of them put it, that 'he's the only white man in there'. In the following month 74% of those questioned by Gallup said they agreed in general with the Birmingham speech. It was not true, though, that Heath's action was motivated by expediency. He detested the Powell speech. So did key figures in the shadow cabinet. James Prior, his PPS, recalls that:

'The letters to Mr Heath after he sacked Mr Powell just didn't arrive in bundles, they arrived by the sackful, and 95% of them or more were obscene, and very much against Mr Heath in every way ... I'm quite certain that if Mr Powell hadn't been sacked, Quintin Hogg would have resigned, he was so angry about it.' Hogg, the shadow Home Secretary, was furious that Powell had trespassed on his territory.

In the short run, the Conservatives' approach to the Race Relations Bill after Powell's sacking was muted and confused. Boyle and others declined to vote with the party against it. The right, angry that this had been done with impunity, barracked Hogg when he summed up at the third reading. But Powell had succeeded in putting race back on the political agenda. By September 1968 Heath himself had accommodated the right wing to the extent of calling at York for the law as it applied to aliens to be applied to Commonwealth immigrants, and he had begun to stress that assisted repatriation and the sifting of 'immigrants of good character' were party policy.

At the 1968 party conference Powell's supporters were vociferous on the floor as he in his turn called for repatriation. When he was rebuked by Quintin Hogg, who selected the tag 'moderation in all things, nothing to excess' for the former professor of Greek, Mrs Powell was seen by lip-readers of the television screen to say some very hard things about Hogg. Powell himself smiled broadly. He had moved the locus of the whole debate. Two consequences flowed from this. First, Powell had allowed the previously unsaid to be not just uttered but shouted from the rooftops; others, who lacked his range, would feel emboldened to set out their own darker fears after hearing them expressed by such a man. Second, Powell's new stature, as an independent force on the right, now guaranteed saturation media coverage, also assisted the other causes he espoused, as he set forth a critique of the

Labour government which was markedly more hostile than anything which came from Edward Heath. The Monday Club, founded in 1961 by opponents of the Macmillan/Macleod Tory radicals, expanded its influence in the party well beyond the initial simple creed of Queen, country and capitalism. Powell never joined it, but some of its publications and pamphlets (notably 'Who Goes Home? Immigration and Repatriation' by George K. Young) spoke in the accounts of what was now called Powellism. The party's liberals came under threat. Boyle, unpopular with the right wing for his views on both race and education, left his Birmingham constituency for what was (even then) the more tranquil life of a vice chancellor. Another liberal Tory, Nigel Fisher, challenged in his constituency by a group whom Harold Wilson was quick to dub 'the skinheads of Surbiton', survived. Macleod provided a model of how a friend in need should behave, with his crisp note of support: 'If you go, I go. And so I will.'

At the height of the confrontation with Powell, Heath could draw comfort from the fact that the Labour government was massively unpopular. By-election victories, the drip-feed life-support of opposition parties, flowed in. In May 1968, after the sacking of Powell, the Conservatives were a record 28% ahead of Labour. Yet there were still worries for Heath. Wilson, in his second phase, was occupying more and more of the centre ground. The Heath model for making life better was beginning to look oddly like the Wilson version. When the Labour government applied for entry to the EEC, Heath had imposed a three-line whip in support. To some of his backbenchers this seemed odd behaviour for an opposition. When Wilson alternately went through the motions of tightening sanctions on the Smith regime in Rhodesia and then attempting to negotiate a settlement with it, Heath was persistently wrongfooted. Only Home's determined attempt to keep the 'Rhodesia lobby' in check saved him from major revolts at the hands of backbenchers who argued that the Smith regime should be recognised – indeed would be if Ian Smith could be persuaded to accept the terms dangled before him first on HMS *Tiger* and then, in 1968, on HMS *Fearless*.

It was on trade union and tax reform that Conservative hopes for a distinctive presentation were pinned. Robert Carr had chaired the Conservative study group on the trade unions for the last three years before it reported. They had wanted to wait for the Donovan Commission to report, but eventually published their own proposals two

months earlier. 'Fair Deal at Work' had been carefully researched.
Carr asserts:

'We did our homework very thoroughly indeed. It wasn't just a
study group of politicians; we had people from industry, actually from
both sides of industry . . . certain members who would have been very
embarrassed to have been published, [including] a leading official of
the TUC in his private capacity.'

The detailed proposals expanded on earlier policy statements:
collective agreements would be made legally enforceable; there would
be a registrar of trade unions and a new system of industrial courts.
Sympathetic strikes and inter-union disputes would be excluded from
legislation.

All this looked to be an emphatic contrast to Donovan's advocacy of
steady, undramatic voluntarism. The position changed when 'In Place
of Strife' appeared. It was not a carbon copy of 'Fair Deal at Work',
but it looked close enough to confuse the public and astonish the
Tories. Carr reflects:

'We were caught out by that, because we certainly weren't expecting
a Labour government to introduce legislation of that kind. And there's
no doubt that in the end the fact that they first of all tried and then gave
up made our life very much more difficult when we came into power in
1970, because everything was compared to "In Place of Strife" . . . and
the trade unions, having fought and won a battle with a Labour
government on that issue, were much more likely to fight even harder
and believe they could win against a Tory government.'

But by the same token, trade union power would remain high on
the Conservative agenda, its position shifted to the right by what
Wilson had tried and failed to do.

In other fields of domestic reform the Conservatives again suffered
from the inability to produce a clear and dramatic theme to excite the
nation. The mid-term manifesto 'Make Life Better' was as uninspired
as its title. This was not just because it was burdened by excessive
detail, but also because of disagreements behind the scenes between
the out-and-out free marketeers and Heath's more technocratic
approach, arguing that growth was the key to reversing economic stag-
nation rather than the reduction of government action. Heath wanted
structural and institutional reform to make for the better and less
wasteful use of government aid. In this way, it was hoped, expenditure
could be reduced while the level of services was sustained. Powell, now
challenging on all fronts, was among those who clamoured for

widespread and rapid denationalisation – a stand designed to show up Heath's apparent lack of interest in the ideological approach. He made an impression on Sir Keith Joseph, but had few other disciples within the shadow cabinet. The main concern of the Tories' economic policy group was with the reform of taxation so that it would not penalise initiative. As the national tax burden rose as a proportion of GNP following the austerity of Callaghan and Jenkins, the cost of reducing direct taxation to the desired levels rose ever more sharply. The 1966 Callaghan measures had included SET (Selective Employment Tax), which the Tories were pledged to scrap. But the yield from SET was high (it reached £600 million by 1970) and the economic policy group was left with the alternative of VAT (Value Added Tax), which their business allies insisted should not be accompanied by a payroll tax. Fears that VAT would raise inadequate revenue left the policy planners involved in another hurried search for savings.

Another crucial issue was not thought through, as Brendan Sewill realised:

'The Conservative Party never got down to resolving the intellectual question of whether you needed an incomes policy or not. Several times in the late 1960s I tried to get Ted Heath, Iain Macleod as shadow Chancellor or Reggie Maudling, who'd been Chancellor, to come together and talk about whether one needed an incomes policy . . . each time they were reluctant to do so, and therefore the question was never really properly discussed.'

Maudling inclined to favour incomes policy; Macleod did not. The party went into the 1970 election arguing against any form of statutory prices and incomes policy. Heath was content to campaign on the notion of firm but unspecified guidelines, while belittling the use of the Prices and Incomes Board.

The main draft of what was to be the Conservative election manifesto had been substantially written by Michael Fraser and his aides in 1969. However, a much publicised conference was held at the Selsdon Park Hotel in January 1970 with the aim, in Sewill's words, of getting 'the shadow cabinet together for a weekend to go over all the details of all the various policies, and make sure they were committed to all of them'. Some difficult questions (including those raised in a paper by Sewill examining the possibility of a voluntary incomes policy) were put at the bottom of the agenda. Those present deny that Selsdon Park represented any kind of dramatic move to the right or the setting in concrete of what later became known as the 'No Lame Ducks' attitude to public subsidies to industry.

It was felt, though, that the differences with the government should be most stressed. Wilson's move to the centre had eclipsed the Liberals and pushed the Tories into a different orbit. As David Butler and Michael Pinto-Duschinsky remark in their study of the 1970 election:[5]

'The Labour Party adopted so many Conservative policies that it left Mr Heath little room for manoeuvre if he did not wish to break the consensus by moving to the right. The electorate was denied a direct choice between grammar schools and comprehensive schools, between lower taxes and fewer social services on the one hand and higher taxes and benefits on the other, between neutrality and British membership of the Western Alliance, between large-scale immigration and restriction, between retention and abolition of capital punishment, and even better British support for Nigeria or Biafra.'

The publicity for Selsdon Park therefore stressed the novel and the different. A tougher line on law and order, enthusiastically promoted by the shadow Home Secretary, Quintin Hogg, was given prominence. Wilson was quick to seize his opportunity. 'Selsdon Man', he declared at Birmingham – waiting for the gale of laughter – 'is not just a lurch to the right, it is an atavistic desire to reverse the course of twenty-five years of social revolution. What they are planning is a wanton, calculated and deliberate return to greater inequality . . . The message to the British people would be simple and brutal. It would say, "You're out on your own."' Heath found that his opponent's description of Selsdon was believed by those on his right who wanted unsentimental free-market alternatives to what they saw as welfare corporatism. Their disappointment was all the greater when they found that Selsdon Man, at the time of his birth, had been a fictional character. Heath had never believed it all, although he was happy enough to use the rhetoric of freedom versus state interference. In private he was cautious. 'Are you moving at all to the right?' a close friend asked him in 1970. 'Just a bit,' he replied, 'but we have to stay in the centre.'

There were clues enough to Heath's real priorities. Andrew Alexander, writing from a Powellite position, quotes with a dismissive sniff an interview Heath gave to the *Guardian*'s Terry Coleman during the election:[6]

'He had said, "The key to everything is the creating of more national wealth." Was this the key to everything? "Yes." "Without exception?" "Without exception." "What about such things as freedom?

Did that depend on wealth?" At this he came alive and spoke with a direct strength I had not seen on the previous two days. "If you've ever been poor you will know that." '

This was the real Heath. Sara Morrison sums up his position at the time of Selsdon Park:

'The caricature version . . . of Selsdon Man never ever played a real part in Ted's vision of his premiership . . . I think he wanted the UK to be competent and contemporary, and he wanted the Tory Party with that in mind to become caring and compassionate.'

The problem for Heath went further than the gap between these views and his rather wooden presentation of views further to the right, one of whose champions – Powell – continued to bait him. In addition, there was the difficulty that the government also stood for a caring and compassionate society. And, from 1969, it stood for wealth creation as well. Things had begun to come right for the Wilson government.

Labour in the home straight: 1969–70

In early 1969 Labour had still appeared woefully adrift. Its supporters were disaffected over Vietnam, industrial relations and race relations. Abroad, it had looked foolish in the comic-opera 'invasion' of the tiny Caribbean island of Anguilla, politically helpless after a real invasion – of Czechoslovakia by the Warsaw Pact – and devious in its continued attempts to get a settlement with the Rhodesian regime. The economy did not initially improve after the devaluation of the pound. In the absence of temporary import controls, the balance of payments remained depressing for a full year, forcing Chancellor Roy Jenkins into yet another deflationary package. After a brief rally in the economy in January 1969, the deficit increased once more. Each time, taxes were raised, hitting personal consumption.

Then at last exports began to rise. The Chancellor was at the Export Services Exhibition at Earls Court, which he had just opened, when startling news reached him from the Treasury. The August trade figures showed a surplus of £48 million. The cabinet seized on this with huge relief; they had staked everything on the balance of payments. It would provide a surplus to pay off international debts, and it was a powerful talisman of good husbandry. All the indicators of Britain's economic performance began to turn round. By the time of the Labour conference, the Chancellor was confidently predicting a £500 million surplus. Wilson was rejuvenated. He had had what he describes as a 'chilly reception' at the TUC, following the debacle over 'In Place of Strife'. Now he was able to mock the Tories, who had, he claimed, talked Britain down. Long lists of national technological achievements were recited at an almost computerised pace. The opposition had been:

'. . . dining out on the prospects of our failing to get the balance of payments into surplus. Now as Britain moves from long years of deficit into surplus, their champagne is turning into gripe-water.'

Wilson's own self-projection, by which he set such store, had improved. He was, Crossman thought,[7] 'back at the peak of his form, brilliant, gay, on top, and overpowering Heath'. He had not been as damaged in the country by his failure over trade union reform as had been expected. His chirpiness, his Chaplinesque quality of picking himself up after every disaster, won him a good-humoured tolerance. From cartoonists and commentators alike, he had been through the pain barrier in 1968. The government was also helped in 1969 by the firm action taken in Northern Ireland, when troops were despatched to protect the minority in the province, and the reserve army of the Protestants, the B-Specials, were disbanded (see chapter 8). It was a major rehabilitation for Home Secretary James Callaghan and, for the first time, he, Wilson and Jenkins were seen to be working together, rather than divided, either in rumour or in fact. Wilson could rest easier from his own fear of coups. He had always feared Callaghan most:

'Roy Jenkins and James Callaghan both – and it's perfectly natural and it's very healthy – hoped they would be Prime Minister one day. It's happened in one case. To that extent they might make common cause, but Roy was never quite so serious a politician . . . [James] was full time on it. He wasn't giving dinner parties every night.'

By 1970 the Chancellor's dinner parties were in celebration of a pound which was bursting through its $2.40 level and official reserves standing at over £1000 million. Jenkins's April budget resisted back-bench demands for a general reflation with limited tax concessions, and cast a cautious eye on the steady increase in the level of wage settlements, which threatened to pass an annual rate of 10%. Jenkins thought that 'the British electorate had got absolutely fed up with pre-election budget bonanzas', but rejects the view that this budget's fiscal orthodoxy was eventually to cost Labour dear: 'With the benefit of hindsight I would have been a few hundred million pounds more relaxed than I was.' Jenkins did not forfeit the good opinion of the public, which appeared impressed by his prudence.

Throughout the spring of 1970 the polls still showed a Conservative lead, though it was shrinking. Not until April did any poll show Labour marginally ahead, but by mid-May all were agreed in doing so. Labour gains in the 8 May local elections, followed by a Gallup Poll showing Labour 7% in the lead, convinced Wilson that he could make a dash for safety. From his centrist position as a 'national' leader, he believed that he had pushed the Conservatives into acrimonious irrelevance, as well as entirely neutralising the Liberals. Selsdon Park had seemed a bonus. Powell was providing another. In January 1970 he had said at Scarborough that special aid for areas of high immigrant population did more harm than good, for it encouraged 'all concerned to deceive themselves for longer and longer as to the true magnitude of the prospect'. It was, Heath retorted, 'an example of man's inhumanity to man which is absolutely intolerable in a Christian civilised society'. He was continually goaded by Powell's attacks on the Conservative policy on Europe, and by the publicity which Powell received. With some impudence, Labour strategists now prepared a poster for summer release, in anticipation of an autumn election. 'Yesterday's Men – They Failed Before!' showed six dwarfish mannikins: Heath, Macleod, Hogg, Maudling, Home – and Powell. The poster, now a collector's item, was never fully released, although it was to achieve a later notoriety when its title was used for a BBC documentary film on the (by then) Labour opposition.

As the Tories slumped in the polls, and Heath's regular warnings that the good news of the trade figures could not last were mocked by each new Treasury release, their nerves were worn ragged. The 7% Gallup lead for Labour had produced hysteria at Westminster. Politicians may profess to believe that opinion polls are no better than a heap of entrails, but they pore over every fresh offering. In May, elated Labour MPs with marginal seats behaved like men and women reprieved from a death sentence, Conservatives as though they had just received one. Barbara Castle confided in her diary:[8]

'The truth is that we've all been caught on the hop by the sudden swing of opinion our way.'

Wilson told his colleagues on 14 May that he wanted a June election. He would have a newish register, even more important for Labour now the mobile eighteen-year-olds had the vote. He would avoid trouble at the test matches if there was rioting as a result of Peter Hain's planned campaign against the 1970 South African cricket tour (in the event, it was cancelled). There would be summer weather. England were in the World Cup once again. 'Many Tories will be on holiday in June,' Wilson told his colleagues; the Labour Wakes weeks were to follow. So the election should be on 18 June.

The election campaign was an extraordinary contest between a boxer and a puncher. Wilson took good care to surround himself with the trappings of government. The Prime Minister, in his grey suit and green tie, sat among the tulips in the garden at Downing Street to tell a deferential interviewer that he had gone for June. Why had the polls turned his way? 'Because many people are proud that Britain is strong and paying its own way,' he replied grandly. This was to be his theme, combined with attacks on what now seemed a divided and uncertain Tory leadership. The Labour manifesto was entitled 'Now Britain's Strong Let's Make it Great to Live In'. It laid heavy stress on a strong economy as the basis of welfare spending. Neither there nor in the compendious 'International Briefing – Labour and the World 1964–1970' was there a single mention of Britain's retention and deployment of an independent nuclear deterrent, or condemnation of American policy in Vietnam and Cambodia – issues high in the priorities of the Labour left. His colleagues watched Wilson's progress around Britain with suppressed scepticism. Benn remembers:

'He really did think that his reputation, Doctor Wilson, the man who was above party, would carry the day, and he was much impressed by the Queen's walkabouts in Australia, and therefore the walkabout was used – he would walk about and people would see him.'

Joe Haines, the shrewd *Daily Mirror* journalist who had become Wilson's press secretary, offers another parallel:

'One of the things we did was to run through the commercials for Lyndon Johnson, and Harold thought he should have a fairly quiet campaign; it would be the old seasoned Prime Minister, the man that you know and love so well, against the rather nasty Tory Party. And the idea of the walkabout, the wave from the windows, the doing away with any discussion of policy . . . was initiated by Lady Falkender, Marcia Williams as she then was.'

In contrast, the Conservative leader looked stiff and uncomfortable, lacking in both matiness and assurance. He had not sung a duet with Ena Sharples at the *Sun* television awards dinner.[9] He had not been on *Sportsnight with Coleman*. His close circle knew his doubts and difficulties, recalled by his PPS, James Prior:

'Ted was very quiet and uncertain of himself, and I remember him just before the election going to speak at a great lunch of the Industrial Society where he was putting forward the views of the party on industrial relations . . . It was a pretty grim experience, and Michael Wolff* took me aside afterwards and said, "Look, many more performances like that and we're beaten before we start. You've got to tell him." The problem was, in the words of party chairman Anthony Barber, that "while he was respected . . . because he was reckoned to be a man of integrity . . . the warmth which he undoubtedly exuded in private didn't really come across to the public at large".'

Heath's problem was not lack of a programme or of professional help. The manifesto 'A Better Tomorrow' set out the institutional reforms Britain needed in the long term. There should be no more twisting and turning. The policies for a modern Britain should be stated clearly, even brusquely, then adhered to. One such statement led to much trouble later: 'We utterly reject the philosophy of compulsory wage control.' Heath's personal introduction of the manifesto caught a note picked up at all his meetings: 'During the last six years we have suffered not only from bad policies but from a cheap and trivial style of government.'

Conservative election broadcasts concentrated on rising prices, using a duo of experienced television professionals, Christopher Chataway and Geoffrey Johnson-Smith, and the threat of a coming wage freeze. Images of the snipped 'ten bob pound' and the frozen wage packet 'in the family size' were used recurrently. The BBC programme *Election Forum* was successfully saturated with postcards putting to Harold Wilson the proposition that he was a twister and a liar.

All this took time to break through. Television appeared to show a relaxed Prime Minister enjoying himself among the people and a strained opposition leader lecturing indoor meetings. At Sunderland, Wilson enjoyed himself hugely with hecklers when he saw a number of black 'Enoch' placards among the crowd. 'Your leader isn't coming to Sunderland, is he?' he taunted. 'But then it's sometimes hard to know who your leader is. Heath or Powell, which do you want?' The question touched a raw nerve for the Conservative leadership. Powell's election address had fulminated against Commonwealth immigration and the Common Market in that order. Anything he said in the campaign was guaranteed press headlines and broadcasting

* Wolff was Heath's principal speech writer in opposition.

coverage (of which he received more than the Liberal Party leader and 15% of all coverage of the Conservatives). Heath was left to explain the differences with Powell as best he could, being saved by an inept onslaught from Tony Benn:

'The flag of racialism which has been hoisted in Wolverhampton is beginning to look like the one which fluttered twenty-five years ago over Dachau and Belsen . . . Enoch Powell has emerged as the real leader of the Conservative Party . . . He speaks his mind; Heath does not.'

Heath was able to repudiate the attack, Powell to reiterate his war record against fascism. Powell's remaining speeches were in violent language. In one he warned of 'the enemy within', a massive 'attack by forces which aim at the actual destruction of society as we know or can imagine them'. In another, two days before the poll, he called on the electorate to 'vote Tory' because the national contest was far more than one between 'a man with a pipe and a man with a boat'. He was bitter about the man with the boat:

'This at least has been made crystal clear, over and over again, by the leader of the party, that if there is a Conservative government after Thursday, I shall not be a member of it.'[10]

The most he could hope for was to be returned to Parliament 'on one side of the House or the other'.

It seemed the speech of a man who believed that his party would lose. In the event, it helped the Conservatives to win. After two weeks of adverse opinion polls, which did not tally with the private reports going to Barber at Central Office, there was a palpitation. Heath's dogged talk on prices was getting through. A newspaper strike, inevitably more noticed by the general population than most strikes, was a reminder of past industrial trouble. When, on 9 June, Labour reported yet another record surplus – £606 million – the papers were not there to record it. They were back, however, to make the most of a sudden deficit in the monthly trade figures for May – £31 million – Britain's defeat in the World Cup, and the final Powell speech on 16 June. No published poll then put Heath ahead, but he was already on the brink of a surprise victory. The ground had shifted under Wilson's feet, although he did not feel the tremors until he sat watching the first televised results in his room at the Adelphi Hotel in Liverpool. He was to come back to London with the lost, vulnerable look of a man who has had a stroke. Heath had won an overall majority of 30, with a swing of 4.7%. He could turn in vindication to colleagues who were, in Sara Morrison's phrase, 'lying like stink immediately after the victory, saying that they'd known all the time that they were going to win'. He had known, all along. Wilson was out. The opinion pollsters had lost their deposit.

Wilson blames the result on the weather:

'I think what really did us was the heat. It was very hot weather . . . the combination of the heat, and the opinion polls did us.'

The weather was the least of it. Wilson's revival in the opinion polls had been put to the test when there was no certainty that it would be sustained. As soon as the polls turned, the government went on the hustings, leaving a month for a professional and well-prepared opposition to discredit it. 'Three years' freeze and two months' sunshine', their party political broadcasts warned. Peter Shore, who wrote the Labour manifesto with Wilson, realises with hindsight that:

'The nation needed to be thawed out rather longer in the new warmth of national success that we were enjoying in 1970, before their allegiance could be won, and I think we lost the election largely by abstention, if you like, of Labour votes . . . Wilson could have fought a more dynamic campaign but I'm always reluctant to criticise him as an election campaigner because he's the only Labour leader I know, in my lifetime, who's actually won elections.'

Others were more forthcoming with their criticism. Ian Mikardo had been on the NEC which had passed the anodyne Labour manifesto. He did not think it appealed to party workers:

'They looked at Wilson, they looked at Heath, they found great similarities between them as well as similarities between their policies, and they said, "Well, you know, this is not something to man the barricades for, or even to walk down to the polling station for." They felt it was a matter of indifference what government got in.'

This was true of many of the younger voters. Their idealism had not been touched by the Wilson government. Those on the left had seen the failure to confront capitalism at home. The giant multinationals had been favoured and flattered. The small-time speculative entrepreneur had grown rich. It was the heyday of the industrial merger, and of Slater-Walker's asset-stripping activities, designed, as Jim Slater put it in his autobiography,[11] to 'liberate' assets. Abroad, support for the US, active or tacit, in Vietnam and Cambodia, had bred a bitter disillusion. The authors of the 1968 *May Day Manifesto* wrote:[12]

'The Labour Party, though by no means its whole membership, has redefined itself to fit in with new capitalism and managed politics. The party created, as it was thought, to transform society . . . faces us now in this alien form: a voting machine; an effective bureaucracy; an administration claiming no more than to run the existing system more efficiently.'

Active members fell away, by 150,000 between 1964 and 1970 in the party's published estimates, which exaggerated twofold the real strength of membership.

The increased proportion of GNP spent on education, greater now than that spent on defence, the expansion of higher education for a new elite, left the young unmoved, or challenging the still-unegalitarian provision. Wilson had passed beyond their sympathy. One of the youngest ministers, Shirley Williams, says:

'We got to be a very boring government. People became more and more sceptical about Harold Wilson's brilliant linguistic feats [and] endless weaving of words.'

For the mass of the population things had got better, but not fast enough. More than half of all householders were now home-owners; colour television and motor cars were becoming commonplace. Better provision had to be, and was, made for a population which was expanding at both ends – more young people and more pensioners than ever before. Total personal income rose in the Wilson years by 40%, but in the same period tax and national insurance contributions rose by 80%. This cut into the real income of the average wage earner, who saw public expenditure as a proportion of GNP increasing by the year (it rose between 1958 and 1968 from 40.6% to 52.1%) without commensurate benefits, either to them, or in terms of help for the worst off.

If Labour had been able to demonstrate that this increased public expenditure had improved national planning, and thus increased the rate of growth, and therefore released resources to help the worst off, it could have carried the moral conviction of its 1945–50 predecessor. It did not do so. The National Plan was stillborn, the Industrial Reorga-nisation Corporation a rescue bay for ailing industries. Britain chug-ged along with a rate of economic growth averaging just over 2% – not low by historic standards, but lower than in the last five years of Macmillan and Home, and well below that of the six member states of the EEC. It was not enough to pay for the social programmes which Labour's promises entailed. The more painful alternative – major redistribution of the existing national wealth – was not tried to any significant extent. The richest 1% of the population owned 25% of the national wealth in 1964, 24% in 1968. The poorest 50% increased their share in the same period from 8% to 10% of the total. Among them, the poorest 10% of male manual workers actually earned *less* as a percentage of average incomes by 1969 than they had in 1964 (68% against 71.6%).[13]

The 1970 election, with its wider franchise, had the lowest turnout of any election since 1935: 72%. The result was, in Butler and Pinto-Duschinsky's words:[14]

'The reluctant decision of just enough electors that the Conservatives were, marginally, the lesser of two evils.'

Dr Wilson's plastic surgery on his party and programme had almost come off. He had pushed back the natural centre party, the Liberals. He had held off the nationalist challenge in Scotland and Wales. But in the end, not enough of Labour's natural constituency thought it worthwhile to go to the polling station on 18 June. Wilson would have another chance, but he would never see a second dawn like the one Labour had relished in 1966. His achievements and his own personal resilience and kindness would have to wait for reappraisal. For the moment the Labour Party was to mull over what went wrong. One who thought hard about his own experience in office was the youngest cabinet minister, Tony Benn:

'Our failure to win has always been that we are not able to mobilise our natural constituency, and our defeat is reflected more in the low turnout than it is in the people who vote for the other party . . . Power just slipped through our fingers, because we were saying nothing very useful to people . . . The radicalisation of the Labour Party began from 1970. It wasn't just later. It began then.'

Wilson had tried to find a new constituency in the centre ground of British politics. His failure meant that the old neglected constituency of Labour would come into its own again. The seventies were not to be contested by a social democratic centre party led by Wilson and Jenkins and a Tory Party established still further to the right by Heath's overthrow. That was postponed. Powell had been asked after his 16 June speech in Wolverhampton if he was 'seeking to become leader of the Conservative party'. 'There isn't a vacancy,' he replied. After 18 June, he was right. 'Only one man has really won this election, and that man is Mr Heath,' said the *Economist* on 20 June:

'All parties are alliances, and in the end it was Mr Heath who held his unruly, strained and unconfident Conservative alliance together. No one did it for him.'

Few looked beyond their mutual antipathy to note that Heath and Wilson shared far more objectives and assumptions than fundamental divides. Opinion differed among Conservatives about whether their leader had been elected because of, or in spite of, his presentation of managerial reform and 'efficiency'.

For the moment Heath had won, on his own terms. But if he faltered, the very different approach favoured by his critics would be deployed again – and if not by Powell, by others. The conventional clamour of British politics was to hear from its flanks opposed and harsher calls to battle. Those from the right would find their way better prepared, and the terrain more favourable, than anyone five years earlier would have believed.

3

PREPARING FOR EUROPE

Edward Heath's career has not been blessed with that attribute which above all others Napoleon demanded of his marshals: luck. He lost three out of four elections, more than any other Conservative leader since Balfour. His greatest political success, entering Europe, was soured by changed economic circumstances which he could not have foreseen. But on Waterloo Day, 1970, he had won a great victory – and there were many in his own party who believed him lucky at that hour. In the febrile atmosphere of the previous two months the Conservatives had watched with mounting panic the swing against them in the polls and Wilson's apparently successful attempt to play king-of-the-castle with the balance-of-payments surplus. But Heath had kept his nerve throughout.

The victory was therefore very much his – his triumph and his vindication. As his former PPS Jim Prior, whom he brought into the cabinet shortly after the election, remembers, it greatly increased his standing as Prime Minister:

'The fact that he had won gave him a much stronger position than anyone else would have had under similar circumstances. So he was able to come into government... knowing absolutely what he wanted to do, and being prepared to push it through very toughly indeed.'

This toughness had its bad side: an abrasive manner which could easily be mistaken for stubborn inflexibility. Heath, whose first nine years in Parliament had been spent grappling with the rigours of the Whips' Office, had never acquired the mellow friendships of clubland and the Smoking Room. Lord Croham, Permanent Secretary to the Treasury in 1970, found the new Prime Minister 'a lonely man, also because he was a bachelor, and I think this added to the pressures on him and probably affected his performance, because he was not very able to judge people's reaction to him ... and of course he was very demanding'. Among those who served him, however, he always inspired respect and often devotion.

Heath came to power determined to achieve a number of clear objectives, evolved from the long and assiduous studies of policy options he had seen carried through in opposition. This operation had been managerial in spirit and fact-finding in purpose: a reappraisal, though not of an essentially philosophical kind. The 1970 manifesto set out the managerial plan for Britain. Later, the contrast between policy goals and ideological consistency in achieving them was to open up a long debate between Heath's supporters and their critics on the right of the party. In essence, Heath was a problem solver first, an ideologue only a distant second. He approached the recalcitrant problems of modern Britain like a chief executive, the great civil service departmental head he could have been, rather than as an intuitive populist leader. Enoch Powell, speaking from a very different tradition, makes the point:

'[Ted] believes there is an answer to all problems which can be worked out by proper bureaucratic means – I'm not using that word abusively for once – by the proper approach. If all the relevant facts are assembled and put together by competent people, and logical analysis is made, then that will provide the answer.'

The satirical magazine *Private Eye* caught the Heath style early on, with its fortnightly 'Heathco' bulletins, couched in the hectoring language of a managing director to his workforce. And Heath's public pronouncements often did less than justice to his concern, compassion or comprehensive mastery of facts, as his aide Douglas Hurd recollects:[1]

'. . . introduce a rostrum, a microphone or a few thousand people, and the result could be disastrously different. The voice might change its quality. The vocabulary might become stilted, the tone defensive. The thread of the argument might become lost in a mass of detail. Instead of speaking to people, Mr Heath would too often speak at them.'

These were flaws, but Heath had a strong talent for administration and this was his supreme opportunity. It was inevitable that Powell would be excluded after the events of the previous two years; otherwise, the cabinet contained all the party's talents. The 'Yesterday's Men' prematurely derided by the Labour Party filled the principal posts: Home, Maudling, Macleod, and Quintin Hogg, now re-ermined as Lord Chancellor Hailsham. On the next tier were the key appointments in the new leader's image, men upon whom he relied to see his strategy through: Anthony Barber in Europe, Robert Carr at Employment, Geoffrey Rippon at Technology, Lord Carrington at Defence, and William Whitelaw in charge of the Commons. To provide a second opinion should there be obfuscation by the Whitehall mandarins, the Central Policy Review Staff, vulgarly known as the Think Tank, was set up. Its irreverent reports on the departments culminated, in the early days, in presentations by its chief Lord Rothschild to the cabinet at which, in Douglas Hurd's phrase, he 'rubbed ministers' noses in the future'.

The future which Heath believed would work lay in Europe. To this belief he brought the commitment of a lifetime. His Oxford friend Madron Seligman, who had often travelled with him in Europe since their student days before the war, noticed that, on his postwar visits:

'He was always struck by the speed at which Europe was modernising and everywhere we went he pointed out the way in which Europe was investing in new transport, in new facilities and generally higher standards in many ways, and he felt Britain was falling behind.'

In his maiden speech in 1950, before the silence of the Whips' Office engulfed him, Heath had pleaded with Britain to 'go into the Schuman Plan to develop Europe and to co-ordinate it'. The rapid economic development of the Community in the sixties, and the advantages to its constituent members, together with the weaker political and economic growth of Britain in the same decade, reinforced his determination to achieve this end. Britain must modernise or perish. Community membership would bring more than modernisation, however. To Heath, the strongest arguments for EEC membership had always been the political ones. A united Europe was a guarantee of peace through collective strength, and a counterbalance to the superpowers. Though Heath himself never openly put such an argument into words, friends frequently refer to it, citing his lack of faith in America's international judgement. As Jim Prior observes:

'For Heath, it was never a matter of as it were making Britain's role in Europe that of a lesser power. He saw Britain in Europe as the way back to being a great power again.'

So the imminent negotiations with Europe (set up by the outgoing Labour government) inevitably preoccupied the new prime minister. Community entry fitted into his overall strategy. The key points of this strategy were that the burden of taxation should be switched from the direct to the indirect; that trade union reform should sweep away ancient restrictive practices; and that, from Whitehall ministries through to the National Health Service, government, national and local, should be restructured for efficiency. (Denationalisation was not a major concern.) Incomes policies were forsworn and the Labour government's Prices and Incomes Board sent packing.

Heath consciously reacted against the Wilson style of buying the hours with beer and sandwiches at No. 10, and the years with Royal Commissions and similar postponements of executive action. A vigorous new climate of industrial growth and competitiveness would, he believed, bring the dynamism Britain needed to enter Europe and to survive in its rugged but bracing atmosphere. Robert Carr catches the spirit of the time:

'We believed that Britain had got boxed in. We weren't doing well relative to other countries and we had to make a definite attempt to break out of a vicious circle . . . The first key point was to join the European Community . . . Coupled with that we had to stimulate growth in our economy, and no one will understand the Heath government unless they understand the degree of our commitment to economic growth . . . The Industrial Relations Act fitted into this pattern.'

Heath came before the Conservative conference in October 1970 as its conquering hero. In a comprehensive speech, which reciprocated the warmth that greeted him, he set out his theme of radical change in a free society in which the British would come to appreciate that 'no one will stand between them and the results of their own free choice'. He went on:

'If we are to achieve this choice, we shall have to bring about a change so radical, a revolution so quiet, and yet so total, that it will go far beyond the programme for a parliament to which we are committed and on which we have already embarked.'

The consequences, for the party and the nation, did indeed go far beyond the parliament. Some were revolutionary; none was quiet. On the platform at that Conservative conference one familiar face was absent, another face appeared for the first time. Iain Macleod, convalescent after appendicitis, had collapsed and died of a heart attack in 11 Downing Street just a month after achieving the office he had awaited for so long. This meant not simply the loss of a Chancellor of the Exchequer who had prepared himself for office, for Macleod had no special talent for macro-economics. His gifts of communication, the ringing counter-tenor voice at the party conference, the political flair that went with the gambler's instinct at Westminster: all were unmatched. Robert Carr sums up the loss:

'Politically he was our trumpeter. Ted Heath was never a great

Staunch allies: Harold Wilson at the first of many meetings with US
President Johnson, who later described him as 'a man of mettle'

Left: Trying to beat the ban: Kenyan Asians with British passports arriving at Heathrow in the week of Labour's bill to exclude them

Below: Making the traitors tremble: Protestant fundamentalist Ian Paisley campaigns against the taint of Catholicism

Dreaming of a hat-trick: Harold Wilson at a general election press
conference, June 1970

Right: Unions on the march: demonstrators against the Industrial
Relations Bill, December 1970

Left: The big day spoiled: Edward Heath doused in ink at the formal signing ceremony of the Treaty of Rome by Britain. Sir Alec Douglas Home looks on

Below left: Back to candle power: the impact of the 1972 miners' strike

Below right: The new viceroy: William Whitelaw arrives in Northern Ireland, April 1972

Not to be overlooked: 23-stone Cyril Smith arrives at Westminster after winning the 1972 Rochdale by-election

Holding on to union rights: Vic Feather and his successor as TUC General Secretary, Len Murray

trumpeter, and any party, any government, needs a great trumpeter. And Iain Macleod had a skill unsurpassed in men of any party in my generation of raising issues in a big way which commanded attention, not only amongst his own party supporters, but amongst the country at large . . . His loss was a terrible blow, and of course caused a very early dislocation of the government set-up, a reshuffle within the first two months, just when we were all getting settled into our jobs. That was a great disaster.'

On the evening of Macleod's death, the Prime Minister, his PPS Tim Kitson recalls, hurried round to No. 11 to bring what consolation he could to Eve Macleod. Heath had lost, according to James Prior, 'the one man above all others that [he] would have listened to', a politician who, whatever his performance as Chancellor, would never have allowed the presentation of the government's case to appear heartless or bureaucratic. Heath's advisers recall his long uncertainty about whom to appoint to the Exchequer. Eventually he recalled Anthony Barber, who had had just six weeks in charge of the European negotiations. Tim Kitson remembers Barber's arrival at No. 10:

'When he arrived he looked very surprised and said, "Good gracious me, what's the Prime Minister want *me* for? Not to look after the Treasury, I hope."'

For Barber, a naturally modest man, the Treasury was beyond the pinnacle of his ambitions. It was also to be a formidable test of his capacities. Although he had earlier held office as a junior Treasury minister, he was unprepared for the tussle which was to follow between an expansionist Prime Minister and the ever-cautious Treasury. Geoffrey Rippon replaced Barber as negotiator in Europe, where it had become plain that the key decisions hung on a summit meeting between Heath and the French President.

There was a further consequence of Macleod's death, of greater import. With just a few weeks experience of Westminster, John Davies was plucked from the backbenches to be Minister of Technology, and then almost at once put in charge of the massive new super-ministry of Trade and Industry established in October 1970. It was an appointment the Prime Minister was to regret. One senior colleague who had pushed for Davies recollects, 'I recommended him, and I was a hundred per cent wrong. He couldn't cope in the House.' Nor was he able to delegate within the new ministry whose overlord he became.

John Davies had had exceptional practical experience of a kind welcomed by the new managerial-style administration. He had been a senior industrialist and the first Director General of the Confederation of British Industry. Unfortunately he also suffered from a species of political foot-in-mouth disease which usually eliminates its victims early on in the cruel natural selection of politics. Within months of his appointment he made two speeches, often confused, which were to become rhetorical deadweights. As the government's new champion at the 1970 conference he promised:

'Not to bolster up or bale out companies when I can see no end to the process of propping them up . . .'

And, in the House of Commons in November 1970, Davies hung another phrase around the neck of the government when he said:

'We believe that the essential need of the country is to gear its policies to the great majority of people who are not lame ducks, who do not need a hand, who are quite capable of looking after their own interests, and only demand to be allowed to do so.'

Davies believed that he was speaking in the context of an industrial policy which would break with the postwar consensus of planning and intervention. Heath in opposition had set out a prescription for industrial expansion which was based on lower taxation and less state interference. Institutions which seemed to represent that interference – the Prices and Incomes Board, the Industrial Reorganisation Corporation, the Consumer Council – were speedily wound up. Anthony Barber's first package as Chancellor cut both income and corporation taxes, and roused Labour fury by proposing the abolition of free school milk – giving an early notoriety to the then little known Education Secretary, Margaret Thatcher – among other public expenditure savings. In this context John Davies and his junior ministers, John Eden, Nicholas Ridley and Fred Corfield, believed that they were there, as one of them said, 'to leave the restructuring of industry to market forces'. John Eden has no doubt about the role he thought his department should have played:

'We concluded that a number of companies should not be rescued through the injection of public funds if they could not achieve success in the competitive environment in which they were operating . . . It marked a very considerable change from the practice of the previous administration.'

The early touchstones of this policy, such as the decision not to bail out the Mersey Docks and Harbour Board, did not give adequate indication of the troubles to come. In November 1970 Fred Corfield received an approach from Rolls-Royce. The blue-chip company was in the red. It had superb products and the engineering hubris that went with them. In the aero-engine field the stakes were ever higher. Rolls-Royce knew it had in the prototype RB-211 engine a quantum leap in the technology which would keep it at least abreast of its two American rivals. In the cut-throat competition to place the engine in the US civil aviation market, Rolls-Royce, enthusiastically backed by the Labour Minister of Technology, Tony Benn, had taken a great risk. Blocked from Boeing, and unable to secure a contract with the second largest US airframe manufacturer, McDonnell-Douglas, because of senatorial pressures to buy American, Rolls-Royce concluded an ultimately punitive contract with the third firm, Lockheed, then equally desperate to break back into civil aviation. The contract was fixed price, with heavy time penalties. By 1970 it was clear that technical delays and failures in the experimental carbon fibre intended for the engine fan blades would put the company at Lockheed's mercy.

The government's recent rhetoric had led the nation to believe that lame ducks would be left to die – whatever their size. Rolls-Royce was not. First, in November, it received a further £42 millions in state aid. Then, when the arrival of the Lockheed chief signalled his intention to invoke the penalty clauses, in a single day in early February 1971 the government allowed the company to go bankrupt and then national-ised it, to re-emerge as Rolls-Royce (1971) Ltd. This freed the com-pany of its contractual debt to Lockheed. (It also increased the public sector, which the Conservatives had warned against in their 1970 manifesto.) The unfortunate junior minister, Fred Corfield, whose handling of the affair was not appreciated by his leader, had said that the RB-211 engine was a loser 'significantly behind its competitors'. Now he had to throw his support behind an attempt to renegotiate the RB-211 contract with Lockheed on the best terms available. Rising unemployment, which the Rolls-Royce and sub-contractors' work-forces would have substantially swollen, and the potential blow to national pride if Britain was forced out of an area of high technology where she excelled, caught the government unprepared. The RB-211, and the family of engines derived from it, survives to this day. It was Corfield's political career which nose-dived. Publicly, the Rolls-Royce affair could nevertheless be passed off as aberrant, as conditioned by international defence commitments and Foreign Office anxieties ab-out Britain's standing in the US. There were more problems to come, but for the moment the Prime Minister's thoughts were elsewhere: with Britain's standing in Europe.

Europe: Joining the club to change the rules

In early 1971 Edward Heath's priority was Europe. He wanted to see British entry within the span of a parliament, and he threw his personal weight behind the effort. So successful was he that the whole process of entry took only two and a half years. The price came later. In his timing Heath for once had more than his share of luck. During the 1970 election campaign the Common Market had not been a major issue between the parties. Harold Wilson had resolved to try again, and his negotiator, George Thomson, already had a timetable for the late summer. The Liberals had long been almost rapturously in favour of entry. Only the resolute anti-Europeans stirred uneasily. George Thomson's round of the European capitals in the last days of the Wilson government had even produced a firm date for negotiations to commence: 30 June 1970 – only twelve days after the election. By then, however, it was the Heath negotiators who opened talks with the Commission, which had been making comprehensive preparations for the past six months. The British knew that they must begin with the riddle of France's intentions.

General De Gaulle had departed the political stage in 1969, and life itself a year later. The British negotiator Sir Con O'Neill is candid about Britain's good fortune:

'I don't myself believe that we would ever have got into the Common Market while De Gaulle remained in power. He'd blocked us twice. I think he was perfectly prepared to do it again. But, mercifully from our point of view, he vanished in April 1969, and one must add that it was quite a good thing for us that he died in November the next year, because while he was alive he was a potential brake on Pompidou's freedom of action.'

The new President, Pompidou, was prepared to do business with the British on the basis that those elements of the Community which best suited France, such as the Common Agricultural Policy (CAP), were safe from British meddling. O'Neill sums up Pompidou's attitude:

'He didn't really want to go on having to fight this frightful rearguard action, not only against us, but against the Germans, the Italians, the Belgians and the Dutch, who all sincerely wanted us in. And Pompidou also thought, as the others did, that having us in would be advantageous as being a contributor to the Community budget. There were good reasons for having us.'

These good reasons included the fact that, in early 1970, the transitional phase of the CAP came to an end. In the words of the British historian of the negotiations, Uwe Kitzinger:[2]

'The French had tied down their partners to a system of finance that would for a long time involve transfers in France's favour by helping to pay for agriculture out of the superior productivity of the Community's industries.'

Given this state of affairs, Pompidou could with perfect accuracy tell the residual Gaullist opposition in France that it made sense to admit another net contributor to the club. It is not surprising that the British negotiators reminded themselves (and visiting MPs) of the fable of the Sibylline Books. For Britain, as Heath knew, the price of entry was rising and the economic benefits shrinking with every delay. Heath knew too that the Foreign Office masterplan for prising open the Community – succinctly summed up by ex-diplomat Douglas Hurd as 'isolate the French' – could not work. The Six had gone too far together. Painful as it had been for some of the British Labour ministers to accept, even the anglophile socialist Willy Brandt would not put enlargement, well as he argued for it, before his country's relationship with France. So Pompidou held the cards. It was with him that the game must be played. That meant ensuring that French suspicions about the Anglo-Saxons were assuaged without provoking more protests from a British public mindful of its Commonwealth links of trade and sentiment.

The convivial Geoffrey Rippon, as the new principal negotiator, had both to obtain the best transitional terms he could for Britain and provide guarantees for those Commonwealth countries – particularly the New Zealand farmers and the Caribbean sugar producers – whose markets were imperilled. Sometimes these two interests clashed. Rippon's chief civil service negotiator, Sir Con O'Neill, believes that Britain paid a price:

'I feel confident that, if we hadn't had to get as good a settlement for New Zealand as we eventually got, we could have got more favourable arrangements for ourselves over transitional periods and sums in our Community budget.'

As the year turned, and 1971 saw the growing unpopularity of both the Heath government and EEC membership in the polls, the question of what sort of deal British public opinion would swallow loomed. O'Neill felt trapped by his terms of reference:

'There was not much room for manoeuvre . . . The Community had decided that they would only let in new members provided they accepted everything that the Community had already done . . .'

So there could be no new Common Agricultural Policy, negotiated with British interests and British participation in mind. The British ambassador in Paris, Christopher Soames, who was to play a key role in the negotiations, puts the dilemma bluntly:

'After all, we were trying to join them, we weren't asking them to join us. We were joining the club, with its rules, on the understanding with the other members that if the rules proved to be unfair they must be rendered fair.'

Having to swallow this camel did not prevent the British delegation from straining at some irritating gnats. For ten months the French raised points which stung a *soi-disant* world power. They wanted to see the British begin to shed their role as world banker to the sterling area and to give a commitment to EEC monetary union. They aired their suspicions about Britain's defence links with the USA – an old Gaullist grievance going back to Macmillan's Polaris deal – and about the fact that the Commonwealth's interests were contrary to Community preferences in agriculture. There were differences within the French delegation, and different interpretations of Pompidou's motives. No heir to the Gaullist tradition could afford to let the nationalist card be played against him at home. The best interests of France lay in drawing out the negotiations and maintaining a tough line in public.

By March 1971 discussions in Brussels were deadlocked – on special arrangements for the Commonwealth, on timescales, and on the budget contribution. The French had added the role of sterling to the agenda. The British were being tested as thoroughly as they had been twice before by De Gaulle. Pompidou had been at those earlier summits. He was less marked by historical scars than the general and more relaxed about the Anglo-Saxons. He knew that the world importance of the Commonwealth was receding. He had the Force de Frappe to assuage French sensitivities about Anglo–American nuclear weapons. He was prepared to give sterling time to become a European currency rather than an alternative world reserve linked to the dollar. When he sensed that Heath's patience was running out, along with that of his EEC partners, Pompidou moved. France, wrote Uwe Kitzinger, had:[3]

'. . . made it clear that it was in her power to insist on conditions which no British government was likely to be willing to accept . . .

Pompidou could reckon to obtain the maximum advantage from a direct approach by Edward Heath.'

Heath was not slow to make that approach.

The intermediaries were Ambassador Soames and Michel Jobert, secretary general at the Elysée Palace. They bypassed the French foreign ministry. Heath and Pompidou were kept in touch, but they neither made commitments nor risked personal intervention until a tight agenda had been drawn up, containing what the French wanted to hear from the British. 'The big question,' recalls Soames, 'was how Heath and Pompidou would get on when they met, because they didn't know each other.'

In fact the two leaders had met in the early sixties, in the shadow of De Gaulle's and Macmillan's mutual incomprehension of one another's position.

Could Heath now do better than his predecessor? He prepared himself for his viva voce with formidable application, briefed by Hurd and his aides on what 'carried particular weight with the banker who was President of France'.[4] Heath's mastery of detail was an advantage when so much could hang on one or two days of talks. He landed at Orly airport on 19 May 1971, and made a game attempt to explain, in tortured French, what the *'moment historique'* meant to him. The newsreels unkindly showed Premier Chaban Delmas struggling to keep a straight face, as some of his advisers, less successful, moved hastily out of camera shot. Heath dined that night with Soames, to prepare for the sessions at the Elysée. The British team were gratified by the outcome of that first meeting, as Con O'Neill remembers:

'Heath and Pompidou clicked. They liked each other and they trusted each other. I think they were together having a *tête-à-tête*, nobody there except interpreters, for ten of those twenty-four hours. They broke for meals; nothing else.'

It was the 'greatest single feat of [Heath's] premiership', in the judgement of Douglas Hurd, who served him throughout. He was able to convince Pompidou that the British had come to make friends, not trouble.

Pompidou made a very public demonstration, for domestic French consumption, that he could probe British intentions. It was harder for Heath to explain what he had agreed. Pompidou is dead. Neither Heath nor his interpreter at the Elysée, Michael Palliser, have broken silence. It was left to the man who was later to 'renegotiate' Heath's terms, James Callaghan, to give a mocking version of the concessions some months later, contrasting them with the opposition response:

'"Do you accept the CAP?" Mr Heath said, "Yes." The Labour Party says, "No."

'"Do you accept the unanimity rule – that alterations can only be made by unanimous agreement?" "In the case of the CAP we do not accept it."

'"Do you agree to work for an economic and monetary union?" Mr Heath said, "Yes." The Labour Party says, "No."

'"Will you turn away from the open seas and moor yourself to Europe?" Mr Heath said, "Yes." We say, "No."'

Whatever Heath had agreed, it had an immediate effect. On 7 June the French Finance Minister, Giscard D'Estaing, blandly accepted all the vague assurances offered earlier in the year by Rippon. The British had written themselves into the Treaty; they had not rewritten it. There was a price, as Con O'Neill concedes:

'We realised that our contribution to the budget would be a very severe strain . . . disproportionate. We realised we'd be paying more than anyone else. We hoped . . . agriculture would become less burdensome for the Community as a whole . . . The Community gave us an undertaking that if an unacceptable situation should arise the very survival of the Community would require that its institutions find equitable solutions . . . They refused to incorporate it in the treaty. But it was on the record.'

There was one other safeguard: that member countries would not attempt to overrule any single country in pursuit of what that country believed to be its vital national interests.

No vital interest was thought to be at stake by the British negotiators during the hard slog of negotiations after the Paris summit. The New Zealanders got fair terms, as a special case. The Commonwealth sugar producers pondered the formula that the French would '*avoir au coeur*' their interests, not knowing that those who would have their interests least to heart in future years would be the British farmers who switched into sugar beet production. The British budget contribution was set to rise from 8.64% to 18.92% of the Community total in the five years of transition. Fishing rights were to threaten the whole negotiations late in the day, but by the autumn of 1971 the debate had shifted to British internal politics. Would Britain give 'full-hearted consent' to the terms which in the other three applicant countries, Norway, Denmark and Ireland, was to be sought by national referenda as well as parliamentary debate?

Full-hearted consent: the national debate 1971–2

Heath was often to be reminded that his commitment in the 1970 manifesto had been 'to negotiate, nothing more'. In a carefully phrased statement in May 1970 he had said:

'I do not myself believe that Parliament will approve a settlement which in the opinion of its members is unequal and unfair. In making this judgement they will have in mind, as is natural and legitimate, primarily the effects of entry on the standard of living of those whom they represent. Nor would it be in the interests of the Community that its enlargement should take place except with the full-hearted consent of parliaments and peoples of the new member countries.'

It was clear how this would happen in Scandinavia. But the British abhorred the referendum as alien to parliamentary tradition. The Labour Party NEC had itself voted 15 to 1 against a proposal for a referendum put up by the TGWU. The sole supporter was Tony Benn, from whom more would be heard on the subject. Although there was an all-party parliamentary majority 'if the terms were right', there was no such majority in the country at large. All the polls showed a majority against entry from May 1970 until June 1971.

Following the publication and mass dissemination of the government's White Paper in July there was a brief surge in support of entry, but majority public opinion reverted to hostility for the rest of 1971. In part this reflected the general unpopularity of the government at the time. However, entry became more popular with declared Conservative voters, who had been hostile in the sixties: a 54:34 balance against entry in February was converted to 68:19 in favour by late July. This was helped by the distribution by the Conservatives of 800,000 copies of the shortened version of the White Paper to party members. Also, the overwhelming majority of national newspapers supported entry, and co-ordinated their efforts with that of the lavishly financed European Movement. Broadcasting was influenced by producers who came largely from the group most favourable to entry: young, university-educated professionals. Not all of them would have attended the planning 'media breakfasts' of the European Movement as did the editor of ITN, Nigel Ryan. But they were there in spirit.

The unanimity in the 'quality' press reinforced the rally of the constituencies to the government's case on Europe. This in turn helped Heath with his own recalcitrant backbenchers, one in ten of whom had expressed opposition to entry in their 1970 election addresses. The dissidents had powerful figures among them, including Enoch Powell, and backbenchers of character such as John Biffen and Neil Marten. Early estimates of the number who would vote against varied between 60 and 40 – perhaps up to a sixth of the parliamentary party. However, the government could count on pressure from the constituency associations, and it was decided to leave the vote of principle on accession until October, after the party conference, to maximise these pressures. At the conference Powell gave tongue to the dissident view:

'I do not believe that this nation, which has maintained its independence for a thousand years, will now submit to see it merged or lost; nor did I become a member of our sovereign parliament in order to consent to that sovereignty being abated or transferred. Come what may, I cannot and I will not.'

They were powerful words. They fell on deaf ears. The leadership prevailed, in a well-disciplined conference, by a majority of more than 8 to 1.

The dissidents knew, however, that they might still have the last word. There were enough of them to defeat Heath, who now had an overall majority of only 25, if he was unable to find support elsewhere in the House. He knew he could depend on 5 of the 6 Liberals. But, unless he could wear his own rebels down to single figures, he would also need the support of the Labour pro-Europeans. Much hinged on the attitude of the Labour Party.

Harold Wilson had no natural affection for Europe; he was a European of the head rather than of the heart. Had he won in 1970, he would have pursued his own application for entry without delay. Roy Jenkins, whose fervour for Europe equalled that of his Balliol contemporary Heath, would have been Foreign Secretary. George Thomson would have carried out the negotiations, and would have negotiated similar terms to the Conservatives – he was quick to declare that those brought back by Geoffrey Rippon were acceptable. But Wilson was not in Downing Street. He was in the wilderness, writing his memoirs. For as long as possible he said nothing about Europe, but he was attuned to the changing mood in the party. Resolutions hostile to British membership of the EEC had almost been passed at the 1970 conference. The unions, resentful of the Tory government's industrial relations policy, needed no prompting to reject the terms now offered. When James Callaghan, who had outmanoeuvred Wilson over 'In Place of Strife', seemed to be putting himself at the head of the anti-Europeans with a much-trailed speech at Southampton on 25

May, Wilson, always suspicious of his colleague, feared he would be outflanked. Most of the left and much of the right of the party was already hostile to Europe. Labour's then spokesman on Europe, Harold Lever, recognised his leader's dilemma:

'If Harold Wilson had turned and resisted those who led the fight against Europeanism, even if he'd won, he would have been left without his home in his own constituency in the Labour Party. I'm not charging him with cynicism in any way, but it's inevitable that leaders don't become leaders or stay leaders if they're indifferent to majority support in the parliamentary party.'

Lever knew better than his fellow pro-marketeers why Wilson would not fight their corner for them:

'[In] a strong and bitter battle, his only real allies would have been the Jenkinsites; when the battle was over, he would have been in – shall we say – a precarious condition, even though some of them would have wanted to reward him for his fight by sustained support. The temptation, if they had won, to discard Harold in favour of Roy would have been very strong.'

Some of the Jenkinsites said so to Lever. They had wanted to cut Wilson's throat. They still did. In response to the Prime Minister's glowing endorsement of the terms on television Wilson responded with the theme that he was to offer to his party: 'Are they fair terms . . .?' Some of his left wing were suspicious. The more he talked of the terms, the more they counted their principles. The press wrote him off with derision. David Watt had written in the *Financial Times* in May:

'If the leader of the Labour Party starts at this late stage to discover a sudden burst of indignation on behalf of Caribbean sugar producers, Scottish fishermen and New Zealand farmers, many of us will be quietly sick.'

Ignoring this offstage retching, Wilson began to set out his objections to the terms. Others trod the Damascus road, Denis Healey twice within months. He had been a late convert to entry, writing in the *Daily Mirror* on 26 May:

'I know it's unfashionable. Some of my friends think it's politically inconvenient too. But the world has changed a lot in the last nine years, and so has the Common Market . . .'

Four months later Healey too was opposing the terms, in the language of Ernie Bevin:

'Will it put an extra pat of butter on the plate of the ordinary man and woman in Britain?'

That mountains of the stuff were to descend on the people of Britain may have been less apparent then than it is now, but Healey's turnabout brought him some ridicule. He now says:

'I would regard the episode as probably the most damaging to me of my entire career.'

Rival pro- and anti-market adverts signed by Labour MPs appeared in the press. (One MP of easy persuasion, Michael O'Halloran, signed both.) Anthony Crosland announced that the issue ranked low in importance with him, and found his friends unforgiving. For others it ranked high, above the unity of the party itself, as Peter Shore remembers:

'There were those who longed to drink the waters of national oblivion . . . who wished to merge into a union in western Europe, and there were others who passionately objected to this and who felt that this would be totally destructive of all that had been and all that could be. Now that's not a light issue and of course it racked the Labour Party, and it had to be played out, this drama. But in no way – and this was the dilemma – could people who felt strongly on this issue be persuaded simply and meekly to accept the majority decision.'

In the absence of a referendum, the internal Labour debate had many of the characteristics of the wider national argument: nationalism against internationalism, free trade against protection, capital against labour. The Labour pro-Europeans, increasingly a minority, felt that Community entry was an issue above party. A majority of the last Labour cabinet was in favour; they saw no reason to abandon their commanding positions through resignation on a single issue. Harold Wilson edged away from his former cabinet colleagues, but left them a long rope. He announced that he would pronounce on the terms, but not until after the special party conference on 17 July. Thus he was able to use his influence against a vote being taken at that conference: he must listen to the arguments, he said, without prejudice. And the arguments were called, that hot day, for and against, in an even-handed confrontation. Roy Jenkins was silenced by virtue of his position on the NEC, but the pro-Europeans made the most of the equal treatment they received.

John P. Mackintosh put the pro-market case, echoed by others, that growth at European level would avoid a repeat of the forced devaluations and economic failure of the last Labour government. Michael Foot, and Peter Shore at his most Churchillian, replied that the terms were appalling, the burden intolerable. The Labour marketeers were so encouraged by their success (disproportionate to their numbers at the conference) that they overplayed their hand within the party. At the next PLP debate on the issue Roy Jenkins's demolition of Barbara Castle was greeted by such a drumming of desks by the Jenkinsites that the majority rumbled with rage. The NEC proposed to put a motion to the October conference opposing entry. The constituencies were being mobilised. A televised confrontation between the pro-European Dick Taverne and his hostile general management committee in Lincoln warned wavering members of what might be in store. At the October conference Wilson gave a veiled hint to the pro-marketeers that the coming vote of principle was 'not an end but a beginning'. The bill would follow:

'I cannot imagine a single Labour member who, faced with this legislation, will not be in the lobbies against the government.'

Delegates' anger when the press at once predicted a big rebellion boiled over in a hostile reception for Deputy Leader Roy Jenkins.

The responsibility for those uncannily accurate stories lies with William Rodgers. He had convened meetings throughout the autumn to raise the spirits of the pro-Europeans. A hard, truthful man who had been the organising force behind the Gaitskellite Campaign for Democratic Socialism, Rodgers was trusted by the oddly assorted pro-Europeans. He kept them steady under fire. He also opened communications with the Tories, and this became a factor in Heath's calculations about the parliamentary strategy. As Rodgers recalls, he wrote to the Prime Minister:

'It was wholly personal, and I didn't tell anybody either before or after. I said, "Look, have a free vote. I've always been committed in favour of Britain's membership of the Community. I'm going to vote in favour. But why don't you go first of all for the biggest majority you can get, because you can get a bigger majority with a free vote than without one? And secondly, why don't you see that it's such a great occasion that it must be positive . . .?"'

The government had already postponed the vote of principle in order to have more time to roll up their own dissidents. The Chief Whip, Francis Pym, was also an advocate of a free vote, calculating correctly that the Tory dissidents were outnumbered by those on the Labour benches. With some difficulty he persuaded Heath. The Labour Party persisted with a three-line whip. The gamble of the free vote paid off for the government. On each side the dissidents (69 Labour, 41 Tory) felt the strain, thumbed through telegrams from their constituents, and went through the lobbies in unfamiliar company, murmuring the last words of Sidney Carton. Perhaps 40 on each side either abstained or conformed because of party pressures, but these cancelled each other out. The majority in favour was 112. The vote represented a fairly accurate view of the balance of opinion in the Commons, though it did not at that point represent the feeling in the country.

The treatment of the European Communities Bill, a short measure acceding to the European Treaties, was another matter; this was party politics, in style and content. Pressures to conform were now intense, as the immovable Enoch Powell remembers:

'It only scraped through by 8 votes on second reading after a probably more intensive brainwashing operation on the potential dissenters than any Prime Minister, reverting to his previous character as Chief Whip, has ever carried out. I'm told that those who went into Ted Heath's room in the week before the second reading came out looking more like ghosts than men.'

The rebels were reduced to a small band, nicknamed the 'Dirty Dozen' in their party. Most Labour pro-marketeers followed the lead of Deputy Leader Roy Jenkins in voting against the second reading. (His stance provoked the most offensive mail which the fastidious Jenkins had ever received.) Twelve Tory rebel votes might therefore have been enough to ditch the bill. There was however a further arrangement. The government knew that it could rely on a group of elderly Labour MPs who were not seeking re-election. At each stage as the twelve-clause bill passed through the Commons enough of them were absent, on a rota. The most momentous bill of modern times passed the Commons without amendment. (Many of the tabled amendments, by seeking to amend the treaties, would have prevented their ratification.)

The frustration of the opposition at this procedure – 'full-hearted contempt', Michael Foot called it – helped Labour's incoming chairman Tony Benn when he revived his campaign for a referendum on the issue of entry. The Labour shadow cabinet reversed its previous position and backed him. Roy Jenkins and some of his closest associates promptly resigned, yielding territory to the Labour left which they never recovered. Ironically, in view of their relative success and failure in the 1975 campaign, Jenkins was as apocalyptic in his warnings as Benn was optimistic. And yet Benn would have the last laugh. He had found the issue upon which a coalition could be built that would reduce the old Gaitskellites to a permanent minority. Their dawning realisation of this was to have profound consequences for Labour's schism in the years ahead.

For the moment, Britain went into Europe, with a muted fanfare. Heath, with his characteristic ill luck, was drenched in black ink by a woman protester when he arrived for the signature of the Treaty of Accession. His then PPS remembers him 'going up and down in the lift, looking like something from one of those minstrel shows' while arrangements were made to wash him down, and the statesmen of Europe waited. On this issue, as with little else in his premiership, he had had just enough time, and just enough good fortune, to carry out his grand design. The arguments of both sides in the great debate now embarrass those who put them so passionately. It remains true that entry to Europe brought consequences as profound as both sides had imagined, but rarely what they had foreseen, either in hopes or fears. Heath had taken Britain in, and in doing so had fulfilled his abiding ambition. Old alliances had been fractured; new ones cast. For a few it was the end of the political road; for more it marked the beginning of a new era. And Wilson preserved the option of keeping Britain in Europe, if the premiership by chance should come to him again. He thus contributed to the principle of entry what Heath had given in 1967 – the best that the leader of the opposition could offer, in his fashion.

4

HEATH AND THE SEARCH FOR SOLUTIONS

The Conservatives believed that, if Britain was to be modernised, to achieve real economic growth in the bracing climate which awaited its industry in Europe, they needed simultaneously to reform industrial relations and to break away from the muddled compromises, restrictive practices and wildcat strikes which, in their view, had characterised the Wilson era. Their manifesto had promised a comprehensive bill, which they knew would be bitterly opposed. Employment Secretary Robert Carr, who had more shop-floor experience than most of his colleagues, was to take it through Parliament:

'Wherever you looked in Britain we were an old country in desperate need of physical renewal. We could only do this if we could get economic growth, and the Industrial Relations Bill fitted into this pattern, because we believed we would not succeed in getting growth going [without it]. One of the conditions was to bring a greater degree of stability and orderliness into the conduct of our industrial relations. I don't think that people realised the nature of the British industrial disease at that time. It wasn't too much trade union power; it was really too little constitutional trade union power. The shop floor had taken over.'

Jim Prior, with the hindsight of a later stint at Employment, remembers the compendious hopes placed in it:

'I think enormous faith was placed in the Industrial Relations Act, because really it was the means of bringing about a regulation of the economy, without having to go back to all the old problems of incomes and prices policy all over again. The general thesis was that the trade unions had too much power; they exercised that power in a monopoly situation which enabled them to push up wages without pushing up productivity . . . and this was a way of getting rid of it.'

The government had set its face against incomes policy in the 1970 manifesto. In that year, wage and price inflation were accelerating at 13% and 8% respectively. The Heath government proposed to combine firmness on the wages front where it was itself the employer with a legal framework in which the unofficial strike could be dealt with and the powers devolved or ceded to shop stewards taken by 'registered' unions. Heavily influenced by the Society of Conservative Lawyers and the American Taft–Hartley legislation, the Industrial Relations Bill, published in 1970, was a complex package. Robert Carr had hoped for something simple, written in workaday language, but the lawyers and the parliamentary draftsmen had got at it. Carr himself got into difficulties:

'I had to have a brief in order to understand the purpose of the clause I was talking about. So it was complex to me, one of its main authors. What it seemed to other people I dread to think.'

Comprehensiveness had its virtues, but to the unions the bill sounded and looked alien. Even the legal profession was uneasy; rather than rely on the existing courts, they set up a brand-new Industrial Relations Court, infamously known as the NIRC, to deal with offences under the bill. The approach was the reverse of the piecemeal strategy Prior was to adopt nine years later, and he argues today that:

'If we had simply taken Mrs Castle's legislation and put that into operation in 1970–1, it would have been very difficult for the Labour Party to resist.'

The trade unions had no such difficulty with the new bill. At first, as their academic adviser Lord Wedderburn remembers, the sheer complexity caused delay:

'You see, the three little proposals in "In Place of Strife" were very easy to understand. This great big new bill, with hundreds of clauses and so on – that was much more difficult.'

This bill, the trade union leaders felt, struck at cherished immunities fought for over seventy years. At best its advantages would put them back in the position of the trade union bosses of the fifties, but clamped in corporatist embrace and legal restraint. They were told that the 'pillars' of the bill were non-negotiable.

The substance of the bill offered the trade union leaders a mix of advantages and limitations. It enshrined the right to belong to a trade union, but also the right not to – which struck at the heart of the pre-entry closed shop which many unions had established. Trade unions won the right of recognition and improved protection against unfair dismissal, but they had to pursue these as 'registered' unions, through the National Industrial Relations Court and the Commission on Industrial Relations. The concept of registration in exchange for favours and in fear of penalties was unpopular with the unions, who saw it, in Wedderburn's phrase, as 'state licence'.

Unregistered unions lost tax concessions and were open to unlimited claims for damages where they were accused of the 'unfair industrial practices' set out in the bill. Collective agreements were assumed to be legally binding unless the contrary was stated in writing within them. Fixed limits were set to the amount which could be levied on registered unions in compensation. Unregistered unions had no such limits. Registered unions could avoid liability in actions brought against them if they could show that they had used their 'best endeavours' to prevent repetition of the actions which had caused the complaint. In disputes where the minister judged that a strike would damage the community at large or national security, he could apply to the NIRC for a cooling-off period of up to sixty days and for a secret ballot to test the union membership on the issue.

To the government the bill seemed to provide a portmanteau solution to what they saw as the chaos of British industrial relations. But Vic Feather of the TUC said it turned the unions into 'centralised corporate business enterprises with authority resting at the top'. They saw themselves being required to act as the government's special constables against their own members.

The proposals were debated against a background of industrial bitterness and mounting unemployment. The TUC brought 140,000 demonstrators into central London in February 1971 to the chant 'Kill the Bill', and at a special conference the following month advised member unions to de-register. (All recognised unions had been assumed by the government to be automatically registered.) In Parliament much of the bill passed through the guillotine procedure without being debated at all; the opposition – led ironically by Barbara Castle – on one occasion voted solidly for twenty-four divisions against a mass of clauses which there had been no time to discuss.[1] The opposition were incensed, the trade unions more hostile than ever.

The Industrial Relations Act was duly placed on the statute book. The government believed that opposition would become largely ritual; the unions would fall in with the new framework of law. But in the autumn of 1971 unemployment was creeping up to the million mark and there had been a series of bruising clashes over pay with the public sector unions. These had been conducted with states of emergency used to heighten the sense of crisis. Strikes in the docks and among local authority workers were followed by a tussle with the power workers and their militantly moderate leader Frank Chapple. The power workers had a giant's strength, and this time came close to using it, before the December power cuts were followed by a court of inquiry chaired by Lord Wilberforce. Its findings were not quite in line with the government's recently enunciated 'N–1' pay policy (roughly, that each settlement should be lower than the one before), but the government was relieved. The power workers could have given them a bloodier nose, under different leadership. Wilberforce, they thought, had done a good job. He should be used again. Then the Union of Post Office Workers were worn down in a two-month dispute early in 1971. Everyone liked Tom Jackson but no one rallied to his side. The Post Office Workers went down. So, claimed the government, did the trend of pay settlements. And all without either the Prices and Incomes Board or the old procedures of arbitration and conciliation. There was a price, though: the government's unyielding image made trade union concessions on the Industrial Relations Act highly unlikely.

At the TUC conference in September 1971, Hugh Scanlon of the engineers' union came to the rostrum to call for a tougher line on de-registration: the TUC should *instruct* its member unions to de-register. Despite the misgivings of the TUC General Council, this vote was carried, and over thirty unions were later expelled for the duration of the Act. Robert Carr confesses that the government was caught out by non-compliance:

'I certainly had a blind spot about this. I never expected the trade unions would oppose the bill on the question of registration . . . And from their narrow short-term point of view it was a damnably effective tactic.'

Scanlon believes that his intervention prevented 'an avalanche of registration'. But lack of registration cost a union dear, exposing it to the risk of liability for unlimited damages. Taking account of legal fees, dispute benefits, fines and sequestrations in actions such as that brought by the aptly named Mr Goad of Sudbury, Scanlon calculates that the Act cost the engineers over £8 million, running over into the next parliament, when the NIRC had a brief life-after-death.

All this lay in the future. The government could still claim in the autumn of 1971 that their industrial relations policy was intact. 1972 would be different.

In September the miners put in a 47% pay claim. Over the years of Lord Robens's chairmanship of the National Coal Board they had seen many pits closed, while they slipped down the national earnings league. The union had folk memories of the trauma of 1926, and the splits that had followed. A minimum 55% balloted vote in favour was necessary before strike action could proceed. The NUM's leaders were new and unknown. Robert Carr recollects that:

'Our judgement turned out to be wrong. There was no doubt about it, our intelligence about the strength of opinion within the miners' union generally was not as good as it should have been. The miners really do walk on their own . . . We just didn't know the miners. They hadn't been to St James's Square, the old home of the Ministry of Labour, for nearly fifty years.'

This optimism based on inadequate intelligence continued even when the miners rejected an NCB offer of less than 10% and voted, just – by 55.8% – for strike action. The NCB chairman, Derek Ezra, believed the NUM President, Joe Gormley, to be 'a man who wanted a settlement rather than not to have a settlement'. Gormley was good at giving this impression, and it was partly true. The *Economist* announced in bullish mood that 'there is plenty of coal stock to ride out a strike'. In fact, there was less than two months' supply. Perhaps the NUM executive's intelligence was better than their opponents'. With considerable public opinion behind it, the NUM brought out every one of its 280,000 members. Even right-wing Tories who represented moderate mining areas called for a better offer from the NCB. The government remained publicly calm. Sir Denis Barnes, Carr's Permanent Secretary, saw no plans in preparation:

'Heath, having called two national emergencies in the last nine months didn't want to declare another, so nothing was done to plan electricity cuts until the last moment, and things ended with industry in a fair sort of shambles . . .'

The NUM Secretary, Lawrence Daly, agrees:

'I think if they'd moved quicker it's possible we might have been defeated. But they waited a few weeks.'

Daly and his colleagues were able to accelerate the run-down of stocks by using a new weapon: the flying picket.

'Suggestions for flying pickets came from a Scotsman who was a Yorkshire area official, Jock Cane, and he and others, like Sammy Taylor from Yorkshire, pressed for the idea of using miners on strike . . . to go and ensure that supplies weren't getting to power stations, etc. We didn't have to picket pits at all, because the lads were with us solid. . . . It was surprising how effective it was.'

The great set-piece confrontation of the strike was at the Nechells Works of the West Midland Gas Board, Saltley. This episode has long since passed into legend, and its assumed lessons have been absorbed and endlessly reworked by both sides. In February 1972 the depot held 100,000 tons of coke. As lorries queued in the cramped triangle of access roads to take out the coke, the local NUM pickets sent out for reinforcements. The call was answered by 400 Yorkshire pickets, led by an unknown area officer named Arthur Scargill. Scargill had the supreme advantage of knowing exactly what he wanted to do:[2]

'It was an El Dorado of coke. There were a thousand lorries a day going in and you can imagine the reaction of our boys fresh from the successes in East Anglia ... We wished to paralyse the nation's economy. It's as simple as that ... We were out to defeat Heath and Heath's policies because we were fighting a government.'

The police faced mounting difficulty as they were daily crushed by fresh reserves of pickets – 'panzers without tanks', recalls ex-Chief Inspector Brannigan. Whereas the local union leaders went home at teatime, Brannigan remembers Scargill staying there with his men throughout, building up the mass which eventually grew to more than 15,000. On the final day, reinforcements of Midlands trade unionists, men and women, arrived at Saltley like Prussian columns at Waterloo. Alan Law of the TGWU was there on that day:

'We all stood and moved towards the Saltley gate. Ten thousand voices took up the cheer: "Close the gate, close the gate, close the gate." It had to close, it had become a fixation – that gate was the object of so much feeling on the part of the multitude.'

Saltley gate had become a fixation elsewhere, too. Jim Prior was in cabinet that morning. Home Secretary Maudling had reported that the chief constable of Birmingham was determined to hold firm:

'In the middle of cabinet a note came in to Reggie Maudling which he read out to colleagues. It was a message from the chief constable saying that about 15,000 people had turned up at the gates and he was frightened the police would have been totally overrun; the gates had therefore been closed and the lorries turned away. Now that was a very dramatic moment as far as cabinet was concerned, and I think a sad moment as to the future conduct of the strike because it really meant we were beaten by intimidation and force.'

Arthur Scargill saw it differently. He told the massed cameras ecstatically:

'Here was living proof that the working class had only to flex its muscles and it could bring governments, employers, society, to a complete standstill.'

In the end, though, the significance of Saltley lay in the lessons that each of the protagonists thought they had learned from it and would live to use again. (In fact Saltley did not have much coke left, and the gates could have been opened again on the following Monday.) The miners won for other reasons, as the NUM-sponsored MP Dennis Skinner explains:

'We were absolutely confident that we would win, and we won, as you know, in seven weeks . . . It wasn't based on some super confidence by the miners. It was purely on the fact that there was only seven weeks' supply of coal . . . I tend to the view that we were well on the way to victory by the time of the Saltley closure. It was symbolic, it was psychological, and it helped to impress the establishment . . . they set up the Wilberforce inquiry.'

The establishment was indeed thrown off-balance. On the day after Saltley gate closed behind the chief constable, Douglas Hurd noted in his diary:[3]

'The government is now vainly wandering over the battlefield looking for someone to surrender to, and being massacred all the time.'

Brendan Sewill, in the Treasury as a special adviser, recalls:

'The lights all went out and everybody said that the country would disintegrate in a week. All the civil servants rushed around saying, "Perhaps we ought to activate the nuclear underground shelters and the centres of regional government, because there'll be no electricity and there'll be riots in the streets. The sewage will overflow and there'll be epidemics. The result of all that was that the government had to give way and pay up to the miners.'

The government turned to Lord Wilberforce, who had served them well before. He reported within the week: 20% for the miners, phased over sixteen months. The miners needed further concessions, served up at No. 10, before they accepted. They could have had the N–1 incomes policy for dessert, for they had well and truly cooked it. Heath's ministers believed that, as Carr puts it, 'the court of inquiry blew us to pieces'. Anthony Barber thought it 'a disaster' which was never again far from the government's mind when dealing with the miners. The Prime Minister, however, came out of the candlelit conclaves of the cabinet determined to try a fresh approach: 'a more sensible way to settle our differences'. But before this could come about he was to have other rebuffs from the unions.

First, there were various body blows for the NIRC, which cumulatively undermined the rationale of the Industrial Relations Act. Before the coal dust had settled on the Wilberforce Report, the three rail unions submitted a pay claim which the government resisted. It was much lower than that of the miners, as were most others that spring, but the government wanted to resist. The new Employment Secretary was Maurice Macmillan, a tense, shy, thoughtful man, who lived on nerves and black coffee – in outlook very much his father's son. Macmillan was intended to be a conciliator. He offered arbitration. When its findings were rejected, he went to the NIRC under the IR Act to get a cooling-off period of fourteen days, followed by a ballot. The result was decisively in favour of strike action. Even the moderate staff union, the TSSA, voted 2 to 1 in favour. The strike was now legitimated in the government's own terms. Sid Weighell, the new General Secretary of the NUR, watched the law officers arguing before the NIRC:

'They didn't understand what made the trade union movement tick.'

But they did understand now that any ballot would be treated as a vote for or against the act and the NIRC. The compulsory ballot was not used again.

The NIRC's main tussle was with the largest union in the land, the TGWU. The dockers, traditionally at the heart of this union, were embroiled in one of the great issues of industrial change during the seventies: containerisation. It had become quicker and more efficient to load goods into containers outside the docks. New ports were springing up to deal with this traffic as the pattern of British trade shifted. The established docker in a traditional port such as Liverpool felt particularly threatened. Dockers began to picket the new container terminals and the transport firms which serviced them. One of these firms, Heaton's, had recourse to the NIRC, who fined the TGWU £5000 for the action of its shop stewards, and £50,000 when it ignored the court and continued the blacking. The union was urged by the TUC constitutionalists to go to court. Len Murray believes that the union was content to be pushed in this way; the initiative did not come from its side, but it tacitly accepted his view. So the unregistered TGWU went not to the NIRC but to the Court of Appeal.

What happened next was a 'torpedo below the waterline' for the government, in Robert Carr's phrase. Lord Denning in the Court of Appeal found for the union, agreeing that it could not be held responsible for its members. He picked up with cruel accuracy the flaw in the Act which had been exposed by de-registration, saying in judgement:

'If registered, the shop stewards would be guilty of unfair industrial practices but the union would not . . . Why then, should the union be mulcted in heavy fines and large compensation, simply because it was not registered? If the legislature had intended that an unregistered union should be so penalised, it should have said so . . . But Parliament has not said so.'

This meant that the NIRC would not in future be acting against great unions, whose funds could be sequestered, but against the individual shop stewards who had been forcing the militant pace. Robert Carr saw at once the scale of the 'disaster'. He and Geoffrey Howe had tried 'to draw up proposals which would make it as difficult as possible for anybody to be sent to prison under the Act . . . I remember we both felt we might as well jump off Westminster Bridge that morning.'

The imprisonment of individuals, with all its emotive overtones, was now a probability, as the NIRC went rolling on. Heaton's appealed against the Denning judgement to the House of Lords. In east London, workers at two depots were bringing actions against named dockers' shop stewards involved in picketing them. One action was brought by Tony Churchman, a shop steward inside the Chobham Farm depot, who found that his rivals outside the gates were delighted that the NIRC had ordered their arrest for contempt:

'It was like a holiday, a bank holiday. They were sitting on the roofs, on the balconies. All the traffic was stopped. I've never seen anything like it in my life.'

There was some fast footwork. The TGWU leader, Jack Jones, was well aware that the shop stewards' action was implicitly critical of the union, which had paid fines, and gone to court. He had members on both sides in the dispute. He did not want martyrs from the far left. Two barristers who had acted for the TGWU before saw Lord Denning privately, and the unlikely figure of the Official Solicitor appealed for the prison orders to be quashed. Denning concurred. The government was made to look doubly foolish – first for getting into such a position and then for apparently using such an arcane escape route. In fact, it was Denning's own political judgement:

'We were influenced perhaps by the state of the country, by the realisation that there would be a general strike, which would paralyse the whole nation ... I disclaim any political considerations whatsoever. We've got to construe the Act of Parliament in relation to the whole system of society as it is, and that is what we did.'

The shop stewards were widely quoted as being dismayed that they had been snatched from the prison gates. 'It's a bloody liberty, they had no right to do it,' said one. Another, Bernie Steer, remembers how the TUC hierarchy wanted them to go to court rather than prison:

'We were asked unofficially by Vic Feather whether we wanted to go to court and told that they would deal with the expense, provide the lawyer and so forth – which I thought most strange coming from the General Secretary, when the TUC's policy was not to have anything to do with the court.'

A fresh action was brought against the dockers for picketing Midland Cold Storage. Again the NIRC pronounced, was spurned, and issued a committal order. By now there was national publicity, as another Dickensian figure, the Tipstaff, trudged bravely into the crowd to remove five of the pickets to Pentonville. One of them was seen shouting, 'How can they arrest me? The Union Jack grows out of my bloody head.' The widespread support for the men sprang from the view that it was unBritish to jail men for taking industrial action. There were sympathetic strikes. The TUC broke off its tentative talks with the government about the economy and threatened a one-day general strike on 31 July. Mass demonstrations outside Pentonville were organised.

The government were now desperately anxious for industrial peace; above all, they desired trade union cooperation and restraint for their new policy of reflating the economy. The Act had to be put on the back burner. With fortunate timing for the government, the House of Lords swiftly ruled against Denning in the Heaton's case, and restored the status quo ante. That meant that the union rather than the shop stewards was held responsible. The Pentonville Five were released by the NIRC and came out of prison to a heroes' reception without having purged their contempt.

The NIRC's time had passed, though it lingered on through other controversies such as the Goad case. The portmanteau approach to trade union reform had been discredited. Those who had resisted the act without compromise were vindicated, though they did not fully realise how much they owed to events outside their control. The Denning judgement taught those who had drafted the Act a sharp lesson, as Sir Denis Barnes concedes:

'The fact that the judiciary could take such different views of its meaning implied that the Act wasn't as well drafted as it might have been.'

It had acquired a reputation for actually worsening industrial relations, within a very short life-span.

Thus, by mid-1972, the Conservatives' policies on pay and trade union reform were in equal disarray at the hands of the unions. Well before this, a third front had been opened up against Heath's promise of a 'quiet revolution'.

The industrial U-turn and the dash for growth

The government's policy of disengagement from industry had been dented by its nationalisation of Rolls-Royce. But that could be presented as a unique aberration, necessary to fulfil world obligations. The case of the Upper Clyde Shipbuilders' yards seemed at first sight totally different. This consortium, put together during the previous government's phase of belief in strength through merger, now had debts of £28 million. In opposition the Conservatives had considered a document, attributed to Nicholas Ridley, proposing the 'butchery' of the yards, and the sale of the carcass. Ridley, a junior minister in the DTI, sat beside John Davies in the House of Commons in June 1971 when Davies declared that this lame duck was for the slab:

'The government has decided that nobody's interest will be served by making an injection of funds into the firm as it now stands.'

Closure loomed, and the liquidator was called in. The UCS workers, however, got in first. They organised a work-in, which generated enormous publicity, and found a voice in the shop steward Jimmy Reid, then a leading member of the Communist Party. The strategy was simple:

'The best way of demonstrating what we were demanding, namely the right to work, was by continuing to work no matter what anyone said. So if they said, "You're sacked", we'd say, "No, we're not sacked, and we're continuing to work."'

The work-in caught both parties by surprise. Tony Benn was quick to show his support by visiting the shipyards – an action that initially

drew criticism from his shadow cabinet colleagues. But their opinion
rapidly changed. So, more slowly, did that of the government. At first,
the DTI ministers held their ground, but they began to find themselves
isolated. The UCS workers shrewdly invited the media into the yards
to chronicle the work-in, whose significance was emphasised by the
shadow of the workless outside. Unemployment was rising fast, and
nowhere faster than on Clydeside. The local chief constable, David
McNee, warned the cabinet that violence on the scale then becoming
familiar in Northern Ireland was a real possibility. If there were to be a
million jobless by the turn of the year, no one would feel more guilty
than the Prime Minister and his close colleagues, who had come to
maturity in the thirties. Whitelaw, who had cut his political teeth in a
Clyde constituency, warned that there was a point beyond which you
could not push the Clydesiders.

Jimmy Reid gambled on a belief that the decision on the yards would
be taken above the level of the DTI. He was right. In 1972 a further
£35 million was injected into UCS; all four yards were saved, one
switching later to offshore rig construction. Heath's critics accused
him then, and have since, of reacting to unemployment by throwing
money at it in 'Pavlovian' fashion. He brushed aside such criticism in
his own party at the time, arguing that he was not in office to create
what then seemed like the last word in mass unemployment; he would
use the power of the state to prevent it, and personal persuasion. His
impatience with the industrialists whose response to his bracing new
climate of confidence seemed to be to push Britain into slump was
seldom hidden. Campbell Adamson of the CBI was a recipient of
frequent thunderbolts:

'I couldn't count on the fingers of both hands the number of times
that Mr Heath told us that everything had been put right that the
government could put right, and still industry didn't invest enough.'

The Chancellor had admitted in July 1971 that a mini budget was
needed:

'In spite of a recovery in the second quarter, taking the first half of
1971 as a whole, the level of output was probably more than 1%
below the level assumed at the time of the [March] budget.'

He welcomed the CBI's offer of voluntary restraint on prices, and
went for further stimulus of the economy, with cuts in purchase tax,
easier credit and better allowances for industrial investment. The
nationalised industries were to restrain their prices – a course of action
that would provoke fierce wage battles later. Output was planned to

grow by 4% between the first halves of 1971 and 1972. Inflation was running at 13%. Unemployment, however, also continued to rise. In January 1972, with the European legislation in the Commons and the miners at the gates, Heath faced tumult. Jim Prior remembers that time:

'When the figure reached a million and there was uproar in the House, he was very shaken, and I think this had a marked effect on his wish to reflate the economy. And of course from having started off with a tough public expenditure programme . . . we found ourselves as an anti-cyclical measure freeing up the economy and spending a great deal of money.'

The money did not go into British industry. Already in early 1972, as Access credit cards 'took the waiting out of wanting', the cash registers rang to the tune of Japanese electronics, German cars and Italian deep-freezes. It was only just beginning.

In the opening months of 1972 Heath must have thought sometimes of Baldwin's dictum, recalled for him by the old Earl of Swinton: no wise prime minister ever takes on any of these three – the Pope, the Treasury or the miners. Heath had taken over responsibility for Northern Ireland after Bloody Sunday. He had been humiliated by the miners. The first rumblings about the inflationary consequences of his growth priority were audible in the Treasury. To fashion a new industrial strategy, if industrialists and ministers could not do it, seemed a minor challenge compared to such as these. Even at the 1971 Conservative conference press speculation had suggested that the right-wing junior ministers at the DTI were themselves lame ducks. In late 1971 a committee of officials was set up to devise a framework for industrial expansion. It was chaired by Sir William Armstrong, the determined and somewhat messianic head of the Civil Service. Armstrong had been Permanent Secretary at the Treasury. He had been in at the creation of the DTI and the other super-ministries. Now he was itching for a renewed involvement in economic policy. As the Treasury drifted out of favour with Heath, his opportunity came. Armstrong brought together a strong team consisting of members of the Cabinet Office and the Think Tank, and the Treasury mandarin Sir Leo Pliatzky, who thus describes their task:

'The concept was that we must strengthen our industrial capacity so as to take advantage of membership of the Common Market. And those really were the terms of reference of the exercise.'

The outcome was to be a new Industry Act. Very few of those whose departments were to be profoundly affected by the 'exercise' knew about it, Pliatzky says:

'. . . so of course when conclusions were reached, and the wraps came off, it was a very great shock to some of the other members of the government, and some of those who were most committed to the market economy philosophy were really quite taken aback by the whole thing.'

The bad news was broken to Eden, Corfield and Ridley by John Davies, as Corfield remembers:

'We were told out of the blue that the Secretary of State was very sorry he hadn't been able to tell us before, but he'd been given strict instructions from the Prime Minister that he was not to do so . . . The Industry Act was to restore the power of government to channel finances of companies which were in difficulties. In other words, it was a complete reversal of the policy which we had been elected upon.'

The Industry Act gave wide-ranging powers to the DTI to disburse money to companies not just in the assisted areas but throughout the country. These powers were supported by an Industrial Development Executive uncannily like that Industrial Reorganisation Corporation which the Tories had abolished less than two years previously. Corfield and Ridley became martyrs for the free market reformation and were dismissed from the government. Eden was translated to Telecommunications. Their passing cannot have been made easier by the widely reported hopes of Tony Benn that the Industry Act would be 'spadework for socialism'!

The conjunction of the 1972 Industry Act and the 1972 budget marked the watershed of the Heath government. In his budget speech Anthony Barber made it clear to Parliament that, while the previous year had been 'dominated by the twin evils of inflation and unemployment', he was not one of those who 'look[ed] to unemployment as the cure for inflation'. His critics in his party later charged that he erred in the opposite direction. Barber said that a 'further boost to demand is required'. This was to be the real spur in the 'dash for growth'. The aim was to have achieved 10% growth between the first half of 1971 and the first half of 1973. That was to be lift-off: 'a rare opportunity to secure a substantial and faster rate of growth over a considerable period of years'.

Barber believed that such a boost would not be 'inimical to the fight against inflation'. It was possible to believe in 1972 that, on the evidence of its first decade, the Common Market would give greater opportunity for growth. There was spare capacity in the economy. There was a potential growth in productivity if industrial relations improved. Public expenditure, now to be increased, would later decelerate to allow expansion in the private sector. If the pound was floated, and allowed to find its own level, a sterling crisis, which had so often intervened as the British economy heated up, could be avoided. The strong element of wishful thinking in these five strands is more apparent now than it was then. Barber's budget cut income tax by a billion pounds, with additional tax cuts. All investment in plant and machinery other than passenger cars would receive 'free depreciation' – that is, a 100% first-year allowance. The regional development grants abolished under another name in 1970 were re-introduced, and the White Paper 'Industrial and Regional Development' was unveiled the day after the budget, rapidly to become law as the Industry Act.

These policies bore Edward Heath's personal stamp. They were his attempt to exploit the opportunity of Europe and to reduce unemployment – if not at a stroke, then at least faster than his advisers believed wise. The Prime Minister had taken on the Treasury. Brendan Sewill, drafted in as Barber's special assistant in 1970, says:

'I was very worried about the 1972 budget. I realised it was too big – too big tax giveaways. And I think a lot of people within the Treasury were worried too.'

John Nott, then a junior minister in the Treasury, is adamant that 'the so-called Barber Boom was the responsibility of the Prime Minister, Edward Heath'. A senior Treasury civil servant of those days confirms this view:

'The enthusiasm for the increase in expenditure certainly came from the Prime Minister and one or two of the spending ministers, rather than from the Chancellor of the day. The Chancellor went along with it. But quite a lot of the organisation of it was not actually done under the Chancellor; it was done under a programme which Heath took a very close interest in. You certainly can't blame Barber for the expansion.'

Barber himself has remained loyal to his old chief in public, although there was a hint in his *Financial Times* review of Sam Brittan's *The Economic Consequences of Democracy* in 1977 that he had later contemplated resignation. Of the 1972 budget he now remarks:

'You can say with the benefit of hindsight that that budget was too inflationary. That's a fair criticism. But the fact is, at the time we thought this was in all the circumstances not unreasonable.'

A strong Prime Minister could carry the cabinet against an amiable Chancellor. Sometimes Barber's endorsement of the strategy did not cover all the decisions:

'There were one or two occasions when I really felt we were taking decisions on public expenditure where I felt I should have had more support. I got rather depressed and I used to come back and talk to Jean, my wife, and say, "Oh God, I'm fed up with this bloody job" . . . but I never put pen to paper or anything like that.'

To do so, he felt, would have been 'to announce to the world that the spenders had won'.

The spenders were winning in a Keynesian world, where today's emphasis on controlling the various money supplies had not developed. In May 1971 the Bank of England had published its consultative document, 'Competition and Credit Control', proposing 'new techniques of monetary policy'. Later that month, the Governor explained that it was:

'. . . a new approach to credit control designed to permit the price mechanism to function efficiently in the allocation of credit . . . It is hoped these changes will favour innovation and competition and in their way make some contribution to faster and sounder economic growth.'

Changes in the methods used to control credit were introduced in September 1971 and produced some transitional distortion of the monetary aggregates, particularly M3. (M3 is the money in circulation plus both current-account bank deposits and such things as deposit accounts held by UK residents; M1 excludes the latter.) The growth in M3 was 28% in 1972 and 29% in 1973, but the narrower aggregate, M1, grew by only 14% in 1972 and 7% in 1973. Critics in the Conservative Party began to speak out. In June 1973, Enoch Powell warned:[4]

'The flow of money is increasing at such a pace that it would increase by one fifth in a single year. There is no doubt what this means . . . inflation.'

Did the government genuinely believe that such an increase in money supply was not dangerous? Or was it simply holding on for growth at all costs? They undoubtedly regarded monetary policy as subordinate to fiscal policy, and primarily as an instrument of demand management rather than for the control of inflation. The Chancellor argued that high growth of output 'will entail a growth of money supply that is high by the standards of past years'. He was advised that some of the increase in M3 was the consequence of the new system of credit control. But there was no preparedness to follow through the logic of the new system. Since it was based on the price mechanism it involved the will to raise interest rates when monetary restraint was needed. The Chancellor was held back by the Prime Minister. Determined to see investment increase, Heath refused to countenance higher interest rates for a further year – until their abrupt hike from 7% to 11% in July 1973. Jim Prior explains why:

'[Heath had] to pump money into the economy in what he knew was a risky business, in order to try to break through to the sunnier uplands of higher growth.'

The decision to float the pound in 1972, following the American decision to suspend dollar convertibility into gold, inevitable though it was, carried its own snare. Previously, inflation had caused an exchange crisis and the fall of the currency against the dollar. Now with the floating pound those warnings were muffled, just when they were most needed. Meanwhile the falling pound had an immediate inflationary effect on the prices of the imports which were being sucked into Britain in increasing numbers.

The tripartite talks and the U-turn

After the 'disaster' of the defeat by the miners, Edward Heath had said that the country needed 'a more sensible way to settle our differences'. If he was to see his growth policy through, he believed he had to have some agreement on prices and incomes. It could not be statutory; the 1970 manifesto had utterly rejected the philosophy of compulsory wage control. And as the incomes policy lobby, principally identified with Reginald Maudling, became vociferous once more, Heath's Wolverhampton scourge lashed the government for this flirtation with wages and prices control:[5]

' "Do we really," one groans aloud, "have to go through all that once more? It is bad enough to have seen the X-film once, but is it necessary to stay in our seats through another and yet another performance? We know how it finishes; and it will finish the same way, however often it is played through." '

Heath, however, believed he had a different cast, and could script a different conclusion. After several overtures and false starts, owing to the dispute over the shop stewards imprisoned in Pentonville, Heath brought together a working group of ministers and trade union leaders to discuss urgently 'the problem of conciliation, low pay, a link in collective agreements to the cost of living, and the improvement of the UK's competitive position'. Influenced by the extent to which European leaders such as Helmut Schmidt seemed able to take their unions into their confidence, Heath made a major personal effort to win over the TUC leaders. Formal tripartite talks between the three sides opened in September 1972. Robert Carr sets out their aim:

'We really did bring the trade union movement and employers into . . . the guts of macroeconomic policy and we really did open the books . . . to look at the national income figures, the expected growth in national income over the coming year . . . to get common agreement that that was the most growth we could expect and how best to distribute it.'

For nearly two months Heath brought to this task his command of detail and his fixity of purpose. In spite of themselves, the trade union leaders came to respect him for it. Jack Jones seems to have rediscovered behind the mask the man who had been on the same side as him in the Spanish Civil War:

'. . . a very decent man, there's no question about that. He was prepared to be patient and listen to our point of view and our arguments, and, within his limits as a Conservative Prime Minister, I think he did try to respond.'

The CBI representatives agree that, as Sir Richard O'Brien puts it:

'He conducted the talks with great sensitivity . . . [his] great quality was that he listened.'

As the talks went on, Campbell Adamson of the CBI reflects:

'One got the growing feeling . . . that he loved the trade unionists more than he loved the industrialists. And not only did he consider them by far the more important partner but that actually he even seemed at times to be more able to agree with them than with his own kind as it were, the industrialists . . .'

Throughout September and October the two sides sparred. Heath opened the bidding by offering an attempt to limit price increases to within 5%, if pay increases could be kept to £2 per week, plus a new body to help the low paid, an increase in pensions, and a device that was to haunt his successors, 'threshold payments', which would be triggered by a rise in inflation above the anticipated rate. The TUC wanted more: the withdrawal of the Industrial Relations Act and the specific recognition of the Common Agricultural Policy, VAT and the

Government's Housing Finance Act as factors driving up the cost of living unacceptably. What was to be done about dividend income and speculators? they asked. (These demands for political gains could infuriate Heath; O'Brien remembers his outburst after one such meeting: 'Her Majesty's government negotiates with no one.') After all the days of talking there was one immovable object, as Lord Croham, formerly (as Douglas Allen) Permanent Secretary at the Treasury, remembers well:

'It looked as though we might succeed, but every time we kept coming back to square one – you must have a total freeze on prices – and that killed it.'

As the quid pro quo, Heath wanted a wage freeze. And on that neither Jones, nor Scanlon, nor their colleagues could deliver. Scanlon believes that the 'hatchet man' preventing any deal was Anthony Barber, and that in the end Heath was stuck:

'I don't know anyone who listened to us more than he did. But I equally don't know anyone who ignored what he'd listened to more than he did.'

This is to underestimate the strain on any Prime Minister if the central tenets of his policy are demanded 'on the table' in negotiations. Croham feels that some of Heath's colleagues 'were much more concerned about the government being deceived'. Why should Jones and Scanlon give up to a Conservative government, who, they felt, had recently chastised them with scorpions, that right to collective bargaining which they had protected from a Labour government who, by contrast, had merely flicked them with a very small whip?

The talks finally broke down on 2 November. Tripartite discussion was not seen as having been a futile exercise, however. Much of the proposed package re-emerged in a subsequent statutory offer which the unions could not refuse. Also the TUC leaders had developed a taste for this sort of negotiation. Jack Jones was enthusiastic:

'We thought we were in the business of developing an understanding that could be applied. And that understanding, incidentally, was very much the sort of pattern that the Labour party promised in their election manifesto of 1974 . . . a general framework of good social legislation plus control of prices.'

Ironically, Heath's tripartite talks led to the Social Contract unveiled to no small effect by his opponents at the next election.

After the breakdown of talks, Heath and his close advisers deliberated. The tortuous details of an all-embracing statutory incomes policy were a challenge to be relished by civil servants such as Sir William Armstrong, upon whom the Prime Minister increasingly leaned. Armstrong, the intense and driven child of Salvationists, was a political civil servant not so much in the ideological sense as in his ambitious desire to embrace a policy without the civil servant's ultimate detachment. Heath, on the other hand, had the pragmatism of the true civil servant – what his old antagonist Powell calls the 'civil servant's ability to execute somersaults unselfconsciously'. The most prodigious of these somersaults was now at hand. On 6 November the government announced a statutory incomes policy, beginning with a ninety-day freeze on prices, pay, dividends and rents. The new Leader of the House, Jim Prior, had to 'produce the unwanted child like the tragic heroine in a barnstorming melodrama', as the *Guardian* sketch-writer Norman Shrapnel put it. The Prime Minister was savaged by Powell: had he taken leave of his senses? Heath was asked on television if, as a man of principle, he should not now resign.

It looked like a spectacular U-turn. In fact it had come about gradually: the early rejection of compulsory wage control had never been founded on belief in its antithesis, the monetarist theory of inflation, and the Heath government had always tried to control public sector pay. Robert Carr claims that they were 'operating from the very beginning an informal incomes policy' in the hope that the industrial relations legislation would have a benign effect on wage claims and unofficial strikes, so that no formal policy would be needed. By the end of 1972 any such hopes were at an end. So, Carr argues, the government:

'. . . made tactical U-turns reacting to events as they occurred. But the strategy remained very strong and coherent, and we felt it was much better to make U-turns in tactics than make U-turns in strategy, which we never did.'

The show might be going in a different direction, but it was still on the road, and the destination remained the same: growth.

Confirmed growthmen in the Heath image were now in charge. The hapless Davies had been moved from the DTI as an act of kindness. (Christopher Chataway, for six months one of his juniors, recalls that, 'He was finding it extremely difficult to function any more in what had proved to him a surprisingly alien environment.') In his place came Peter Walker, the epitome of the self-confident businessman who stood high in Heath's esteem. The government would continue its dash for growth without internal dissent. If that meant an incomes policy, then so be it. The Chancellor came into line with foreboding, as he now recalls:

'I felt, as I think all of us felt, very sad. After all, we'd set our hearts and minds against it; we'd announced at the election that, under no circumstances, or some words like that, were we going to introduce statutory incomes policy. Therefore it was a very very big decision to take. On the other hand you can say, and I think in fairness one ought to say this, that a good government will always do what it believes to be best in the national interest, even if it's highly embarrassing.'

The question which most embarrassed Heath in Parliament had not been Powell's; it had come from a man with whom he had had far more in common, over many years: Roy Jenkins. Had he abandoned his view that statutory policy would only make inflation worse in the long run? asked Jenkins. Or was the short-term prospect so disastrous that he could no longer afford to look at the long term? The answer which could not be given was that, with inflation rising, the government's eyes were on what the short term offered. If it could only continue the pace of reflation, the government believed, it would pass Go and collect the rewards. But what was really happening in this national game of Monopoly, the great property and takeover boom which was now under way?

Making money: the boom and the bonanza, 1972–3

It has been suggested that the British economy is like a supertanker in the Solent: it takes a considerable time to turn around. Previous attempts had run out of time. There had been 'over-heating'. Overseas misgivings and balance of payment crises were never far from the policymakers' thoughts. Heath therefore attempted a new course: straight ahead, regardless. Instead of the old stop-go-stop it would be go-go-go, despite the scepticism of the Treasury. It was now up to the industrialists. They had the new market – Europe. They had a more favourable business climate. So they should invest in manufacturing. But the industrialists were sceptical and gloomy; there was more, rather than less, trouble on the labour front. Cecil King, the fallen press tycoon, records in his 11 May 1972 diary, after the reflationary March budget, a lunch with Lord Plowden, then chairman of Tube Investments:[6]

'Plowden very depressed and looking forward to retirement. The heavy engineering side of TI is about 80% of their business, and this shows no sign of picking up. The nearer their products are to the retail consumer the better they are doing.'

Eight months later, King lunched with Plowden again. The gloom was still there:

'No serious investment is to be looked for until industrialists have confidence that the new investment will earn an adequate profit for a period. They have no such confidence at the present time.'

The problem which was so to distort the dash for growth was threefold. The first phase of the reflation was expanding the public sector, sometimes at the expense of the private sector in the competition for skilled men and women. The rewards of the non-industrial investment were far higher than those of the industrial. And the failures of British management and industrial relations meant that they could not compete with, and were further demoralised by, the success of the asset strippers and property speculators who left their mark on the period.

The growth of the public sector was considerable. Heath's spending ministers were hard at work. In 1972 Margaret Thatcher, Secretary of State for Education, had continued her predecessor's policy of expanding education. The 1972 White Paper 'Education: A Framework for Expansion' envisaged a large increase in higher and further education, to admit 22% of the eighteen-plus generation to higher education by 1981, as against 15% in 1971. It talked of education as 'valuable for its contribution to the personal development of those who pursue it', as well as a national investment in human talent. Talent already trained, faced with the choice between Oxford and Cowley, Lanchester or Linwood, knew where the future seemed brightest.

Setting aside the Redcliffe Maud Report's proposed fifty-eight unitary authorities as unwieldy, Peter Walker had completed his reorganisation of local government, to bring the nation the benefits of two-tier local government in places with strange-sounding names such as Dacorum, Tameside and Gwynedd. The intention, with well-meaning origins dating back to the Tories' period of opposition, was to reform the managerial structure of local government and the allied public services. Some services, it was thought, should be brought down to district-level administration; others should go up to the six metropolitan and thirty-nine non-metropolitan counties. Some naturally linked services, such as housing and social services, thus became separated at different levels. In every town clerk's department, local government understrappers weighed up the rival attractions of redundancy and promotion to do the same job by a different name. Planning and publicity departments proliferated. Authorities left with few functions invented new ones. The financial memorandum issued with the legislation in 1971 had said that it 'would have little direct effect upon either local authority finance or expenditure overall'. That may have been the aim; the reality was expansion of personnel, which the initial policies of the next government were further to intensify.

Sir Keith Joseph was absorbed with a parallel reorganisation of the National Health Service into an elaborate new three-tier system. Regional and Area Health Authorities and two hundred Community Health Councils below them; the latter were described by Shirley Williams as a 'seraglio of useless and emasculated bodies'. To this reorganisation, with its attendant increase in administrators proportionate to medical staff, Sir Keith brought all the enthusiasm he was to show for the dismantling of the system a mere ten years later.

Central government was not behind in making its contribution to the proliferation of administrators, from the setting-up of the VAT inspectorate onwards. Numbers increased by 208,000 in education, 97,000 in the Health Service, and 98,000 in national and local government: 400,000 in all, according to the Oxford economists Robert Bacon and Walter Eltis, who later analysed the effect of 'too few producers' for the British economy. Their thesis was that, if this figure was markedly greater than the increase in total national employment – as it was – then human resources were being drained away from the productive sector.

Not all the brightest and the best flocked to the non-productive sector. Some, productive after their fashion, believed, with Jim Slater, that it was better 'to make money than to make things'. The City of London was reluctant to invest in British industry in the early seventies, and hostile to the 'smoking industrial background'. The institutions, notably insurance and pension-fund managers, knew that in time of high inflation industrial shares gave a poor return on capital compared to property or gilt-edged stocks. They did not want to put capital into old-established industry, but to back the new whizz-kids who sought to 'liberate' what was already there by breaking up a company wherever its paper value was less than the sum total of its assets. Slater, John Bentley and their kind were fawned on by the City editors. They received breathless treatment from the profile writers and instant historians. Anthony Sampson, for example, wrote:[7]

'Slater is (like Walker) the very paragon of the new Heath-type Tory – self-made, hard-working, unsentimental, competitive.'

At the time Heath shared this view. (Slater Walker advised Heath's merchant bankers on his own investments, though, according to Slater, he 'had no knowledge of the investments made by Slater Walker on his behalf'.[8]) Sir William Armstrong was packed off to watch Slater in action, to pick up tips about 'oomph' which he could apply in Whitehall. And Campbell Adamson remembers a dinner at Chequers when the Prime Minister made much of Jim Slater:

'. . . as if to say to us, the other industrialists, now here is the kind of industrialist I like, he is doing the things you are not doing. He's investing, he's being successful.'

These illusions about the new entrepreneurs did not last long. When Heath tackled another of them, Nigel Broakes, at one of the Chequers dinners about his failure to invest 'north of a line from Bristol to the Wash', he received the disarming reply:[9]

'As far as I'm concerned, Prime Minister, Trafalgar would not invest north of Oxford Street the way things look now.'

The new entrepreneurs did not need to bask in the favour of the Prime Minister. They merely needed the climate which his government had inadvertently created for them. In the late sixties a breed of secondary or fringe banks had been spawned, from a combination of the credit-finance boom and the restrictions imposed on lending by the big clearing banks; some of these enterprises had grown from hire-purchase companies, others from successful stock-market raids and asset redevelopment of the Slater–Walker variety. People wanted to borrow, and if they could borrow at less than the rate of inflation they could hardly go wrong. The fringe banks began to hurt their bigger brethren. So the Bank of England's aim in bringing in its Competition and Credit Control Scheme in 1971 was to encourage competition by putting the banks' lending limits on an equal footing. The scheme benefited the prodigal at the expense of the prudent. Provided banks maintained a 12% minimum reserve of assets to liabilities, they could lend as much as they liked beyond that – virtually to whomever they chose. Happily for the Bank, the scheme fitted well into the government's picture of a healthy free-enterprise economy, liberated from tiresome restraints. As mentioned above, the new system soon produced distortions in the money-supply figures. Worse, it created a situation in which the only effective way to control credit would be to raise or lower interest rates, which (linked to mortgages) are always politically sensitive.

So the rush to the new Klondyke began. In the two years after the new relaxed controls came in, bank advances doubled, private borrowing trebled, and loans to the property and financial markets quadrupled. All the banks joined in, from the seediest bucket shop to the mighty National Westminster, which was particularly prominent in lending to property men. The men who then ran the clearing banks are reluctant to discuss their role in what followed. Why was the fourfold increase in property lending – highly inflationary in that it pushed up existing assets rather than output – not matched by an equal increase in investment in industry (up 73% in the same period)? One prominent banker of the day has claimed that they received 'messages from Whitehall that we were being beastly to manufacturing industry' – so they waited for industry to come to them. When it didn't, frightened of the burgeoning secondary banks, they pumped money into property. The big four banks benefited greatly: their profits rose from £278 million in 1971 to £580 million in 1973. Other conditions, too, favoured a property boom at this time – after Labour's planning restrictions in the sixties, and with the need for new office space in the cities. All coincided with the advent of the new entrepreneur. John Plender has summed it up:[10]

'Security, marketability and potential for a rising income made property an ideal asset with which to confront rising pay-related commitments or insurance-policy bonuses.'

The property man brought his own security with him – the rising value of his assets – and borrowed short on the expectation that they would continue to rise, rather than borrowing long and relying on the ability to meet interest payments from existing rents. As, in Plender's acid judgement, they could depend on 'the willingness of British chartered surveyors to put a value on any given building by reference to comparable recent transactions in the property market', the property bubble was self-inflating. Jack Walker, of English and Continental Property, bought Bush House for £22 million, had it revalued as four separate buildings and immediately raised the value to £28 million. He described this as 'creative thinking'.[11] The Crown Agents plunged into the lending spree. Many of the most notorious losers, some of which had politicians on the board, secured Crown Agents' finance, from Gerald Caplan's London and County Securities (Jeremy Thorpe on display) to John Stonehouse's London Capital Group. When the bubble burst, the follies of the Crown Agents cost the taxpayer £85 million in reconstitution.

A good example of the bubble at its most inflated was the deal done in August 1973 by Jack Dellal and Stanley Van Gelder of Keyser Ullman. They persuaded Town and City Properties to acquire for £97 million a company they owned called Central and City Properties. Keyser Ullman cleared a £28 million profit on the deal. Only £2 million of the purchase price came from the buyers. £95 million came from the obliging banks, while the City looked on in admiration. Van Gelder later told the Department of Trade inspectors:[12]

'What you bought for a million pounds one day you sold for two the next, and that person sold for three the day after.'

Keyser Ullman's luck did not hold. When the music stopped in late 1973, it had lent over £300 million. About a third of this had gone to four borrowers quite unable to pay, including William Stern, who was to achieve bizarre notoriety by going bankrupt with debts of £104 million, and a young Slater protégé, Chris Selmes. Selmes, for reasons never properly explained, was released from his huge debt in exchange for a Henry Moore sculpture, £16,000 worth of shares and a debt of £114,000 curiously described as 'binding in honour only'. Others paid up. Edward Du Cann MP, chairman of the 1922 Committee, and director of Keyser Ullman, had borrowed £7.5 million from it, which he repaid with interest.

Long before this, the boom was becoming an embarrassment to the government. It fuelled inflation. A 70% increase in house prices over the two years put new strains on first-time buyers. Conspicuous greed embarrassed a government which talked of rectitude and restraint. Heath had lost his Home Secretary, Reginald Maudling, forced to resign as Home Secretary when the corrupt architect John Poulson came under investigation. The Prime Minister had denounced Cayman Islands tax havens, uncovered when the affairs of Lonrho and its consultant Duncan Sandys MP came to public knowledge, as 'the unpleasant and unacceptable face of capitalism'. But the government was slow to move against the property men. The Treasury adviser Brendan Sewill sums up the reason why:

'It's rather like pulling a pint of beer, I suppose . . . you're liable to get some froth at the top, especially if you're not very good at pouring beer. It was felt that the property boom was a bit of froth on the top, and that if you were going to get the output of industry up then this was undesirable . . . but perhaps inevitable.'

The government's reluctance to interfere with the dash for growth continued into 1973 and ran parallel with the first and second phases of its incomes policy. The first stage, the ninety-day freeze, was followed by a Stage 2, operated through two bodies with a family resemblance to their Labour predecessors, the Prices Commission and the Pay Board. They were intended to limit rises in pay, prices and profits more tightly than any previous postwar government had done. Regulations were drawn up with a care and reverence for detail characteristic of medieval theology. Pay rises were limited to £1 per week plus 4%, profits to the average of the best two of the last five years.

Barber's 1973 budget did nothing to restrain the increase of demand in the economy. 5% annual growth was still the target. In fairness it should be remembered that Barber was urged on to further reflation by the opposition, much of the press and bodies such as the National Institute for Economic and Social Research.

Unemployment still stood at around 3%. It was assumed that a boom in consumer spending would lead to a rapid increase in domestic output. There was to be neither a curb on lending nor an increase in interest rates. Short of investment (private sector investment in buildings rose by 83% in these two years, that in plant and machinery by less than the rate of inflation) industrialists turned surly when Heath lectured them. There is a remarkable account in the June 1973 issue of the *Director* of what some of his hosts must have seen as one of the rare and rather awful visits of Edward Heath to the Institute of Directors. He was greeted by a group which included Don Ryder of Reed and IPC, Graham Dowson of Rank, Neil Wates the builder, and Denys Randolph of Wilkinson Sword. They were worried about Stage 2. Their attitude angered Heath, who said:

'When we came in, we were told there weren't sufficient incentives to invest. So we provided the inducements. Then we were told that people were scared of balance of payments difficulties leading to stop-go. So we floated the pound. Then we were told of fears on inflation; and now we're dealing with that. And still you aren't investing enough.'

He went on to berate the industrialists for their fear of change:

'Industry isn't keen to have the products of the universities for fear they might bring new ideas.'

He denied that there was excess demand or strain on capacity:

'Every government has to go for full employment – no government could exist on any other terms.'

In case there was any doubt where he now stood, he left his battered hosts with a moral from the dying Disraeli's murmur to the young Hyndman:

'"England's a very difficult country to move" – that was absolutely bang on.'

The industrialists listened, but their hearts were not always in it. A huge discrepancy was opening up between imports and exports. Import prices were increasing at three times the rate of export prices, offsetting by a long way the impressive 1973 increase in industrial output. The balance of payments was in deficit by over £1 billion. World commodity prices soared, to feed increased world trade, and also to provide a hedge against inflation. In June 1973 the *Economist*'s commodity indicator was 76% up on the previous year. As these prices rose, Britain – because sterling had fallen in value since the 1972 float – suffered proportionally more than other countries. Rising prices at home, especially of foodstuffs, placed further strain on the incomes policy.

The critics of the policies of printing money and clamping down on wages found their voices. Milton Friedman, who had met Heath but had no influence in those days at Downing Street, thought that the consequences of the dash for growth were crystal clear:

'What Mr Heath should have known was that the attempt simultaneously to prop up the money supply, to provide more government spending while putting a supposed lid on prices and wages through price and wage control, would result in a temporary boom followed by a price explosion, followed by inflation.'

In May 1973 Peter Jay, a convert to Friedman's views from the Gaitskellite wing of the Labour Party, wrote in *The Times* of 'the boom that must go bust':

'We have got the most acute prospect of general overheating on the back of the weakest balance of payments in the postwar period.'

That same month the dash for growth began to falter, and there were some public expenditure cuts before its end. In July the government (which only in April, and in the face of the Chancellor's protests, had subsidised mortgage rates to prevent them reaching politically undesirable levels) now had to raise the minimum lending rate from 7% to 11% in eight days. As always happens when such action is too long delayed, the sour smell of panic hung in the air. On 27 July the government lost two by-elections on the same day, both to the Liberals, in what were thought to be impregnable Tory seats which had been represented by impeccably double-barrelled knights of the shire. To lose one would have been thought incompetent; to lose two looked like disaster. The Liberals had already won Sutton and Cheam. They would be in the hunt at Berwick, where Lord Lambton had been forced to resign as both a minister and as an MP after pictures of his sexual acrobatics with a brace of Maida Vale prostitutes had been hawked round Fleet Street. And, while the Liberals rampaged through the shires, Labour had shrugged off its own troubles in Lincoln – where the rebel MP, Dick Taverne, had held his seat in the by-election he himself called – to win all six of the new metropolitan counties created by Peter Walker, and the GLC.

Heath's government was in trouble. There was still Stage 3 of the incomes policy to be negotiated. That August, the Prime Minister went yachting at Cowes, where luck again deserted him. *Morning Cloud* was slowed by alternate gales and lulls in the Fastnet race. He had told his hosts at the Institute of Directors that, in ocean racing, if you run into rough water over submerged rocks, then either 'you tack and go off, losing direction and the race; or you go through and come out on the other side.' The Prime Minister still believed that, as far as his incomes policy was concerned, he could come out on the other side. He also believed that he could steer across the biggest submerged rock ahead, on which he had come aground before: the National Union of Mineworkers.

5

THE OIL BURN: HEATH'S GAMBLE FAILS

As he prepared for the autumnal argument on pay and prices with the unions, Heath recognised the scale of his difficulties. The General Council of the TUC had registered no more than a resentful acquiescence to the transitional Stage 2. Rapidly rising prices increased shop-floor resistance to imposed pay restraint. And the months of the administration's life were numbered. Another year, and all deals would be off until the election of 1974 was decided. Douglas Hurd had written in his diary in the previous March:[1]

'Prices should come right slowly after mid-1973, and unemployment come right too fast. Balance of payments will get worse, then better. If no horrors occur, autumn 1974 might be best [for an election].'

Things had not come right, but if the government could clinch a flexible Stage 3 incomes policy they might yet do so by autumn 1974. The worse 'horror' which they could envisage was defeat by a single union powerful and determined enough to burst through the statutory policy.

Heath and Armstrong therefore took great care with Stage 3. On pay the policy was to include redress of anomalies, compensation for 'unsocial hours', and special threshold payments which would be triggered by cost of living increases. A further acknowledgement of inflationary worries was the fact that the plethora of percentages and flat-rate maxima outlined in Stage 3 were all higher than in Stage 2. Certain exemptions were clearly aimed at winning over the miners and electricity workers. As a further gesture to fairness, the first steps were taken to reduce the swollen levels of bank profits.

Could such a policy hold? One hot day in July, after receiving the Portuguese dictator Caetano at the front door of No. 10 amid a flurry of protesters carrying 'Grocer Welcomes Butcher' banners, Heath slipped away to the garden with Sir William Armstrong. They had a secret date with the NUM president, Joe Gormley. Gormley was there without the knowledge of his executive; Heath and Armstrong, for their part, had chosen not to tell the NCB chairman, Sir Derek Ezra, what was afoot.

Gormley, a cunning negotiator, was riding scout ahead of his troops. If there was to be a Stage 3, he could best avoid a strike against it if the NUM could be seen to have got a better deal than anyone else. As he remembers it, he put a proposal to Heath and Armstrong which would allow a deal:

"'Of course, wages aren't the only thing we'll be claiming from the Board. For example we shall have a claim for an increase in payments for unsocial working hours." As far as I was concerned, I had given them the biggest possible hint as to how they could find a way round the problem. And I was convinced that they had both taken the hint, because they turned to each other and said, "We never thought of that. We never thought of that at all."'

It was not a deal. It was an understanding, in the minds of Heath and Armstrong; but they fatally underestimated two things. First, Gormley had to carry his executive; they had merely to report progress to the cabinet. Second, by the time Stage 3 was launched, the miners' own demands might outreach whatever was then 'on the table'. The progress was reported back. The Chancellor remembers that the draft proposals had qualifications:

'. . . which were put in there with a particular eye on the miners, and the general feeling was that they were going to do pretty well out of Stage 3, certainly compared to every other group of workers.'

Meanwhile, the NUM's pay claim went in on 12 September, with an item concerning 'enhanced shift payments' in addition to the flat-rate claim.

Could the miners be induced to settle within the still-unveiled Stage 3? The question was blown away by a desert war. On 6 October, the outbreak of the fourth Arab–Israeli conflict took the West by surprise. Egyptian troops crossed the Suez Canal on the Jewish festival of Yom Kippur. For once, the Israelis seemed to have the worst of it. Already the Arab-dominated Organisation of Petroleum Exporting Countries (OPEC) had agreed to hike up the price of a barrel of oil from its then level of $3. As the war turned against Egypt and Syria, the Arabs increased pressure on Israel's Western backers, first by curtailing the supply of oil, and then, in mid-October, by raising the price to $5 per barrel. Two months later it was more than doubled again, to $11.63.

In Britain, such a quadrupling in price of a major industrial import was both massively inflationary for the retail price index – it caused a 2% jump – and deflationary for the industries which would find their markets shrinking as their costs rose. But the rise would be to the advantage of those who had substitute energy, in the form of alternative fossil fuels, to offer. The point was not lost on the coal miners. A few voices in Britain had already warned that oil was ridiculously underpriced in the world economy. Lord Rothschild's was among them, but he was at that time in bad odour with the Prime Minister for suggesting in a public speech that Britain might be one of the poorest countries of Europe by 1985. So the oil-price rise, despite the noises that had been coming from OPEC in September, was as unexpected as it was calamitous, hitting Britain especially hard at the economy's two weakest points: the balance of payments and the accelerating commodity import prices.

Heath's Stage 3 had been 'put to bed' at the printers on the eve of the Yom Kippur War. Publication was planned for 8 October. It was thus almost impossible to withdraw or alter the terms of the new pay policy, even if it had been possible then to understand that the world had changed utterly. Stage 3 was launched by Heath at one of those Lancaster House 'presidential' press conferences characteristic of his later premiership. He was obviously preoccupied, and his presentation has been described even by the loyal Hurd as 'incomprehensible' to the journalists.[2] In one aside on the threshold payments which were to be the inflationary curse of government for the next twelve months he said:

'It is right that people should have an additional safeguard against the possibility – and I put it no higher – of world import prices rising exceptionally fast in the year ahead.'

For his part, Joe Gormley saw that what he had thought would be available only for the NUM had been written in for all. The NUM had not been given unique treatment but used as a marker for cases where flexibility within the policy might be needed:[3]

'The hint . . . had been taken up all right, but not for us alone. It applied to everybody. I must say that I wasn't best pleased. I had gone there to solve our problem, not to give them help in running the country as a whole. Whether it was through stupidity or deliberate policy I never knew, but they had effectively blocked a loophole by which our position relative to the rest of industry could have been restored.'

If there had ever been an understanding, it was a dead letter now.

On 10 October the NCB made its formal reply to the NUM's 40% wage claim. It was just within the outer limits of Stage 3 (which was not to be endorsed by Parliament until November).

The miners were offered a complex package amounting to 13% – the full basic permissible increase of 7% plus 4.5% for unsocial hours and 1% under the flexibility clause. The only other things that could be offered in addition within Stage 3 were a productivity agreement, which could have been worth a further 3.5%, and the possibility of NCB threshold payments. With hindsight, members of cabinet believe that Norman Siddall, deputy chairman of the NCB (Sir Derek Ezra was in hospital at the crucial time) offered too much, too soon. Robert Carr:

'The negotiating tactics of the Coal Board at that time were most unfortunate. As I recall it, they put everything into the shop window at the beginning, and they had an unusually long bargaining period to get through . . . [that] left no room for negotiation and bargaining in the future.'

(The union had put in its claim in September but, as a consequence of the timing of Wilberforce, the settlement was not to come into effect until 1 March.) On this view, a lesser offer would have allowed the cunning Gormley to chivvy further concessions out of the Board which he could then have presented to his executive and to the delegate conference as victories.

The case against the NCB is not persuasive. As October rolled on, the miners took in the implication of the oil-price rise. They knew that 13% was a long way short of 40%. The junior minister of the day whose job it was to oversee the coal industry, Tom Boardman, defends Siddall:

'One of the problems of having a code is that it fixes the ceiling up to which offers could be made, but it also fixes the floor, because to offer someone, a group of workers, less than they knew they could be offered within the code would have been treated as offensive and would have been quite counterproductive . . . So I think they were right in their tactics to offer the maximum amount that could be given by the code, provided, as was the case, they kept up their sleeve a number of concessions that could be given outside the code.'

The union picked up the concessions. But they flatly rejected the basic pay offer. The NUM leaders knew that the oil-price rises strengthened not only their case but also their tactical position. The government had tried to learn from its 1972 defeat and, as Tom Boardman remembers, it had contrived to 'build up what at that time had been record coal stocks both at the power stations and indeed at the pitheads'; stocks were thought to be adequate until May 1974. Now, however, the situation had changed:

'This was thrown completely out of gear by the Middle East war and the consequent cutting off of virtually all oil supplies from the Middle East. That meant that, instead of a massive oil burn to replace the coal burn, it had to be reversed . . . and there had to be a massive coal burn to reverse even the normal level of oil burn. And this put very considerable pressure on the stocks and very much strengthened the miners' hands.'

In a deputation to Downing Street on 23 October, the miners put their case, following the oil crisis: Britain needed all the energy it could get, yet six hundred men a week were leaving the coal industry. Heath was polite but unyielding. He would not accept that a fundamental reassessment of the proper economic cost of coal, and thus of miners' wages, was now needed. Lord Rothschild had put the argument to him, but he had been bawled out and told he had no understanding of politics. To demonstrate his mastery of this art, the Prime Minister now told the miners that Stage 3 was not negotiable. The government feared that one special case would lead to others. The electricians' leader had made clear to Boardman his views about the Stage 3 settlement his union had accepted:

'Frank Chapple rang me up and said, "Tom, don't forget what I said. If those buggers get one farthing more [than] me, then all bets are off. And I could stop the country in forty-eight hours. It'll take them forty-eight weeks, you know."'

So, at the beginning of November, the Coal Board was permitted to offer only pence, when pounds might still have turned the trick. The NUM executive, fortified by a unanimous decision of a delegate conference, called for an overtime ban to begin on 12 November. The government, with 1972 in mind, responded with the precipitate declaration of a state of emergency. Coal output began to fall.

It must have been clear to Heath and Armstrong by this time that their hopes of Joe Gormley were misplaced. The NUM president was being carried along by his membership. The rest of the NUM executive were unknown quantities to Downing Street, yet the NCB, who did know them, were now effectively excluded from the negotiations, as Ezra recalls:

'The NCB were not really involved at all and we were very unclear right through this period, from the time the overtime ban started to bite, exactly what was going on . . . Our relationship with the NUM throughout this period . . . remained very good, and every time they had a meeting with the government they immediately came round and told us about it.'

This exclusion continued to the bitter end. Ezra was not at Downing Street when, on 28 November, Heath called in the NUM executive and appealed to them to call off the overtime ban in the national interest.

It was not a meeting of minds. Heath, Barber, Armstrong, Boardman and Employment Secretary Macmillan put the government's case. They were greeted by a mixture of down-to-earth bargaining and tough political argument. Two memories catch the mood. Armstrong later recalled 'a little man . . . at the very back' saying to the Prime Minister:

'"Why can't you pay us for coal what you are willing to pay the Arabs for oil?" And although it was put in that way, not put as an economist would put it, that was bang on the economic nose . . . And the Prime Minister really had no answer.'

Anthony Barber remembers an outburst from the Communist vice-president of the NUM, Mick McGahey:

'It was abundantly apparent at the end of that meeting that the strike was political, because I remember McGahey, who'd been rather curt in his answers . . . I remember Ted saying to him, "What is it you want, Mr McGahey?" He said something to the effect, "I want to see the end of your government!" There was a long silence and Ted, who was genuinely trying to reach some understanding, didn't reply. Then after a little while I remember Joe Gormley saying, "Well, come on lads, let's go." And that was the end of the meeting.'

In Gormley's account, he intervened to tell the ministers that the strike was about wages, nothing more. In a separate room, the executive voted then and there to continue the overtime ban, and left Downing Street in high good humour. Boardman was left with a sense that the NUM president and those who shared his view on the executive 'believed that everything that could be extracted had been extracted' and that the final offer might be put to the miners in a ballot, without recommendations.

At this juncture the Prime Minister brought William Whitelaw back from Ulster. Heath and Whitelaw had been engaged in the complex parallel negotiations to set up the new power-sharing Stormont executive, and to prepare for the Sunningdale conference due to open in early December. Whitelaw's affability, his ability cheerfully to burble through tense situations and so to defuse their explosive potential, had stood him in good stead in Ulster. Might he not be the man to talk to the miners instead of the hypertense Macmillan? In fact, as his colleagues noted at once, Whitelaw brought not a fresh but a fagged-out mind to the problem. Twenty months in Northern Ireland had drained him, perhaps more than he knew. 'Willie was a danger to shipping throughout,' is the memory of one of those who now had to deal with him daily. Nevertheless he plunged in with the enthusiasm he would have brought to a walkabout in the Crumlin Road for a 'man-to-man' talk with the NUM leaders, who formed the impression that there might yet be more on the table, dressed up as payments for 'bathing and waiting time' outside the shifts.

Events, however, were closing in on the beleaguered government. Heath had taken too much on himself. So had Armstrong. Douglas Hurd gives an example of the Prime Minister's diary at the beginning of the critical week of 8 December:[4]

'The Prime Minister entertained the Italian Prime Minister to dinner at Chequers. The meal was hardly over when Mr Heath flew to Sunningdale by helicopter to preside over the last stages of the conference on the future of Northern Ireland. Three days later it was time for the state visit of President Mobutu of Zaire. Two days after that the European Summit began in Copenhagen. . . . They all involved talks, travel, long meals, extensive briefing beforehand; yet none of them had anything to do with the crisis which was swallowing us up.'

That week, dour but determined, Heath went on television to announce a three-day week for industry to conserve coal supplies. The government was digging in. Four days later a deflationary emergency budget was brought in, cutting public expenditure by £1200 million and introducing a belated attempt to control hire-purchase credit and to tax development gains. Only weeks earlier the director general of NEDC, Sir Ronald Mackintosh, had been denounced by the Prime Minister almost as a traitor in the camp when he had suggested that personal consumption must be cut back and the overheated economy damped down. The Chancellor's advisers now prevailed. He carried the cabinet for the cuts, once the consequences of the oil-price rise had sunk in:

'[I] realised very quickly that all we'd been trying to achieve was really coming to an end . . . I only had to point out to them what the consequences for our balance of payments were of the fourfold increase in oil prices and . . . they rode in right behind the general proposition which I was putting to them, namely that we had to make very substantial cuts in public expenditure.'

Other critics also had to be assuaged. There had been a lag before the excrescences of the speculative boom led to criticism from Conservative loyalists; now it was widespread. Heath's long-time admirer and biographer George Hutchinson burst out in *The Times*:

'Who will readily forget the brazenly swollen profits of the banks, of the ghastly band of usurers trading in second mortgages, of the property speculators (all working together very often)? . . . The activities of a grasping minority, socially insolent, politically illiterate, are becoming extremely offensive to a good part of the nation.'

That had to be set against the demands of the miners, and made it easier to beat the speculators just a little in the December budget. (The first tremors of the developing secondary banking crisis, as the great edifice of credit crumbled, were already felt in the City.)

This mood of austerity and emergency, which its critics saw as contrived to win back public support for the government, made Whitelaw's negotiations with the miners more difficult. His instinct was to break Stage 3, as he was empowered to do under the legislation. The cabinet would not let him do it. Whatever illusory hopes there had been for a settlement based on 'bathing and waiting time' evaporated before Christmas, when Harold Wilson, who knew how matters stood, made the proposal public, thus ensuring that the government would disown it. In the cabinet the hawks were more than ever in the ascendant. Whitelaw, desperately tired and with no coherent alternative, was pushed aside. The Prime Minister's close allies, Lord Carrington and Jim Prior, the chairman and deputy chairman of the party, saw the partisan advantage in standing firm, and then putting matters to the electoral test. Douglas Hurd reports that:[5]

'During the next five weeks, from 2 January until 7 February, only two topics were of any interest in the political office at No. 10. Would we have an early election? If we did, how could we win it?'

Carrington was appointed Secretary of State for Energy on 8 January, when the Trade and Industry Department was split up. A fresh and crucial opinion was added to the key group of ministers dealing with the miners. With Carrington arrived the effervescent junior minister Patrick Jenkin, whose appeal to people to save energy by brushing their teeth in the dark was somewhat spoiled by the press photographs of his house – which revealed every light blazing. How serious was the crisis? How much was being manufactured with an early election in mind? The TUC General Council feared that the government were stage-managing the run-up to a crisis election. The opinion polls now showed the government 4% ahead of Labour in spite of its by-election disasters. The TUC decided to intervene with a snap offer the government would have to accept.

At the routine NEDC meeting on 9 January, chaired by Anthony Barber, the NUR leader Sydney Greene, then chairman of the TUC's economic committee, proposed without prior notice that if the miners were made a special case other unions would not use that as a precedent in their own pay negotiations. Existing Stage 3 settlements would thus be safe. Why, if it was to be taken seriously, was this offer sprung on the government? Len Murray describes the TUC's dilemma:

'Should we tip them off? Should we alert them? The reason why we didn't was because we were afraid of a leak . . . And we wanted it to be face to face, men to men, a bang-bang kind of situation.'

If this was the intention, it backfired disastrously. Barber had listened with incredulity as the mild-mannered Greene mumbled through the offer. Barber says:

'First of all I felt that there was a little bit of trickery in this, because normally when anything really major was likely to be proposed, as I was chairman of the NEDC I would have known beforehand . . . I felt immediately suspicious of this because I could see all sorts of implications . . . The TUC had repeatedly said in the past that they could not promise that other unions would not do this, that or the other; that wasn't in the nature of the TUC. So it seemed obvious that they couldn't bring home the bacon anyway.'

Whitelaw, the government's peacemaker, had been assured that the miners' dispute would not be discussed at the NEDC meeting, and had not attended. In his absence, Barber's suspicions prevailed. He slipped out to call Heath from a pay phone – his mistrust extended to the NEDC officials – and checked that he would be right to turn the offer down. Heath concurred. In the course of the following week, Barber consulted his colleagues and Armstrong. Most agreed that the TUC offer should be rejected. Whitelaw, who disagreed, did not press his dissent hard enough. When the TUC came to see Heath himself, the last of their series of meetings was long remembered by those present for the Prime Minister's gloomy silences, interrupted, in the account of

Stephen Fay and Hugo Young in the *Sunday Times*, by 'the cavilling Barber'.

When asked directly by Hugh Scanlon, 'Is there anything, anything at all we can do or say that will satisfy you?', Heath said nothing. Len Murray thought this a fatal error:

'There are times when you've got to be silent for half a minute, you know. There are times when you've got to say "Snap". With great respect to Mr Heath, a man of considerable ability, great ability indeed, I felt at the time, and I've felt since, that either a Harold Macmillan or a Harold Wilson, certainly a Jim Callaghan, would have snatched Hughie's hand off across the table and said, "You're on?"'

Could the TUC have delivered? They had offered a great deal. In effect they were endorsing Stage 3, almost policing it. For the government there would have been political dividends in being seen to have forced such a role on the TUC; equally, if the TUC defaulted later, there would have been dividends in condemning it for a bargain broken. The government would have avoided impalement on an inflexible Stage 3, in the changed circumstances. In other days, at the time of the tripartite talks for example, Heath would have made something of what was offered. Now, he could not. He stood by Stage 3, wanting the electoral rewards of firmness, but hesitant to seize them through a snap election. Enoch Powell had fired a warning shot on the eve of the NEDC talks, when he had said in Derby:

'The supposed issue in the conflict which bids fair to divide the nation today is a wholly bogus issue, a figment of the fevered imagination of politicians in a tight corner of their own manufacture.'

Powell's solution was to admit that the statutory policy had failed, and to pay the miners their economic price.

This view had no supporters in the cabinet. But it was deeply split. While the TUC came and went, 'the battle for an election on 7 February was lost' – by 17 January, Hurd estimates. In this argument Heath's closest associates were themselves split. Prior and Carrington wanted an election. The former recalls that he 'couldn't see any other way of the dispute ever ending'. Whitelaw and Pym, who knew what was at stake in Northern Ireland, were opposed. Pym was shrewd in his advice:

'The country was supporting him. I could feel that. It was a three-day week; we seemed to be producing almost as much in three days as we normally did in five. There was no question of the public not supporting the government. They clearly were. And my instinct was that if they were asked to vote for it they would wonder why . . .'

Although Pym's advice was very much in tune with the Prime Minister's own instinct, an election was almost called for 7 February. (It would have been on the old register, a further advantage for the Conservatives, who were best organised to follow up voters who had moved.) The pro-election hawks tried to keep their quarry in sight. Heath's PPS Tim Kitson watched the manoeuvres after cabinet:

'It was thought that the following morning they were going to make the decision to announce the election and then [Heath] was going to have dinner in [his] flat. Peter Carrington had asked me what he was doing and I said, "Oh, he's staying in tonight," and he said, "Oh well, that's good." Then in fact he went out and had dinner with Mr Whitelaw. Things seemed to change round. I actually didn't get many marks from Peter Carrington over that!'

The Prime Minister had decided against a snap election. He would soldier on, and rely on the power of reason to convince the NUM executive that they should even now abide by Stage 3. The 17 January deadline came and went. No Prime Minister finds it easy to contemplate the awesome risk of losing office a year early; this one was reluctant to fight a bitter class-war election, despite his reputation for confrontation. At Westminster Conservative backbenchers had been preparing with nervous elation for the trenches. Now the elation was transferred to their opponents. Prior came back from the Commons to tell Heath that: 'The Labour Party and the people in the Tea Room are raising their hats to you this afternoon, and saying you let them off the hook.'

So he had. Within a week the miners had gone for a strike ballot: authority for a frontal attack on Stage 3. The vote was 81% in favour; the mood was expressed by one young miner interviewed during the overtime ban: 'We've poleaxed Ted Heath before, an' we shall do it again.' The cabinet hawks could now fly unrestrained; their point seemed to have been made. 'The miners have had their ballot, perhaps we ought to have ours,' said Prior at a press gallery lunch on 6 February, while members with marginal seats scuttled from their places to phone spouse, agent and stockbroker. The battle would be on uncharted ground. There would be a brand new electoral register, which helped Labour. There would be a national strike in progress, in which violent unrest could play into the government's hands.

For Heath there was a further, personal blow. He had relied heavily on the advice of Sir William Armstrong. In the first week of February

Armstrong suffered a total physical and mental collapse. He had been at Ditchley on 27 January, talking wildly of coups and coalitions to his alarmed fellow guests. Campbell Adamson remembers himself and the president of the CBI being harangued by Armstrong at this period:

'We listened to a lecture about how Communists were infiltrating everything. They might even be infiltrating, he said, the room he was in. It was quite clear that the immense strain and overwork was taking its toll, and two days later of course he had to give up and have a rest.'

Downing Street insiders talk of him as:

'. . . really quite mad at the end . . . lying on the floor and talking about moving the Red Army from here and the Blue Army from there.'

The smoothest piece of the Whitehall machinery had broken down. Sir William was taken away from Downing Street. He never returned.

In those last days one further opportunity to settle with the miners had come up. The Pay Board's long-awaited report on relativities had been published on 24 January, proposing machinery which would allow exceptions on grounds of fairness for special cases under Stage 3. William Whitelaw missed the chance to use it at once for the miners – an error he later regretted:

'Before the report was published I never thought through the implications of it. Barbara Castle said on the day it came out that she couldn't understand why on earth I hadn't used it to settle with the miners. She was quite right. I had never really thought of it.'

It was typical of the muddle in which hostilities now broke out that, having refused to make a reference to the Relativities Board until the NUM strike ballot had been called and held, Heath made such a reference on 8 February – the day after he had called a general election.

The February 1974 election

Edward Heath must have known the contradictions in his position. He was calling an early election, yet his three-week delay had given the opposition parties time to prepare and the electorate time to ponder. He was fighting in last defence of a policy which his party had eschewed in 1970. He was forced to ask who governs Britain; the voters were more interested in how Britain was governed. His strategists leaned – some, such as Barber, too heavily – on alarmist talk of extremists in waiting, yet the miners needed only token pickets, and, apart from occasional verbal toughness from Mick McGahey, declined to oblige the media. The campaign was short, but with the previous three weeks' phoney war it was too long for one issue to predominate. Douglas Hurd noted that, by 7 February, 'the government found the initiative slipping from its hands'.[6]

The opposition parties had troubles of their own. Labour had to switch the focus of the election from 'who governs?' to rising prices, in the knowledge that they were behind in the polls (and remained so throughout the campaign). The resurgent Liberals, who had won four by-elections in a spectacular year, hoped for a record vote, but no one knew from whom it would come. Jeremy Thorpe, who had recently resigned from the doomed London and County Securities, was a wild card. In the event, both he and Harold Wilson were to play out their roles in the election by the simple avoidance of error; they needed do nothing more, for the government seemed suddenly pulled down by Murphy's law: whatever could go wrong for them, did. The first blow came from Wolverhampton. On the day of the dissolution Enoch Powell wrote a letter to his constituency chairman; it was nothing if not blunt:

'I consider it an act of gross irresponsibility that this general election has been called in the face of the current and pending industrial situation. The election will in any case be essentially fraudulent, for the objective of those who called it is to secure the electorate's approval for a position which the government itself knows to be untenable, in order to make it easier to abandon that position subsequently. . . . I shall not therefore be seeking re-election for Wolverhampton South-west . . .'

Loyal Conservatives shaken by this may have been further puzzled when Heath lifted the television curfew imposed in the state of emergency, and referred the NUM claim to the Relativities Board. So what was the crisis upon which he based his case when he asked rhetorically in his first broadcast if the struggle against rising prices should be abandoned under pressure? Were the miners extremists who had to be beaten or claimants with whom there might yet be arbitration? Bank profits, revealed a week into the campaign to be up by 40% to 50% for the big clearing banks, seemed to strike at the heart of the Conservative claim to fairness, to be the 'trade union of the nation as a whole'. On 15 February, the RPI showed a record rise for a single month. From this moment on, Barbara Castle in the supermarkets and Shirley Williams on the platform always had the housewife's shopping bag in their sights when the TV cameras picked up the prices issue.

Then, on 21 February, a week before the poll, the Pay Board's recommendations on the NUM entitlement were released at an off-the-record press conference taken by its deputy chairman, Derek Robinson. As the figures came out in a Press Association report, it appeared that the miners were actually 8% worse off than other workers with whom they had been compared. Ministers were caught flat-footed, and as they struggled to establish the true position they were mortified to hear Harold Wilson declaim, 'There's something funny going on.' Robinson, who was known to be a Labour sympathiser, was held responsible for producing figures which seemed so much at variance with the government's case. In fact, he and his chairman, Sir Frank Figgures, had wanted to highlight how difficult it was to establish a consistent basis for assessment of workers' wages. But the Press Association leak did not convey this point. By the time the basis for the figures was established, the government's credibility had been knocked. 'If I didn't know you well, I'd have had difficulty believing you,' Jim Prior's farm manager said after watching his boss's explanations on TV.

Powell did not watch his old rival's discomfiture in silence. He spoke at rallies of the 'Get Britain Out' campaign, and poured sarcasm on Edward Heath. To a cry of 'Judas' from the gallery he rounded in a flash with his own cry of pain: 'Judas was paid. I made a sacrifice!' Labour observed this unlikely ally with mixed feelings as he revealed two days before the poll that he had already voted by post for the Labour candidate in Wolverhampton South-west. On the same day, Campbell Adamson said at a management conference that the Industrial Relations Act had soured the atmosphere in industry and ought to be repealed by the next government – unknown to him, the remark was recorded. Heath was not amused, but it had been no more than an insider's indiscretion. More serious for the government were the January trade figures, which showed the largest deficit ever recorded – as a Labour spokesman gleefully noted, it was twelve times the figure for June 1970.

In spite of this cascade of misfortune, it was still hard to see Heath losing. The polls consistently put him ahead. The Liberal surge, helped by the public's distaste for the slanging match between the big parties, eroded Labour and Conservative support equally. The Tories kept their eyes on the gap between themselves and Labour. It had not closed – quite – by polling day. Harold Wilson, however, had narrowed it skilfully. He had phased the Labour campaign, reacted swiftly to the cards he was dealt, and turned some of them into trumps. If, by polling day, the electorate did not quite believe that his proposed social contract would effectively tackle inflation, they agreed with him about rising prices and an end to industrial confrontation. He did not invite them to make a full examination of Labour's ambitious programme, and mentioned socialism only twice in his campaign speeches. He had begun dubious of victory, making private arrangements for a discreet exit from the count at Huyton if things went badly. Now he was in with a chance.

On 28 February 1974 the electorate voted – inconclusively. If it had been a jury it would have been discharged. The ambiguous verdict, on a high poll of 79%, gave the Conservatives almost 1% more of the popular vote than Labour but four seats fewer: 297 against 301. There had been heavy swings against the Tories in the West Midlands, and in Wolverhampton most of all. The Liberals had acquired six million votes and fourteen seats – a discrepancy they were not slow to publicise. In Scotland and Wales it was the nationalist parties which benefited in seats and support from that disillusion with the big parties which had helped the Liberals in England. In Northern Ireland the pro-Sunningdale Unionists were swept away, as Francis Pym had warned. Eleven hardline Protestants accompanied the solitary power-sharer Gerry Fitt back to Westminster. On 1 March the news of the election result was received with grim satisfaction at his house in Pimlico by Enoch Powell:

'Having risen at my customary hour of seven, going down, tiptoeing down, and seeing the paper slanting through the letterbox, and reading the words "Heath's Gamble . . ." Heath's Gamble? I thought. *Gamble?* So I pulled it through and it fell out flat on the mat: "Heath's Gamble Fails". So I took it up with me to the bathroom and sang the Te Deum.'

Heath remained at Downing Street. He did not go to the Palace. It might still be possible to stitch together an anti-socialist coalition. He did not know the new Ulster MPs. He had no reason to love them, or they him. ('There is nothing that makes Ted so angry,' Powell was to say later, 'as an Ulster Unionist.') These eleven hardline Unionists were not appealing as potential coalition partners. Their price would be the dismantling of all Heath had achieved at Sunningdale. Cecil King claims that, in spite of their wide differences with Heath, they were prepared to offer support.[7] The Scottish Nationalists who had been returned had every interest in a new election while the political temperature in Scotland was high and still rising. If the Liberals could be locked into an arrangement with the Tories, however, a minority government might survive with no more than the day-to-day support of the Unionists. So the target was Jeremy Thorpe. The Liberal leader had ebulliently proclaimed, 'We are all minorities now.' He led a torchlight procession through the streets of Barnstaple, and hurried home to await the call. In the end he had to make it himself – the local telephone exchange was out of order! Thorpe took the London train on the Saturday, giving interviews as he went. Wilson, who had expected the telephone to ring, but from Buckingham Palace, retired to his home in Great Missenden with his Labrador, Paddy. The weekend would be Thorpe's, but the prize would be Wilson's. The Labour campaign team were in close touch with a mole inside the parliamentary Liberal Party who assured Bernard Donoughue that while 'Jeremy is of course very keen to get his knees under the cabinet table . . . there are enough of us who won't have it to stop it'.

What was Heath able to offer Thorpe? According to Norman St John-Stevas, who had been an intermediary between the two men, 'I would have asked for Jeremy Thorpe to become Foreign Secretary,' and something would have been found for the other Liberals. It did not happen.

As the weekend ebbed away, some of the Wilson entourage became nervous that they might be cheated of victory. Joe Haines sums up their reaction:

'Ted Heath had been beaten and he should have given up. They were outraged that there should be a deal with the Liberals. There were at least two senior members of the party who, had Heath done a deal with Jeremy Thorpe and made him Home Secretary, would immediately have exposed Jeremy Thorpe's association with Norman Scott, the association that finally brought him down a couple of years later.'

(On the eve of poll, letters had been purchased from Scott through an intermediary by Thorpe's close friend, David Holmes, acting on his own initiative.)

In the event, unsavoury tactics were not needed. It was clear that the Liberal MPs wanted nothing to do with coalition. Thorpe was dispatched back to the Prime Minister:

'I told him that while it wasn't clear who had won the election, it was quite clear who'd lost it.'

For Heath, there was no alternative but resignation. His gamble had indeed failed. He had sacrificed sixteen months in office. The policies he had followed were either to be jettisoned or to be packed away as part of the nation's unfinished business.

6

THE SOCIAL CONTRACT

Harold Wilson took possession of 10 Downing Street once more on 4 March. It was characteristic of his new cautious approach that he did not make it his home this time. During the election he had told a newcomer to his campaign team, the LSE academic Bernard Donoghue, that he intended to hold office for only two years, if the chance came, and to be a more relaxed leader of the team; the sweeper rather than the striker. Even to achieve this ambition he would need to secure a parliamentary majority by winning a fourth election, and to bind together a party which enjoyed only 37% electoral support (its lowest since the war) and had been seared by three years of ideological dispute. The cabinet he formed was therefore a tribute to the peace-maker's art. The two men who might be the most serious challenge within the PLP, Healey and Callaghan, had their energies fully absorbed by the Exchequer and the Foreign Office. Roy Jenkins and Barbara Castle, who had fallen foul of elements in the parliamentary party for very different reasons, were given posts below what their experience and ability would have justified. And in a significant gesture to the two groups on which Labour's strength in the country rested, the trade unions and the party activists, Michael Foot and Tony Benn went to Employment and Industry respectively. Jack Jones had requested the appointment of Foot to Employment rather than the blunt and combative Reg Prentice (who, ironically, was TGWU-sponsored):

'It was made clear to the Prime Minister that Michael Foot would be very acceptable as Secretary of State for Employment.' Tony Benn, as chairman of the Home Policy Committee of the National Executive, which had nurtured the 1973 programme, with its far-reaching proposals for industrial regeneration, had a natural claim to execute the programme in the appropriate department.

The new government took office under circumstances of great gravity. There was still a state of emergency and an unfinished strike. Wage settlements were nudging 20% and the effect of quadrupled oil prices was working through fast into the economy. The Stage 3

threshold payments were being automatically triggered by this unprecedented inflation, leaving the lucky recipients feeling, as Tom Jackson
puts it, as though they were 'in front of a gigantic Las Vegas slot
machine that had suddenly got [stuck] in favour of the customer'.
Unemployment was high by the standards of the recent past, but the
public expenditure which might combat it by the stimulus of demand
and production was already running unquantifiably high. The shock
waves buffeted the plummeting adventurers of the Barber boom, as
secondary banks and property companies collapsed into bankruptcy.
All this had to be faced by an administration without a parliamentary
majority, which – were the opposition parties to combine against it –
could be turned out of office at any time after the first vote on the
Queen's Speech.

The constraints within which the government operated, however,
were not merely those of Parliament or the world economy. It had to
take serious note of what both its trade union allies and its own rank
and file wanted. The events of the previous three years ensured that
there could be no cavalier disregard of either. On the union side the
virtual separation which had followed the rupture of 1969 had
become a re-marriage under the threat of the Heath shotgun. As
Barbara Castle noted wryly:

'He had driven the unions back into the arms of the Labour Party.'

It was not, however, the traditional relationship, which the union
movement's historian Colin Crouch has described as a formula in
which the unions supported the parliamentary leadership while the
latter left alone 'the sacred preserve of free collective bargaining' so
each 'would respect and preserve the autonomy of the other'.[1] Well
before 1974, with the increased radicalisation which followed attacks
on their powers and immunities, many of the union leaderships had
moved left. Their demands had changed. So had their sensitivities.
Jack Jones had proposed in 1971 a Labour Party/Trade Union Liaison
Committee. The party had welcomed it, as Foot says:

'. . . for the very purpose of trying to avoid the disruption between
the party and the trade unions which had occurred in the latter days or
months of the [first] Harold Wilson government.'

The union leaders' desire to talk at the top table had been strengthened by their ultimately unsuccessful discussions with Heath in the
tripartite talks, of which the Liaison Committee discussions became a
kind of opposition shadow. Len Murray describes the mood of those
discussions:

'We said, "Right, let's sit down and try to visualise what it looks like; what the circumstances of a Labour government coming to power are and what can be done."'

It was taken for granted that the first things which could be done were the repeal of the Industrial Relations Act, the restoration of trade union rights, and the establishment of a new Advisory Conciliation and Arbitration Service (ACAS) to mediate in disputes on a voluntary basis without the intervention of the law. But, as Barbara Castle wrote in her diary:[2]

'... the biggest hurdle remained. What were the unions prepared to do to help overcome inflation? ... Incomes policy was anathema. Labour's leaders gave solemn pledges that they would never return to a statutory policy, but this was not enough. So bruised and sensitive were the trade unions that any mention even of a voluntary policy was taboo ... The unions insisted that the problem of inflation must be approached from the other end by keeping prices down. Gradually the consensus emerged that the right answer was government action to create a "climate" to which the unions would respond.'

In February 1973 the constituent elements of this 'climate' had been revealed by the Liaison Committee in 'Economic Policy and the Cost of Living'. The paper called for 'a wide-ranging and permanent system of price controls', including subsidies for essential items such as foodstuffs, redistribution of wealth and income through taxation, improved pensions, health, housing and transport, and widespread extension of public ownership in industry, land and capital. The document concluded that:

'The problem of inflation can be properly considered only within the context of a coherent economic and social strategy.'

Labour politicians, Castle records, were 'still uneasy' about the omissions in the document, but felt the terms were the best they could get. Thus the Social Contract was born. (This appellation, borrowed from Jean Jacques Rousseau, had been used by both Benn and Callaghan in the early seventies before it stuck as a short and simple description of a non-binding compact, whereby in return for an array of measures designed to benefit their members economically the union leaders would use their best endeavours to moderate wage claims.) The Labour leadership had tried to cover itself in the radical 1973 programme against an inability of the unions to deliver:

'We accept that a policy of wage restraint cannot succeed for very long if wages and salaries are moving out of line with the growth of productivity . . . The need is for a far-reaching social contract between workers and the government – a contract which can be renewed each year as circumstances change and new opportunities present themselves.'

The 1973 programme had been so phrased, however, that, in return for the party's giving 'firm and detailed commitments which will be fulfilled in the field of social policy, in the fairer sharing of the nation's wealth, in the determination to restore and sustain full employment', the unions would 'confirm how they will seek to exercise the newly restored right of free collective bargaining'. Thus the Social Contract which had been presented by Labour in the February election as a formula for industrial peace was unbalanced from the start in what the two parties to it could promise and could deliver. For the new minority government to deliver, it could be argued that it had to implement the whole range of ambitious policies to which it was committed. It would in any case have to answer for these to its rank and file.

What had happened – not for the first time – was that Labour had moved sharply left in opposition. The movement gained momentum in Tony Benn's year as chairman of the party, 1971–2. At Westminster his colleagues marvelled at the dexterity with which Benn won support for his proposal for a referendum on membership of the EEC, further splitting the disheartened pro-European minority in the process. What was less apparent but equally far-reaching was the effort he put into energising the party activists. As Benn saw it, the 1970 Labour defeat had been caused by a government's drifting too far from the wisdom of its supporters; to regain lost ground, the parliamentary party had to come back to them, as he himself had done to the Glasgow shipyard workers who had jeered him in 1969 as the Minister for Mergers, but welcomed his solidarity with their successful work-in in 1971. Though opinions in the party differed about whether Benn was the sorcerer or the apprentice in what followed, he achieved an explosion of activity in the National Executive. A hundred sub-committees bloomed in the exercise 'Participation 72' and the chairman was everywhere, encouraging here, prompting there. To work with him, an impartial chronicler of those times has written, was 'exciting, inspirational, sometimes dangerous'.[3] By contrast, the party leader's reputation was at a low ebb. To the constituency activists Wilson stood condemned on the record of his government and his lack of enthusiasm for those, from Clydeside to Clay Cross, who subsequently took on Heath's ministers, and sometimes beat them. To the pro-European right of the party, Wilson had sold the pass and left them helpless before the new forces who had destroyed their old hegemony. In May 1972 the *New Statesman* went so far as to say that he had: '. . . sunk to a position where his very presence in Labour's leadership pollutes the atmosphere of politics.'

A week later, unabashed by the blitz of readers' letters headed by one from Michael Foot, the weekly suggested that Wilson should stand aside to let Foot himself and Crosland contest the leadership. Under this pounding, Wilson's special skill was to preserve himself by fast footwork rather than by making a stand.

The way was clear for those who believed with Benn that they had no business providing 'intensive care for capitalism'. The problems of the sixties had been caused by the failure to invest coupled with the failure to listen. New forms of public enterprise must be found which would be an advance on the old Morrisonian monolith and able to intervene directly at the level of the existing or new enterprise. The committees deliberated. The National Executive listened. In December 1971, the Industrial Policy Committee of the Labour Party had set up a Public Sectors Group chaired by Judith Hart, and powered by a group of young researchers who were later to become members of the parliamentary left: Stuart Holland, Tony Banks of the AUEW, and Margaret Jackson from Transport House. In proposing wide powers of intervention and control which would go far beyond Keynesian demand management, the group went with the grain of the times. Even the Conservatives had abandoned their 1970 programme in favour of the Industry Act, the nationalisation of Rolls-Royce, and the re-creation of public-investment agencies. (Benn wrote in the *Sunday Times* on 25 March 1973 that Heath had 'performed a very important historical role in preparing for the fundamental and irreversible transfer in the balance of power and in wealth which has to take place, even if only to allow inflation to be tackled successfully'.[4]) Labour now set forth its most radical programme since the war, centred on a National Enterprises Board and a system of compulsory planning agreements with private industry. (Judith Hart argues that the NEB had a long ancestry, going back to Crossman's plans for the expansion of industry and science in the early sixties.) The NEB was to be a state holding company with a stake in all sectors of the economy, rather than the merger bureau which it was felt that the old IRC had been. Its multitudinous functions were set out in a Green Paper in April 1973. It was to attack unemployment through job creation, promote exports and assist import substitution, sustain investment and technological change, help the regions, combat the multinationals and aid the spread of industrial democracy. Where Heath was vainly exhorting the private sector to invest, the NEB would come in and do the job – with the private sector, if they were willing; for them, if they were not. Stuart Holland hoped that the competitive public enterprise would also act as an investment leader, 'breaking from the pack' when the private oligopolies held back for fear of being caught with surplus capacity. The failure to invest identified by Heath would thus be tackled, but by pull rather than push.

To show that they were deadly serious about the scale of their intervention in the private sector, the Public Sector Group drafted a key passage for the proposed 1973 programme:

'For the range of tasks suggested, some twenty-five of our largest manufacturers would be required, very early in the life of the Board. These companies would be selected on the basis of the use to which their resources could be put. The NEB would be wholly state-owned and would always take a controlling interest in its participating firms.'

The document was just as quantitatively explicit about the second string of the industrial strategy, planning agreements. Like the NEB, these had their inspiration in continental practice. They were the brainchild of Holland, who had made a particular study of the economies of Western Europe; he had high hopes for them:

'Agreements would be entered into with remaining, and in practice majority, private companies in a sector, so that their broad investment plans more or less coincided with the direction of the government's objectives.'

The draft programme stated that such agreements would certainly be expected to cover the hundred largest companies, all of which would be involved in the disclosure of information on future investment, pricing, product development, marketing, exports, and import requirements. The industrialists received these sweeping plans without enthusiasm. The right wing of the Labour Party also began to stir; Harold Lever remembers their deep scepticism:

'[The proposals were] predicated on the assumption that the government of Britain is able to interlink in a helpful way all the plans of all the different industries, and all the different components of each separate industry. The thing is a naive dream . . . of an omnicompetent, all-seeing eye in government, which can then act to inform,

instruct, guide and persuade the hundred thousand different entrepreneurial components of private industry into one harmonious
equivalent of the Russian Gosplan.'

These ambitious intentions were not to the liking of Harold Wilson:
no Gosplanner he. In office he was to warn the No. 10 Policy Unit,
headed since the election by Bernard Donoughue, that he did not want it
'prowling like a wolf through the economy'. Wilson tried to keep any
mention of numbers out of the policy. At a meeting of the National
Executive on 31 May to finalise the draft document which would go to
conference, he argued through many hours for the deletion of references to twenty-five companies. The crucial amendment for deletion
came from Denis Healey. Time and the bell had taken their toll;
members drifted away and the final vote was 7 to 6 against deletion.
Wilson abstained. Even more surprising was the key vote for inclusion
from the moderate Co-Op MP John Cartwright. He had been bruised
by the pugnacious Healey, who had said that he supposed that
nationalising Marks and Spencer would make it as efficient as the
Co-Op. On the following day Wilson issued a statement which
enraged the left, outlining what he had said to the NEC:

'Those in the majority – comprising less than a quarter of the full
executive – yesterday adopted a proposal to nationalise an unnamed
twenty-five of the one hundred biggest companies in Britain . . . A
substantial majority of the parliamentary committee had already
made its position clear both on compensation and on the twenty-five
companies, and I emphasised that in my view the shadow cabinet
would not hesitate to use its veto at the appropriate time. It was
inconceivable that the party would go into a general election on this
proposal . . .'

Wilson was on flimsy ground referring to the small numbers on the
NEC who had voted. Over half of the NEC had been present, but
enough had abstained, as he had, to let the proposal through. Now
what had been a statement of intentions became an issue of principle.
Many weary months passed before the issue could be fudged over at
the annual conference. Wilson's threat of a veto cast doubt on the
partnership implied by Clause 5 of the party's constitution which
provided for the manifesto be drawn up jointly by the NEC and the
PLP. That set off a ripple of discontent in the constituencies which led
to the formation of the Campaign for Labour Party Democracy, a
pressure group for accountability. The CLPD was one day to dislodge
many Labour right-wingers – including John Cartwright, whose vote

had carried the 'twenty-five companies' through the NEC in the first place.

The February 1974 Labour Manifesto did not specify how the NEB and the new planning agreements would operate. But it promised an ambitious programme of nationalisation:

'We shall also take over ship-building, ship-repairing and marine engineering, ports, the manufacture of airframes and aero-engines into public ownership and control . . . sections of pharmaceuticals, road haulage, construction, machine tools, in addition to our proposals for North Sea and Celtic Sea oil and gas.'

According to opinion polls, the proposals were not electorally popular, at a time when the party was struggling to regain lost support. Over the next three years they were to be at the centre of Labour's parliamentary struggle. In the short parliament of 1974, however, they could not command a majority, and the government was preoccupied by the attempt to implement measures which, it could claim, fulfilled its side of the Social Contract.

Writing out the Social Contract: March–October 1974

The Wilson government settled the miners' strike within days. In the words of its author, Michael Foot, the deal was:

'. . . an intelligent settlement which prepared the way for co-operation with the miners [and] the Plan for Coal which we devised within a few weeks.'

The settlement was well above the Stage 3 guidelines, which the TUC recommended should otherwise run until July 1974, except for special cases who should receive substantial 'catching-up' increases after inquiry or arbitration.

If there were to be further voluntary restraint thereafter, with inflation and expectations about future inflation rising by the week, the government would have to show that it could deliver on its part of the Contract. There was an immediate freeze on council-house rents, subsidies on basic foodstuffs, and a bill to tighten up controls on prices – but not the price freeze which the unions wanted. Shirley Williams, the Prices Secretary, thinks in retrospect that, though the food subsidies were 'economic nonsense', they could be justified in that they brought the unions back on board. Barbara Castle, at the DHSS, used the increase in pensions and health and welfare benefits to urge on the unions the benefits of the often disregarded section of the payslip – the social wage. She saw that the social wage would only be valued as highly as the money wage if it could be directly compared, so she:

'. . . got some of my experts to put an actual financial calculation on the value of the social wage, in money terms, to the person on average earnings. And we worked out, even as way back as 1974, that it was worth a thousand a year.'

Of more worth, to the trade union leaders at least, was the honouring of the pledge to repeal the hated Industrial Relations Act and abolish the NIRC. The provisions for protection against unfair dismissal were retained, and the new conciliation body proposed by Jack Jones set up as ACAS. The Trade Union and Labour Relations Act (TULRA) swung the balance of power back towards trade union rights. The argument now centred on the closed shop. Was it right that an employee should be open to dismissal from a firm where a closed shop operated because he or she refused, on principle, to join the union? Foot was prepared to concede exemption on religious grounds; the Conservative opposition inserted the blanket provision 'any reasonable grounds' and in the bill's passage through the House of Lords inserted rights of appeal for individuals who were refused entry to, or expelled from, any particular trade union (a Donovan recommendation). TULRA owed its substantial amendment to the first of many voting muddles in the parliaments of 1974–9: although he was absent, unpaired, Harold Lever's name was added to those voting. This was revealed and exploited later, to invalidate the bill as passed, and allow an open season for amendments. Attempts by Michael Foot to extend the effectiveness of picketing by a requirement that the police should stop vehicles so that pickets could talk to the drivers never came to the vote. The Home Secretary, Roy Jenkins, had been told that the Metropolitan Commissioner, Robert Mark, would resign over the issue, which he believed to breach the neutrality of the police. Supporters of the proposal argued that it might make the lot of the police easier: if pickets could put their case, the frustrated anger which caused unruliness or violence at some mass pickets could be avoided.

In the end, the strengthened TULRA of 1976, when the government had a tiny overall majority, affirmed that there was a legal right to picket at the workplace 'or any other place where a person happens to be, not being a place where he resides'. The Act's critics point to this as the legitimising of secondary picketing. Professor Wedderburn, the academic who helped to draft the bill, dissents:

'The effect . . . was to make industrial action lawful (give or take a wiggle of a boundary here and there) roughly over the area that it was lawful under the Act of 1906. And no greater. It's one of the great myths that has been built up by the Conservative Party that it was wider.'

In one area where the closed shops might prove to be a threat to liberty, the rights of newspaper editors, Foot came under intense pressure both from some of his backbenchers and from the newspaper publishers in the House of Lords. Foot, an ex-editor of *Tribune* and the *Evening Standard*, was unhappy to be tagged as a menace to editorial freedom (especially by proprietors whom he thought had a better claim to that title) but opted for a voluntary code which could be written into the revised Act. It was agreed that this would include the editor's right to commission and publish any article, from any quarter. In the event, the proposed charter of press freedom was never written; no formulation could be agreed by the parties.

In tandem with the TULRA, the government pushed through an ambitious Employment Protection Act, giving new rights which included reinstatement after pregnancy leave, and a Health and Safety at Work Act. Organised labour stood to gain from both. It was hoped that they would be seen as further down-payments to the account of the Social Contract.

As the government wrote in their clauses to the Social Contract throughout 1974, the TUC took up the challenge. Jack Jones looks back on that first year:

'We tried to persuade the trade unions first to accept that wage claims should be put in not more than once every twelve months, and that they should be related to the movements of the cost of living – not excessive claims on and beyond the movement of the price index. I wouldn't say that was entirely successful; there were some exceptions.'

The exceptions made themselves felt as inflation gathered pace. The first of the threshold payments promised under Heath's Stage 3 was triggered by the April Retail Price Index. Government food subsidies kept the price index below the level of wage rises. (The October 1973/October 1974 figure for the rise in the RPI was 17%. Wages rose in the same period by 22%; between February and October alone the figures were 8% and 16%.)

Ministers placed great faith in the social wage, improved health care, pensions, health and safety at work. But the middle section of the payslip is hard to read, when it cannot be translated into cash terms. While some union leaders argued in good faith that the social wage and better working conditions should be quantified instead of increases in money wages, their members saw it differently. Ministers explained to Treasury officials why public expenditure in this area now would stem inflation later, as Leo Pliatzky* recalls:

'The workers would take home not merely the wage in their pay packet, but they'd also get cheaper food because there were food subsidies, cheaper housing because of the rent freeze and increased housing subsidies, free school milk, and so on. And because of this social wage they'd be content with a smaller real wage. Well, of course, it wasn't like that at all. They said thank you very much, or no thank you very much, to the social wage, and still went on demanding real wages.'

The middle figures on the payslip did not pay the rising bills at a time of inflation. Only money in the pocket would do that. Bernard Donoughue, head of the Downing Street Policy Unit, thinks that it was worth a high price to re-integrate the trade unions and involve their members in a counter-inflation strategy, but the social wage 'didn't mean as much to them as it cost us'.

The cost was indeed high, against the background of rising world prices which had forced other industrial countries in a less parlous condition than Britain into severe deflation already. The oil-price hike had the effect of simultaneously inflating prices and deflating domestic demand. Denis Healey recalls that on becoming Chancellor in March he was at once confronted with reports from both the neo-monetarists of the London Business School and the Keynesians of the National Institute. They agreed on one thing: the crisis was insoluble. This was not Healey's view. He believed that he could avoid the further increase in unemployment which deflation through demand management threatened to bring. His lieutenant at the Treasury, Joel Barnett, says:

'[Healey] made the fundamental decision to react to the oil crisis in a different way from the Germans and Japanese, and indeed from many other developed countries. Instead of cutting expenditure to take account of the massive oil-price increases of 1973, which in our case cut living standards at a stroke by some 5%, the Chancellor decided to maintain our expenditure plans and borrow to meet the deficit.'

He also tried to persuade other countries not to deflate, knowing the risks of going it alone. That, however, he had to do. (The strategy was initially tried later by the Mitterrand government in France, but it operated in Britain from a weaker base, both in Parliament and the

* Pliatzky was Second Permanent Secretary at the Treasury.

economy). The end result was that Britain deflated later, and with more serious consequences, than Germany, Japan and the rest.

There was no shortage of nominations for increased public spending, which was set to rise in real terms by 9% over 1974–5. In Healey's first budget, in July, £1240 million was earmarked for pension increases, £500 million for food subsidies, £350 million for housing. Increases in the basic rate, and in higher rates of income tax, with some increases in indirect taxation, brought an additional tax yield of £1500 million. The Chancellor describes himself at that time as 'too inexperienced . . . to appreciate the full horror of the situation'. As Britain got out of step with other industrial countries, the error was magnified rather than corrected by Treasury forecasts of the gap between revenue and expenditure: they underestimated the public sector borrowing requirement (PSBR) by £4 billion. Healey says now:

'In my first year the Treasury itself was wrong by 5.6% of GDP about the size of the gap – it underestimated it by 5.6% just as in 1976 it overestimated it by £3 billion. I think it took time for some of the older people in the Treasury – perhaps I would say Sir Douglas Wass – to recognise that fine tuning is not possible unless you have reliable figures.'

In his book *Inside the Treasury*, Joel Barnett, no whimsical romantic, judges that:[5]

'The whole course of the next five years might have been different had we decided we could not plan for such a high PSBR and therefore not increased public expenditure to the extent we did.'

But the government had commitments to full employment, to increasing the social wage, to extending the welfare system, to action on the RPI through subsidies. 'We just took the manifesto,' says Barnett, who soon came to see himself as a junior gamekeeper in a cabinet of poachers, 'and my ministerial colleagues started spending in accordance with that manifesto.' That, of course, was what they believed they had been elected to do. The main internal and external factors, the threshold payments and the oil-price increase, helped to destroy a policy which had always depended on a reciprocity from the unions which, because of inflation, they could not now give.

Healey's July budget cut VAT to act on the RPI and extended food subsidies up to the next election, for which the favoured date was 10 October. Demand was stimulated; unemployment would fall. What happened was a further boost to inflation. The TUC's guidelines 'Collective Bargaining and the Social Contract', agreed in June and

endorsed at a pre-election TUC Congress in September, did not
prevent wage claims continuing to escalate. Len Murray, who poured
much scorn at the Congress on 'those who sneer at the Social Contract', carried the day, although some union leaders, such as Scanlon of
the AUEW, still sat in silent disapproval.

Election countdown – and the binding of Benn

It was a tragedy for the country, as well as for the Labour Party, that a
minority government held office, thinking always of an election that
could be only months away, vulnerable until August to the threat of
parliamentary defeat. (It was in fact defeated eighteen times in the
House of Commons.) Bernard Donoughue claims that the government was marked by:
'. . . the almost complete absence of discussion of economic policy. I
think it's true that the cabinet never really discussed economic policy
before the October election; indeed didn't, as I recall, discuss it until
early 1975.'
If the government waited on events, the mandarins were content to
let them. That summer, Donoughue lunched with a very senior Treasury official and asked him why there were no Treasury papers on the
inflation crisis:
'He said, "Oh no, of course not, Bernard. Politicians never deal with
serious issues until they become *the* crisis. So at the Treasury we're
waiting till the crisis really blows up."'
Throughout the summer Wilson maintained his new, unobtrusive
style. He avoided a final confrontation with the militant Loyalists in
Northern Ireland by a failure to break their strike, preferring to lash
them with broadcast insults rather than intervene to save their quarry:
the power-sharing executive (see chapter 8). Foreign Secretary James
Callaghan conspicuously omitted to take up Britain's responsibilities
under the Treaty of Guarantee when the Cypriot president was
overthrown in a coup inspired by puppets of the junta in Athens. The
Turks were not slow to take advantage of the situation. Meanwhile
Callaghan pursued his renegotiations in Brussels in a low key, doing
enough to convince the Europeans that he meant Britain to stay in,
while leaving his party still hoping that he did not.
Harold Wilson had come through a prolonged press campaign
against his political secretary, Marcia Williams, over the involvement
of her brother, Tony Field, in Lancashire land deals. Labour was

vulnerable to any such connection, in view of its vehement criticisms of land speculators. Field had been buying slag heaps and re-selling the land and the industrial spoil separately – 'not speculation but land reclamation,' said Wilson loyally. The projected scandal was deflated by the exposure and conviction of one Ronald Milhench for forging Wilson's signature on the key document in the case. Later Milhench went abroad. Marcia Williams went to the House of Lords as Lady Falkender: her boss's contemptuous rejoinder to the Fleet Street muckrakers. In the same month Wilson's deputy leader, Edward Short, had to fend off press comment when it was revealed that he had once (twelve years previously) received a £250 cheque for consultancy from T. Dan Smith, recently gaoled for corruption in the Poulson case. It was the year of Watergate. Any whisper of corruption and cover-up was well received in Fleet Street, and brought little comfort to the party in power, which suspected a concerted attempt to thwart its election preparations.

Throughout the summer Wilson and his advisers were embarked upon a careful exercise: mellowing the manifesto. A flood of Green and White Papers poured from Whitehall: sex discrimination, devolution, pensions, land, consumer protection. The crucial area of internal party conflict was industry policy. Although legislation on such a controversial matter was ruled out until an overall parliamentary majority could be won, Tony Benn and his advisers had set to work in March on a draft Green Paper which would float the full range of ideas and powers envisaged for the NEB. The task was entrusted to his junior minister, Eric Heffer, and a group of trusted Benn aides, including Stuart Holland and Francis Cripps. Two civil servants who were to go on to high posts outside the civil service, Alan Lord and Ronald Deering, sat in, aware that the Permanent Secretary, Sir Anthony Part, regarded the whole strategy as disastrous for British industry. From Downing Street this committee was watched with a jaundiced eye. Richard Graham of the Policy Unit was the appointed 'Benn-watcher'. He remembers the alarm in the Prime Minister's entourage:

'The view was taken very early on – I think earlier than Benn realised – that there was no way we could go into another election with a Green Paper floating about which contained such very radical industrial ideas . . . so we'd better have a White Paper.'

Whereas a Green Paper could include all the ideas of the 1973 programme, and perhaps embellish them, a White Paper would keep the actual legislative proposals under tight controls: it would be put through the cabinet's Public Enterprise Committee.

Wilson and Benn now behaved in a manner which only makes sense in the light of their extreme mutual mistrust. Benn toured the country declaiming at rallies and galas the size of public subsidy to private industry. His memorandum to the Liaison Committee setting out the extent of NEB intervention and compulsory planning agreements for one hundred firms was leaked to the press. Some sympathetic ministers were taken aback by how far these proposals went beyond the manifesto. Others disliked the tactic of appealing to the party over their heads, as Barbara Castle complains:

'If he'd come to his like-minded cabinet colleagues and said, "Look, this is what I'm proposing, I'm meeting resistance on this, that, and the other," then he could have mobilised our support . . . But instead of doing that, Tony did what he's very fond of doing, appealing to the party rank and file and the party in Parliament over the heads of his cabinet colleagues. He did this by issuing his proposals through the NEC before they'd been to cabinet. That swung sympathy against him, because it put Harold Wilson in an impossible position.'

Was the policy that of the government or of the party tribune? When the draft White Paper, which Benn had attempted to tone up rather than down, came before the Public Enterprise Committee, Wilson's reaction was watched by Joe Haines: 'Harold read it briefly, quite angry, said it was woolly rubbish and he would have to do it himself.' In his memoirs Wilson does not spare the draft White Paper:[6]

'As I had feared, it proved to be a sloppy and half-baked document, polemical, indeed menacing, in tone, redolent more of an NEC Home Policy Committee document than a Command Paper.'

Benn, whose whole political appeal in the 1970s was based on the premise that that was what Command Papers published by government should look like, if party policy was to be carried out, now had short shrift from his senior colleagues on the committee. He challenged the Prime Minister, who was chairing the committee:

'That was a period of very great tension, because I took to that committee the speech he had made to the 1973 conference, and I quoted it line by line at him when he tried to reduce the commitments in the White Paper, and it was a very very tense and difficult period. But we got 90% of what we'd said we'd do into the White Paper.'

Benn's memory plays him false here. The White Paper was much altered. The Prime Minister had been seen by the CBI. So had the

Chancellor. Campbell Adamson had never known the CBI so united as in their hostility to the draft White Paper:

'I remember going through with the council at one meeting a whole list of actions that our side might have to take if Benn really got his way in a White Paper . . . We certainly discussed an investment strike . . . the possibility of industry withholding its investment. But we also discussed various things about not paying various taxes, and a list – I don't know that I want to be very specific – but a list of things which in themselves would not have been legal. I want to make the point hastily here that the CBI never got anywhere near actually to doing anything which wouldn't be legal.'

Such measures proved unnecessary. Adamson found Wilson 'sympathetic' to the CBI's view. (Wilson was not averse to orchestrating these protests himself, as he told Terry Coleman in a *Guardian* interview two years later.[7] When 'a sub-committee of a sub-committee of the NEC' produced nationalisation proposals he disliked he would send the intended victims two draft letters, one to himself and a reply to it, which could 'then be published to show that the proposal was not government policy'. The letters 'got a reply almost as quickly as if they had bounced off a satellite, for obvious reasons'!)

When the White Paper, 'The Regeneration of British Industry', appeared in August, it was much changed from the original draft. According to Richard Graham:

'Wilson went around telling everyone that the NEB was going to be the IRC* again, and the civil servants took their cue and the committee altered the NEB, watered it down . . . and of course the planning agreements were to be made voluntary. And the moment that Benn accepted that they should be voluntary, the policy had lost its teeth.'

The role of the NEB was still emphasised in the October manifesto, but what Wilson called its 'marauding role' as a major power in the economy was gone. In the short term, Wilson had laid what he saw as the Benn bogey. Whitehall had certainly got the message. Bernard Donoughue saw the balance shift against the Minister:

'I'm sure that Tony Benn felt himself betrayed by his Prime Minister, because the moment the word got around, as it rapidly did in Whitehall – and the Cabinet Office made sure that it got around – that the Prime Minister was not giving his support to Tony Benn, then the

---

* The Industrial Reorganisation Corporation, abolished in 1971.

civil servants began to back off from their minister. Although in this case Mr Benn had backed off from them in the beginning.'

Benn himself claims that 'wholly contradictory assurances' about what the White Paper meant were given on successive days to the TUC and the CBI. In October the Tory cartoonists still portrayed a Wilson mask being peeled from the face of a demonic Benn. Wilson had taken extravagant care to ensure that the voters would see it otherwise.

Wilson could thus treat September as though it was his Indian summer in politics. His political rivals had problems of their own. Jeremy Thorpe's gimmick-ridden hovercraft tour of the coastal resorts had not been a total success. 'I'm Jeremy Thorpe,' he announced to one holidaymaker. 'That's your problem not mine!' was the dour reply. The hovercraft sank at Sidmouth, an early warning of the risks of living by the media. Edward Heath suffered a personal tragedy in another sinking in the same week. His yacht foundered and his godson was among those drowned. It was a grim preliminary to a fourth and last contest with his old adversary, while Tory discontent with his leadership gathered around the born-again Conservatism now being offered by Sir Keith Joseph.

Why, therefore, was Wilson's fourth election victory so narrow? Labour gained only 17 seats from the Conservatives and had the lowest share of the vote of any majority government since 1922. Wilson's own explanation in *Final Term* was the fact that the decline in the Liberal vote had benefited the two big parties equally.[8] The Scottish and Welsh Nationalists made further gains to the alarm of both Labour and the Tories, but on balance they hurt the latter most, especially in Scotland. The Conservatives switched tactics twice with some success. One of their strategists recalls:

'When he'd recovered from a rather catatonic state, [Heath] was keen to win the next election. He was much influenced by advice from Pierre Trudeau who told him that, whatever happened, he should just offer people enough to win, and that it was ridiculous to go round telling the electorate they had to wear a hair shirt. So Ted thought we should give the electorate some prizes. Hence 9% mortgages and the abolition of domestic rating . . .'

Hence, too, the emergence of a new star. Margaret Thatcher had made a parliamentary reputation that year on the Finance Bill committee. Now she went national, as the party's prizegiver. Heath's own style was less sure. His 'catatonic' condition that year was explained much later when he was diagnosed as suffering from a thyroid deficiency. In the last days of the campaign he switched to a new theme: a government of national unity in the face of the crisis.

In the end it came down to what Butler and Kavanagh call 'an unpopularity contest'.[9] The campaign had run too long, with tired old faces to the fore. The electorate gave Labour an overall majority of 3, in a Parliament where the minority parties held 49 seats between them. Labour would be unlikely to run a full term with such a slender majority – though few in the party would have predicted that two of those three, Prentice and Stonehouse, would depart in such spectacular fashion (the former, in Gerald Kaufman's phrase, 'running the four-minute mile on the road to Damascus';[10] the latter soon to make his epic swim to Australia). Wilson, with his mind set on the two-year deadline he had given himself, could now settle back to watch the political nemesis of his old rival Heath, contrive the downfall of his inner-party challenger Benn, and plan the strategy for his 'fifth election': the Common Market referendum. Only the inexorable rise in inflation would not wait on these events.

7

THE PARTY'S OVER

Three major policy debates marked Harold Wilson's last administration. Although each was played out with no ostensible reference to the others, all were linked. Within a year of the October election, the Wilson administration had completed a triple evolution of policy which must have left Edward Heath wondering why he had been criticised for U-turns. Before Wilson left office he had turned the Labour Party back towards consensual reformism. There was full-hearted consent to EEC membership in the popular endorsement of a referendum. There was a voluntary pay policy of rough and ready justice endorsed by the trade unions. And there was an industrial policy of mild interventionism lukewarmly supported by the private sector, rather than the full-blooded public ownership associated with Tony Benn. After this Harold Wilson could safely stand aside and make way for an older man.

Before the Prime Minister felt he could grapple with either inflation or his turbulent Industry Secretary, winning the EEC referendum was paramount. The pledge to renegotiate British terms of membership, and to submit the result to the people, had been a key element of Labour's appeal in February, the promise which had allowed Powell to make his 'vote Labour' plea from a position of constitutional principle. In the struggle against the European Communities Bill, Powell had seen the Labour Party as allies, almost comrades, in the lobbies. The fundamental renegotiation was entrusted to Foreign Secretary James Callaghan, who did not so much get down to fundamentals as drift away from them. He had begun with a tough bluster on 1 April 1974, which fastidious British diplomats still remember with a shudder of horror. The Europeans were lectured on what was good for the British housewife and what was not, from the CAP downwards. This phase soon passed. The British government started to become serious about continued membership. It is possible that Callaghan was, as Powell believes, 'turned by the Foreign Office within a month'. More plausible is that Callaghan was playing the tough negotiator for domestic consumption, but as far as the Community itself was concerned, signalling as soon as he judged it wise that his stance on membership was the reverse of 1971; it was now to be: *'Oui, merci beaucoup.'* By June 1974 he was able to assure the EEC foreign ministers at Luxembourg that:

'The proposals I shall put before you, if accepted, would not require changes in the treaties.'

The argument would be confined to the terms available under those treaties, rather than focusing on the major issues of sovereignty and the non-acceptance of the CAP which the anti-marketeers wished to stress. As the summer slipped away, there were flickers of unrest in Transport House. Worries intensified when the formidable Helmut Schmidt arrived at the Labour Party conference to say:

'Your friends in Europe want you to stay in . . . when you talk of solidarity, that is something you will have to weigh.'

There were some splutters. 'Why should this patronising Hun lecture the great British Labour Party?' asked the hunting barrister John Ryman MP, eager to make a reputation as a small British eccentric. But that October the anti-EEC majority in the Labour Party still believed that it would prevail. Better terms would not be forthcoming. The EEC would look even less attractive as the cost of contributions and the visible trade deficit with it both rose. The British would resist the loss of their sovereignty, and, as Douglas Jay wrote in the *Spectator* on 28 September, refuse:

'. . . to be entangled, like a fly in a cobweb, as one state in a plutocratic Little-Europe federation, with Germany as the inevitable senior partner.'

After the October election Wilson and Callaghan speeded up the negotiations. They were pledged to let the British people decide, within twelve months, 'whether we accept the terms and stay in, or reject the terms and come out'. Ian Mikardo, who had known both of them longer than any other member of the NEC, judged the results of Harold Wilson's renegotiation cynically:

'I never believed at any time from the very beginning of the discussion that his position was genuinely agnostic . . . All those people with whom Harold Wilson was negotiating knew that he was decided that in the final issue whatever he got or didn't get he was going to say yes. So that being so there was no great occasion for him to be given much, and he knew he wasn't going to get much.'

The new arrangements allowed the negotiators to say that they had preserved the power to pursue effective regional policies, and to control capital movements where necessary in the national interest, together with a commitment to refunds if the British contribution to the EEC budget went 'significantly beyond what is fair in relation to our share of total Community gross national product'. There were some marginal improvements for Commonwealth products. Agreement was struck in Dublin on 11 March. At midnight the assorted heads of state, orchestrated by James Callaghan, burst into a rendering of 'Happy Birthday to You'. It was Wilson's fifty-ninth birthday. On his own preference and forecast, he had one year of office left.

Back home, Wilson's approach remained low key, as it had been throughout. His policy adviser Bernard Donoughue knew this was a deliberate tactic to handle his party:

'. . . slowly to bring the government and after that the party round to it, never himself expressing enthusiasm, and that was quite important, because that enabled the anti-Europeans in the party in the country to feel that Harold understood their reservation, and so they could continue to identify with him.'

The terms were put to the cabinet, and accepted there by 16 to 7. The government had already announced in January that the test of the terms 'at the ballot box' would be by referendum. The seven dissenting ministers – Benn, Shore, Foot, Castle, Eric Varley, John Silkin and William Ross – were permitted to differ, provided they did not speak against the party in the House. This applied to junior ministers too, only one (Eric Heffer) courting dismissal by so doing. When the Commons debated the new terms, the *Guardian*'s sketchwriter Norman Shrapnel reported on 8 April 1975 the Prime Minister's tepid introduction:

'Short of sinking to his knees, Mr Wilson could hardly have achieved a lower profile than in his "stay-in-the-Market" speech . . . and this was sensible of him in the circumstances.'

He was not on his knees at the NEC, however, when, prompted by heavy Transport House criticism of his White Paper on the terms, it recommended rejection. Wilson threatened to resign. He says in his memoirs:[1]

'For only the second time since 1963 I laid my leadership of the Party on the line, and a formula was produced with the help of the General Secretary.'

The 'formula' was that all party members would have the right to differ from a decision of the special conference called for 26 April, just as the dissenting ministers were free to differ from the government. The conference was therefore only able to give a muted roar when it voted by almost 2 to 1 against the terms. There were none of the highlights of 1971, only Callaghan's visibly mouthed 'Rubbish!' from the platform when Peter Shore proclaimed, 'I come to you as a Secretary of State for Trade who can never sign a trade treaty for Great Britain,' and the last known mention of socialism by Roy Jenkins on a Labour platform. Sovereignty, he said, was not the ark of the socialist covenant.

Wilson had carried the cabinet only. He could not command a majority in the PLP, nor in the party in the country, now formally committed to campaign against him. The party's leading orators, Foot, Benn (and, on this subject, Shore) stood by to lead that campaign. Benn, though a recent convert to the sovereignty camp of anti-marketeers, was bitterly at odds with Wilson over industrial policy, and the idol of the constituencies. But the Prime Minister had Benn to thank for victory without bloodshed when it came. The referendum had been Benn's idea and his alone. When the shadow cabinet had adopted the notion in 1972, provoking the resignation of Jenkins and his close allies, Jim Callaghan had shrewdly said, 'Tony Benn may have launched a little rubber dinghy into which one day we shall all wish to clamber.' The former petty officer's metaphor was apt. The cabin boy had found the dinghy, but it was his shipmates who were carried to safety. In the next two months normal politics – and that meant the gathering inflationary crisis – was almost shut out. Even in March Barbara Castle had noted in her diary:[2]

'No Cabinet. Cabinet government barely exists any more, and is certainly going to be broadly in abeyance until the Referendum is over.'

Two opposing umbrella organisations, Britain in Europe and the National Referendum Campaign, were set up, each with a government grant. The former had most of the money and a classy style. The latter had passion and eloquence, hampered by the evident discord of some unlikely allies, which the cartoonists seized upon. This alliance, from far left to far right, was, Enoch Powell concedes, 'a motley crew', which made the best it could of its disparate elements:

'After all, all sorts and conditions of men can resent the destruction of their own country's independence.'

The two sides were allowed to circulate written versions of their arguments, in opposed but politically neutral colours, but these were accompanied by the government's case, at greater length, in patriotic red, white and blue, like some prototype SDP leaflet. The national press was also heavily in favour of Britain staying in Europe, providing a 54:21% bias of sympathetic column inches, on subsequent calculation. Much of the feature material included sustained attacks on Tony Benn linked to his activities as Industry Secretary – 'Bye Bye Benn', 'Now Benn Grabs Ferranti', 'The Minister of Fear', being typical. Benn's habitual preference for a high profile was obliged, but he was drawn with horns and tail.

The pro-Europeans stressed Britain's changing balance of trade, employment prospects (ironically, 'Jobs for the Boys' was the heading on the principal poster) and the need for Britain to play a major part in the new and powerful Europe. They outspent the National Referendum Campaign by a factor of ten. (They collected in subscriptions and donations £1,356,583; the antis raised £8,629.81.) Their all-party presentation, with Thorpe and Heath flanking Jenkins, laid a heavy stress on men of sense and moderation come together, accompanied by Kennedy-style TV programmes from the American film-maker Charles Guggenheim. For the anti-marketeers Benn made much of the running. His allegation that the Common Market had already cost Britain 500,000 lost jobs forced Wilson to take centre stage, attacking the judgement and the mathematics of his own Industry Secretary. Mostly, the Prime Minister and the Foreign Secretary stayed out of the struggle, on the pretence that they were still in some sense above an equally balanced argument. This led James Callaghan into difficulties when he was confronted on the BBC Radio 4 programme *Referendum Call* by a Mrs Levy, who wished to know why she had received two pro-EEC leaflets and one against.[3] No, said Callaghan, the third one was the government's view, 'which comes down in favour, on balance, of Britain remaining a member of the Community'. Was that not two to one, Robin Day insisted from the chair? 'No, that is not correct. I am not pro, nor am I anti . . .' said Callaghan. 'You are not pro?' 'No, I am not.' This was too much for Day: 'What are you doing on this programme?' 'I am here because you asked me, Mr Day.' 'You are here to advise people to vote yes, aren't you?' 'Now, Mr Day, we are not debating this issue. The Prime Minister has taken the same line; it is our job to advise the British people on what we think would be the right result.'

The right result for the government was never in doubt. The size of the margin was. The anti-marketeers had hopes of a late swing, as their case got across. It did not happen, and some of them had a bruising time, none more so than Barbara Castle at the televised Oxford Union debate, when she was asked by Jeremy Thorpe if she would remain in the government if the pro-Europeans won. The 'stain of the misery of failure' which she confessed to her diary that night[4] (though her mail was congratulatory) must have been deepened by the adulation for Edward Heath, whose triumph in the Oxford debate was remarkable. The referendum brought him in from the cold, even if only as a battalion commander in Harold Wilson's grand strategy. The Prime Minister's agility was acknowledged by the two most prominent figures in the National Referendum Campaign. Enoch Powell sees the result as a kind of bonus election for Conservative voters, able to cast a vote against the Labour Party 'even if Harold Wilson has got on the bandwagon . . . We'll deal with him later.' For Tony Benn, it was the presence of Wilson discreetly pushing the bandwagon that made it move:

'His role in it was decisive. If he'd come out against the renegotiation, people would have voted no . . . I regard the referendum in the summer of 1975 as the third election, general election, in which the Labour Party was defeated, but Harold Wilson won.'

The yes vote was overwhelming: 17,387,581 (67.2%) against 8,470,073 (32.8%). Wilson, in election-winning style, announced on the steps of Downing Street that 'fourteen years of national argument is over'. The result was replete with ironies. Roy Jenkins told his fellow campaigners as they celebrated at the St Ermin's Hotel that it had been a famous victory. It had been a victory in a contest which on principle he disliked, and for which he had already thrown away his chance of leading the Labour Party. Now he had found new allies, a fresh and congenial audience, as crowds flocked to the meetings. 'It did have a certain effect on making some of us, certainly including me, believe there was something a bit beyond the high banks of these narrow canals of traditional party politics.'

For the moment, in spite of the public differences of the referendum campaign, Labour's fragile internal coalition held together. Wilson had avoided the catastrophe which had overcome his Norwegian contemporary Bratteli: a result which both isolated him and split his party. Now he could deal with the one challenger whose high profile during the campaign had irritated him, after a full year of discord. On

9 June he made his dispositions. Barbara Castle was summoned in the next day to be told, 'When it is over you will say that the old boy has not lost his touch. It is pure poetry.' He was able to settle his scores with Tony Benn, the real loser of the referendum.

The castling of Benn: 1974–5

In the short 1974 Parliament Benn's cherished industrial policy had been curtailed by the White Paper rewritten by the No. 10 Policy Unit. But he did not believe it had been castrated. The essentials were still intact: a National Enterprise Board (NEB) with a billion pounds of capital, planning agreements, albeit voluntary, and the power to buy into profitable firms or rescue those in difficulty. The creators of the NEB saw its scale as the only proper response to the magnitude of the British industrial crisis. The NEB had to achieve public representation in all the multinational-dominated sectors of British industry, to, in Stuart Holland's phrase, 'reinforce and promote success rather than simply to underwrite or subsidise failure'. There would be failure enough as well – notably British Leyland – before the Industry Bill had even reached the Commons. Throughout 1975 firms large and small crashed, in an economic climate which made the small-scale attempts at rescue through workers' co-operatives doubly difficult. Difficult too would be any incursion by the Department of Industry into the private sector, a prospect which drove the CBI to despair.

The CBI had united in their fear and loathing of Benn during the 1974 Parliament. His style made few concessions to them. Campbell Adamson, then Director General, remembers with fastidious distaste:

'You know, those endless sort of huge enamelled cracked cups which Benn used to drink tea out of – I never liked tea – and occasionally taking telephone calls to trade unionists while the meeting was going on – all part of the scene.'

The CBI dreaded a policy which might shift power fundamentally towards trade unions and away from management. Symbolically and practically, Benn seemed to be telling them that that was what he would do. So more representations poured in to the Prime Minister, who was well briefed through the Treasury on what his Industry Secretary planned. And when the Industry Bill was published compulsory disclosure of information to unions or government had simply vanished from it. Such disclosures are not thought particularly subversive in the European models from which the Industry Bill was drawn, but they had not been introduced in an atmosphere which was – on both sides – so partisan.

Inside the Department of Industry the atmosphere was tense. Benn describes the reaction of Sir Anthony Part, the Permanent Secretary, when he first arrived:

'He said to me, in effect. "I take it you're not going to try to implement the policy." And I said, "Yes, I am." And from that moment there was a certain, ah, chill between us, because he had all sorts of plans which would have made it look as though we were implementing without really doing so.'

The naming of Part here may not be entirely fair. The Permanent Secretary's dilemma was that the policy of his department was systematically rewritten in the Cabinet Office or at No. 10. If he pointed out the need for compromise, he alienated his minister. If he did not, he lost more of the policy, or face in Whitehall, or both. The key was Wilson's attitude. Wilson regarded Benn as on a tight rein, gathered in at the Treasury. He expected civil servants to let the Treasury know what Benn planned:

'While a civil servant should never be as it were disloyal to his minister, naturally they would have to tell the Treasury because of the finance required and so on, so it usually filtered through pretty quickly.'

Benn's disquisitions on the powers, rights and wisdom of trade unions made the Prime Minister bored and restless, as he remembers it:

'Tony Benn came and disclosed to us one day the complete change in his thinking. He said, "I want to tell this to the cabinet . . . most wonderful experience in my whole life." Well, we wondered what that could be. He'd been at a meeting where the shop stewards at the Bristol aero-engine factory passed a resolution saying they should have the right to sack the whole of the management at a week's notice. Deep sighs from all the shadow cabinet, but I was in the chair, so I said, "Well what we can't understand, Tony, is why these people you're talking about should have a whole week's notice. Wouldn't two days be enough to thank their secretaries for past services, take them out to dinner, clear their desks, and so on?" "No, I think it should be a week." So I said, "A week, let it be." He took that dead seriously. It was from that moment I knew he was moving his philosophy.'

Tony Benn's view of the liberating effect of power and respon-

sibility on the workforce was most evident in his enthusiasm for the
co-operative as rescue mechanism. He had announced in 1974 that
there would be government funding to raise new worker co-ops from
the ashes of failed companies. Very soon he was claiming on television
that this new force was 'sweeping the country: . . . the most exciting
thing since the war'. He began with the *Scottish Daily News*, based on
what was left of the personnel and plant of the defunct *Scottish Daily
Express*, and Norton Villiers Triumph at Meriden, a typically British
compendium of great names and obsolete design. Later these were
joined by a third, KME at Kirby, which made variously motorcar
parts, radiators, and orange juice. The money allocated was, as Benn
claims, 'peanuts' compared to government support for sections of
private industry. Unfortunately for him, the co-operatives were
doomed in the dire climate of the recession. They were unlikely to have
the time to search out a new market. Richard Graham of the Policy
Unit, whose job was to monitor the Department of Industry, sums up
the dilemma of Meriden:

'Here was a factory producing a product for which there would be
no market, except as some kind of memento of the past . . . The bikes
they were going to produce were really 1950s' bikes for which there
might be a small specialist market, but, no, this wasn't a product of the
future.'

It was a point put to Benn in cabinet, especially by the financial
wizards, Lever and Barnett. The Chancellor, Healey, was more sympathetic, but alarmed when he heard from Benn's union supporter
Jack Jones that '. . . you didn't need research and development for
motorbikes'. Co-operatives needed the same mix of skills, investment
and market research as any other new industrial enterprise. They did
not get it.

In January 1975 matters came to a head between Benn and Sir
Anthony Part over the co-operatives. The civil servants did not agree
with Benn's decision to provide £3.9 million funding for the Kirby
scheme. The minister was to be nailed:

'[Part] sent me a technical thing called an accounting officer's
minute, which in effect was reporting me to the Public Accounts
Committee, leaked it – or somebody leaked it – to the press; and the
Prime Minister sent a note, and I had to respond, about what had
actually happened. Now that was an act of war, if you know what I
mean.'

As the story appeared in the *Financial Times*, its import was that

Benn had ignored his Accounting Officer's warnings (he had not) and forced his civil servants to report him to protect themselves. A week later Sir Anthony Part was taken to hospital after a heart attack, following a row with the Industry Secretary. His colleagues settled to the yoke. If they chafed, they concealed it in public. Campbell Adamson remembers their demeanour when he visited the department.

'I knew that they loathed the policy. I thought I knew them well enough, and I think I did – they were friends – to know what they would feel about this kind of policy. But I have to say that in all the discussions we had about it, although it was impossible, I suppose, for them at times to disguise their worry and distaste about the policy, they were perfectly loyal in defending it at that time.'

Benn saw his civil servants differently, after the 'act of war':

'The civil servants had ways of mobilising parliamentary opinion, business opinion, media opinion, and public opinion – with the help of the Prime Minister, who could have stopped it instantly if he wished – in order to prevent ministers from doing things.'

One of the suspects felt that he was holding a long rope which Wilson had let out for Benn:

'Wilson certainly didn't want Benn to resign. He wanted him in the government. So he had to decide on how many occasions he was going to let him have his way, and how many not. I don't know what went through the PM's mind when he let the co-operatives go through. Maybe he thought it would be a good idea to let them go through and then fail. But I mustn't impute that to him . . .'

In cabinet, therefore, the Industry Secretary often found himself isolated. As the Industry Bill ploughed through committee, Tribune Group backbenchers tried to reinstate its lost teeth, fighting for powers of compulsory acquisition, ability to increase the NEB stake in private companies to 51%, the duty rather than merely the power to make planning agreements with private companies. All such amendments were defeated. The minister originally in charge of the Bill, Eric Heffer, had resigned over the EEC. A series of signals from Wilson made it clear that proposals for acquisitions by the NEB would have to pass a committee chaired by him, and that he would decide the membership of the Board. Michael Meacher was the junior minister taking the Bill in committee when:

'One of the Tories got up and asked on what basis £50 million only was going to be made available in the first year. Well, it was the first I'd heard of that figure and in fact it had been inserted in one of the financial red books. If it was going to be effective, it probably needed about £1 billion in the first year, and a further billion in each of the next five . . .'

The role of the NEB as initiator of intervention in an unwilling private sector was soon to be a matter of purely academic interest. A queue of ailing private companies waited at the door for out-patient treatment.

The Ryder Report, drawn up by the Prime Minister's nominee for the NEB chair, Sir Don Ryder, came to cabinet in April. It recommended that British Leyland should continue as a volume car producer, separated into its constituent parts, with an input of nearly £3 billion investment over the next seven years. There could be only one source for such munificence, and the government announced that it would take a majority shareholding for the NEB in the reconstructed company. Thus at its very beginning the NEB found its much reduced funds appropriated for the biggest lame duck of all. Leyland had been preceded by Ferranti, which had requested and received £15 million in equity finance and loans from the Department of Industry to help it through its 1974 cash crisis. A majority shareholding in Ferranti was transferred to the NEB later and the company was successfully reorganised and in substantial profit within three years. Rolls-Royce, Alfred Herbert Ltd, ICL and other smaller enterprises were either brought, or collapsed, into the arms of the NEB in 1975–6. Without the Board, the ravages of the industrial depression would have been even more sweeping than they were. What the NEB could not be, with its slender finance and heavy burden, was the investment primer for the whole economy which Benn and his aides had envisaged. Instead, it was left dealing with the walking wounded of the industrial collapse.

Except for one with the National Coal Board, the only planning agreement ever signed with the government came after Benn's departure, when the American multinational Chrysler threatened to close down its UK operations, with 27,000 redundancies, or to transfer its assets to the British government to see if they could do better. The Scottish Secretary, with one eye on unemployment and one on the rampant SNP, threatened to resign if Chrysler's Linwood plant closed; the new Industry Secretary, Eric Varley, threatened a counter-resignation if the problem was transferred to him. Harold Lever, brought in as universal fixer, arranged a compromise. Instead of taking over Chrysler, the government would bear a proportion of the losses of Chrysler UK for the next few years. What it got in return was a planning agreement, and the postponement of Linwood's closure! Lever, the most astringent critic of planning agreements, thus became the only Labour minister to get one agreed and signed. The British government was taken to the cleaners by American business. Chrysler ran through £150 million of the subsidy, and sold out to Peugeot Citroen, without waiting for British approval. (The lesson was not lost on Mr John De Lorean, singing siren songs of gull-winged sports cars to the Northern Ireland Office.) Lever still defends his agreement for the years of employment it bought, and the international obligations it honoured. The Chrysler planning agreement was little better than farce. The next Minister of State at the department, Gerald Kaufman, was scathing about the whole concept:[5]

'In the fifteen months during which Labour held office with a commitment to introduce planning agreements, no one seemed to have sat down and worked out what should actually go into [one] . . . Many Labour MPs felt they should be imposed compulsorily . . . The trouble was, they were called agreements. How do you compel somebody to agree and still claim they have agreed? . . .'

All this lay in the future as Benn sallied forth from the Department of Industry to do battle in the referendum. If Barbara Castle's diaries are to be believed, his allies in the cabinet found his insouciance about the automatic benefits of massive further investment plus workers' involvement unconvincing, without some acceptance that workers' wage demands were affecting the rate of return on current investment. Castle's diary records on 19 May:[6]

'I suddenly saw why I distrust Wedgie. He is right about certain of his themes, such as the need for a crash programme of positive hope through investment and for the involvement of working people in the decisions of industry. But what is so wrong about him is that he never spells out that responsibility involves choice, and that the choices facing this country are by definition grim for everybody. He really cannot eat his seed corn and sow it. But his whole popularity rests on the belief that he is spreading around: that he – and those he seeks to lead – can do just that.'

The dissenting ministers, or DMs as they cosily referred to themselves, also felt that Benn's tactics in the referendum were losing support for their anti-market cause.

When that cause was lost, the DMs attended cabinet with some trepidation. Nothing was said that morning. Then the blow fell. Castle hurried to see Benn:[7]

'Tony Benn was sitting at his desk, a figure of tragedy, surrounded by a cortège of political advisers: Michael Meacher, Joe Ashton, and other figures I could barely make out, because the curtains were drawn against the brilliant sun. The heat was stifling. "Have you heard anything?" I asked. "Yes," he replied, "I am to be moved to Energy." I was staggered, my first feeling being that this was the cleverest move that Harold could make.'

Benn changed places with Varley, also one of the DMs, one anti-marketeer swapped for another.

Few in Downing Street believed that Benn would take Energy. He would either resign, and leave the government, or he would get his friends to fight for him. They did very little. More effort was made to save Judith Hart before she chose to resign. In the event, Benn resolved matters by accepting demotion to Energy within a day of being offered it, despite noises offstage by Jack Jones and on stage by Michael Foot pleading his cause. His colleagues felt that, if he had not actually been sacked, they need not fight too hard to keep him when, as Castle wrote:[8]

'We have all suffered from his habit of writing Labour policy by ministerial edict. The Department of Industry enabled him to be all things to the Labour movement with none of the restraints the rest of us face.'

Benn himself says:

'It was very difficult being in that subsequent cabinet, but I felt that, provided you were putting forward with integrity and honesty the arguments that you believed and that were in line with party policy, you were there to fight it out.'

This view was endorsed by his constituency party.

The Department of Industry marked the high point of Benn's ministerial career. Few Labour leaders have ever had his gift for communication, or his restless energy. His mastery of the party's decision-making processes gave him a sway over the industrial strategy which Harold Wilson would have been bound to fear. It was one thing to tease Benn as an Old Testament prophet: quite another to see him snatching the leadership of the Israelites to lead a commando raid on the Promised Land. The prophecies brought him a mass following in the party, and he was hailed by admirers as 'the most important leading Labour statesman since Nye Bevan'. They also

brought him widespread distrust, from the suspicion that he intended
to capture the leadership by Labour populism – a picture which led
one review of his book *Arguments for Socialism* to be headed 'Arguments for Me'. The scepticism of his colleagues, relayed to an avid
press, resulted in the pop-eyed caricature with which he was vilified.
And the more he was vilified, the greater his hold on the party rank and
file, the more eager they were to learn from this betrayal. As with all
other infatuations, that between Benn and the Labour activists inevitably excluded proper considerations for others, for their difficulties,
doubts and hesitations. Benn had the ability to be the most creative of
cabinet ministers or the most effective tribune of the party outside. He
believed he could be both. Had it been 1945, he might have been right.

In the strained circumstances of 1975 he was wrong.

The rebirth of incomes policy

Throughout the spring of 1975, as the government settled into its
renegotiations with the EEC, and Harold Wilson measured the length
of Tony Benn's ambitions in the Department of Industry, the inflationary situation worsened. The position at the end of 1974 was summed
up by Michael Stewart in *The Jekyll and Hyde Years*:[9]

'Retail prices were 18% higher than a year before; but weekly wage
rates were 26% higher, and on top of this most wage and salary
earners were now receiving eleven threshold payments, totalling £4.40
per week. As a result real personal disposable income in the fourth
quarter of 1974 was in fact 2% higher than a year before – an absurd
situation, given the 10% worsening of the terms of trade in the same
period, and one made possible only by a large increase in the balance of
payments deficit.'

The situation caused sleepless nights at Nos. 10 and 11 Downing
Street. In the Policy Unit, Donoughue remembers concern that:

'. . . inflation was rocketing, the government deficit was rising, the
trade deficit was rising, so it was there in the numbers, in the tea
leaves.'

But the comings and goings to Europe, caused interruptions:

'. . . endless renegotiations, summits in Paris and Dublin and so on,
long ministerial discussions . . . kept pushing back the time when the
Labour government finally confronted economic reality.'

There was another problem too. The reality that the government
had to confront was partly of its own making. Large wage increases for

worthy and responsible groups in the public sector, all of whom had impeccable claims to catch up, were seen as an integral part of the Social Contract, and were so described by the ministers responsible. These rises, sometimes preceded by independent arbitration and inquiry, were duly noted by those unions which had the industrial muscle to get their way by simpler means. With the rises came an expansion of public sector employment following on from the reorganisations under the Heath government. Such expansion of the public sector in health, education and welfare would anyway have been inevitable if the country was even to maintain standards of care for fast-growing populations of both old and young. British levels of provision in these categories were not high by the standards of continental Europe, but it was hard for a sluggish economy to generate the wealth to pay for them. And to the public the increase in numbers often seemed to be of administrators rather than practitioners. For example, by 1975, administrative and clerical staff in the NHS outnumbered hospital medical staff by 3 to 1 – 105,000 against 33,000. On all sides the bills were mounting.

Throughout the first six months of 1975 the situation deteriorated. The Chancellor, Denis Healey, recalls this period as 'the most intense course of adult education in economic management I think anyone's ever had'. In his April budget he had pressed for a package of cuts in planned future public expenditure which had worried the spending ministers who, like Castle, regarded themselves as 'custodians of the Social Contract'. In that 'de-natured cabinet', already split into cabals by the coming referendum, Healey got his way. He remembers that the Prime Minister said to him, 'You know, Denis, I'll support you in everything you want to do except incomes policy.' There could be no interference with collective bargaining, especially when the very contract of which it was part seemed threatened by any attack on public expenditure. Healey raised the problem constantly with the trade union leaders at the Liaison Committee. The Committee could not act, and the government was committed against an incomes policy by the very programme which had brought it to power. In the 1975 wage round the union negotiators knew that they were playing a game of pass-the-parcel, in which the size of the parcel seemed to increase each time round, as one wage settlement exceeded another, but the real weight, in real money, stayed the same. Len Murray says:

'I remember those conferences passing resolutions calling for wage increases of 30%, 40%. I also remember in tea rooms, in bars, sitting and having a cup of tea, having a glass of beer, the delegates – the same delegates who were voting the 30% wage increases – saying to me directly, "Look, we've got to do something about this. You've got to do something about this. We can't go on like this."'

Barbara Castle records the plaintive complain of Sid Vincent of the NUM when the Labour Party NEC considered staff wage demands:[10]

'Even an increase of 20% means an additional bill of £700,000 a year! We must have a paper on the state of the Party's finances if inflation carries on.'

Wearing his other hat as a member of the NUM executive, Vincent had happily gone for, and got, a settlement which allowed pay increases of up to 33% in February 1975. The electricity supply workers followed with 31%. Then came a claim for the railway unions. Sid Weighell of the NUR led for his union:

'We had noted the 30% settlements of power workers and mine-workers and so that was our target. And of course when we were offered 21%, it was disturbing our long-establishing relativity and therefore we were ... caught in this difficulty that railwaymen couldn't afford to let themselves slip in comparison with these other comparable industries. And we eventually got 30%, not without first going to Downing Street . . .'

The NUR had turned down a 27.5% award from arbitration, and its executive voted for strike action. The union's claim hung over the cabinet during the first weeks of that rainless June. Eventually the extra cash was found by the Prime Minister. Outside Downing Street, Weighell said blandly that he was within the interpretation of the Social Contract laid down by other public sector unions.

The General Council of the TUC had rebuffed attempts by Healey to tighten the pay guidelines. Wages had risen by 30% in the previous year. If the current pattern continued, it would mean an annual rate nearer 40%. The economy was slipping into hyper-inflation. The unions' adherence to free collective bargaining, in which the strong seemed to gain most, came under vituperative attack from Paul Johnson in the *New Statesman* in May, then beginning his long march to the right:

'Free collective bargaining necessarily excludes huge sections of society. They are not organised. They cannot be organised. Rapid inflation inflicts the greatest possible suffering on the very poor, the old, the very young, the sick, the helpless, the physically and mentally handicapped, all the outcasts and misfits and casualties of society.

Collectively they number millions. Collectively, from a trade union point of view, they are powerless . . . They cannot batter the public with their fists. Old people open their newspapers with dread, knowing they will read of 30%, 40%, and even 60% wage increases, leading inevitably to monstrous rises in the cost of essentials, like electricity and gas, transport and food, and compulsory charges like rates . . . This may be good trade unionism, but it is not socialism as I understand it.'

In that same month, as the sun shone and the referendum rolled on, the cabinet's most articulate champion of growth through public expenditure, Tony Crosland, who knew of and feared the further spending cuts being prepared in the Treasury, spoke out. To the still burgeoning empires of local government he gave notice that the days of expansion had ended. Local authorities 'with their usual patriotism' should realise that 'the party's over, at least for the moment'. In June, although Michael Foot begged him not to go public, Crosland turned on the railwaymen with whom he had been negotiating as Environment Secretary:

'Principles of social justice should determine the distribution of our national wealth. But all government efforts to increase social justice are lost in the crazy haphazard lurches which characterise pay settlements under conditions of rapid inflation. The most extraordinary thing is that most wage and salary owners agree with everything I have said . . .'

The party was over when Jack Jones, the most influential voice in the trade union movement (and later described in one opinion poll as the most powerful man in Britain), came to realise it. He had brooded for months over the threat to a Labour government if what it tried to do for working people and the less well off under the Social Contract was destroyed by a failure of that same contract on the wages side. He says:

'I recognised that something further would have to be done to try to persuade in a voluntary way the trade unions to hold their wage claims within reason, otherwise we were going to have hyper-inflation . . . and that was no good to the working people of this country.'

At roughly the same time Jones and Wilson's aide Joe Haines came up with the idea of a voluntary flat-rate policy. It would be clear, unmistakable, difficult to breach. ('A fiver; everyone can understand a fiver!' said Joe Haines.) It would help the lower paid most, by rough, egalitarian justice. The wealthy would get nothing, which would commend the point to those on the left who were still smarting at

A sign of the times: petrol shortages in 1973

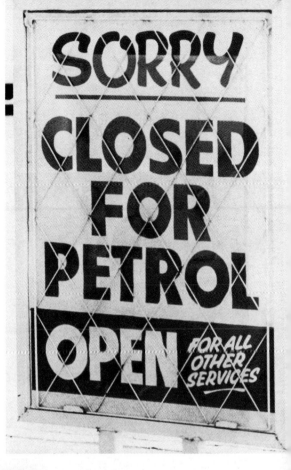

Below: The new face of Nationalism: Margot MacDonald MP, SNP victor at Govan, with her daughters

'We want to bring down your government': Mick McGahey, Joe
Gormley and Lawrence Daly leave Downing Street with the NUM
executive, including Arthur Scargill

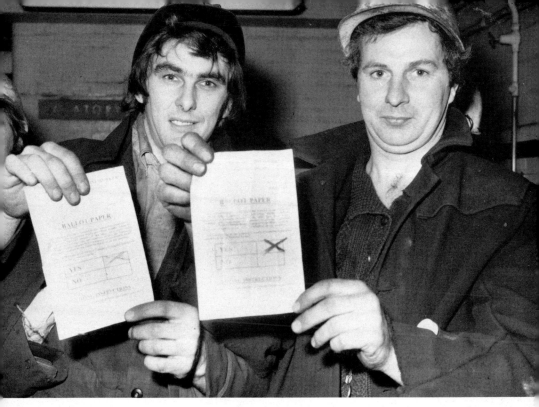

Yes to strike action: the miners voted 81% in favour in 1974

In February 1974 'Who governs?' was a slogan that boomeranged

'I'm not sure that "Who governs Britain?" is a question we should draw attention to!' 18 January 1974

A moment of influence: Jeremy Thorpe at Downing Street for talks with Edward Heath, March 1974

'We certainly threatened an investment strike': CBI leaders arrive in Downing Street to talk with incoming Prime Minister Wilson

Get Britain out: Enoch Powell campaigns on an anti-market platform

Keep Britain in: Helmut Schmidt pleads with the Labour Party conference, November 1974

A press view of the anti-marketeers

Join the professionals

Opposite: Changing the set: Margaret Thatcher helps to clear up after a Conservative rally in 1974

Embarrassing intruders: a streaker at Twickenham

...and Tony Benn's campaign against the cabinet majority in 1975

Labour's failure to introduce a wealth tax (the proposal had vanished in a cloud of Wilsonian pipe smoke into a Select Committee, which produced enough minority reports to excuse permanent inaction). Finally, the policy would be voluntary – not only, as the wags said, in that you could settle for less than the flat rate if you wanted, but also in that settlements might come about by consent among the unions. Jones is happy to claim paternity of the flat-rate limit:

'I produced the idea of a rate right across the board. I suggested a slightly higher figure but we settled on six.'

The government were delighted to sell it as his.

To win round the TUC there came an unexpected ally. The international money markets turned on the pound. On 30 June sterling fell like a stone, losing 5 cents in the day. This was the crisis for which the Treasury had waited. Wilson returned from the Midlands that Monday to an action replay of past scenes in his life at Downing Street. The Governor of the Bank of England was waiting. Armageddon was at hand. Joe Haines and Bernard Donoughue remained outside as the Governor made his pitch:

'Drastic measures, painful but inevitable, had to be taken. The government had to be seen to be in charge, etc. And what were the drastic measures? Well, it so happened that the Treasury had them handy. So handy, in fact, that it would be possible for the cabinet to discuss and endorse them at their meeting next morning (in breach, incidentally, of the rule that cabinet papers must be circulated forty-eight hours at least in advance of a cabinet meeting).'

The package called for an immediate statutory incomes policy. The Prime Minister emerged converted. Throughout the evening, against the background of a reception for the Belgian Prime Minister, the fight for Wilson's ear went on. Haines and Donoughue persisted. Then, the latter remembers:

'Around midnight the classic Treasury bounce, the draft of their policy, arrived, and it was a draft for a statement by the Chancellor of the Exchequer the next day, announcing a statutory policy, criminal sanctions ... and then there was to be a second White Paper in a week's time with massive public expenditure cuts.'

Such a policy would have split the cabinet. The Chief Whip had advised that he could not carry the PLP. The advisers drafted a response; the choice was not between statute and chaos, but between a statutory and a voluntary policy. They had been working on a voluntary policy; it should have its chance. The Prime Minister was converted back, and telephoned Haines at 1.40 a.m. to tell him so: 'When the cabinet turned up at half past nine the next morning they didn't have anything to consider.' The Treasury mandarins retired wounded – so wounded that when the voluntary policy came to be drafted it was largely done by the No. 10 Policy Unit.

The gravity of the crisis and the narrow escape from the hated statutory policy made it easier for the Chancellor and Employment Secretary Michael Foot, acting together, to urge a flat-rate voluntary policy on the TUC, at NEDC meetings. The union leaders were shaken, and came back chastened. Sid Weighell, fresh from almost the last 'pay victory' of the old free-for-all, was still a tyro union leader then:

'Jones and Scanlon came back and Scanlon said, "I have looked into the abyss," and what he'd seen had frightened him to death.'

On 3 July the General Council endorsed a flat-rate £6 policy, with zero increases for those earnings above £8500 per annum, by 19 votes to 13. Scanlon's AUEW voted against, well aware that this policy would hurt differentials and the better-off skilled workers relative to the lower-paid. Scanlon, who was 'taken struggling and screaming in to the first round of wage restraint', knew the problems which would arise in his union. The engineers did not give a grudging acceptance to the policy until the end of the year, after it had been endorsed at both the TUC and the Labour Party conferences. The reserve statutory powers prepared by the government were dropped on the insistence of Michael Foot.

The government had achieved an incomes policy of last resort, not imposed upon the trade unions, but publicly identified as the creation of the most powerful union leader in the land. Jones still speaks of it with pride:

'Surprisingly for twelve months that policy operated without in my knowledge any breach, people accepted it, and for many many workers up and down the country it was a decided advance.'

The man and his creation were dramatically denounced at the Labour conference. On the Tribune platform in the Spanish Hall at Blackpool that year, Ian Mikardo launched a sombre attack on the policy. On the left of the platform were Benn and Heffer; on the right Foot and his young ally, Neil Kinnock. Barbara Castle had shown an advance copy of the speech to Jones, who says:

'Perhaps that's why I was enraged. I felt that some protest ought to

be made at the point where the attack was being directed, at the point
of its being said.'

He stormed down to the front of the hall, and seized the microphone. For some minutes of confusion, he could be heard bellowing
at Mikardo, 'I detest these attacks on the trade union movement.' It
was a clear if brutal demonstration to the Tribune left that, for the
moment, the tanks were on their lawn.

Did the policy work? It stuck; it helped to reduce the level of
inflation over the next three years. It was a rejoinder to those in the
labour movement who continued to pretend to themselves in 1975
that wage costs had nothing to do with inflation. It was also the only
alternative left to a government which thought that it would thereby
avoid massive further cuts in public expenditure to sweat the excess
demand out of the economy. But it came too late. It did not prevent the
1976 sterling crisis, for which June 1975 had been a mere dress
rehearsal, and the agonising cuts which followed. And it piled up
discontents and anomalies which led to later variants being rejected by
the unions within two years, as its union backers were in turn rebuffed.
Caught between its rhetoric in opposition on the one hand, and the
frustrations of its supporters on the other, Labour could not expect an
ad hoc incomes policy to be credible for the course of a parliament.
Wilson did not solve his economic problems. He bought time. And
time, in July 1975, seemed a very scarce commodity.

By the end of the year the cabinet was wracked by the further cuts in
public expenditure over which it had agonised throughout the autumn. That Christmas the Prime Minister knew that one present he
had long promised his wife and himself remained under wraps:
retirement at sixty, before he got stale. His Downing Street aides
remember a long and ferocious battle by Lady Falkender to persuade
him to stay on 'at least for two more Honours Lists', but he was
adamant. At the 1975 party conference he had asked his staff to draw
up a timetable for countdown to resignation on his sixtieth birthday,
11 March. But for a week's delay, he kept to it. The delay was to have
an influence on the succession. He had told his advisers that he thought
James Callaghan the likely heir, but that he was not averse to Healey.
Callaghan had been forewarned, in broad hints, in time to make his
dispositions. Healey had not. The 5 March sterling crisis (see chapter
9) caused Wilson to spend his birthday in office. On that day a brawl
between Healey and the Labour left over a rebellion on the public
expenditure White Paper confirmed the Chancellor's high status in the

demonology of the Tribune Group. The government's defeat at the hands of the rebels forced it to table and carry a vote of confidence. This further delayed Wilson's resignation, and added an air of sensation to the public announcement. Why was he going? What was to come out? The only news at the press conference was that in a last bizarre act of patronage the outgoing Prime Minister had made his PPS a minister.

When, on the morning of 16 March, Wilson told a stunned cabinet that he was to resign, Healey hesitated. Callaghan had been told in detail of the Prime Minister's intentions on the preceding night, but Healey had been given only a five-minute advance warning. In the end there were six candidates. Crosland, who came bottom, Jenkins, who polled badly, and Benn, who threw his weight behind Foot, all disappeared at the first ballot. Healey went out next, and in the third round Foot was defeated by 176 votes to 137. Whether he meant to or not, the Prime Minister made way for an older man – the man whom he believed would be the best guarantor of the party's deal with the unions. Callaghan saw off his Oxford-educated rivals with unruffled ease. For all of them the moment was inopportune, for Jenkins and Healey most of all. For Callaghan it was exactly right.

The press farewell to Wilson was to a character, an English worthy – 'a palliator of crisis, not a man who could solve great problems . . . Labour's Baldwin,'* was the view of the right, who had come reluctantly to relish his innate conservatism. In his memoirs Wilson quotes with approval a different epitaph, that of Peter Jenkins in the *Guardian*:

'. . . The country does have now a kind of National Government appropriate to a deep economic crisis . . . His Government does not dare, and probably never will, to speak openly the language of German Social Democracy, but that is the direction in which their policies are now pointing. Like it or loathe it, the face of British politics has been virtually transformed, all in the space of less than nine months.'

It had not. That much was illusion. But Wilson had contrived to turn his party away from the fundamentalist socialism of the 1973 programme, towards Europe, incomes policy and the mixed economy, while preserving, for a few more years, the internal Labour coalition. Had he not once had a majority of 100, it would have been said that his skill in sustaining government without any firm majority at all showed

---

* Patrick Cosgrave in the *Spectator*, 20 March 1976.

how much more he might have achieved with firm parliamentary support. If that cannot be argued, at least he combined the lessons he had learned and the limits which constrained him in 1974–6 to lead his party by consent. He did not confront the storm, as Tony Benn would have preferred, but he was not afraid to leave port and use the winds where he could. That much will outlast the final images of the shuffling figure in the Garter robes, the ludicrous 'lavender list' of figures from the shadows who received 'honours' at his resignation. He won four elections – matching Gladstone, as he was not slow to point out – and all before the age at which the Liberal patriarch had formed his second administration. Unlike Gladstone, he could remind his party, he had done it while leading a party which before his advent was said to be in a terminal decline – to which the party responded by damning the achievement as mere legerdemain. Those who would have sacrificed the Gladstonian electoral record for more of the Gladstonian rectitude, and formed the view that Labour out of office might be better than Wilson in, were to have their chance in the 1980s to make a different party. Few of them realised that Wilson did not create the tension between a socialist party and government in a weak mixed economy. He demonstrated it, with feats of elision which became more strained, less credible, the longer he went on. In such a dilemma, it was a sensible resolution to lower his personal retirement age to sixty.

8

THE OTHER ISLAND

While the political problems of the mainland all came down to economics, Northern Ireland additionally faced a crisis of legitimacy for the state itself. Its political contradictions had come to notice in a time of upheaval.

1968–70: The claim for civil rights

1968 was a year of marches, and a year of muffled drums. All over the world – it seemed, from the vivid images of television – young people marched against discrimination, brutality and oppression. In May it was Paris; in August Prague. In Britain the new student radicalism overflowed at concert and campus, and in the mass protests of Grosvenor Square. Everywhere, there seemed to be an idealistic new generation who believed that justice and freedom were attainable by direct action, if only their torpid elders would somehow get out of the way. Nowhere was more obviously open to this new wave than the British state's forgotten backwater: the six counties of Northern Ireland. What began there in hope and fraternity as a crusade for all was to become a nightmare struggle for a whole generation caught up in the fury of Ireland's two competitive nationalisms and displaced minorities. In the course of it, the British and Irish states, each almost parodied by the rival identities established by ballot or bullet in the North, have been drawn further into the conflict. As the life of Northern Ireland has been poisoned by sectarian violence and the repression which follows it, so has the bacillus entered the bloodstream of the Republic and mainland Britain.

For forty years the British had hidden the anomalies of Northern Ireland in the recesses of the national conscience. In the 1920s they had accepted a compromise based on two conflicting principles: they must come to terms with Republican nationalism, but they could not coerce the Northern Protestants into a unitary Irish state. They left a device for the two Irelands to find their way back together – a Council of Ireland – but they did not activate it. And they fuelled Ireland's perpetual problem of the minority which feels threatened by an alien majority when they allowed the Northern state to contain all the six counties of nine-county Ulster in which there was a bare majority for the Union. One third of the Northern population was Catholic. Over the years some of this minority accommodated to their position and identified with, and served, the government of Northern Ireland. Many more did not. By 1968 the Province – like the Republic to the south, which had grown ever further away from it culturally and politically – had forty-five years of separate existence behind it – as much as the new nation states of central Europe. Perhaps, if the Irish of both traditions had been more like the English, believers in muddled compromise and crisis avoidance, they would have come closer because of the sheer practical advantages of doing so. Under the long dominance of Lord Brookeborough to the north, and De Valera to the south, each state energetically multiplied the symbols and trappings which made it uncongenial to the other. Minorities were always out of step, the Unionists for resisting the nation of the Gael, the Northern Catholics for 'disloyalty' to the Orange order. Here was a state where every agitator could wave the bloody shirt, be it orange or green, worn in 1694 or 1916.

The northern Nationalists for many years boycotted Stormont, unwilling to walk up the long drive past Carson's melodramatic statue into what Carson's successor had called 'a Protestant parliament for a Protestant people'. Discrimination abounded. In employment, few Catholics found work in the great shipyards which had been synonymous with Ulster prosperity. Elsewhere, in newer factories, the Union flag on a man's machine proclaimed – as emphatically as did the huge murals of King Billy at the Boyne which emblazoned his neighbourhood – that he dug with the right foot. In local authority employment there was a conscious policy of Protestants first and foremost; the Catholics got less rewarding jobs. Local government rested in the hands of Unionists, even where there was a Catholic majority, as in Londonderry. This was the result of two devices: the local government franchise and the straight (or, more accurately bent) gerrymander. The local government franchise was of Victorian complexity. Instead of a universal franchise, local voting was restricted to ratepayers, while businessmen had an additional vote. In this way some were disfranchised, others pluralists. The former were largely Catholic, the latter Protestant. In areas where the Catholics were easily the majority – such as Londonderry, which in 1966 had 14,000 Catholic and 9000 Protestant voters – this would not have been enough for Protestant dominance. So, by use of blatant boundary-fixing of which even Elbridge Gerry would have been ashamed, it was possible to have one Catholic ward and two Protestant, and thus eight Catholic councillors and twelve Protestant.

With resentment always a bony presence, new grievance was piled on ancient wrongs. The British knew little of these things, and cared less. The BBC left local affairs to its regional office. The occasional national programmes which ventured criticism were received with such outrage by the Unionists that they were withdrawn or scrapped. The historian of Irish broadcasting, Rex Cathcart, describes the rule for the early sixties:[1]

'Questions were not asked because they were the concern of another place. So the greater British public learnt little of what was going on in its own backyard.'

In 1966, when a new Prime Minister at Stormont, Captain Terence O'Neill, had made cautious attempts to thaw the permafrost in which the Unionists had preferred to keep their relations with Dublin, a Protestant backlash began. Republican demonstrations against a visit by the Queen were evidence of smouldering passions beneath the surface. So were the first assassinations of Catholics. The BBC (whose incoming Controller Waldo Maguire was reduced to meeting television men from London in hotels, since he believed his telephone to be bugged by senior Orangemen on his staff) ignored these passions for a further two years, by design. So did ITV and most of the press, with a few honourable exceptions.

The impact of the Northern Ireland Civil Rights Association (NIC-RA) was thus all the greater when it burst upon Britain's and the world's television screens in 1968. Founded in 1967, on the American model, NICRA called for an end to discrimination in housing and employment, universal suffrage and an end to gerrymandering, the repeal of the Special Powers Act, and the disbanding of the exclusively Protestant armed police reserve, the 'B Specials'. Within five years, NICRA was entirely successful in these aims. Few civil rights campaigns have been so effective, and in the country of the blind alley, where political failure seems endemic, it is all the more remarkable. Yet its achievements are remembered now not as the closure of a chapter of injustice, but as the beginning of the troubles which have torn the country apart. NICRA was at first middle class, and avowedly non-sectarian, its Republican nationalism only latent. 'There was no question,' Gerry Fitt believes, of 'demanding a United Ireland.' For

Fitt, the former Merchant Navy man who represented the Catholic enclave of West Belfast at Stormont and Westminster, that may have been true. He wanted an end to discrimination against his constituents, who, like him, were Catholics. Others, just as naturally, spoke in the idiom of the Republican tradition. Bernadette Devlin, the student Pasionaria who formed the People's Democracy Movement at Queen's University, remembers that on the first Civil Rights march the crowd, when urged to sing, broke out with 'A Nation Once Again', and had to be hastily reminded that the theme now was 'We Shall Overcome'. When Devlin appeared on television, her own references to 'the Unionist minority' made it clear that she thought instinctively in an all-Ireland context.

The Protestant reaction to the advent of NICRA was bitter. O'Neill's government was a classic victim of De Tocqueville's dictum that the most dangerous moment for a repressive government is when it begins to reform. O'Neill's instinct was to respond to the Civil Rights movement. In the Orange lodges they saw it differently. Although the first march on 24 August 1968, from Coalisland to Dungannon, passed off peacefully to the (eventual) strains of 'We Shall Overcome', a second one on 5 October in Londonderry flashed the face of police violence around the world. The march was initially banned by O'Neill's Home Affairs Minister, William Craig. The marchers persisted, and were batoned for their pains. O'Neill pressed ahead with reform of local government, and of housing allocation with the appointment of an Ombudsman. He appealed directly to the people of Northern Ireland on television: 'Ulster is at the crossroads . . . What kind of Ulster do you want?' He made it plain what he wanted, by sacking Craig from his government, and appealing to moderate Catholic opinion. He did so in vain. Northern Ireland is littered with the bones of those who believed that a moderate non-sectarian majority was always there to be roused. The momentum of action and reaction was to shake to pieces O'Neill's frail and belated initiative. Protestant Ulster reverberated to the stentorian tones of Ian Paisley, a fundamentalist Presbyterian who had founded his own church and a newspaper *The Protestant Telegraph*. The Ulster Hall on Sundays rang with Paisley's revised version of the Sermon on the Mount, beginning: 'The marching feet of the people of Ulster will cause the traitor to tremble.' The traitor, O'Neill, must be dismissed, he argued.

NICRA responded to these intoxicating times in its own way. After calling a truce over Christmas to give O'Neill a breathing space, it was outflanked by the young activists of People's Democracy, who staged their own march right across the province. The march was ambushed at Burntollet Bridge by a Protestant mob, some of whom were members of the B Specials taking off-duty exercise. Rioting followed in Londonderry, with the police attacking the Catholic enclaves. O'Neill now lost more support within his own party by setting up the Cameron Commission to look into 'the causes and nature' of the violence in Northern Ireland. His ablest minister, and deputy, Brian Faulkner, resigned. Faulkner, whose character included an uncanny mixture of the qualities of Heath and Wilson, never gave a satisfactory reason for his action, saying in his autobiography that the report was 'an initiative to avoid initiatives, a backdoor method of abolishing the ratepayers' franchise'.[2] His resignation fatally weakened O'Neill and with him the gentry of the ascendancy who had run the Unionist Party. O'Neill called an election, made no headway, and was humiliated by a massive vote in his own constituency for Paisley, the new voice of working-class Unionism. For the first and last time a Unionist leader appeared in the Catholic enclaves to a guarded but friendly welcome. They welcomed him, but he came from the wrong tribe, while in his own he was suspect. In a by-election two months later the victory of Bernadette Devlin ensured a spectacular new voice to stir Catholic hopes and Protestant paranoia. In the wake of further police riots and clumsy bombings by Protestant paramilitary groups, O'Neill resigned in despair. His cousin James Chichester-Clark had helped to precipitate the resignation by leaving the government. O'Neill then had the dubious pleasure of casting what turned out to be the decisive vote between Faulkner and Chichester-Clark for the leadership. He voted for his cousin. It was a mistake. Chichester-Clark was caught up in events beyond his comprehension, let alone his control.

The British were now pulled centre stage. It was the marching season once more, when MacNeice's 'grocer drunk with the drum' came into his own. Riot and counter-riot followed. The Apprentice Boys of Derry got a rough reception on 11 August, and the police were rough in their turn. To prevent pitched battles between Catholics and B Specials, Home Secretary Callaghan agreed to send troops to Londonderry on 14 August. All chance of limiting their role to one city at one time vanished immediately when riots broke out in Belfast, devastating some Catholic districts. Gerry Fitt telephoned Callaghan. He wanted troops for west Belfast:

'I did so because there was great hysteria and emotion abounding in the streets of the Falls Road at that time, where many of the Catholics believed they were under very serious attack from Protestant extremists . . . He said, "Gerry, I can get the army in but it's going to be the devil of a job to get it out." How correct he has proven to be.'

The troops were at first welcomed in the Catholic districts with cups of tea; they were seen as protectors, even liberators. The Labour government contributed to the euphoria by announcing that the B Specials were to be phased out. The Protestants were to be appeased by a solemn and binding declaration that Northern Ireland was and would remain an integral part of the United Kingdom unless its population wished otherwise.

At this juncture the classic misunderstanding between the two islands appears. What seems to the British to be part of the solution becomes on the other side of the water part of the problem. While the Protestants smouldered at yet another report recommending the disbandment of the B Specials and a drastic overhaul of the Royal Ulster Constabulary, the old masked face of militant Republicanism was appearing in the cramped enclaves of Belfast and Londonderry. With a mixture of sentiment, opportunism and muddle, elements in the Republic's Fianna Fail party had crossed the line between the relief of distress in the Six Counties and the purchase of arms for the IRA. (Charles J. Haughey, later a controversial Taoiseach – Irish Prime Minister – was one of three ministers acquitted of gun-running at a murky trial in Dublin in 1970: an incident never forgotten in the North.) The Provisional IRA had friends, funds, and an old cause. A cause was not the same as a *casus belli*. The Brits had arrived to provide that. To show that the army were not protectors against Protestant violence but the ancestral enemy of the Gael stalking the streets, the IRA needed only to demonstrate that the troops and their government were as the Republican tradition portrayed them. From 1970 through 1972, the British obliged them.

1970–72: Downhill all the way

In the next two years Northern Ireland was changed utterly. It changed in the level of murder, ranging from the sectarian to the psychopathic. The number of deaths by violence rose from 20 in 1970, through 172 in 1971, to 467 in 1972. It changed in the nature of government, with the suspension of Stormont, never to return in its old form, and its replacement by direct rule from Westminster – revived colonialism as the least bad alternative. And it changed in the men who spoke for the two estranged communities, pushing aside the blundering squires and sentimental nationalists of yesteryear.

When the new Heath government took office in June 1970 it was seen, inevitably, as a victory for the Ulster Unionists too. The Unionists at Westminster at the time, who included the Northern Ireland premier's younger brother, worked closely with, and were almost indistinguishable from, the Tory backbenchers. The new Home Secretary, Reginald Maudling, who had responsibility for Northern Ireland security, was much to their taste. Amiable, shambling, a slow-burn politician, he was not going to get over-excited about Northern Ireland. Already, in March, three young Scots Guardsmen had been slaughtered in cold blood, in a deliberate IRA act of provocation. The army and the Catholic ghettoes were being taunted and turned towards mutual suspicion and hate. Maudling declined army advice to ban the traditional Orange parades of the summer. Sectarian riots and killing followed. The Home Secretary visited the province. He was not impressed. 'For God's sake bring me a large scotch,' he groaned on the plane home. 'What a bloody awful country.'

It was to become more bloody yet. During his visit Maudling had agreed that the security forces, bitterly criticised by the Protestants, should assert themselves. Arms searches and a curfew in the Falls Road, CS gas and panicky shooting by the army as the IRA's scattered gunmen opened up on them: all left Catholic Belfast convinced it was under the heel of oppressors, not protectors. The protection would have to come from elsewhere. And the Provisional IRA was at hand to provide it, with a fivefold increase in membership in 1970, and a network of gunmen who could now find a haven in the embittered ghettoes. The more they emerged as the voice of the Catholic ghettoes, the more they appeared to fulfil the Protestant nightmare of uprising and treason, so that assorted factions of terror gangs from the majority community took to the streets in their turn. Their trade was murder, their 'justification' what the other side were doing. The bloody shirt could be waved again, the tribal identity as fixed as in the childhood of Louis Macneice:

> One read black where the other read white, his hope
> The other man's damnation.

For many it was to be not damnation but a death warrant, hooded bodies discovered at dawn, shot through the head, often tortured.

In this gathering mayhem the hapless Chichester-Clark resigned in

March 1971. The nimble Faulkner at last ascended to the office for which his abilities fitted him, if his record did not. Faulkner's tragedy was that, by the time his opportunity came, the gestures to the minority which he now favoured, including further reform of housing and local government, and committee responsibilities for the opposition at Stormont, were no longer enough. The minority community was split. Constitutional nationalism had produced the Social Democratic and Labour Party (SDLP), itself a coalition between those such as Gerry Fitt who were socialists first and Republicans second, and those who were more in the green tradition of Irish nationalism, such as the Derry schoolmaster John Hume. But just as Unionist politicians looked over their shoulders at Paisley and Craig, who in turn kept watchful eyes on the paramilitary gangs, so the SDLP could not neglect the support enjoyed by politicians closer to the IRA, and by the gunmen themselves. Army shootings in Derry led to the deaths of two of Hume's constituents during riots. He called for an independent inquiry. When he did not get it, he had to persuade the SDLP to boycott Stormont. If the level of violence could only be raised enough by the paramilitaries there was always a point at which community leaders could be forced back within the tribe.

That point was not far off for Faulkner. As a young man in Lord Brookeborough's cabinet he had seen internment used against the ineffective IRA campaign of the late fifties. It had also been used in the South, simultaneously. There was no chance that the South would co-operate this time. Jack Lynch, the Taoiseach, would not, and could not, seem to be Faulkner's poodle now. The British government, however, despite opposition from army commanders, eventually consented. 342 men were rounded up on 9 August for internment without trial. Because intelligence on the IRA was so patchy, many of those 'lifted' had no connection with the gunmen. Over the next two days 23 people were killed in riots across the province. Brian Faulkner's widow Lucy remembers that he thought internment 'the only possible step', but realised afterwards that:

'. . . the security forces and the police did not have, it turned out, the information that they should have had at that time. Mistakes were made in the people that were picked up.'

Even had the intelligence been perfect, however, internment would have been counter-productive. Imprisonment without trial (accompanied as this often was by interrogation without benefit of civil rights) left the minority further alienated from the state. Another piece of the

Ulster tragedy, another anniversary for the cycle of protest, demonstration and death, was in place. The leader of the opposition, Harold Wilson, intervened with his own response to the crisis of the North when he produced a fifteen-point programme, which could lead to a solution. It was not, he said, possible to see a solution:

'. . . in which the agenda does not at least include consideration of, and which is not in some way directed to finding a means of achieving, the aspirations envisaged half a century ago towards a united Ireland.'

The word was out. Labour's position was changing. The campaign against the Northern state could succeed. So there was every incentive for the IRA to keep up the pressure, to which the Stormont government's only response seemed to be to call for more troops. By the end of the year there were 15,000 British troops in the province. Soon they were to provide concrete evidence that they contributed to the problem rather than to the solution.

On 30 January 1972 a protest march in Londonderry against internment set off under the banners of the Northern Ireland Civil Rights Association. It was defying a ban on all demonstrations. The British troops deployed to contain the inevitable rioting came under fire. The Paratroop Regiment, especially, had gained a reputation for a rapid reaction time and twitching trigger fingers. By nightfall thirteen civilians had been shot dead, their bodies carried past the watching TV cameras to a chorus of grief and imprecation. Condemnation was worldwide. In Dublin the British embassy was burned down. At Westminster Bernadette Devlin bore down on the huge bulk of the Home Secretary like a pocket battleship, and battered him into something approaching wakefulness. It was not just the fourteen dead men of Derry (another had died later) who lost their lives in 1972. The old Northern Ireland state died with them.

The road to Sunningdale

The inevitable consequences of 'Bloody Sunday', as it was instantly dubbed in the Irish press, the retaliatory havoc of IRA bombings in Northern Ireland and on the mainland, concentrated the mind of Edward Heath remarkably. When he had shaken free of his preoccupations with the European legislation at Westminster and the first NUM strike, he called Faulkner to London. Faulkner was abruptly told that he must accept a transfer to Westminster of security powers, a series of plebiscites on whether the border should remain, co-operation with the SDLP in a community government, and the appointment of a Northern Ireland Secretary of State. Such a re-organisation would have left the Stormont government with fewer powers even than a large local authority. Faulkner was taken aback. Only three weeks earlier Heath had dismissed predictions of such moves as 'speculation' in a telegram to the Unionist Council, itself already rocked by the defection of the dissident Unionist hard-liner, William Craig, to form the new Vanguard movement. Faulkner turned down the offer. Lucy Faulkner remembers his mood when he returned:

'It was a blow below the belt to the whole Unionist population . . . He felt betrayed by the British government. And the Unionist popula-tion felt betrayed by the British government. Had it happened, I think, with a Labour government, they would not have been so surprised. But there was this intense shock and almost disbelief that a Conservative government could act in that way, having given assurances to the contrary.'

The Conservative cabinet was deeply divided about the wisdom of direct rule. Even those who argued that the army could no longer serve two masters, while Britain took the blame for a policy not always of the government's instigation, accepted this further responsibility with foreboding. They knew that they who called loudest for 'Brits out' would relish the short-term advantage of seeing the Brits further in. They knew too that Faulkner, for all his misjudgements, was a better bet than the assorted collection of Orange zealots who now stood ready to exploit the 'betrayal' of Stormont. Now he was gone. Faulkner flew home that Thursday night, putting a brave face on his humiliation. Heath and his intimates talked into the night. At 3 a.m. Whitelaw accepted the job of Secretary of State, and was presented to a startled and half-empty House of Commons on the Friday morning. By that evening he was doing the rounds of startled officials and policemen in Belfast, beginning with a governor whose post had just been abolished.

The new Secretary of State plunged into the routine of walkabouts and think-ins which characterised his political style. Again, briefly, a British initiative met grassroots Catholic goodwill ('You'll always be welcome in the Creggan,' housewives cried, as Whitelaw plunged down the shopping streets of Londonderry.) At the same time secta-rian killings, in the ratio of two Catholics slaughtered for every Protestant, reached new heights. The IRA killed more soldiers. The

Ulster Volunteer Force (UVF) and, later, the Ulster Defence Association, killed more Catholics. A minority of these murders were undoubtedly the work of psychopaths, but many were, in the words of Sarah Nelson, carried out by 'young working class men between seventeen and twenty-two who differed little from others in their area in terms of education, employment and police records'.[3] They heard some of the leaders of their own community say that in the last extremity they would shoot to kill for Ulster. In the circumstances of 1972 they believed the last extremity was at hand. Ulster Vanguard, founded by the dissident hard-line Unionist William Craig, was at the peak of its influence, and was, briefly, dignified by a public handshake from Faulkner on the last day of the Stormont Parliament. Craig was to argue, as the year went on, that Ulster's loyalists might have to be 'prepared to kill'. On Craig's flank stood a still more uncompromising figure. Ian Paisley had been at Westminster since 1970. He was not taken seriously there. In Belfast he was a force, the kind of figure to whom the Protestant working class traditionally turned (though the advocates of Irish unity perennially forget it) when their identity is threatened. Whitelaw, as a Conservative, an officer and a gentleman, got the benefit of the doubt from some of Ulster's traditional Orange leadership. He got none at all from Paisley.

A British viceroy, for such he was, has some examples and initiatives open to him. Whitelaw tried most of them. He established special category status for the internees (in effect, as political prisoners), and set in process the phasing-down of internment with an amnesty for many. After the IRA announced a temporary truce on 25 June, Whitelaw met the IRA leadership secretly in London. David O'Connell, Seamus Twomey and Sean MacStiofan (born in England, like many other Republican leaders, as plain John Stephenson), and the youngest and cleverest, Gerry Adams. The IRA could feel the future was with them. In two years their campaign and the backlash they had provoked had ended fifty years of Stormont. They had come from a huddle of gunmen, regarded as primitive thinkers by the old Official IRA, to a seat at the negotiating table. Or so it must have seemed. (They had already met the Labour leader Harold Wilson in Dublin in March.) The Provos went back empty-handed, but the news of their visit was success enough, in increasing the bitterness of the Loyalists.

Whitelaw tried to deflect some of that bitterness by sending the army into the 'no-go' areas which had existed by tacit agreement since the early police riots. But he stuck to his plan for wide constitutional change. After a conference at Darlington attended by the Official Unionists, the SDLP, and the new middle-of-the-road Alliance Party, the British government published a Green Paper. It proposed a new assembly elected by proportional representation, with a power-sharing executive. Law enforcement and security would remain with Westminster. There would be a Council of Ireland, the tangible reminder of Ulster's position within Ireland and the need for Dublin to underwrite it. The Protestants, their most acute observer Padraig O'Malley comments:

'. . . had to confront the unpalatable fact that their autonomy was to be much diluted, and that . . . they were to be at once a bit more British and a bit more Irish.'

Neither was easy for them. What might seem masterly compromise in Darlington looked like a sell-out by the time it reached the be-leaguered Protestant minority in Dungannon.

To reassure Northern Irish opinion that malefactors would be brought to justice, the British government implemented the recom-mendations of the 1972 commission, chaired by Lord Diplock, which had looked into methods of combating terrorism. The power to arrest without warrant and detain for up to seventy-two hours suspected terrorists was supplemented by special courts to try them. In the 'Diplock courts' the judge sat alone without a jury. The intention was to prevent intimidation – of both juries and witnesses. Convictions soared, but it was not long before the confessions obtained under intense three-day interrogations became as suspect as some of the evidence by the new class of witness/informer. Once again the attemp-ted solution simply became part of the problem.

The real solution had to be political. For this Whitelaw pressed ahead with his initiative. There were many things going for him. In Britain he had all-party support. In the Republic he had a government willing to pay quite a high price to be seen to be involved in the destiny of the North, and this did not change when Lynch was replaced by Cosgrave of Fine Gael after the 1973 Irish election. Finally, among the Ulster politicians, Faulkner had the courage to see that the British proposals offered something back, after the trauma of direct rule. Whereas Craig and Paisley vied in their absolute opposition, Faulkner saw that powers might be transferred back in time to a functioning assembly, in which the Unionists would still be the majority. In his memoirs he wrote:[4]

'By nature I was attracted to businesslike and practical arrangements and quite welcomed what I saw as a modernisation of the legislative style.'

He knew that the SDLP leader Fitt was also prepared to try to make the assembly work. Between them they surely spanned enough of even Ulster's rainbow spectrum? At first it seemed so. The new assembly was elected by proportional representation on 12 June 1973. It had a majority for power-sharing. 50 of its 80 members belonged to the three parties represented at Darlington: Unionists (23), SDLP (19) and Alliance (8). The rest were opponents of any form of power-sharing, who set about disrupting the new assembly when it met in the Great Hall at Stormont. (The Chamber, with its statue of Lord Craigavon of the 'Protestant Parliament for a Protestant people' was not auspicious.)

Faulkner was shaken by the enmity of men who had been so recently his associates. His wife says that:

'The scenes which took place then were in Brian's opinion an utter disgrace to the politicians of Northern Ireland. There were scenes of violence, street politics, guttersnipe accusations. And he was filled with horror partly because these were people with whom he identified in that they had the same determination to remain in the United Kingdom that he had . . .'

Such people could express that determination with all the simple vehemence of traditional Ulster politics. It was enough that they were against power-sharing. Faulkner had to show it through a quite different route: compromise and trust. It would never have been easy. Senator Conor Cruise O'Brien, up from the South to look at this strange new hybrid, commented:[5]

'The task assigned to them is a daunting one, requiring all their skill and nerve, and a great deal of patience. They are not necessarily helped by being told they must act reasonably. What sounds reasonable in one community sounds supremely unreasonable in the other, and people who try to sound reasonable to both tend to be rejected by both.'

At first, reason prevailed. Under Whitelaw's bonhomous chairmanship, a power-sharing executive was set up: 6 Unionists, 4 SDLP, 1 Alliance. (In this Faulkner already went further than his position in the assembly elections, where his party had accepted power-sharing in the committees.) The SDLP dropped their support for anti-internment rent strikes as a gesture of goodwill. In return Faulkner agreed to a tripartite conference to set up a Council of Ireland. The SDLP would not formally enter the executive without it.

So there came to Sunningdale Edward Heath and his Secretary of State of a few days, Francis Pym, the new Taoiseach Liam Cosgrave, of the Fine Gael/Labour Party coalition now in power in the Republic, and the members of the putative executive with their advisers.

What they agreed was to be the Irish Historic Compromise. Indeed, it was presented as such. But they all wanted different things. The British wanted the Republic to co-operate in security and agree to mutual extradition, and most of all they wanted a broadly based coalition to outface terror and extremism in Northern Ireland. The Unionists wanted the Republic to recognise the legitimacy of their state, and the British to let them continue governing it with minority representatives who, in this new climate, would give up their tiresome insistence on Irish unity. The Republic wanted a Council of Ireland which would count, and be consulted. So did the SDLP, who saw this as their guarantee, portrayed as the first stage in all-Ireland institutions, when they went back into their communities to face out the gunmen. The British, for a few months, perhaps got most of what they wanted, thanks to intense lobbying by Edward Heath. A Council of Ireland was to be set up, to consider a bill of rights, common areas of law enforcement, and an all-Ireland court. The Republic solemnly agreed, after forty drafts, that:

'The factual position of Northern Ireland within the United Kingdom cannot be changed except by the decision of a majority of the people of Northern Ireland.'

The Unionists would have to be content with that.

Could the Council of Ireland be sold on that basis? The doubts were not only among the Unionists at Sunningdale. Gerry Fitt shared them. He thinks now that the Council of Ireland was always going to be seen as 'being a step down the road, the thin end of the wedge, into an Irish Republic'. That was the problem. Two different accounts had to come out of Sunningdale. The Unionists had to say that the Council of Ireland had scuppered Irish unity, the SDLP that it advanced it. Enoch Powell points up the anomaly:

'It was very typical of Ted Heath that he thought he achieved something by dragooning people at Sunningdale into accepting something that they not only didn't mean, but which those upon whom they depended, the electors upon whom they depended, couldn't possibly mean.'

It looked different then, for a hopeful moment. Lucy Faulkner remembers her husband's elation on his return, that he had a workable

compromise. He was soon to be disabused of this notion. Three
hammer blows in succession fell on the men of compromise. First,
within days of taking office as chief executive, Faulkner lost a bitter
debate in the Ulster Unionist Council. It rejected Sunningdale, and
Faulkner resigned as party leader. A week later the second blow was
struck in the South. Kevin Boland, one of the Dail trio charged with
gun-running (but acquitted) in 1970, did his bit for harmony in the Six
Counties by bringing a lawsuit against the Dublin government. Its
recognition of Northern Ireland as an entity, he said, contravened the
constitution. The government's mumbled defence in the courts, that it
had made a declaration not an agreement, clarifying what it would
have preferred to blur, was noted down grimly in the North. Behind
Cosgrave's stilted recognition, it seemed, lurked the old irredentism of
the claim to a thirty-two-county Republic, regardless of what the
Northern Protestants desired. This was a body blow for the executive,
who faced angry demonstrations at Stormont. Paisley was ejected by
force. 'The demon doctor who preaches God knows what,' Faulkner
called him in a bitter impromptu television interview. The power-
sharing coalition tottered, but it did not fall. If it could buy time, all
might yet come right. Time, however, was the one thing it had not got.
For reasons wholly remote from Northern Ireland, and against the
passionate pleas of the past and present Secretaries of State, Heath
declared an election in the United Kingdom. In the twelve constituencies of Northern Ireland that meant first-past-the-post contests which
would not be about the British miners' strike. There were no miners in
Northern Ireland. There, the question 'Who Governs?' was asked at
every election. It concerned the very basis of the state. So the February
1974 election would be a referendum on Sunningdale.

1975: A failure of will – the collapse of power-sharing

For those committed to the new executive the results of the general
election were dismal. A United Ulster Unionist Coalition was formed
out of the Protestant parties opposed to Sunningdale and Unionist
politicians who had peeled off since. A tired old Unionist warhorse,
Harry West, was hauled out to lead it. Coalitions which are simply
against something have their own cement; those who have to defend it
find their interests diverge. The members had to say different things to
their separate constituencies, and the Unionists among them were
dogged by the opposition slogan 'Dublin is just a Sunningdale away'.

This of course did not harm the SDLP with their own community, but that vote too was split. In a skewed result, the anti-Sunningdale candidates got 51% of the vote – but 11 seats out of 12 – and, as Gerry Fitt remarks with wry humour, 'The 49% got me.'

In the unpropitious circumstances the executive could point to something near majority support. It might have shrugged off calls for fresh assembly elections in the wake of the general election result. But that result had also brought a minority government into office at Westminster. In the calculations of high summer, Ulster's agonies would not count for much. The incoming Labour government would be further fazed by the new factor which now surfaced in the province: raw working-class power.

Before 1973 working-class Protestants had joined the various shadowy paramilitary bodies. Some of them had taken part in sectarian killings. They had not organised as a political force, still leaving that to the traditional standard bearers of Unionism. When they saw some of these figures return from Sunningdale to sell them a Council of Ireland, they came down, crudely but effectively, into the political forum themselves. Since 1971 the Ulster Defence Association (UDA) had co-ordinated the paramilitaries, had gloried in its tough image as the Protestant backlash incarnate. The UDA now came together with the Loyalist Association of Workers (LAW), trade unionists cut off by the sad sectarianism of Ulster from their natural outlet in Labour politics. (The Unionist leadership had systematically played the Orange card against the Northern Ireland Labour Party in the 1940s, helping to destroy it; in such ways was the Irish time-warp exploited and preserved.) The leaders of LAW, trade unionists such as Hugh Petrie and Billy Hull, had long urged industrial action against 'betrayals' by London and by the security forces. Until 1973, however, the appeal of the UDA (especially to the unemployed, to whom it gave a certain dismal status) had been stronger. The object now had changed: it was to coerce an executive still Protestant-dominated, and the London administration which backed it.

The Ulster Workers Council which emerged in 1973 was a formidable body. It contained a wide group of the Protestant working class, from men such as Petrie and Hull, to Glen Barr, an articulate young assemblyman from Londonderry, the saturnine Andy Tyrie, supreme commander of the UDA, and Billy Kelly, a Bible fundamentalist whose knowledge of the Ulster power stations was to be more important to the UWC than his familiarity with the Good Book. After the February election the 21-member executive of the UWC felt strong enough to carry through the strike it had threatened since Sunningdale. The assembly was due to ratify Sunningdale on 14 May. The UWC announced that it would call a general strike if the vote went through. It did. No one took calls for general strikes all that seriously. They had been made before. The UWC called a strike for 15 May. Not entirely to their surprise, the UWC found it was not greeted with enthusiasm, as Andy Tyrie of the paramilitary UDA remembers:

'On the first day of the strike there was no strike. When I appeared at the headquarters for the strike there was no activity. The workers were going to work. Most of the UDA personnel were out in the streets. I contacted quite a lot of people. I knew their heart was in the strike but they thought it was just another farce, it was something that was talked about, planned, but would never go into action.'

This time there was a difference. The UWC contained within it the Protestant private armies, a powerful instrument of coercion. Whether or not they liked it, the mass of the population could be persuaded. Tyrie and his friends got to work. A lunchtime mass meeting in the shipyards was told that all cars remaining in the car park would be burned. Since the paramilitaries were capable of much worse than arson, very few cars stayed put. Their owners left in them. Barricades were set up, manned by armed and masked UDA men. Rows of these worthies were shown on television picketing places of work. Tyrie makes a nice distinction, in describing the effect on the province:

'Nobody was being beat up or forced not to go to work, but what we did do we used very subtle intimidation.'

It did not seem so subtle to Lady Faulkner, at the chief executive's residence:

'With hindsight it's very easy to say that here was a population which rose in its wrath and put out the executive, but that was nonsense. I was actually at the end of a telephone during that strike, and for the first few days the telephone line was constantly occupied by people ringing up from housing estates, places in the country, to say, look, we can't get into our work, there are people with sticks and staves and masks at the end of our road, and what is the government going to do about it?'

The answer seemed to be: precious little. Westminster was responsible for security, but the soldiers and police under its control did not move against the road blocks. Secretary of State Merlyn Rees and his junior minister Stan Orme were nervous of using the army to break a strike and unsure of the loyalties of the RUC, some of whom, says Rees, openly sympathised with the strikers, arguing, 'They were speaking for our people. They are our lads; we are not going into the South.' There were newspaper pictures of fraternisation between strikers, police, and even troops. Gerry Fitt was close enough to the Labour ministers to see how they were caught by their own assumptions:

'It was a totally political strike, but it was called the Ulster Workers' Strike, and I think as such even the name of it had an intimidating effect on Harold Wilson and the Labour cabinet.'

By the morning of 16 March, the UWC, with considerable skill and expertise, began to put into effect Billy Kelly's plan gradually to shut down the province's electricity grid. Only the big Ballylumford plant, which produced 70% of Ulster's electricity, was to be left in operation. Next they demanded that industry be excluded from the grid. Shops and garages were only allowed to open at certain hours. Human blockades seemed omnipresent. As effectively as the student demonstrators had done in the sixties, the UWC grasped that broadcasting, with its urge to cover a 'running news story', could help them. One UWC leader was quoted by Robert Fisk of *The Times* as saying:

'The BBC were marvellous. They were prepared to be fed any information. They fell into their own trap that "the public must get the news". Sometimes they were just a news service for us; we found that if the media were on our side we didn't need a gun.'

Only later was the BBC's then Director General to muse that his Northern Ireland region had 'clearly allowed local parliamentary democracy to be overturned with little comment'.

The broadcasters would argue in their own defence that the parliamentary democrats did not maintain a high profile in defence of parliamentary democracy either. Merlyn Rees buzzed this way and that in personal anguish. He flew military technicians in plain clothes to Ballylumford to see if they could operate the power stations. The technicians found it all too complicated:

'They said they could only run it with the co-operation of management, middle management and above, which was not forthcoming.'

Without electricity, even those workers who wanted to work could not do so. By 24 May the executive were desperate. Faulkner flew to see Harold Wilson at Chequers. Unless the British government assumed control of petrol supplies, and used troops to do it, he would resign. He left believing that this would be the burden of the British Prime Minister's broadcast on the following day. But that was to be remembered for something else. Wilson, according to Joe Haines, had just made a tentative decision that he would call a second 1974 election on 10 October. Nothing must rock the boat before then. So he took refuge in rhetoric, and heaped abuse on the strikers in language Churchill might have used about Mussolini, emphasising the subsidy – 'taxes poured out almost without regard to cost' – which supported Northern Ireland. He continued:

'Yet people who benefit from this now viciously defy Westminster, purporting to act as though they were an elected government; people who spend their lives sponging on Westminster and British democracy and then systematically assault democratic methods. Who do these people think they are?'

The only possible comment on the feelings of both bitter opponents of the strike and the strikers came from Andy Tyrie: 'He couldn't have done us a greater favour.' All the Ulstermen's bitter feelings of rejection and resentment boiled over. Now it was their cause.

From then on the strike was solid. The British army did take over the petrol stations, but to no avail. Electricity supply had fallen to 50% of normal output, so gradually that no plant was damaged. It seemed inexorable. By this time it appeared to be only days before essential supplies to hospitals, and to the pumping of the sewage system, would be cut off. A mass demonstration swept up to Stormont. Many of those who took part wore sponges in their lapels. They were there to hear Craig and Paisley call for the resignation of the executive. To the rear of Stormont, at the same time, Faulkner and his colleagues were taking their leave. The executive had fallen. The UWC had won. Faulkner never held office again. (He was later killed in a riding accident.) The ablest man thrown up by the majority community in the political history of the state could perhaps have transformed it. He was destroyed by the Loyalists to whose assumptions he had pandered in his earlier political life. Now he had changed his views. They had not changed theirs. He was destroyed too by the weakness and ineptitude of the Labour government. As his widow says bitterly:

'The British government itself was intimidated before the people of Northern Ireland were intimidated, in my opinion . . . Merlyn Rees . . . was a man with a very deep sense of conscience, and I think he was very gravely disturbed by the strike. But that didn't actually motivate him to take firm action when firm action was necessary.'

Rees would argue that the power stations were the key to the strike. Once they were lost military intervention could not regain the initiative. Within that small and exclusive club, the ex-Secretaries of State for Northern Ireland, there is general unwillingness to criticise Rees. The difficulties on the spot are always far greater than they seem to the armchair critic in London. The failure to move against the first barricades, however, was fatal. It allowed the UWC to be seen to be calling the shots. The strikers continued as they began. One of their leaders, Glen Barr, has admitted that the strike could have been broken in the first few days. The strikers' victory cost more than the executive. It ruled out power-sharing for so long that, when it could be rationally considered once more, the demands of the minority had moved well beyond it. And it left the Labour government for the next few years unwilling to take risks with the Unionists, who were much keener on a firm hand. The IRA obliged in its turn, extending a bombing campaign of such frightfulness that it had already provoked the Prevention of Terrorism (Temporary Provisions) Act. Like most things temporary it has endured long beyond what brief cosmetic life-span it should have enjoyed. For a time, security, rather than solutions, became the prime concern of Westminster. Harold Wilson's fifteen points seemed far, far away.

1975–80: 'Acceptable levels of violence'

After the fall of the power-sharing executive there was no real initiative in Northern Ireland politics for a long period. What Sarah Nelson calls 'the zero sum game'[6] between majority and minority – each being able to advance only at the other's expense – went on. The British held the ring, aware that, while direct rule might temporarily be seen as the least unpalatable option by the ravaged province, it too dealt in zero sums. Merlyn Rees stayed on for two years, phasing out internment and special category status for those who had been convicted – usually but not always properly convicted – in the courts. One plus and one minus to each militant tradition: the zero sum observed. A new Constitutional Convention was elected, to recommend the one thing which could not be allowed – a return to majority Unionist rule. Talks with the IRA leadership in 1977 produced another makeshift truce, at a time when the Provisionals were at a low ebb, their momentum temporarily lost and their ranks depleted by bloody feuds with their rivals, the old Official IRA, now politicised and more

sophisticated in their approach to the two-nations problem of Northern Ireland. Truces never last when the cause for war remains. The
causes of the IRA's 'war' with the British army remained. The British
army was omnipresent in Catholic areas, nervous soldiers with guns at
the ready, plastic bullets to fire at rioting crowds, police stations and
barracks forlorn fortresses in alien territory.

In 1976 Roy Mason, who as Defence Secretary had been well aware
of Northern Ireland as a security problem, replaced Rees as Secretary
of State. He continued to see it as a security problem. He and his
juniors built up better relations with the Unionists at Westminster
(two of them, Harold McCusker and John Carson, even voted with
Labour in the final 1979 vote of confidence). He was less accommodat-
ing to the SDLP. Gerry Fitt remembers the Mason regime without
affection:

'Roy Mason acted as a Colonial Secretary in that situation. He wore
safari jackets in Royal Avenue in Belfast. He acted as if he was in
Leopoldville rather than Belfast.'

In the battle for hearts and minds this was not an advantage. There
was an immense weariness of violence in Northern Ireland in the
mid-seventies. The people had suffered too much. The sectarian
assassinations nauseated both communities: the young Catholic murdered on his way home to the Short Strand, the Protestant farmer
gunned down at the plough in the border farmlands of Fermanagh. In
1976 this aversion to violence produced the Northern Ireland Peace
People, founded by Mairead Corrigan and Betty Williams. Mairead
Corrigan's sister, Ann Maguire, had seen her three children killed
when a car ran out of control after the gunman at the wheel had been
hit by shots from a British army patrol. She took her campaign onto
the streets. For two years there were mass marches and demonstrations for peace. The Peace People won the Nobel Prize in 1977. For a
while they seemed to take their community by storm. It did not last.
Winning the prize was perhaps unfortunate for them. There were
splits, well-publicised quarrels, consistent denigration from the IRA.
And in a land of so many martyrs people began to forget the three
Maguire children. There were others to mourn, other sources of rage
and grief.

The success of the Provisional IRA in these years was to persist, so
that in 1979 a British army report made this sober estimate of their
continuing capacity:

'The Provisionals cannot attract the large number of active terrorists they had in 1972–3. But they no longer need them. PIRA's organisation is now such that a small number of activists can maintain a disproportionate level of violence.'

Internment left many families with a son, a brother, an uncle incarcerated in 'the Kesh'. Already schooled in a different tradition, the youngsters of the community had a model to live up to, a status to aspire to in the rigours of ordinary life. Their families might not like it, but the house-to-house searches in their areas – 34,000 in 1976 alone – stoked resentments, made people more tolerant of what 'the boys' whom they had seen grow up were now doing. The IRA were adept at inviting the kind of reprisals which would suit their cause. They could deploy a more powerful weapon yet, and a peculiarly powerful one in the tradition of Irish nationalism. They could suffer. If they suffered enough, they would become objects of sympathy as well as passive acceptance to many in the Catholic communities and of passionate admiration to some.

First, there were the investigations. IRA members had been tried in Diplock courts. They were roughly treated during interrogation before they made the confessions upon which they were convicted in those courts. In 1976, as Roy Mason took over from Rees, the British government suffered the severe embarrassment of being found guilty of 'torture and inhuman and degrading treatment' by the European Court. Only the torture count was dropped on appeal. The mud stuck. And, although Mason ferociously defended his security forces and the RUC, misgivings mounted throughout 1977 about the interrogation methods used at Castlereagh, Gough Barracks and other centres, especially after an atrocity such as the La Mon restaurant bombing. An Amnesty International report in 1978 found that:

'. . . maltreatment of suspected terrorists has taken place with sufficient frequency to warrant the establishment of a public inquiry to investigate it.'

The government was compelled to commission an inquiry, chaired by Mr Justice Bennett, which produced within its narrow terms of reference recommendations for the better protection of the rights of prisoners in custody, and accepted that ill-treatment had taken place:

'[Some injuries] sustained during the period of detention in the police office were inflicted by someone other than the prisoner himself. This is indicated beyond all doubt by the nature, severity, sites, and number of separate injuries on one person.'

The Bennett Report caused a storm of protest. It was taken up by the

Irish Americans in the USA. It was cited by Gerry Fitt when he refused to vote with the Labour government in the 1979 vote of confidence. It cast doubt on the convictions of all those who came before the courts charged with terrorist offences. (One RUC interrogation office told the journalist Peter Taylor in 1979 that, in his opinion, 2% of those convicted were in fact innocent.[7]) The IRA were thus able to claim that the whole process whereby they were brought to trial was a political frame-up. If they evaded capture on their missions of murder, they could be lauded in *An Phoblact*. If they were arrested, they would mix with the innocent and benefit from, as well as sharing, the rough treatment the latter were seen to have received.

Second, there was detention. In the Maze prison H-Blocks (so-called because of their distinctive layout) after 1976, the IRA were treated as ordinary prisoners, a necessary corollary of abolishing internment without trial. They claimed to be political, to have the rights of prisoners of war to organise themselves, to wear their own clothes, to do no prison work. They began to go 'on the blanket' in 1976, wearing only a prison blanket, and, later, smearing their cells with their own excrement in a perverse attempt to create the shocking squalor which would most publicise their case to the world. Outside, a prison culture grew up, every rally accompanied by gaunt sympathisers in the symbolic blanket, every pub a collection point for the victims in the Maze. Cardinal O'Fiach came to see them, supported their case:

'The authorities refuse to admit that these prisoners are in a different category from the ordinary, yet everything about their trials and backgrounds indicates that they are different.'

O'Fiach was much impressed by the prisoners' fortitude, by the words of Irish smeared on cell walls in toothpaste, by the fact that they did not come from criminal backgrounds. They were in the conscious tradition of the blood sacrifice, the separateness of Pearse, who proclaimed (though born himself of English parents) that 'the Gael is not like other men' and went on to create his own potent myth by dying at English hands in the Easter Rising. The assassinations carried out by the IRA and its even more murderous imitators continued to claw out at the highest in the land, as well as the humblest. They had no effect. Even shock was numbed by sheer repetition. Sacrifice was different. If the terrorist turned his violence upon himself, suffered as others had been made to suffer, his cause would prosper. As the new British government took power in 1979, still mourning the murder of Airey Neave – its spokesman on Northern Ireland, blown to pieces in

the precincts of the House of Commons by a car bomb planted by the
Irish National Liberation Army (INLA) – the men in the Maze were
considering the last shot in the Republican locker. If the 'dirty protest'
could bring no more dividend, there remained the fast unto death.
That was to be the answer to Margaret Thatcher.

The tragedy of Northern Ireland in the seventies was that tribalism
prevailed. It was treason in one community to acknowledge any
aspiration on the part of the other. Terror and counter-terror brought
their own legacy: economic deprivation, loss of human rights, repressive measures, sometimes adopted on the mainland after their
introduction in Northern Ireland. The British governments switched
between political initiatives and a dogged determination to reduce
violence to 'acceptable' levels. Moderate majorities were sought, but
never found, for positive policies. In the end, there was always the
tribe, greener, or more orange, by the year. In the Republic, as in
Britain, unstable or minority governments compounded the problem,
dependent on votes they could not control wielded by men they did not
like. The largest party in the South, particularly when it fell under the
sway of the most frivolous and irresponsible of Irish leaders, Charles J.
Haughey, could not desert its roots in the armed Republican struggle.
As one Irish historian, Padraig O'Malley, puts it, harshly but
accurately:[8]

'The call for the end to the guarantee, the veiled references to the
desirability of a declaration by Britain of its intent to withdraw, the
insistence that unification is the only solution and inevitable, imply
that Fianna Fail does not dispute the aims of the IRA, only the means it
employs . . . The aim of Fianna Fail is to induce consent; the aim of the
IRA, to make Northern Ireland ungovernable. The more successful the
IRA is at the latter, the more susceptible Northern Protestants are to
the former.'

In fact, the greater the coercion the more the Unionists clung to the
guarantee that their status could not be changed without their consent,
the more they cried 'No Surrender!' and thus vitiated the possibility of
changes which might make the minority sufficiently satisfied with an
altered Northern state to abandon tacit support for violence. In the
zero sum game, it may seem that progress can only be made if the table
is knocked over. As long as the IRA could say that its activities alone
provoked talk of 'solutions', and that such talk would vanish in a
reassured Orange hegemony if it was defeated and obliterated, some
small part of every irredentist nationalist who longed for the unitary

thirty-two-county state would want the IRA to continue. As long as Paisley could tell the faithful that any concession on any front was the start of a slow slide to a Rome-ruled United Ireland, some part of every member of the Unionist tribe accepted the crudity and violence with which the Protestant extremists set their face against change. The window of opportunity prised open in 1973–4 might have been slammed shut in any event. But it was let go without any real attempt to hold on.

9

THE ROAD TO THE IMF

By common consent among his colleagues, James Callaghan was a resourceful Prime Minister, who filled the last great office of state with rather more resolution and effect than they had expected from his ministerial record in the sixties. The hour found the man, though neither seemed meant for the other. To get through the trauma of Britain's forced application to the IMF without provoking a still-graver crisis, a Labour administration needed a figure who combined emollience and experience with ultimate toughness. This Callaghan now did. His response to monetary crisis was very different from that of the almost piteous figure groaning 'I am the Selwyn Lloyd of this government' described by Richard Crossman in 1964. His challenger for the leadership, Denis Healey, analyses Callaghan's initial advantages:

'He was regarded – and I suspect rightly – as the best of the candidates. He had been outside the really unpopular departments for some time and very often in these elections it's more important to have no enemies than to have a lot of friends.'

The Labour leadership contest had provided a flash of colour in the otherwise leaden political landscape. The new Prime Minister settled scores and paid debts with the deliberation which always lay beneath that avuncular exterior. Roy Jenkins had already been offered the EEC presidency before Wilson's resignation. It was made clear that he need not wait upon the order of his going; the Foreign Office was not for him, who had done less well in the leadership contest than would have been thought possible five years earlier. It went instead to Tony Crosland, whose leadership campaign had veered between tragedy and disaster in its brief span, but who had the admiration and trust of the new Prime Minister. Barbara Castle was as unwelcome to him as a private patient on a NUPE picket; she was returned to the backbenches, though not to obscurity. The newcomers were trusties those on whom Callaghan believed he could rely. The Northern Ireland Secretary, Merlyn Rees, called on his leader, who said to him, only half-believingly, 'I'm Prime Minister of the greatest country in the world.' He, and it, were soon to be tested, on ground which (to the Chancellor of 1964–7) was all too familiar.

Callaghan came into a bleak economic inheritance. In November 1975 the Chancellor, backed by the Prime Minister, had presented a package of cuts totalling £3 billion. In the outcome, after protracted agonising, Healey settled for £3 billion in the February 1976 White Paper. This led to a storm in the parliamentary Labour Party, the resignation of Joan Lestor, and the government's defeat at the hands of its own backbenchers on Harold Wilson's sixtieth birthday. The government had recourse to, and won, a vote of confidence, the last of several during its life.

There was a great gulf fixed between the Labour Party's hopes, in the country and at Westminster, and Whitehall's view of the economic realities. For the Labour left, anxious to press an alternative economic strategy on the government which involved increases in expenditure on industrial investment, as well as import controls, concern with the Public Sector Borrowing Requirement (PSBR) and the reaction of the international markets was Treasury fetishism. Inside the Treasury the view was that things were out of hand. Leo Pliatzky, the senior Treasury official responsible for public expenditure, has written:[1]

'The failure to stick to any public expenditure plan had in fact gone a long way towards discrediting the whole process of government.'

In the severe recession after the 1973 oil price hike the British economy had not only stopped growing but had actually shrunk. At the same time public expenditure was rising fast. In the first two years of the Labour government, it took up a greatly increased proportion of national income: between 1973–4 and 1974–5 the proportion rose by 5%, from 40% to 45%, provoking fears that such an appropriation of resources would distort the whole economy. As well as the deliberate increases in public sector wages and social benefits, there was the additional increase in payments inevitable in any recession. The Treasury did not have an adequate monitoring system to deal with such rapid changes in expenditure and assumption. So, by early 1976, it had decided to introduce cash limits and stabilise expenditure programmes from 1977–8 onwards. In theory, government spending would level off in the years after April 1977.

The cuts were not, therefore, the 'massive and immediate cuts . . . which would increase both unemployment and the cost of living' set out in the critical Tribune motion on 10 March. Pliatzky and his

Treasury colleagues, who believed expenditure was still growing, watched with delight as their political master the Chancellor tore into his critics:

'Denis Healey was right to describe his Labour critics as out of their tiny Chinese minds, a sentiment with which I agree.'

To those critics, however, cuts in future spending betrayed their pledges and their hopes. If the party was over, the Party was finished too. Healey pitched his appeal to them in terms which in essence followed the Keynesian resource argument:

'We must make room in the next few years for a big shift of resources into manufacturing industry or our relative economic performance is bound to decline still further.'

But when he rounded on the Conservatives it was to attack their 'monetary profligacy', in terms which would have fitted the continuum from Mr Barber's stewardship to the first year of his own.

Sterling was under severe pressure too. In February 1976 the view had been taken in the Treasury that sterling was overvalued, making the pound less competitive. Sir Douglas Wass, the Permanent Secretary, and Sir Brian Hopkin, the chief economic adviser, were in agreement that something should be done to bring about a controlled devaluation. Technical discussions went on between the Treasury and the Bank of England, the traditional supporter of exchange stability. Both institutions were deeply divided about such a policy. For obvious reasons it could not be explicitly admitted, even in private, that the objective was to depreciate the currency. The hope was that Britain would thus regain the competitiveness for her exports which she had lost through her rapid rate of inflation, without the use of the chosen weapon of the alternative strategy – import controls.

Opponents of devaluation pointed to the risks: there was no guarantee that it could be controlled; it would fuel inflation through rising import prices; it would be a national humiliation. The pound could fall, but it should not be pushed. Better by far to go for the traditional methods of improving competitiveness: fiscal and monetary restraint, to keep down wage rises and increase productivity. One senior Treasury adviser remembers the Chancellor as 'delphic' throughout this debate. Healey's own recollection is cautious:

'Well, I think I'd come to the conclusion that the pound was a good deal too high and it would be helpful if it were lower. But I learned from bitter experience later on what I think later governments have sometimes learned, that once a trend changes it's very difficult to check it where you want it . . . So I would say that the way things actually went that Easter, I had mixed feelings, like the chap who saw his mother-in-law go over Beachy Head in his new car.'

The pound went over Beachy Head on 5 March, the day after the Bank of England's dealers had intervened in the markets to prevent a rise in its value. The markets got the message. Healey says:

'There is no doubt that the Bank of England made everybody feel that we wanted the pound to fall, by selling sterling at a time when other people were already selling it . . . therefore the pound would fall, therefore everybody wanted to sell their pounds before they lost more value. And I think this technical accident or mistake by the Bank of England was responsible for the acceleration of the trend. But it wasn't the cause of the whole thing.'

The Bank's officials deny that they breached the cardinal principle 'don't intervene in the direction in which the market is moving', but that is what the markets saw. There were rumours of indiscreet hints by ministers. The managers of the volatile oil funds kept in sterling balances in London began to move them out, led by the Nigerians. The pound plummeted through $2. When the Chancellor introduced no further public expenditure cuts in his April budget, but pinned his faith on a second round of incomes policy, the markets continued to react with pessimism. By the first week of June 1976 the falling pound seemed about to break $1.70. The Wass policy of controlled deprecia- tion had turned into an uncontrollable plunge. For the new Prime Minister it was an unwelcome return to an old theme. The crisis which was to lead his government to the IMF was under way.

The first relief party was sent out in June. Gordon Richardson, Governor of the Bank of England, and an executive director, Kit MacMahon, put together a £45.3 billion standby credit. $2 billion came from the USA, the rest from the central banks of the Group of Ten, from Switzerland, and from the Bank for International Settle- ments. It was impressive. It was also a failure, for the conditions were short term – three months, renewable for three, followed by repay- ment. If it was not enough, there would be no alternative but to go to the IMF. Healey accepted this in writing, and told the House of Commons:

'My hope and expectation is that drawing on these funds will be only temporary. But if any drawing on them could not otherwise be paid on the due date, Her Majesty's government would be prepared to seek a further drawing from the IMF.'

It was out in the open. The Treasury and the Bank were told by their international counterparts that public expenditure cuts were now essential to 'get your people back on the reservation', as the American Under-Secretary to the Treasury, Ed Yeo, put it.

The standby credit trapped the British government, as it had been intended to do. The conservative bankers who ran the US Treasury knew that if Britain found the short-term loan inadequate she would need to borrow on far tougher terms. That would mean the IMF, which could be relied on to get the 'profligate' British back on the reservation. The only way for ministers to avoid that would be to execute further fiscal measures repugnant to their party. A senior Bank of England official says:

'Our judgement was that it was worth giving them six months to take the necessary measures.'

There was a respite, no more. The senior Treasury official on the international side, Sir Derek Mitchell, returned almost weekly from meetings with his American, French and German counterparts with the unpopular message that the British were expected to make further cuts in public expenditure. The Americans, who combined the greatest influence with the most minimal sympathy, still carried a view of Britain's problems established in the previous year, when the picture was painted by Eric Sevareid, Morley Safer and other American television commentators of Britain's 'ungovernability' and feckless-ness.

What the effects would be of the new system of cash limits for public expenditure and the counter-inflationary rigour of the second year of incomes policy (wage increases limited to 5% with an upper limit of £4), which cut real wages sharply in 1976–7, were not known. Like the oil revenue to come, they were just too far in the future to influence the debate. Even if they had been taken into account later, there would have been other reasons found by the men in the US Treasury to make Healey wear a hair shirt. In June 1976, they were determined upon it, as Treasury Secretary William Simon recalls:

'We were assured that the standby was going to take care of the problem and, if they could weather the storm, it would all be over. I disagreed. . . . I warned Prime Minister Callaghan and Denis Healey that this was throwing good money after bad, and that it would disappear by the fall, in my judgement. They disagreed with that expectation of mine and I just said that, in the absence of attacking the fundamental cause of the problem, monetary policy and the public sector spending, there was no way in which they could continue to support the pound at silly levels. The market would win out. There wasn't enough money in the world.'

So the Chancellor made one more attempt to satisfy the markets.

The July measures

By July the Chancellor was told by the Treasury that he had to cut public expenditure or lose the confidence of the markets. The real state of the British economy was now less important than the impression of it held by those from whom Britain had to borrow. Without their support, it would rapidly become what they believed it to be. There were those in the Treasury who put the Chancellor's dilemma to him with some brutality: either he changed policy in order to avoid the IMF, or he would be forced to go to the Fund, where he would find the policy changes among the conditions. Wass and Pliatzky understood the political constraints on a Labour government, and the way in which the planned course of action would have to be argued. So Healey presented the cabinet with a £1 billion pound list of cuts, to take effect in 1977–8. He needed another contribution to public revenues, to keep down the PSBR. It came from an unexpected quarter: a 2% surcharge on employers' National Insurance contributions. This was introduced, 'over lunch', Tony Benn remembers, as a supplementary package. The Chancellor's officials had told him that the package would not work otherwise:

'Douglas Wass . . . said he didn't think it would be enough, and why not do this; it was likely to have very little effect in the real economy.'

The authors of the surcharge still defend it as distributing its effects quickly among profits, prices and employment, but its negative impact on industry marked how far the markets had pushed a Chancellor whose first priority was Britain's industrial competitiveness. Interest rates were not raised, however, as many of the critics of monetary growth had been demanding. The cabinet was resentful, but acquiesced. So did the parliamentary party. Tony Crosland, whose travels as Foreign Secretary made him less frequently the anchor man of the economic growth faction in cabinet, flew home for the exercise. The Labour left, he told his wife, were:[2]

'. . . totally demoralised. They have no leader because Foot and Benn have not resigned. And the absurd Benn–Holland–Bish strategy is as dead as a dodo.'

In his commonplace book, the Foreign Secretary put down his private thoughts on the consequences of the cuts:

'(a) Demoralisation of decent rank and file: Grimsby* LP . . . (b) Strain on TU loyalty . . . (c) breeding of illiterate and reactionary attitude to public expenditure – horrible. (d) collapse of strategy which I proposed last year . . . Now no sense of direction and *no* priorities; only pragmatism, empiricism, safety first, £ supreme. (e) and: unemployment, even if politically more wearable = grave loss of welfare, security, choice; very high price to be paid for deflation and negative growth.'

The high price had yet to be paid. The Chancellor set out his measures on 22 July in the most politically acceptable terms he could – less jam tomorrow:

'It remains my considered judgement that there is no call for major action in the current financial year.'

He argued that the cuts and tax increases were necessary because otherwise:

'. . . the financing of the public sector will pre-empt private savings which productive industry is likely to require on a substantial scale to finance stock-building and investment [as the recovery gathered momentum]'.

The July measures, Healey believes:

'. . . were sufficient to get our economy into balance, and in fact the current figures show we actually had a balance of payments surplus in 1977 before any of the IMF measures had actually had time to take effect . . . I thought enough had been done, but that didn't mean it was enough to satisfy the markets . . . The markets in the end decide what is the appropriate level of interest rates, whatever the central bank wants to do, and the markets decide what is the value of your currency.'

For the markets the July package was a flop, as Gavyn Davies of the Policy Unit remembers:

'. . . the markets wanted blood, and that didn't look like blood. We didn't understand that in No. 10 at the time, we didn't know that what they wanted was a humiliation . . . trying to avoid the humiliation was a waste of time.'

The view that the humiliation of IMF conditionality should be

---

* Grimsby was his constituency, regarded with awe by the Foreign Secretary for its commonsense judgement.

avoided until the last possible moment was not shared by all the cabinet. Crosland and others held the view that, if the government had to apply to the Fund, it would be better to go voluntarily from relative strength in the summer. The Prime Minister and the Chancellor, hoping to the last that the pound would stabilise after July, decided to hang on. For a few weeks it worked.

Then, on 9 September, the pound weakened further against the dollar. Scarce currency reserves were spent in vain support. Interest rates had to be raised after all, MLR rising to 13%. Inside the Treasury the options for an application to the Fund were under active consideration, but it was understood that the government wanted to hang on at least until after what was likely to be a tough annual conference was out of the way. Wass and Mitchell went to the IMF conference in Manila, where one of their delegation recalls that the British were treated as 'pariahs' when they made it plain that any application would be on the basis of existing policies. No final decision about an application had been made when the Labour Party conference gathered in Blackpool on Sunday, 26 September. On the Monday and Tuesday following, the markets delivered their verdict on the deliberations of the party. The pound fell by two cents, then by four. The Chancellor had not intended to be present for the economic debate. He was travelling to London airport with the Governor of the Bank of England, on the way to Manila. At Heathrow, appraised of the latest news, he consulted Callaghan by phone, turned round, and headed for Blackpool and a fateful decision:

'We had an emergency meeting that evening and decided the only thing to do was to announce that we were going to the IMF, because that was the only thing that would hold the markets, which it did.'

On the first day of the conference, Tony Benn, speaking for the NEC to commend its 1976 programme (and public ownership of banks and insurance), had said:

'We are also paying a heavy political price for twenty years in which, as a party, we have played down our criticism of capitalism and soft-pedalled our advocacy of socialism.'

On the following morning, with the pound in precipitate fall, Callaghan replied in a speech intended for Manila and Washington, as well as the party faithful. It was blunt; the very reverse of the old Wilsonian mix:

'Britain has lived for too long on borrowed time, borrowed money, borrowed ideas . . . For too long, perhaps ever since the war, we've postponed facing up to fundamental choices and fundamental changes in our society and our economy. That is what I mean when I say we have been living on borrowed time. For too long this country, all of us – yes, this conference too – has been ready to settle for borrowing money abroad to maintain our standards of life, instead of grappling with the fundamental problems of British industry.'

He went on to wound Labour's Keynesians when he said:

'We used to think that you could spend your way out of a recession and increase employment by cutting taxes and boosting government spending. I tell you in all candour that that option no longer exists, and that, insofar as it ever did exist, it only worked on each occasion since the war by injecting a bigger dose of inflation into the economy, followed by a higher level of unemployment as the next step. Higher inflation followed by higher unemployment – that is the history of the last twenty years.'

These words are often attributed to the Chancellor's son-in-law Peter Jay, who in his journalism and in his Wincott Lecture the previous December had sought to bring the economic liberals to the aid of the government, in an attack on accelerating inflation and the assumptions about public expenditure and wage bargaining which fuelled it. Callaghan's speech certainly aimed to please the bankers, if not the conference. It was almost an introduction to the discussions now under way in Manila. There could be no turning back. Bernard Donoughue paraphrases the Chancellor's argument to the cabinet economic committee in the middle of that week:

'We needed an IMF loan, because we needed the stamp of approval. The dilemma we were in was that in the current situation the City wouldn't buy gilts, so we couldn't finance public borrowing and the IMF wouldn't make us a loan, and foreigners wouldn't buy sterling in the present situation. And we needed to turn that round . . .'

Confidence: of all world commodities that was the hardest for Britain to acquire. The hard men from the international financial community now had an opportunity to state the terms for acquiring it.

The coming of the IMF

Chancellor Healey appeared on the rostrum at the Labour conference on Thursday, 30 September, immediately after a debate on a motion which called (with much else) for a 'state monopoly of credit and finance with a state bank and state credit corporation under the control and management of the democratic organisations of the working class'. The motion was defeated, but the NEC statement to which it was linked was carried, against the open opposition of Callaghan. Healey, tousled and flushed, spoke for five minutes – the maximum allowed; he might be Chancellor in a grave economic crisis, but here he was just another delegate. After swatting at the 'siege economy' alternative he announced that:

'I am going to negotiate with the IMF on the basis of our existing policies, not changes in policies, and I need your support to do it. But when I say 'existing policies' it means things we do not like as well as things we do.'

It was the least he could say, in a combative speech, during which he was often heckled, before he took his seat to an enthusiastic reception from most of the parliamentary party. Many of his colleagues, even on the right, believed that the Fund, egged on by the ultra-conservative US Treasury under President Ford, would seek harsh conditions. Surely Britain could borrow elsewhere? The Chancellor and his officials thought otherwise, but in public they had to minimise the degree of conditionality they would accept.

This did not make matters easier in Manila, where Sir Douglas Wass led the British delegation. US Treasury Secretary William Simon remembers that:

'The pressures in Manila on the members of my Treasury and Central Bank team were, you know, "Simon, take it easy. We don't want to put our country into chaos. We want to make sure that we work our way out of this problem. We're willing to adopt measures, but you cannot demand measures that will be too severe."'

The civil servants feared that any further package of cuts would never get through the cabinet. The Americans listened with scant sympathy.

No one understood more clearly that the cabinet might break up over further cuts than James Callaghan. He embarked on confidence building. He needed to get the most he could, and concede the minimum possible, while persuading both his party and the IMF, simultaneously, that he had done everything in his power to meet their wishes. He began with a brush with the Chancellor. The pound had continued to fall. On 6 October it fell to little more than $1.50. Healey told the Prime Minister that he would have to raise MLR to 15% to stop the slide. Callaghan demurred. There would be a knock-on effect, from jobs to mortgages. Healey persisted:

'So I said, well, I want to take it to cabinet. And he said, "Well, all right, but I won't support you in cabinet . . ."'

Healey returned to No. 11 looking resignation full in the face. Without Callaghan's support, he had no hope of success. Fifteen minutes before the cabinet, the Prime Minister's private secretary, Kenneth Stowe, came round to say, 'Jim wanted you to know that he was only testing the firmness of your conviction. Of course he'll support you in cabinet.' So what has been described as 'the day the pound nearly died' (and Healey's career with it) turned out differently from expectations. The pound recovered, never to touch $1.50, at least during that administration. It did quiver at $1.55 however when one of the IMF briefing papers about the British economy leaked to Malcolm Crawford of the *Sunday Times*, who wrote on 24 October:

'The Fund thinks that sterling should be let down to about $1.50 to the pound (against today's $1.64).'

The story was hotly denied. Crawford now believes that two depreciation options were being considered, and a senior IMF official remarks, 'At an earlier time the Fund felt the pound should be devalued. So that story was probably . . . kind of delayed.'

The flurry did not increase mutual confidence between the British and the IMF team which arrived on 1 November. They were to discuss the biggest loan request ever made in the Fund's history.

The British respected their compatriot Alan Whittome, a former Bank of England official, who led the IMF team, and his managing director, Johannes Witteveen. They would not be negotiating alone, as Denis Healey knew:

'The IMF inevitably operates as the tool of the American Treasury, and I knew that behind Witteveen there'd be the saturnine tubby figure of Ed Yeo, the American minister . . .'

On Callaghan's orders, the IMF team were left 'kicking their heels in Brown's Hotel for several weeks', before a preliminary meeting where some token offers were made by the British – 'chicken feed really', in the estimate of one senior adviser. The Treasury men stuck to their line that enough had been done; it would be madness to ask for further cuts. A senior IMF official remembers:

'The British took a very tough negotiating position in the sense that they told Alan Whittome that they were under instruction not to discuss changes in policies . . . [Had this continued], the thing was off. The mission would come back to Washington.'

The Prime Minister was using the time consumed in these desultory negotiations to pursue an alternative strategy of his own. Harold Lever was dispatched to Washington in mid-November to try to secure agreement for a safety-net arrangement for sterling, provided by the central banks. He visited Secretary of State Kissinger and President Ford, defeated but still in office, as well as William Simon and the Chairman of the Federal Reserve Board, Arthur Burns. The British wanted the State Department and the Executive Office to understand that, if the IMF pushed too hard, the British government might fall, resulting in chaos in the Western Alliance. Lever was playing a poor hand. The US Treasury, deeply suspicious that the British were trying – as they were – to bypass the IMF and its conditionality, had the last word with the President. He offered Lever only a third of a loaf. A safety net was agreed – but only after an IMF deal was concluded. Lever's mission had even less success in attempting to bypass the Fund to raise money elsewhere in the United States. Nor could the Germans be persuaded to help, either with loans or in further pressure on President Ford. Callaghan was out on his own.

Neither the Treasury nor the Bank of England had been enthusiastic about the Lever mission. Callaghan believed they were undermining his strategy. Downing Street was resentful, as Donoughue remembers:

'There was a feeling around that many people in the upper official levels of government, and in the banking community, didn't want him to succeed, and a lot of effort was put into making sure he didn't.'

One Treasury official involved in the IMF application dismisses Lever as believing 'the whole thing could be done by mirrors'. Callaghan, the ex-Chancellor, had suspicions of his own Treasury, reinforced by Alan Whittome's first reaction to their forecasts for the British economy. The IMF said that the Treasury had exaggerated the likely size of the PSBR. Here was evidence that the mandarins were painting a redder picture of the books than the international bankers were. Whose side were they on? Incompetence rather than a deliberate fiddling of the figures is likely to have been the culprit here, the PSBR being notoriously difficult to estimate. But since the PSBR was at the heart of the loss of confidence, this episode did not improve the atmosphere in Whitehall.

There were darker suspicions too, blurted out on television by the Liberals' economic spokesman John Pardoe, that certain Treasury officials were egging on the IMF to ask for tough conditions. Rumours ran round Westminster that the Fund was being told, 'Don't bail these bastards out.'

Joel Barnett, the Chief Secretary to the Treasury, puts it more moderately:

'I have no doubt in my own mind that there were some senior Treasury officials who felt more strongly than others that the IMF was needed to keep a check on this profligate Labour government. I have no doubt about that. There are some who suspect sabotage by at least one official, senior official. I have seen no evidence to support that view, although I think it's fair to say I would share the suspicion.'

Donoughue recollects that:

'Some American sources would come through to us at No. 10 and report to us what some people in the UK Treasury were allegedly saying to the IMF in terms of "keep firm and really make sure that you impose big expenditure cuts". But I should say, I think the allegations, true or not, were only about some parts of the Treasury [which] contained a whole spectrum of views . . .'

There is no evidence on record of explicit disloyalty, and those whose names were then bandied around as 'traitors' – to their later misfortune – have vehemently denied the charge. But there were implicit hints. US Treasury Secretary William Simon thinks he got a message: be tough:

'The people in the Bank of England and the people in the UK Treasury knew what had to be done. While they would never say it, because they were fiercely loyal, I think that they were secretly rooting for us, that we would hold fast our ground.'

The cabinet debate

The fact that this suspicion was shared in Downing Street did not make progress easier. The negotiations with the IMF dragged on. On 19 November, at a meeting in the Chancellor's room at the House of Commons, Sir Douglas Wass warned that without progress the IMF team would simply pull up stumps and leave the field. An initial Treasury proposal for substantial further public expenditure cuts of £3 billion (the IMF were then asking for £5 billion) as a prerequisite for a loan from the Fund was slapped down in the cabinet. When the Prime Minister went round the cabinet table on 23 November, ten out of thirteen who spoke attacked the proposal, following Tony Crosland's strong lead that cosmetic cuts were all that were needed, since the issue was confidence rather than profligacy. His case, as his wife paraphrases it, was that:[3]

'. . . with one million unemployed nobody could say that there was not enough spare capacity to increase exports. Far from reducing the PSBR the spending cuts would mean higher unemployment, which would in turn mean higher social security payments and lower tax revenue, thus actually increasing the PSBR.'

The Chancellor could not get the Prime Minister's support. The Treasury knights retired unhorsed. By the following Thursday, Crosland reported to his wife that Healey was 'at the end of his tether', and there was talk in Downing Street that he might be replaced as Chancellor by a recalled Roy Jenkins.

Callaghan had kept his own counsel up to this point. His apparent lack of commitment either way was the strongest card he had. Somehow he had to hold together the diverse elements in the cabinet, to get the most that might be on offer for the lowest sacrifice. The expectations of the markets, the estimates of the Treasury and the views of his party stood so far apart that agreement seemed very far away. The IMF now knew that any call for £5 billion worth of cuts was politically impossible. Callaghan decided to let the cabinet range over all the alternatives to an IMF loan, in a debate the outlines of which were known to the Fund negotiators and relayed by them back to Washington. He made two gains in so doing. He stood back from declaring his own hand for a little longer, while the cabinet collectively thought aloud for him, and he demonstrated to the Fund that there was no certainty about a deal. It was not until 29 November, after a European summit at the Hague where he received no more than token support from Schmidt, that he told Crosland, the one minister whose opposition or support could be crucial, that he had 'decided to accept the IMF's terms'.

In allowing the cabinet to debate the alternatives that week, Callaghan took a calculated risk: that an alliance would build up against any loan agreement. The cabinet split into four groups. There were those who wanted the tough Treasury line, seeing no alternative – prominently, Healey, Barnett and Edmund Dell. There was the left group who wanted an alternative economic strategy: Benn, Foot, Albert Booth, Stan Orme, and – with them but not of them – Peter Shore. There was the right-wing group clustered around Crosland, and deeply averse to cuts which would destroy their hopes of redistribution through economic growth: Roy Hattersley, Harold Lever, Shirley Williams, David Ennals and, more sceptically, William Rodgers. And there were the rest, who would wait for Callaghan's lead and then follow it. If the second and third groups combined, they might detach the Prime Minister from the Chancellor, as they had on 23 November. The trusties would swing behind the Prime Minister in that event, and Healey and his supporters would be isolated.

A succession of cabinet meetings followed. Tony Benn was asked to make the first presentation, arguing the case for a siege economy, with import controls – the genesis of what was to become the Labour left's alternative economic strategy. The choice was significant. Benn was the most fluent, but not the most popular, exponent of the left case. He knew Callaghan's game:

'I think Jim Callaghan, who ran the cabinet with considerable skill, realised that the first thing to do was to get the cabinet to reject the alternative, rather than discuss whether we should accept. His strategy was to let me put in a paper on the alternative strategy . . . the whole cabinet was devoted to the examination and ultimate destruction of my paper. And it was a very good debate.'

Crosland reported Benn as 'carried away by rhetoric'. What Benn was saying, in the knowledge that he could not carry the day in cabinet, was that there would ultimately be no alternative to what he proposed:

'. . . They said to me, "You see, your plan, Tony, will mean a siege economy." And I said, "We haven't an alternative to a siege economy. The difference between my siege economy and yours is that in my siege economy we'll have our allies with us, against the bankers. In your siege economy we'll have the bankers with us and our supporters outside. So when the crunch comes, in your siege economy, you'll find that you're being defended by people who are really hostile to you, and the people you depend on will be against you." That's exactly what happened . . . I circulated to that cabinet . . . the published minutes of the 1931 Labour cabinet, in which exactly the same discussion took place . . . to remind them that there was a history in this matter.'

Benn's alternative was savaged by the Chancellor, who remembers it with scant affection:

'He didn't really have alternative proposals. I think that on many of the big issues of the time he was simply agin it.'

Then the other ministers chipped in. One of them, William Rodgers, recollects that:

'Jim Callaghan tipped off a number of people to have their questions ready and [Benn's paper] was completely massacred.'

Rodgers saw that Callaghan wanted not merely to isolate the Benn group, but to isolate Benn within the group:

'Callaghan was brilliant; I mean, one of the great achievements of his period in cabinet as Prime Minister was isolating Benn. One way he did it was, of course, leaning very heavily on Foot as the real genuine voice of the archetypal left in the Labour Party, and the other was in detaching Peter Shore from Benn.'

This tactic worked. Callaghan and Foot were already constructing the close alliance of mutual trust which was to see them through to 1979. Foot was not impressed by the Benn rhetoric either:

'There were others who argued in my opinion more effectively. Because Tony Benn would often argue merely to incite what was in his mind, at least that's what some of us used to think; whereas some of the other people argued in order to persuade.'

The task of persuasion, as the debate went on, switched to Peter Shore, who argued for selective import controls to bring round the balance of payments. He pitched his argument, as he recalls, to the likely circumstances of that particular year:

'We were in a position to do that, first, because we had been hit far worse than any other country and it wasn't just a matter of exporting unemployment . . . and secondly because we were beginning to see the first signs of North Sea oil, and we could have offered our trading partners the prospect not of cuts, but of a standstill, which is a very much more acceptable thing.'

This was a position which some of the Crosland group initially accepted. They had held a series of anguished meetings over the week, and had marked at least one defection (Rodgers) from their number. They still held the view, as Shirley Williams recalls it:

'. . . that the IMF could be faced down to some extent; one had to make some concession to it, but nothing like as much as it asked for.'

Crosland, who came out in favour of import deposits, which were also favoured by the Policy Unit at No. 10, still believed that the Fund's bluff could be called. The Chancellor held his ground, unconvinced:

'Tony Crosland was saying . . . we don't understand economics at all – you can run a much bigger deficit than this without damage. The trouble with theoretical economists is that they don't understand that when you have a deficit you can only finance it by borrowing, and you've got to persuade people that it's worth lending to you, and that they'll get their money back.'

In fact the lenders had already come to Healey's rescue. The cabinet was not to be the only circus in town. Whittome of the IMF had been reporting back regularly to his chief Witteveen in Washington. They did not use the telephone, suspecting it might be bugged by the British. In the last weekend of November, while they conferred in Washington, US Treasury Secretary Simon was in London. He too knew that Healey was under pressure in cabinet. The role played by Simon and his Under Secretary, Ed Yeo, was as curious as it was controversial. Yeo had already been several times to London, pressing the British to accept cuts in the budget deficit. In Washington he joined Simon and Arthur Burns of the Federal Reserve Board in urging the defeated President Ford not to yield to British blandishments. It was a highly unusual intervention by one country in an application by another; the more so for the ties of interest, sentiment and strategy which bound the two. The Americans are much the largest provider of funds to the IMF, but what Simon and Yeo were doing went well beyond a concern for prudent lending. Many thought their actions damaged the neutrality of the Fund. Their controlling influence had worried the Chancellor, when the IMF was called in, although paradoxically they now came to his aid against his colleagues. The Americans argue that they were defending the integrity of the IMF exercise, not pressing their own harsher alternative. It is true that in the end they accepted a compromise, but it was very much one of their moulding.

What was Simon doing in London on 27 November? He had been tipped off about the drubbing which the Treasury had received in the previous week:

'It was felt that I should stop off in the UK and have informal and hopefully secret discussions with the members of the Bank and the Treasury . . . unfortunately the press was hounding me everywhere I went and as a result I had to devise something rather devious.'

He went to the tailors, Wells of Mayfair. Yeo joined him secretly to discuss their game plan:

'Then we met the Treasury people and there was generally a small parade of folks in and out of this tailor, and I ended up buying three suits I didn't need; but nonetheless we pretty well set the parameters . . .'

For that, the suits were a small price to pay. With the knowledge he had gained, Simon called Johannes Witteveen in Washington. The

IMF, he said, should close in for a deal, while President Ford could be held. Witteveen packed his bags and came to London himself, with little notice. He saw Callaghan on the morning of 1 December.

Callaghan had already told Crosland that he had concluded that there would have to be a deal with the IMF. But with Witteveen he blustered to some purpose, claiming that Britain was ready to apply to the General Agreement on Tariffs and Trade for permission to impose temporary import restrictions (a position which might still have got majority cabinet support). The meeting was not cordial. Callaghan called the IMF managing director 'Boy', and lost his temper in a rather calculated way. Healey looked, as well he might, uncertain of where his Prime Minister stood. Then the two men left for the cabinet. In the afternoon Healey and Callaghan met the IMF duo again, in the Cabinet Room. Witteveen now found Callaghan talking the language of accommodation. The 'foxy old peasant', as one of his Treasury officials called him, showed his hand. If there could be cuts in the cuts, they would take it. The IMF agreed that there might be a compromise, on a reduced PSBR.

By the evening of 1 December, therefore, a crucial shift in the balance of the cabinet debate had taken place behind the scenes. The last piece to move was the Foreign Secretary. He had been told that evening that some of his supporters, reverting to their free-trade instincts, had deserted any idea of import deposits. Meanwhile he sensed that the Prime Minister had come firmly behind Healey, and baulked at further opposition. He telephoned his wife to say:

'I may well switch my argument halfway tomorrow and say this: that in these circumstances we cannot afford not to support the Prime Minister. He is crucial.'

And so he did, advising Roy Hattersley to do the same – 'No time for heroics – or for you to think that your judgement is better than mine.'

How good was that judgement? Crosland was Foreign Secretary, perhaps less fiercely engaged in immediate events than if he had still been in one of the major home spending departments. He had gone along with other cuts in the past year. He was exhausted; observers at the party conference two months earlier had marked his weariness, the 'lack of bottle' easily described by people whose political courage often comes in smaller containers. Tragically, he had less than three months to live. In other days it is hard to see him not making a fight of it. Now, after the Prime Minister had come in to support the Chancellor's revised package in cabinet (£1 billion worth of cuts in the first year, £1 billion in the second, and the sale of £500 million of BP shares), Crosland spoke. The cabinet should accept, he said. He was unconvinced by the economic arguments but his political judgement was that the Prime Minister should not be opposed. It would smash up the party if this opposition became known. His old friend and pupil Benn was dismayed:

'When you say you've no alternative then you've got to go along with it. And therefore the wobblies in the middle who I thought would support us when it came to the real crunch . . . collapsed. And I think the death of the social democratic wing of the party occurred in that cabinet, when Tony Crosland said at one stage: it is mad but we have no alternative.'

There remained further cabinets to distribute the cuts, while Callaghan and his Policy Unit waited for the letter of intent to be drafted by the Treasury. The first draft omitted the specific money-supply targets, though a complete draft existed in Whitehall. Had Callaghan not insisted on seeing it, his staff believed, the targets would have been tied down still further, and the BP sale excluded from the PSBR reduction. It was the last bounce left in the Treasury. The full letter was sent on 15 December. For a Labour government it was painful. It declared:

'An essential element of the government's strategy will be a continuing and substantial reduction over the next few years in the share of resources required for the public sector. It is also essential to reduce the PSBR in order to create monetary conditions which will encourage investment and support sustained growth and the control of inflation.'

From the IMF point of view, it was 'not especially tough . . . in line with the normal Fund conditionality'. Their negotiators believed that they had dealt with real weaknesses, in a real economy, and not that they had participated in an elaborate con trick on the money markets. They threw their support behind the safety net for sterling which Callaghan so intensely desired, and in exchange for a commitment to 'an orderly reduction in the role of sterling as a reserve currency', a $3 billion facility was arranged. By then, a falling pound was not the problem. Sterling was rising fast. The American Treasury remained unhelpful in this matter until overruled by the President, but even they had no quarrel with the scale of Britain's acceptance of the IMF terms. The British had kissed the rod. 'We were generally happy,' says William Simon, 'with the deal that was eventually made, and I think the proof of the pudding was in the results many months later.'

What were these results? Some of the cabinet critics were surprised at how little damage the IMF package did. Peter Shore accepts that:

'In the event, unemployment hardly moved, and the economy began to move forward again really fairly shortly afterwards . . . It didn't have that dramatic deflationary effect which I so feared at the time, and I have to say that in all honesty.'

For Healey, the IMF visit had been hard to swallow, the draught the more bitter because Whittome's first examination of the Treasury books had demonstrated that the exercise was based on a false PSBR estimate. He concludes that:

'In the end . . . we got a good deal, and we managed our own economy so well that I drew only two slices of the four slices of money available and paid it all back before I left office, or the equivalent back . . . The virtue of the whole thing, even though it wasn't necessary, is that sentiment internationally completely switched round.'

So it had, in terms of international confidence. Callaghan had brought his cabinet around with consummate skill. As the standby loan was about to expire, he was forced to manoeuvre under the guns of the world's bankers, trained not only on him but on the City of London. These were not the circumstances in which he could have lightly allowed his Chancellor to be isolated, much less overthrown. With no parliamentary majority and the shadow of higher inflation falling across his course, he was in a weak position. That the government went on, even recovered its ground, was a triumph of sorts. It was achieved without a single resignation, from a cabinet in which the majority had been, at first, overwhelmingly against any IMF terms unless dictated by Britain.

It was skilful. But deftness is not all. There was a price to be paid. To buy confidence in the money markets was to dissipate it elsewhere. The symbolism of the seal of good housekeeping was matched, inside the Labour movement, by the symbolism of socialism betrayed. It looked to Labour activists then, and seems in memory now, like the death of Keynesian welfare socialism and the birth of monetarism, the external dictatorship of the markets and the American bankers. To the trade unions, which had just agreed to a second round of incomes policy to bring down inflation (and their real wages with it), it was a rebuff, as Jack Jones puts it, '[to hear] Denis Healey totally speaking with the voice of the IMF'. Healey's reckless courage cost him dearly in party terms. The party workers who now felt that their government existed only on sufferance from, and as long as it imitated the motives and methods of, the US Treasury never knew that Healey resented it too. In the coming battle for the soul of the party, the Crosland faction was unable to shake off the accusation that, when the IMF came, they did nothing. As the pound soared in the collective hysteria of the money markets, with a new and sympathetic President in Washington and the oil coming ashore, the bleak November choices of 1976 were hard to recall, even in the following year. It kept the loss of confidence in the party leaders' commitment to their programme fresh in the memory. Both ways, the IMF exercise was about confidence. The judgement of the world of Labour politics might be as irrational as that of the markets. Its consequences were to be just as painful.

PROGRESS DENIED: THE DEBATE ABOUT STANDARDS

The long hot summer of the IMF crisis was notable for another reappraisal, then far advanced. A section of British public opinion served notice that it was through with the questing libertarianism of the sixties. They had had enough of love and curiosity. They were full of freckles and doubt. The sea change in British politics in the seventies can only be understood by analysing how the debate about standards came to occupy the overground of political argument. What were thought in the sixties to be shrill protests by threatened vested interests came together in a grumbling consonance that the line must be drawn somewhere. Permissiveness, collectivism and social reform, it was thought, had produced a crisis of authority. Governments were at best weak, at worst corrupt. Subversives lurked everywhere. The terrorist was at the gates.

The elements of this disillusion were easy to mark. The Heath government had been under constant pressure from the right to toughen up on law and order issues. Quintin Hogg's Selsdon presentation (see page 40) had been rumbustious but unspecific. During the election Powell had outbid his own leadership on this as on much else. In a speech at Northfield he linked together the elements in the Great Conspiracy, the 'enemy within'. 'Forces which aim at the destruction of our nation and society as we know or can imagine them' were about this task of subversion. They included students, 'the mob', those who manipulated the 'combustible material' of race, and the 'civil rights' nonsense' in Northern Ireland. Powell's speech was shrugged off by the Tory leadership, and dismissed as paranoid by the party establishment. It accurately foreshadowed the course of right-wing concern over the next parliament. Within a decade Powell's sentiments were to capture much of the party.

To those who believed in it, the attack on the social order seemed to come from the blithe optimism of the sixties gone astray. First there was the phenomenon of terrorism in mainland Britain. Palestinian hijackers, IRA bombers and disaffected students in the 'Angry Brigade' were merged together in the public consciousness, with some help from the media, as alien violence. When, in 1974, forty-four people were killed in Britain by bombing, the intense public reaction thrust a 'temporary' Prevention of Terrorism Act onto the statute book, where it remains. The scintilla of doubt about guilt which was by repute the safeguard of British justice was forgotten in the haste for convictions. Forgotten already was Britain's tradition as a haven for the political dissenter. The German student leader Rudi Dutschke, disabled by an assassination attempt and living quietly in Cambridge, found that no lifestyle was quiet enough in a Britain nervous of foreign revolutionaries. He was deported.

The student left in Britain paid their critics the compliment of agreeing with them. They too believed that they were now a major force for irresistible social change, that the revolution might be just a heave away. Some sought to turn their campuses into 'red bases', others to challenge what they passionately believed were unsavoury foreign contacts – South Africa, Rhodesia or the US military – and the use of home-bred paternalism against lecturers and students with radical views. Examinations were suspect. Tom Fawthrop, who tore up his finals papers at Hull in 1968, wanted a new system with three characteristics:[1]

'1. The student decides which stimuli to learning are appropriate to his own educational needs.

2. Evaluation of work is neither arbitrary nor status-oriented but is open to discussion and challenge by all concerned ... conducted between equals in terms of power.

3. The results of evaluation procedures will have little permanent significance except as aids to learning.'

Arrogance and intolerance were not the perquisites of authority alone. Student intimidation of speakers such as Professor Hans Eysenck, of university courts, and sometimes of other students who held unpopular views was justified on revolutionary grounds. As three of the student leaders at the Polytechnic of North London put it:

'To the question "Can we have democracy in education?" a revolutionary socialist must answer that under capitalism you cannot have democratic institutions of any sort.'

The argument about democracy raged throughout higher education. Its consequences ranged from the purging of student rectors by authority for raising embarrassing political issues, as happened to

Gordon Brown at Edinburgh in 1975, to Vice Chancellors losing control, as did Sloman at Essex and Adams at the LSE.

From the late sixties onward the Black Papers – polemics against 'the comprehensive disaster' – had begun to circulate. They featured a number of devotees of the grammar schools, themselves often from working-class backgrounds, such as Brian Cox and Rhodes Boyson (a member of the Labour Party until 1966), concerned with what they claimed were falling standards. The gurus of selection – Burt, Eysenck, Szamuely – mingled with critics such as Kingsley Amis who lampooned the new, relaxed style of higher education. Prep-school headmasters contributed letters from parents fleeing the state system; the new infant schools were 'a disastrous experiment' wrote one: 'The accent has been on the reception class being easy going, and simply attempting to make the child enjoy school.'[2] Some of those drawn to the Black Papers had started out with different views. John Marks, later a contributor, says his opinions altered:

'. . . when I began to have school-age children of my own, and began to look at changes on the ground . . . even as a parent governor of the school I was unable to obtain examination results despite asking regularly at governors' meetings for three years.'

What attracted him to the early Black Papers was their opposition to 'a movement to downgrade structure in education, in the sense of discipline in the classroom'. The educational reformers sometimes underestimated the need to carry public opinion with them. Teachers who came out of the universities and into the schools in the expansion of the sixties often displayed a disregard for other opinions which played into the hands of the Black Paper protagonists. Margaret Maden was then a deputy headmistress in Oxfordshire:

'They were very clear about comprehensive education. They were full of zeal and enthusiasm, but there was no sense in their training . . . of an accountability beyond a fairly small and tight professional group . . . They failed to consider how important it was to talk with, and to listen to, people beyond the boundaries of schools, the parents, the local community employers, and all those other stakeholders of whom we're all too conscious now.'

Elderly teachers in ancient disciplines found the new, less structured, informal learning hard to take. One headteacher said wearily on television:

'When the theologians pulled down God the Father, Father the God went too, and with it went the old paternalistic authority of the schoolmaster. We now live in a fraternal society, and some of my older colleagues find it almost impossible. We've had to explain very much more what we do, and why we do it; become very much more patient than we used to be.'

The debate about standards was often a debate about style, Margaret Maden believes:

'The way some teachers dressed, the way some teachers spoke, the way pupils less and less [often] wore school uniform, the way in which corporal punishment was used less and less [often] during the seventies – all these seemed to denote to large numbers of people interested in education a fall of standards. And actually that was a profound illogicality.'

Battle was joined in Islington in 1974. The 'progressive' teachers at William Tyndale Primary School found themselves denounced by their 'formal' colleagues, by the school managers, and by many parents. They saw themselves as victims of the backlash administered by the allies of local Black Paper contributor, headmaster and politician Rhodes Boyson. They argued that:[3]

'Black Paper theory holds that "schools are for schooling" ... envisaged as academic, highly structured, carried on in an authoritarian context, designed to do the jobs western capitalist society requires.'

Their own view was different. They wanted to help the least privileged, to break down 'social control'. To do this 'active rather than passive learning became the accepted theory; subject divisions were blurred'. Classrooms became 'informal workshops, no longer schooling boxes dominated by a centrally important teacher'. Some remedial children benefited from the attention they received. The majority of working-class children, to the dismay of their parents, did not find the three Rs in the informal workshops. When the crisis broke in October 1975, and children were taken away from William Tyndale, Jill Tweedie satirised in the *Guardian* the revolutionaries who had kept some middle-class support, but lost their proletariat:

'Perry and Cressy had such fun mucking about with old egg boxes, and they would eventually read, and anyway the main point was, be happy, wasn't it? The only slight cloud on the horizon was that Perry and Cressy were rather outnumbered by Fred and Marlene, whose parents were bricklayers and dustmen and office cleaners instead of playwrights and barristers and doctors. Parents, in other words, who had not had much of an education themselves and held the quaint old-fashioned view that if Fred and Marlene learned to read, write, do arithmetic, and pass exams, they might go to university and become playwrights, barristers and doctors.'

This was to parody the problem. Deprived children with reading difficulties had engaged the teachers. But the teachers had lost their clientele. Margaret Maden was by then headmistress of nearby Islington Green Comprehensive, a very different environment from Boyson's Highbury Grove. The Tyndale teachers, for all their progressive commitment, she believes:

'. . . absolutely fatally and arrogantly refused to engage in any kind of real dialogue or debate with parents, or indeed inspectors, which was very foolish.'

They lost their jobs after an inquiry. Press headlines on the 'school of shame' ensured maximum panic about the falling standards in Britain's schools. Untypical though William Tyndale was, it helped to make the Black Papers more credible.

The new student power was also excoriated in the Black Papers. Student activists were unsubtly dubbed fifth columnists of the enemy at the gates. Philip Larkin contributed one of his less substantial poems:[4]

> When the Russian tanks roll westward, what defence for
> you and me?
> Colonel Sloman's Essex Rifles? The Light Horse of LSE?

Sloman's Essex Rifles, and the myriad tribes and tendencies of the Trotskyite diaspora, were unconcerned by such attacks. They rather relished them. The student Trotskyists of the International Marxist Group (IMG) and the International Socialists (IS) were never abashed by the bad media coverage they attracted after incidents like the deliberate charge at the police lines in Red Lion Square, in which one student was killed. They drew inspiration from successful working-class action against the Heath government. Both the Upper Clyde Shipbuilders' work-in and the victories of the miners and the railwaymen in 1972 seemed to be the most conclusive evidence possible of class advance. Paul Foot joined *Socialist Worker*, journal of the International Socialists, full-time in the autumn of 1972:

'Our little organisation had grown from zero to perhaps 2000 members by 1972 . . . all through '72 and '73 it was an upward curve all the way. We would get these cheques in. [One] was from a student in York for £17,000 saying. "Today I have received my inheritance."

Stop. New paragraph. "I renounce my inheritance and I declare myself for international socialism." And here was the cheque for his entire inheritance of £17,000. I've often wondered how he must bitterly regret having given this money up.'

The different groups on the far left, who normally reproduce, amoeba-like, by splitting, were now expanding in their own right. Their enthusiastic support for the strikes of 1972 and 1974, taking striking miners under their roofs and joining their picket lines, brought them closer to real political influence. It also meant that by the high point of 1974, when the miners strike helped to bring down the Heath government, they had an inflated view of their own potential. The revolution was at hand. Foot recollects:

'Many of us started to believe that . . . instead of it being a hobby, which it was, there was a possibility of a real mass revolutionary party . . . Various sections of workers just broke through the social contract – smashed it to one side. Inflation of course roared ahead but nobody cared a great deal about that, because the real problem was about power, and what people could do in society. That seemed to be going our way.'

That events did indeed seem to be going their way was one of the major elements in the panic of the middle classes. There were others. Stuart Hall and his colleagues have analysed[5] the extraordinary press hysteria about 'muggings' in 1972–3, which convinced the British public that as well as terrorism and flying pickets mass terror now stalked the streets. One *Sun* editorial encapsulates the voice of the tabloid talmud:

'What are the British people most concerned about today? Wages? Prices? Immigration? Pornography? People are talking about all these things. But the *Sun* believes there is another issue which has everyone deeply worried and angry: *violence in our streets* . . . Nothing could be more utterly against our way of life, based on a common-sense regard for law and order . . . If punitive jail sentences help to stop the violence – and nothing else has done – then they will not only prove to be the only way. They will, regrettably, be the *right* way. And the judges will have the backing of the public.'

Some months later a judge in Birmingham sentenced three Handsworth teenagers who had severely beaten up a man whom they had robbed of 30p: one was given a detention order of twenty years, the other two ten years each. The panic about law and order was under way. In fact the rate of increase in recorded crime had been much faster in 1955–65, at 10% per annum, than it was in the seventies. In 1973, the year in which the panic worked through into the courts, it actually decreased by 2%.[6] But that was not how the public were encouraged to see it. Problems about society were translated into problems about law and order. The press were happy to provide fuel. Mugging stories sold papers, found real anxieties, fed them, and fed upon them. The tabloids, lowering their sights to find the new target area identified by Rupert Murdoch's *Sun*, fought the great circulation war with shrill headlines.

Television, for its part, had embarked on that love affair with the Edwardian past which allowed a rosy light to soften old troubles. The world of the Forsytes, *Upstairs Downstairs* and Edward VII seemed a settled time of order by comparison with the turbulent present. No one dramatised *The Strange Death of Liberal England*. While the tradition of directly addressing contemporary social issues in drama and documentary was not abandoned, it was no longer a priority. Catherine of Aragon came to be more important than *Cathy Come Home*. After the heady times of the Greene era these were more nervous days. Critics who regarded the mass media as a wen of pornography and subversion were beginning to make their opinions felt. Greene had regarded the Viewers' and Listeners' Association as something of a joke. Who could take Mary Whitehouse seriously? he argued, as he tried to open up broadcasting. 'His own preferred culture,' says his biographer, 'suggested sin rather than sanctity.'[7] Mrs Whitehouse had made her national reputation crusading against a culture which suggested sin rather than sanctity. Her critics thought her prepared to go to great lengths to register outrage, but even they had to acknowledge the courage with which she faced ridicule and abuse. She believed that Greene and his disciples were engaged in a brainwashing process:

'Because of the power of the media, people were assaulted by one idea after another, foreign to the basic concepts of our society, but those who would have challenged them were silenced and kept off the medium.'

In the seventies Whitehouse widened her interests into a general attack on pornography and permissiveness. There were some easy targets. Dr Martin Cole's amateurish sex education films, *The Little Red School Book* with its callow advice on how to be a school-age insurgent against the grown-up system, the dottier films of Ken Russell: all were spun together into a web of supposed subversion by the new moral crusaders. At one end there was a real lament for lost innocence. In a public debate with Martin Cole in Birmingham about the proposal to open one of the Ann Summers sex shops in the city, Nora Hinks JP talked of its effects on 'little girls of seventeen, who shouldn't know anything about sex except what is right and what is wrong –' 'Big girls,' Cole interrupted. Mrs Hinks was undeterred. 'She is still a little girl who wants protecting, and is not there for your satisfaction,' she told him. To meet such fears, a Nationwide Festival of Light was organised in 1971. Chief constables and bishops were recruited. Cliff Richard sang in Trafalgar Square. Lord Longford, a social reformer with a talent for backing none too reluctantly into the limelight, was so shocked by the nude review *Oh, Calcutta* that he brought together an unofficial committee of inquiry into pornography. His odyssey among the alien porn made him a media superstar. Other voices were raised too. Malcolm Muggeridge followed the Whitehouse path in attacking sexual licence and the pro-abortion lobby. Ross McWhirter attempted to use the courts against the IBA to stop a film about Andy Warhol, which featured a large lady who painted with her nipples. The targets of what was still a moral minority were frequently fatuous pieces of self-indulgence, the dross that is the waste product of creative freedom. The attacks undermined the belief in liberty which the sixties had claimed in lineal descent from J. S. Mill. And at the same time they contributed to the law and order panic. 'They', out there, were corrupting our children, destabilising society, insinuating the values of the 'trendy' establishment.

Whether these different anxieties were understandable protest or moral panic, they had begun to cohere. They appear in the literature of the time, as well as in the journalism. In the press the new anxiety had many votaries – so many that the veteran feature writer Peregrine Worsthorne was moved to protest that by the time he could chip in on a Sunday with his piece attacking unions who held the public to ransom:[8]

'Paul Johnson has given voice in the *Evening Standard* and the *Daily Mail* – perhaps elsewhere as well – Bernard Levin repeatedly in *The Times*, George Gale in the *Express*, and so on and so on, ad nauseam.'

It was a hard life, to be one of the scribes of doom. Worsthorne also appeared on television with Auberon Waugh, himself the best-read satirist in *Private Eye* as it moved towards the right, to lament, while playing croquet, the decline of the old order. He told Waugh:

'We've all been rather remiss in spurning politics, but most of the bright or intelligent people, who in the old days would have tended to be members of the ruling class, have gone into fringe activities, like you have into satire and I have into journalism.'

This sense of the natural order pushed aside and replaced by a crew of self-serving Trots and trendies became a common theme in fiction. Malcolm Bradbury's *The History Man* brilliantly captured a certain kind of campus sociologist taunting a student of unfashionable right-wing views:[9]

'"It won't do, George," says Howard, intervening, "I'm afraid this is an anal, repressed paper in every way. Your model of society is static, as Michael says. It's an entity with no internal momentum and no internal conflict. In short it's not sociologically valid." A redness comes up Carmody's neck, and reaches his lower face. He says, insistently, "I think it's a possible point of view, sir." "It may be in conservative circles," says Howard, "it isn't in sociological ones." . . . "Nothing I say could ever please you, could it?" "You'd certainly have to try harder than you do," says Howard. "I see," says Carmody, "Do I have to agree with you, Dr Kirk, do I have to vote the way you do, and march down the street with you, and sign your petitions, and hit policemen on your demos, before I can pass your course?"'

Kingsley Amis, in *The Alteration* – his fantasy of a Europe which had never known the Reformation, in which England still groaned under the tyranny of the Inquisition – delighted in giving the names Foot and Redgrave to the sinister officers of the Secular Arm.[10]

What might be jest for the literati was taken seriously elsewhere. By the winter of 1974, with inflation soaring, union power apparently entrenched in Whitehall as well as Congress House, and the Tory Party in its fourth defeat in five elections having polled only 36.7% of the electorate, sections of the middle class felt threatened and unhappy, undesirable aliens in their own country. On the television programme *The Mangling of the Middle Classes*, seeking sanctuary in their orchards and paddocks, they spelt out their fears. One matron explained:

'We're in the mess that we're in because the working classes have, well – this nasty word "class", but how else can you describe a man who works in a factory and brings home a wage? He's got the unions to talk for him, and big industry has got the CBI and various other bodies. Who do we have in the middle to talk about our plight unless we do it ourselves? And this is just what we haven't been doing.'

Now, they did. The Middle Class Association was launched by the Tory MP John Gorst in November 1974. In the same year the National

Federation of the Self-Employed (NFSE) came into clamorous existence to protest at the additional National Insurance, rates and VAT
levied on them. Inflation was the real terror of those on fixed incomes.
Patrick Hutber, another trumpeter of the bourgeoisie, was to write,
quoting Lenin:[11]

'If you want to destroy capitalism, debauch the currency. For
capitalism you might equally write democracy. Because inflation
distributes its apparent rewards and real punishments in so totally
arbitrary a manner, it powerfully reinforces the impulses towards
envy, hatred, malice and all uncharitableness that are already painfully
apparent.' The middle class feared inflation like a plague.

One of the voices which became quickly associated with the new
fears was that of the former Labour minister Lord Chalfont. In 1975,
in an Anglia TV documentary *Who Says It Can Never Happen Here?*
he argued that It was already happening. Poised with his clipboard in
front of Karl Marx's statue, he argued that half of the prerequisites for
a society in accordance with the Communist Manifesto had already
been met in Britain. He believed that he had struck a chord:

'It was mainly a fear of the trade unions. There was a general
unformed fear that we were all, as I say, going to the dogs, that society
was breaking down, that the traditional values and virtues of discipline and respect for authority and respect for the law were being
undermined. And there were some people behind the scenes – they
never came very much to the surface – who were suggesting that
the only answer to this was a military government – a military
takeover.'

Who these figures were is not clear. Chalfont (a former defence
correspondent of *The Times*) says they were sent packing:

'This was not the kind of country in which the colonels take over. So
those ideas never really surfaced, but there was a great deal of it sort of
bubbling, just below the surface.'

Some retired officers did break the surface. General Sir Walter
Walker launched Civil Assistance, a 'Non-Party Non-class' militia to
aid the civil power in the event of a general strike. More melodramati-
cally, Colonel David Stirling seemed to be re-living his army heroics
with GB75, described as 'an organisation of apprehensive patriots';
Stirling said he would 'move in' if requested to do so. Chalfont believes
that plans to train 'a helicopter-borne force of working commandos
to move in and break strikes' were also afoot. In the event the retired
officers never had to strap on their parachute harnesses. The private

militias collapsed ignominiously. In 1976, the year of the IMF, leading activists in both Civil Assistance and the Middle Class Association found a new and more congenial home – the National Association for Freedom (NAFF).

The National Association for Freedom

Modern British politics has never lacked organised groups on the right whose main concern has been economic or individual freedom against collectivism. 'Freedom' has sometimes been for the business enterprise, for unfettered capitalism against the restraints and taxes of the state. At other times the stress has been on individualism, the right to opt out of trade union or state schooling and health services. Well-funded pressure groups flew the flag of private enterprise: Aims for Freedom and Enterprise (AIMS), British United Industrialists, the Economic League. They could run advertising campaigns against nationalisation, keep dossiers on trade union activists, and sponsor resistance to 'creeping socialism'. Industry picked up the bill, its donations not usually classified as political, although it was as clear who they were against as who they were for. On a very different level the Institute of Economic Affairs (IEA) sought to demonstrate that the market could provide better services at lower cost than could the state. *Charge*, the defiant title of one of their best known books, summed up this philosophy.[12]

None of these bodies made a claim to a mass following, though the IEA lived in hope that such an hour would come. It was left to others to try to make individual, rather than economic, freedom a popular cause. Previous attempts had failed. In the sixties Edward Martell's Freedom Group and his *New Daily* had disappeared under a burden of debt and ridicule. In the early seventies, in protest at the apparent growth of union power, and the inability of the Heath government to deal with it, new voices were heard. Ross McWhirter and his twin brother Norris had a history of skirmishes against the left long enough to qualify for their *Guinness Book of Records*. They were litigious, and saw the courts as an instrument of appeal against all those agencies of the state of which they disapproved. Ross McWhirter set up the Current Affairs Press to produce a news-sheet *Majority*, described as 'the organ of the radical right', to instruct what were ambiguously described as 'self-help groups' in the art of strike-breaking. There was something of the small boy in McWhirter, as there was in Colonel Stirling and a similar figure from the sixties, Air Vice Marshal 'Pathfinder' Bennett – a belief that Long Range Desert Group style activities would frustrate the union hordes. It all became hideous reality in November 1975 when McWhirter was assassinated on his own threshold by an IRA terror squad, later surrounded and captured in circumstances of high drama in Balcombe Street, Marylebone.

This atrocity made the inaugural meeting a week later of a new organisation a sombre affair. The National Association for Freedom (NAFF) was intended to bring together the anti-collectivist forces in a new movement. Its chairman was Lord De L'Isle and Dudley VC, war hero, descendant of Philip Sidney and ex-Governor General of Australia. The ruling group included Norris McWhirter, Robert Moss, editor of the *Economist Foreign Report*, and a former army major, John Gouriet. Its council brought together right-wing industrialists, the leaders of AIMS and the IEA, and assorted luminaries from literature and journalism. It listed fifteen freedoms in its charter, some uncontroversial, others plainly aimed at the anxieties of the middle-class small businessman terrified that he was being taxed out of existence and his savings shrunk by inflation while the trade unions rewrote the national rulebook in Whitehall. 'Freedom to exercise choice or personal priority in spending, without oppressive, unnecessary or confiscatory taxation', for example, begged a great many questions. NAFF rapidly absorbed the Middle Class Association and the remnants of Sir Walter Walker's militia. It had a journal, the *Free Nation*, and it had enough journalists in its ranks to ensure a steady flow of publicity for its activities. John Gouriet, the director of NAFF, linked what was happening abroad with what he feared would happen in Britain:

'We felt that 1975 and the years that followed were really a watershed in British politics . . . we had to decide which way we were going to go: down the slippery slope towards communo-socialism and a satellite state of the Soviet Union at its worst, or were we going to claw our way back?'

This apocalyptic tone was deliberate. NAFF's publicists did not stint their language. Robert Moss published *The Collapse of Democracy*[13] to coincide with the launch. It opened with a fictional letter from the London of 1985, by then in a state of 'proto-communism'. The villains were the trade unions, infiltrated by those bent upon the subversion of liberty. Tolerance, said Moss darkly, could only go so far. From the wings Robert Conquest and Winston Churchill the younger inveighed against the Soviet Union and its ambitions. Peregrine Worsthorne told his readers in the *Sunday Telegraph* on 8 August 1976 that soldiers were the last surviving democrats; the only group who believed in obeying orders from the elected government of the day. Class power, he argued, was now the only valid source of authority. If the unions used it, others would have to do so too. Patrick Hutber's elegant tract, also published in 1976, carried the same message in its title: *The Decline and Fall of the Middle Class. And How It Can Fight Back.* Middle-class power, he wrote, should have a twofold aim:[14]

'. . . to make the Labour Party aware of its irreducible demands, and the Conservative Party, which should be its natural ally, more responsive to its interests.'

Peter Jenkins, in a review of the Moss book in the *Spectator* of 3 January 1976, described it perceptively as 'an inverted New Left book'. In their charge of anxiety, their reaction against the trend of the times, these writers and others like them (not all connected with NAFF) became an inverted version of the Left Book Club.

How could power be clawed back? Gouriet, who embarked on an extended round of public meetings, argued that the best way was 'to use the law wherever the law could be used'. And the law stood to hand. British Rail employees who were dismissed because they declined to join the union closed shop established in 1975 were helped to take their case to the European Court at Strasbourg. (They won their case in 1981, when the agreement which had produced their dismissal was declared to be in breach of the European Convention on Human Rights.) NAFF also moved in with legal help when a group of parents opposed to the introduction of comprehensive schools in Tameside, Greater Manchester, took their case to the House of Lords, and defeated the Secretary of State, temporarily. Their elected leaders such as Councillor Grantham spoke in the authentic language of the threatened middle class:

'I believe in competition, initiative and ability, and comprehensive education to me destroys competition, initiative and ability. If we can put socialism back twenty years in the next two years, that's what we'll do.'

They did not do it, but they forced the Labour government, which had taken action to bring the direct-grant schools within the non-selective system, back on the defensive. Many of them opted to join an independent sector which Labour proved unwilling to touch, although this did not prevent a strident campaign to protect the public schools.

With it went a sustained press campaign against the comprehensives. 'Scandal of the Dunces' said the *Express* on 19 October 1976. 'Comprehensives have failed, say the teachers' the *Mail* replied some months later. Not wishing to be outflanked in the debate about standards, James Callaghan, in his Ruskin speech launching a 'Great Debate' about education, sent a scarcely coded message to the educational progressives:

'The balance was wrong in the past. We have a responsibility now in this generation to see that we don't get it wrong in the other direction. There is no virtue in producing socially well-adjusted members of society who are unemployed because they don't have the skills . . .'

His audience was not pleased. The *Mail* was: '3Rs must come, says Jim.' Shirley Williams, who had to pick up the Great Debate and preside over it, offers a different view:

'I remember the *Mail* tended to give a great run to the argument that the schools were falling apart and the standards were declining. It actually wasn't true. Most of the inspectors' reports indicated the opposite . . . In 1978 they suggested that the standards of reading were the highest they'd been for a decade. But with the upsurge of numbers some of the teachers who came in at that time were not very motivated towards the profession.'

Callaghan had noted the extent to which the new middle-class pressure groups were infusing the Conservative opposition with their own spirit. Keith Joseph was one of the first to seize the opportunity provided by public anxiety about inflation, transfers of power and what he describes as the 'baleful consequences' of educational experiment:

'Against this background of incandescent inflation and dramatically rising unemployment, what did Labour do? They handed more and more power to the very people who in the public consciousness were mostly to blame . . . the trade unions . . . As Labour's panaceas failed to work, and as the trade unions asserted more and more power, the climate became worse for the country, but more propitious for those who wanted to turn back the tide of collectivism.'

Joseph embarked on a series of meetings to put 'the moral case for capitalism', getting, earlier than most, a revivalist sense that 'the climate was with us'. The newly elected Conservative leader and Joseph disciple, Margaret Thatcher, shared both NAFF's anxieties and its contempt for the Heath circle she had displaced. 'A bunch of political failures, has-beens who never were', was how Ross McWhirter had described the Heathmen Whitelaw, Prior, Carr and Gilmour, in the last month of his life.[15] This antagonism had been passed on to NAFF. They wanted a different sort of Toryism. Mrs Thatcher attended NAFF's inaugural subscription dinner in January 1977. She gave what was expected of her, a powerful speech on the indivisibility of freedom and the looming shadow of collectivism. She caught the mood of her audience, drew upon it. A hostile critic, Stuart Hall, analyses her appeal:

'She has always spoken quite authentically on behalf of those people who felt they were left behind by permissiveness, threatened by affluence, challenged by the sexual revolution, who never wanted a libertarian society.'

To Lord Chalfont, she '. . . struck a chord which was waiting to be struck . . . all these fears of bureaucracy, of too much government, of the erosion of freedom of the individual, fears of anarchy . . . she just came at the time when all these fears began to coalesce.'

Those who had been fearful, who saw little to choose between Wilson and Heath, were now eager for action.

The opportunity came at Grunwick Film Processing Laboratories in North London. There a dispute began in the summer of 1976 over pay and conditions of work. The employer was an Anglo-Indian entrepreneur with no time for trade union representation, George Ward. His workforce were largely East African Asian immigrants. Believing they had no proper grievance procedure inside the factory, which depended for its competitive edge on the very rapid turnaround of mail-order photographs in the holiday season, the strikers enrolled in the white collar union APEX. They were sacked, as others had been before them. Attempts at conciliation by ACAS were rebuffed by Ward. By October 1976 the TUC was calling for sympathetic action by other unions, and the blacking of Grunwick's services. When this was extended to the blacking of Grunwick mail by members of the Union of Post Office Workers (UPW), Ward sought and received the assistance of NAFF. John Gouriet had the kind of test case he relished. As the 1953 Post Office Act forbade the 'wilful delay' of the mail by Post Office employees, it was possible to sue the union. This Gouriet did. The UPW withdrew the blacking, on the understanding that ACAS would now be able to consult the workforce – strikers and non-strikers – and resolve the dispute. ACAS had been told that Grunwick would provide the necessary names and addresses for consultation, if the blacking stopped.

There was then the expectation, shared by many Conservatives, that this would indeed happen. The union leaders involved, Roy Grantham of APEX and Tom Jackson of the UPW, were widely perceived to be moderate men, running moderate unions. This did them no good. The Grunwick management stalled on releasing the names and addresses until the new year, and eventually ACAS was able to ballot only the strikers and a small proportion of those still at work. If the law was, as NAFF proclaimed, now written by and for the unions, it was ironic that – because union suspicion of its intrusion in their affairs had encouraged the Labour government to keep it imprecise – the law was now working to their detriment. As Joe Rogaly remarks in his account of the dispute:[16]

'Britain is probably the only country in the world that could devise something like ACAS and deny it the legal right to demand the information on which to base its operations.'

From this frustration much followed. ACAS recommended recognition for APEX on the information it had. Grunwick (after a substantial pay rise to workers still loyal to it) countered with an internal opinion poll hostile to recognition, and a challenge to the ACAS recommendations in the courts. In a last attempt to publicise the case through APEX alone, three ministers, Fred Mulley, Shirley Williams and Dennis Howell, appeared on the picket line in May 1977. Shirley Williams has no regrets about going. At the time it had been a little-noticed gesture of support: 'I didn't envisage that the whirlwind would come. I don't think the strikers did. I don't think the union did.'

The dispute had run for ten months. It was about to get rough. In the view of one commentator with no pro-union partiality, Major General Richard Clutterbuck:[17]

'The dispute was a setback for moderation and patience in that they were tried and defeated. The inevitable result was extremism and violence. NAFF must take a great deal of responsibility for this.'

The violent phase of the long Grunwick dispute lasted for only a few weeks. The Secretary of Brent Trades Council, Jack Dromey, had said bitterly, 'This dispute could have been settled a very long time ago, but for the intervention of NAFF.'

He now decided to call in a mass picket, to achieve by intervention what mediation had failed to do. The mass pickets of trade unionists which crowded through Dollis Hill in June and July 1977 were joined by a number of student activists as their term finished, some from the Socialist Workers Party, as the International Socialists had renamed

themselves. There was blanket media coverage, in sharp contrast to
the indifference that had been shown while the picket line had been
small, peaceful and ineffective. As the pickets tried to stop Ward's
workers in their bus, and the police pushed or threw back the pickets,
television had a ready-made theatre of conflict, with guaranteed
matinee performances. The image of a young policeman lying in a pool
of blood on 23 June, untypical though it was even of the level of
violence during the days of mass picketing, did infinite harm to the
union cause. The mass pickets continued until mid-July, when they
were called off to await the outcome of the court of inquiry under Lord
Scarman set up by the government. Ward, unlike APEX, declined
to be bound by the findings. Only the normal courts of the land
could be sure of his compliance, he maintained. On only one occasion
was the APEX leader Roy Grantham allowed into the Grunwick
plant. This was after the mass picket had begun, and he was not encouraged to find that the meeting was to be chaired by the ubiquitous
Gouriet.

Gouriet and NAFF had meanwhile been active in the courts in
another matter. When the UPW proposed in January 1977 to tell its
members not to handle mail and telecommunications for South Africa
during a week of action, Gouriet went to the courts. He tried and failed
to obtain the support of the Attorney General in the case, citing the
1953 act once more. Sam Silkin declined to act, and Gouriet's first
attempt to do so in his own name failed, the court holding that
matters involving public rights and services were for the government.
Undeterred, Gouriet went to the Court of Appeal. There Lord Denning
and his colleagues granted a temporary injunction and rebuked the
Attorney General. Although later the House of Lords performed what
had become almost its traditional function by reversing Denning in its
turn, NAFF had shown that litigation brought considerable dividends
in publicity. Gouriet was now ready for a third and final joust with the
UPW.

During the mass picket at Grunwick the local Cricklewood branch
of the UPW had voted to black the Grunwick mail. Action against the
union nationally was not possible, since it had told the postmen to
desist while it argued for an amendment of the law to allow it the
freedom to act. The men went ahead with their action, and were
suspended, thus closing down the whole postal district. NAFF then
organised its own 'pony express' operation, collecting the backlog of
mail from Grunwick and posting it all over the kingdom. The Grun-

wick strikers had no more weapons to deploy. The ACAS decision in favour of their recognition, upheld in the High Court, suffered the rare distinction of concurrence between Lord Denning in the Court of Appeal and the House of Lords in ruling against them. The Scarman Report recommended the reinstatement of the strikers, and said that Grunwick had acted 'within the letter but outside the spirit of the law'. It did not prejudge the issue of union recognition, then still before the House of Lords, merely observing that 'union recognition, if properly encouraged and responsibly exercised, could in the future help the company as well as its employees'. Ward rejected these findings contemptuously, using language reminiscent of the NAFF tracts. The strikers were not reinstated.

NAFF had won. It had succeeded in finding a surrogate who would not flinch or compromise. It had spun out the processes of conciliation until the unions' frustration led them into a mass picket which distracted attention from the real cause in which they gathered. The outcome was bitterly resented on the left. Playwright David Edgar, with a fine ear of his own for middle-class angst, regrets it:

'All these people came together and said, we are for freedom; and I think that was a very successful political device. In my view it was a hijack, but it was an extremely successful piece of political sleight of hand, to associate the left with authoritarianism and the right with liberty.'

More, NAFF's propaganda was successful in smearing the blood of violent days across the record of many peaceful months, and in influencing Conservative spokesmen to use the same language. Keith Joseph attacked the Scarman Report in strong terms. He had already used lurid language about the demonstrations[18] – '"Moderates" behind whom Red Fascism spreads' – linking the ministers who had appeared on a small and peaceful picket line with the later mass action. The Conservative Party, some felt, had used Ward at arm's length against the government, though it was uneasy about clasping him in too close an embrace. The Conservatives had been used in their turn; their language and propaganda on this issue were now almost indistinguishable from that of NAFF. The demonstrators outside Grunwick had lost. Paul Foot of the SWP acknowledges it as:

'. . . the most appalling defeat . . . This was at a time when we were supposed to be starting the revolution. We were defeated over a cut-and-dried case where most people supported the trade union movement against the employer.'

In all the arguments about standards, over censorship, morality, abortion and education, the sense of progress inculcated in the sixties had faltered, sometimes recovering, sometimes stalling. Grunwick marked a point of counter-revolution. Talk of Marxist fascism, the evil continuum of violence, the road to Auschwitz and the Gulag (these three are from Paul Johnson's farewell letter to the Labour Party in 1977) became part of the rhetoric of politics. The new pessimism spoke in its own tongue, and the leadership of the Conservative Party was to prove quick to learn it. Lord Chalfont was right, the party seemed to say: it *is* happening here. In all the sound and fury few people gave a thought to Mrs Jayaben Desai, and the Asian ladies outside Grunwick, who ended the dispute as isolated as they began, with the condition of their community as unremarked as the cause of their grievance.

11

BLACK BRITISH

In the 1960s the argument had been about newcomers. They were black or brown. They settled in some density in the only areas open to those of their limited means: the inner cities. They were visible, different, and resented by many in the host community, who gave them no thanks for doing the jobs rejected by the British in what was still a full-employment society. Although some even then took up industrial struggles for rights at work, or formed associations inspired by the rising black consciousness of the time, notably in the United States, the majority saw the political battle about their status and future conducted over their heads. The white liberals and the white racists who carried it on did so on their own terms. The former assumed integration in a multi-racial society; the latter racial tension leading to catastrophe.

Roy Jenkins had commended his Race Relations Acts in the 1960s as assisting integration, which he saw as: '. . . not a flattening process of assimilation, but as equal opportunity accompanied by cultural diversity, in an atmosphere of mutual tolerance.'

His colleague Roy Hattersley, who represented Sparkbrook, the first area of Britain to be the subject of a detailed study of race relations,[1] tried to link the desirability of integration with the necessity for controls on entry: 'Without integration, limitation is inexcusable; without limitation, integration is impossible.'

It was easier to achieve limitation, however, by a series of racially discriminatory statutes, than it was to attack the discrimination which fed upon the fears which those statutes were intended to assuage. The very phrase 'race relations' was perceived as a euphemism for the differences between black and white, and the threats, fears and prejudices which poisoned their relationship. After the shameful nadir of 1968, many in the black communities echoed the dictum of A. Sivanandan of the Institute of Race Relations:[2]

'What Powell says today, the Tories say tomorrow and Labour legislates on the day after.'

The black British began to assert themselves, as they found that, even when they had passed the immigration hurdle, even when born in Britain, they remained a problem to be discussed rather than an asset to be utilised – unequal in their diversity, unable to subsist on the tolerance of a minority of their white fellow citizens, unsure when the tacit hostility of the rest would move from discrimination to violence. Some of the white liberal establishment were hurt at this suspicion and resentment.

Sivanandan himself, once the librarian of the Institute of Race Relations, which was splendidly maintained by the white establishment in London's Jermyn Street, engineered its removal from these environs and became director in his turn. The former director, Philip Mason, lamented that it had:[3]

'. . . moved from Jermyn Street, where it was well placed to influence Members of Parliament and civil servants, to premises near Pentonville, where they would see more of black immigrants.'

(Mason himself resided in a farmhouse fifteen miles from Winchester, purchased because it was 'within easier reach of London' than his previous house.) In 1971 the Institute had been attacked by one of its own researchers as 'a minor obstacle in the struggle of black people for freedom, justice, and a better life'. To the chagrin of some of its council, its monthly newsletter Race Today seemed, in Mason's words, 'to take the emotional line and back the underdog every time'.[4] The gap between the underdog and the top dogs of the liberal establishment was not to be closed in the seventies, as the debate about immigration became more and more one of the status and role of black and brown people in a mainly white society, and 'the numbers game' a metaphor for other things.

The 1971 Immigration Act had been about the numbers game. It was the turn of the new Tory government to legislate. In opposition, Heath, with an eye on Powell, had called for immigration to be severely curtailed. A new Immigration Act introduced the concept of 'patriality' by limiting the right of abode in the United Kingdom to those with a parent or grandparent born there. While it was possible that such people might be dark-skinned immigrants from the New Commonwealth, the probability was that such 'patrials' would be overwhelmingly the white denizens of the Old Dominions. It was seen by the black British as openly racist legislation. While more patrials could come in, their kin, as 'non-patrials', would have to join the queue for work permits. Primary immigration from the non-white Commonwealth was stopped by the expedient of patriality. The basic distinction between all Commonwealth citizens and aliens was thus

Private Eye comments: Harold Wilson ennobles his secretary after the row about land reclamation

... and Keith Joseph sees his leadership bid collapse after an unwise speech in Birmingham

'I want to be Prime Minister, of course I do. And 1976 would be a good year for it.' — Mrs Thatcher   9 January 1976

Above: A prophetic guess that the next occupant of Downing Street would be James Callaghan

Waiting for the crisis: Energy Secretary Tony Benn in 1976

The storm breaks: Healey tells the Labour Party conference that Britain must negotiate with the IMF

A powerful slogan for the SNP

Anti-abortion: Malcolm Muggeridge addresses 80,000 demonstrators in Hyde Park

Women say no to the Corrie Anti-abortion Bill in 1979

Jubilee snapshot: The Queen with her husband, four children, Princess Margaret, Captain Mark Phillips and Lord Mountbatten on the balcony of Buckingham Palace. Lord Mountbatten was assassinated by the IRA in 1979

Below: Jubilee street party, Whitechapel

Above: Women strike back: graffiti comments on sexist advertisements, 1979

James Callaghan, now leading a minority government, puts his balancing skills to good use with the skateboard craze in 1977

dropped. The non-whites would be able to come to Britain only with a specific work permit issued by the Department of Employment, unless they were (and could prove they were) the dependants of people already here. Such dependants had further to be under eighteen or over sixty-five, and the waiting and proving process involved led to many of the younger ones passing the age of eighteen, and many of the older ones dying off while they waited to join their families. The principle of racial distinction, and therefore of discrimination, was built into the legislation. For a generation, the number of black and brown patrials would be tiny. The number of white patrials ran into many millions.

The Labour opposition protested at these features of the bill, and promised to repeal its discriminatory features. In fact they went no further than to remove the retrospective power to deport illegal immigrants long resident in Britain, and to allow entry to husbands and fiancés of women already living in the country. At the same time a review of immigration and nationality law was promised, and a new Commission of Racial Equality (CRE) set up under the 1976 Race Relations Act, which attempted to outlaw discriminatory acts on the basis of their effect as well as their intention. The legislation was well meaning, although described by Sivanandan as intended to produce 'a class of collaborators who would manage racism and its social and political fallout'. On the face of it, a country which by 1976 had a non-white population of 1.85 million non-whites, just over 3% of the population, of whom around 40% had been born in the UK, should have been able to achieve better race relations fairly quickly. One rationalisation for immigration legislation had been: stop primary immigration and you placate fears in the host community and improve the lot of the 'immigrant-descended population'. This was not how matters developed.

There was a diversity of reasons for the policy's failure. The immigrants came from the further reaches of an empire built on their labour. In Stuart Hall's memorable words:[5]

'If the blood of the colonial workers has not mixed extensively with the British, then their labour-power has long entered the economic bloodstream of British society. It is in the sugar you stir; it is in the sinews of the famous British "sweet tooth"; it is in the tea-leaves at the bottom of the next "British" cuppa.'

Often they had moved along the sea routes of empire long before their British landfall – blacks to the West Indies, Asians to East Africa,

Chinese to Singapore. When they arrived in the great British cities which had grown with empire, they found themselves in competition for housing with the host population in the inner areas which were already in decline. Ranjit Sondhi, a Birmingham community worker, describes what happened in the city of the Chamberlains:

'It was only in those areas, the transition areas, the twilight areas, where people did not organise against the blacks, that they could get the houses, or where they could live in multiple occupation because nobody would take them as tenants. So they could group together and take over, say, a Victorian dwelling and live six to a house. [New-comers] looked obviously for places where they were most secure, and therefore built around the areas where they first settled, a little community in which their family could move socially and linguistically at ease.'

The process was accentuated by local authorities' lending and rehousing policies. By avoiding dispersal in deference to white fears and prejudices, they actually increased those fears by the visible mass of immigrant concentrations. Lumb Lane, Soho Road, Railton Road: streets, neighbourhoods, changed to multiracial occupancy. Ageing long-time residents, brought up on the vanished certainties of empire, lost in a transferred environment, did not appreciate the pressures and prejudices elsewhere which brought the newcomers among them.

These misunderstandings multiplied. Why was the local park full of Pakistanis of an afternoon? Surely because they had all flocked to England to claim the dole, as a widely circulated scurrilous poem proclaimed. The fact of sweated labour on the night shift, leaving afternoons the only few hours in the twenty-four not occupied by work or sleep, was not appreciated. Why were black youths so visible on the streets, always hanging about, often moved on by the police? Surely they were a threat, a menace. Again the facts of youth unemployment, the sheer impossibility of being anywhere else other than the streets, were not taken into account. The misgivings knotted themselves among more lurid fears, of 'an enemy within'. Stuart Hall marks the outline of this terror:[6]

'"He" is nameless; "he" is protean; "he" is everywhere. He may even, we're told at one point, be inside the Foreign Office, cooking the immigration figures. But someone will name him. He is "the Other", he is the stranger in the midst, he is the cuckoo in the nest, he is the excrement in the letterbox. "He" is – the blacks.'

When in 1972 the Conservative government had allowed Ugandan Asian refugees, fleeing the vile tyranny of Idi Amin, to enter Britain as the citizens of the UK and colonies which their passports proclaimed them to be, the hysteria about a conspiracy on behalf of 'them' was whipped up once more. Even Heath and Robert Carr, it was murmured, must be part of it.

The Ugandan Asians were a brown bourgeoisie in the making. They brought skills, found jobs in accountancy, clerical work and trade, soon settled in, with some becoming millionaires within the decade. In that sense they were untypical. The black and brown immigrants and their British-born children faced considerable difficulties in moving up the scale of employment. The 1976 PEP survey found that their pattern of work was very different from that of the whites. 8% of West Indians had non-manual jobs. 8% of Pakistanis, 20% of Indians, 30% of Afro-Asians had them, against 40% of whites. Only 18% of whites, on the other hand, were semi-skilled or unskilled labourers, as against 26% of Afro-Asians, 32% of West Indians, 36% of Indians and 58% of Pakistanis. This was not just a matter of qualifications. 79% of whites with college degrees were in managerial or professional jobs; only 31% of blacks with the same qualifications had such jobs. Twice as many immigrants were working shifts, on lower wages, with poorer prospects of promotion. Early in the 1970s a number of strikes protested against the poor conditions and discrimination suffered by migrant workers. Initially these often embarrassed local trade unions. The strike of Indian workers at Mansfield Hosiery Mills, Loughborough, in 1972 was for higher wages and equal job prospects with the whites. Their union had to be pushed hard to make the strike official. At Imperial Typewriters, Leicester, where two-thirds of the workforce was Asian, a prolonged strike in 1974 was carried on against the open hostility of many of the white workers. The strike was won, but the factory was subsequently closed down by its multinational owners. Thereafter things changed. The unions became more involved in the struggles of the new black and brown recruits whom they had accepted with some reluctance, as the extent of their exploitation as an under-class became clear. At Grunwick in 1977, there was widespread union support for the Asian strikers, cracked only by legal threats against supportive action and by the counterproductive violence of the mass pickets once frustration boiled over.

Grunwick was a defeat, and a heavy one, for blacks as well as for the trade unions. By this time the shadow of unemployment in the recession was falling across their path. Least unionised, often less skilled, the black and brown workers became the first to be pushed out. The raw despair of that rejection has been brilliantly captured in Linton Kwesi Johnson's poem 'Inglan is a Bitch':[7]

> well mi dhu day wok an' mi dhu nite wok
> mi dhu clean wok and mi dhu dutty wok
> dem seh dat black man is very lazy
> but if y'u si how mi wok y'u woulda sey mi crazy
>
> Inglan is a bitch
> dere's no escapin' it
> Inglan is a bitch
> y'u bettah face up to it
>
> dem have a lickle facktri up inna Brackly
> inna disya factri all dem dhu is pack crackry
> fi di laas fifteen years dem get mi laybah
> now awftah fifteen years mi fall out a fayvah
>
> Inglan is a bitch
> dere's no escapin' it . . .

As the migrants were displaced in the recession, so their children, born British, often found no better way forward. They were an angry generation. For Asian children, with intense and tenacious family loyalties, the achievements had to be earned in a bilingual world: one language at home, the other at school. It took a long time before some teachers and educational authorities realised that for such children bi-culturalism was as necessary as the bilingual skills they acquired. There was no melting pot at the end of the rainbow of cultures. The headmaster who proclaimed in a Schools Council working paper that 'I do not consider it the responsibility of an English state school to cater for the development of cultures and customs of a foreign nature [but] to prepare children for citizenship in a free Christian democratic society, according to British standards and customs' had no sense of irony. His successors learned differently. The Asian child drew strength from his or her cultural identity, though sometimes there were clashes with traditional values over dress, marriage or morality.

West Indian children had a different problem. Their patois was not recognised as a separate language, so they were assumed to be practised in English. Their family relationships were looser, more free and easy. But their homes in the urban centres were three times as likely to suffer from multiple disadvantage as those of the equivalent white child. So they both exhibited and suffered from the stereotype of under-achievement in the classroom. The attitude of teachers who categorised black children to their own satisfaction as difficult, undisciplined and slow learners transmitted itself to their pupils. Low expectations resulted in another generation of low achievement. The classification of their children downwards infuriated many West Indian parents. (A 1973 Department of Education and Science survey found that there were four times as many children of West Indian parentage in schools for the educationally subnormal as their numbers in the population would warrant.) Bernard Coard, who went on to achieve a dubious notoriety in his native Grenada, wrote a book while in Britain entitled *How the West Indian Child is Made Educationally Subnormal*. It found a large readership.

Even when the child of immigrant origin or parentage performed well at school there were problems. As Stuart Hall puts it:

'They've done all the things they ought to have done in order to become good black British citizens. They've been to British schools, they've got the qualifications, they've turned up for those kind of jobs, and they find a kind of systematic denial of the opportunities open to them. Now I think they are really in very deep trouble. [They] can't answer the question "who are they?" They're not West Indians any longer. They're clearly not British, or if they're British, they're British of a very special status, because they're not getting access to all the things that other British youngsters are getting. They feel deeply alienated from the society, and they're without any kind of confidence in their own qualities and characteristics.'

For young West Indians that alienation could be at the same time assuaged and rationalised in a creed of separateness, such as the belief in Ras Tafari with its distinctive dress, dreadlocks and customs – comfort for the young lost in the English 'Babylon'. Rastafarianism offered a powerful image of another way, another style of life, for young people who could identify neither with the West Indian islands from which their parents had come nor with the bleak Britain in which they had grown up. The bleaker that Britain grew, with rising unemployment, the greater the need for escape to something where the rules appeared bent in your favour rather than against you.

For the young blacks on the streets of Britain's cities, it did not need the accoutrements of the Rastas, or the alleged fondness for ganja and loud reggae music, to put them at odds with the forces of 'law and order', both official and self-appointed. Herman Ouseley, now the assistant chief executive of Lambeth, describes what happened:

'As black youth became more prominent by virtue of their presence on the streets because of high unemployment at an early stage during the 1970s, certainly that was a time when the police saw the black presence . . . particularly of youth, as a threat to society, and started to use powers such as sus just to pick people up and bring charges against them.'

'Sus', as it was called, was the offence of loitering with suspicious intent, for which provisions were included in the 1824 Vagrancy Act. Under the Act, the police had the power to arrest a suspect who had not committed an offence but who they said they reasonably supposed might do so. In the nature of the 'offence' there was no proof, save that a policeman was suspicious. Since black youths were abundant on the streets, not easily distinguishable from one another, to a white police force, the power to arrest was much abused. Wholly innocent people felt no better for being assured that they were 'asking for trouble' if they were out on the streets. Freedom of movement is essential to a normal ordered life. One example, shown on television, concerned a schoolboy who was stopped on his way to school and taken to the police station. Why were the police suspicious? Because he was carrying books; and what would a black boy be doing with books at 9.00 a.m. in the morning? A whole population of young people were virtually criminalised by association, in a clumsy attempt to forestall the criminal activities of a minority.

The Metropolitan Police Commissioner of the day, Sir Robert Mark, accepts that relations with the police were linked to the social conditions in the areas policed:

'I think blacks became more resentful of the police because it's true to say that they were mostly part of a very underprivileged minority, quite apart from being an ethnic minority, and were going to have the most unsatisfactory and unhappy living conditions. And this would impinge on the police because the policing becomes more difficult as social conditions become more difficult. There's no problem as far as I know in policing the beaches of Eastbourne. It's much more likely to be difficult to police the streets of Brixton.'

In Brixton, on what the blacks called the 'front line', relations were bad. If Mark felt that some events, such as the so-called Spaghetti House siege involving three West Indian hold-up men in a tense confrontation with police over their hostages, were grotesquely misinterpreted by black radicals, police raids on the haunts of the latter and an over-heavy presence at carnivals and meetings greatly increased the tension. So did the police's relations with a section of the press eager for anything which could be built up as black mischief.

Where there were such activities, the street crimes invariably associated with inner-city areas of deprivation and high stress were presented by the press to fit what Stuart Hall, following Stan Cohen, has described as a 'moral panic'.[8] As described in chapter 10, in the late summer of 1972 the press had begun to talk about 'muggings'. There was some mystery about exactly what a mugging was. The term was American, denoting robbery with violence or the threat of violence, usually in the city streets and subways. The treatment of the offence led to its presentation as a crime usually committed by young blacks against elderly whites. The number of black victims – or white assailants – was not given commensurate publicity. Friendly tips from the police to the press ensured a high profile for this crime and its practitioners. It also associated the young black with the kind of nameless threats upon which moral panics thrive. By the late seventies a National Front poster was able to use the image of the black mugger as a convenient stereotype of the enemy within.

It was not until 1980 that the House of Commons Select Committee on Home Affairs recommended the abolition of 'sus'. In the previous year research done for the Home Office itself had shown that the chances of blacks being arrested under the sus provisions were fourteen times higher than those of whites. The Select Committee suggested the immediate repeal of Section 4 of the 1824 Act, because:

'It is not in the public interest to make behaviour interpreted as revealing criminal intent, but equally open to innocent interpretation, subject to criminal penalties.'

The Home Office held back, and the members of the Select Committee had to threaten to move their own recommendations as a bill before 'sus' was struck out of the statute book. Even then, there was a typically British ritual. The Conservative government repealed 'sus' but then replaced it with a new Criminal Attempts Act open to many of the same objections. In any case, by the end of the seventies, it was too late to hope that the abolition of 'sus', even if wholeheartedly carried through, would repair the damage done over the previous decade to police/immigrant relations.

For the brown British, of Asian origin, the complaint against the police was rather different. It was that the police stood by while all manner of assaults were made against them, while the courts appeared to show more sympathy for the racialist than his victims. While there were numerous examples of individuals of West Indian or African descent being attacked, the attacks on Asians, notably on Bengalis in the East End of London, took on a generic flavour to match their hideous name: Paki-bashing. Sometimes these attacks varied directly in intensity with media coverage of the 'race problem'. Paul Gordon in *White Law*[9] has itemised the attacks in 1976, following press hysteria over a family of Malawi Asian refugees who had been temporarily housed (as had whites) at a four-star hotel through bureaucratic error. (Some sample headlines in the following two weeks were: 'Another 20,000 Asians On the Way' – *Sun*; 'Asian Flood Warning' – *Daily Express*; and 'Another Race War Warning by Enoch' – *Daily Mirror*.) Killings on the streets, or in the home (one seventy-six-year-old Asian woman was tied to her chair and burned to death in Leamington Spa), were only the sharp edge of the hostility. In 1978, after the murder of a young Bengali, Altab Ali, in Whitechapel, an investigation by the television programme *This Week* showed the multiple layers of racial hostility with which the Bengali community had to live. By this time, self-defence groups among young blacks and Asians had formed to try to protect their communities. They believed the police were lax in doing so. And they saw the police presence more often than not apparently escorting the provocative and menacing marches of the National Front.

With the comfort of hindsight it is possible to say that the National Front never amounted to all that much more than 'the tiny band of former Nazis, Empire Loyalists, racists and cranks' (Martin Walker's phrase[10]) which constituted its beginnings. It emerged from the shadows in response to each new immigration scare in British politics – usually the arrival of another group of Asian refugees. It was prone to splits and ferocious internal purges, like other extremist groups. It lived within its fantasies, plausible only to the self-deluded. Yet its presence cast a shadow over the communities which it menaced, and its clashes with opposing demonstrators brought a violence to the city streets which had been unknown since the thirties.

In 1973 the National Front was able to exploit the decision of the

Heath government to allow Ugandan Asian refugees into Britain, both by recruiting from the wilder shores of the Monday Club and the Conservative Party, and in electoral support. At a by-election in West Bromwich the Front candidate, Martin Webster, won 16% of the vote in May 1973, saving his deposit, unlike the assorted NF candidates in the February 1974 general election. Marching through London to protest at the incoming Labour government's amnesty for illegal immigrants, the Front discovered new publicity when a counter-march was taken over by militant elements in the International Marxist Group. In a clash with the police, one student demonstrator was killed – the first such death in postwar Britain. The police were placed in the position of protecting the Front. The NF leadership saw a rich reward in such activity. Its leader, John Tyndall, in a style reminiscent of Oswald Mosley, harped on the need to show the flag, to march through immigrant areas, and not to let 'red mobs' stand in the way. Such marches could serve the double purpose of intimidating the inhabitants but allowing the NF to pose as the upholders of the right of assembly, under police protection. The result was sometimes sickening violence, notably at Lewisham in 1977.

On the surface the National Front was, and remains, an orthodox political party of the far right. It contested local and national elections. In 1976, at the height of the furore about the Malawi Asians, NF candidates polled 43,000 votes in Leicester – an average of 18.5%. Its candidates were shown on television warning doorstepped house-holders that 'rule by the coloureds' and 'a coffee-coloured nation' were imminent. A defector from the NF, Kingsley Read, was one of two National Party candidates elected in Blackburn. Then, in some by-elections in 1977, the NF nosed ahead of the Liberal Party, notably at Stechford. There the anti-fascist Paul Foot, candidate of the Socialist Workers Party (SWP) was mortified to find that:

'It was an utter disaster really, for us, and for me . . . We'd thought there was going to be a big rise in socialist consciousness, that people would be against the Labour government because it wasn't left-wing enough, and therefore that that was something we could catch, if we stood . . . When we said, "Will you vote for us?" a lot of them said, "Well, we're not voting Labour anyway."'

Foot and the SWP canvassers revisited the disaffected on polling day:

'I remember about a dozen people being a bit embarrassed when I came to the door, saying, "We didn't vote for you" (they weren't unfriendly to me at all) "We didn't vote for you – we voted for the National Front."'

The National Front forced the Liberals into fourth place at Stechford, and polled almost 3000 votes. They were third again in nearby Ladywood, where the local Labour Party was so moribund that its former agent was revealed to have been a fascist infiltrator. In local elections in Greater London in the same year, the NF won enough support to make it arguable that, were there a PR system of the type then under discussion for devolved assemblies, the party would win representation. The Birmingham community worker Ranjit Sondhi noted that:

'The National Front were getting powerful in areas which are not dominated by black settlements but which are close to them . . . where people are looking to move up, and are being held back, so they think, by the blacks.'

There was support elsewhere too, among what Martin Webster called the 'robust young men' of the football terraces. Stuart Hall saw this as the NF's main chance to move beyond the frightened and the frowsty to a new generation:

'It sort of plugs itself into the territorial loyalties of those kids who are clustering on the football terraces. It begins to latch into working-class neighbourhood culture, and it affirms the kids' feelings about their locality, their local whiteness. It put Britain and British and whiteness into the vocabulary of youth culture. I think this is a very dangerous moment indeed.'

Against this, a different force was mobilised: the Anti-Nazi League. Its declared aim was to make anti-racism fashionable. The driving force initially came from the Socialist Workers Party, who brought a real flair to its organisation and for once left their dreary sectarianism at home. Peter Hain was one of the founders, who realised that street confrontation with the NF had not diminished its electoral appeal:

'Many of us felt that the kind of throwing a brick syndrome wasn't getting anywhere, and there was the big clash at Lewisham in 1977. And so we decided on a different route, which was militant where it needed to be . . . but at the same time broadened the whole focus of it to have footballers against the Nazis, skateboarders against the Nazis, rock against racism gigs, in an attempt to get through to young working-class kids for whom it had become almost fashionable to be racist.'

This the Anti-Nazi League succeeded in doing. Thanks to pop concerts, carnivals and the involvement of the folk heroes of the young, anti-racism did become fashionable in its turn. The NF's main growth area was suddenly blocked off. It was essentially a movement within the white community. Paul Foot accepts that:

'One of the features of the ANL was that there weren't that many black people in it. The young blacks didn't really respond to the ANL . . . Of course the blacks were appreciative of it and friendly to it, but they didn't mobilise behind it in the way those young whites did.'

One reason for this was that whites and blacks responded to the National Front in different ways. It was easy for the whites to see it as Hitlerism reborn, evil incarnate, which could be isolated and destroyed as prewar fascism had been. The blacks saw the NF as the exploitative, overt part of a pattern of prejudice. To them it was not the only form of racism against which a stand had to be made, as it seemed to be for what Herman Ouseley calls 'the liberal lobby in society; people who were prepared to take to the streets in forms of demonstrations and counter-demonstrations against the National Front as a way of salving their own consciences . . .' The demonstrations had not stopped institutional racism:

'These people didn't go back and alter the way in which their organisations operated or their trade unions or their schools, and as a consequence black people still felt betrayed, because whereas that head-on opposition on the streets was to be welcomed it didn't alter anything. In fact it deflected away from the struggles on the estates, the struggles for greater equality and justice and access to resources which were not happening.'

Racism in the institutions was the fundamental issue. Too often it was shirked. There had been outrage in Parliament when it had been disclosed that Indian brides arriving at Heathrow had been subjected to virginity tests. The practice was stopped, but the mentality which could devise it lingered in officialdom. This mentality could be detected in the incredulity with which bona fide relationships were challenged and tested in immigration appeal cases. An Indian or Pakistani domiciled for a decade or more in Britain sought to bring his wife and their children to join him. Too often the High Commission reaction in Delhi or Islamabad was one of blank disbelief. Challenged to prove the relationship, questioned separately so that anomalies appeared in the different answers of mother and children, the applicants often failed. So did the appeals on their behalf held in distant Birmingham – more often, it seemed to some MPs, after the removal of Alex Lyon as Home Office minister in 1976. It was possible for a Member of Parliament who had known a constituent of Asian origin for years, who had seen photographs proudly displayed of the offspring as they grew, to find himself arguing for the consanguinity of the family members in an adjournment debate to a Home Office minister kitted out with all officialdom's answers as to why it could not be so. For the MP, it produced a vicarious sense of outrage. To the applicants themselves it was deeply felt: a total injustice. What of the courts?

The House of Lords took a restrictive view of cases involving racial discrimination. The obiter of some judges and magistrates revealed to all except themselves the attitudes they brought to the bench. Most notorious of all was Judge McKinnon, who heard the case brought against John Kingsley Read of the British National Party for incitement to racial hatred. At a meeting in 1977, immediately after the murder of an Asian, Gurdip Singh Chaggar, by a mixed group of assailants, Kingsley Read had said:

'Last week in Southall one nigger stabbed another nigger. Very unfortunate. One down, a million to go.'

McKinnon's directions to the jury indicated that he believed Read's speech to be no more than robust argument. Along with some random reminiscences of his public schooldays, he felt able to remark:

'Goodness knows, we have a million and a half or more unemployed already, and that all the immigrants are going to do is to occupy the jobs that are needed by our local population. These are matters upon which people are entitled to hold and to declare strong views expressed in moderate language . . .'

Read was found not guilty as charged, and the judge in 'wishing him well' said, 'You have been rightly acquitted but in these days and in these times it would be well if you were careful to use moderate language.' A parliamentary delegation which went to the Lord Chancellor were told by that urbane figure that there was little he could do.

Although primary immigration from the New Commonwealth had long since ceased, each new scare or scandal brought out a fresh flurry of pledges about curbs. Blacks saw this as a competition in which they would be guaranteed to lose. It seemed to them, as Herman Ouseley puts it, that:

'Immigration remained an obsession, because if you weren't seen to be advocating tight and absolute immigration controls you would be seen as the enemy of the ordinary people of Britain.'

Anthony Beaumont-Dark, then a councillor, subsequently a Tory MP, remembers the time as one when the first question asked – often in traditional Labour areas – was: 'When are you going to do something about this bloody immigration?' That something had been done, and long before, was not an answer that came easily to the lips of politicians. 'Immigration' remained code for the racial mix of British urban society.

It was against this background that Margaret Thatcher, as leader of the opposition, went on television in January 1978 to make what appeared to be off-the-cuff remarks about race. The coloured population was rising; it would be four million by the end of the century:[11]

'Now that is an awful lot and I think it means that people are really rather afraid that this country might be rather swamped by people with a different culture. And, you know, the British character has done so much for democracy, for law, and done so much throughout the world, that if there is any fear that it might be swamped, people are going to react and be rather hostile to those coming in.'

She then mentioned the National Front. People didn't agree with the National Front, but 'at least it's talking about some of the problems'.

The terminology was deliberate. It had not welled up out of her subconscious, as some embarrassed briefings tried to suggest. She had told her advisers beforehand what she proposed to say. One, who 'reacted with horror', was slapped down with the remark that that was what people thought, so why not say it? The electoral dividends were not in doubt. Six weeks later, at the first subsequent by-election, a Conservative gain was registered, with polls indicating that half the voters who switched had done so on this issue. Among the 10,000 letters Mrs Thatcher received after her broadcast were many from Labour voters. In populist political terms this was one of the 'social issues' which pollsters had identified as fertile ground for the opposition. It cut deep into the white working-class vote. It rallied those Conservatives who had been disaffected by Heath's admission of the Ugandan Asians, some to the point of joining the National Front. And it dismayed the black and brown communities, who saw it as what Ouseley calls 'fodder for the racists'. Dipak Nandy, who had earlier been the founder/director of the Runnymede Trust, sees a 'three-year itch' in the politics of race and immigration:

'Politicians have convinced themselves, from the 1960s onwards, that there is a vast mass of racist opinion outside, waiting to be appeased, and if only they can throw another chunk of flesh, the sharks will go away. In fact all it does is to confirm the sharks in their belief that they're on the right track, and there's more where that came from.'

As immigration had virtually dried up, the 'more' for the incoming Conservative government in 1979 could only be achieved by further tightening the regulations on the entry of spouses or dependants, together with tougher methods of policing. 'Operation Swamp' and the riots which followed it were less than two years away. During the 1979 election large-scale protests against a National Front election meeting in Southall led to ferocious clashes between demonstrators and the police Special Patrol Group. Feelings ran high in Southall, where there had been a spate of racial murders. There were casualties on both sides. But, while hundreds of demonstrators were speedily charged with a number of offences, the use of excessive violence by the SPG led to not a single officer being named, disciplined or charged. The schoolteacher Blair Peach had been killed in the fracas. There were no regrets, no apologies. The new Metropolitan Commissioner, Sir David McNee, contented himself by saying:

'If you keep off the streets in London and behave yourselves, you won't have the SPG to worry about.'

The independent inquiry into what happened at Southall provides a sombre epilogue to the decade. It said:[12]

'Those who belong to racial minorities and face repeated public and private expressions of hostility need some rock to cling to, some social institution they can trust to operate impartially, if they are not to be reduced to despair. Of all institutions, those whose impartial operation it is most important to maintain are the police and the law courts. Deprive people of the sense that they enjoy the protection of the law and of the agencies that enforce and administer it, and you destroy their whole feeling of security and any sense that they might otherwise have preserved that they are part of the society within which they live.'

It was never the case that all British citizens who were immigrants or of recent immigrant descent felt alienated from that society. There were spectacular success stories among the East African Asian business community. Burgeoning Asian Conservative groups had needed to be placated by William Whitelaw after his leader's 'swamping' speech. A new bourgeoisie developed, often uneasy at the independence and truculence shown by its youngsters. There was political involvement. A CRE survey[13] in the 1979 election showed a higher turnout rate among Asians than among non-Asians in eighteen of nineteen constituencies surveyed, and pointed out that in eighty-one constituencies the ethnic minority vote was more than 5% of the electorate. Electoral influence would not be long delayed. Nor would black representation, moving from the council chambers to Westminster.

For the new British there was another vertical route to success: sporting prowess. First athletics, then boxing, football and cricket saw the arrival of black and brown stars. The young Daley Thompson, the most comprehensively gifted of all British athletes, presented a very different picture of that 'coffee-coloured nation' mulled over in the neurotic fantasies of the National Front. However, the coloured star on the football pitch or in the boxing ring was often identified with by his young admirers not just for his skills but also for the racism with which he was greeted. The grunts and chants of 'Coon' on the terraces were a perpetual reminder to the young blacks of the society in which they lived. In that society, as it had developed, many of the younger generation, born black and brown British – cut off from both their parents' inhibitions and their parents' dreams – went their own way.

There was, Herman Ouseley believes:

'. . . a split in terms of the approaches to the defence of black communities [between] on the one hand the community organisations which had established black leadership, who would want to work through the established procedures of liaison and negotiation, looking to the police and the other bits of the state apparatus to defend them, by and large; and black youth saying, no, these people have never defended us, in fact they are our oppressors, and we take to the streets.'

In the summer of 1981, at a low point in Margaret Thatcher's first administration, that was exactly what they did. The reason why, out of a hundred thousand reasons, is illustrated by a case submitted in evidence by the National Council for Civil Liberties to the Scarman Inquiry.[14] Errol Madden, an eighteen-year-old art student, was arrested on 9 October 1980 as he walked home from the cinema:

'[He was] locked in a cell and interrogated for three hours during which time he was also subjected to racial abuse and taunts that his mother was "on the game". He was denied the use of the telephone, and claims that he was threatened with a "torture room" and having hot water poured over him . . . He was charged with stealing two dinky cars, for which he had the receipt in his bag when arrested. After three hours of racist abuse Errol signed a statement, written out by a policeman, confessing to stealing the cars.'

Four months later the charge was dropped. Errol had dropped out too, badly shaken, leaving art college. The fate of Errol Madden, and of many thousands like him who suffered much more, explains why, at the conclusion of the seventies, it was some of the black British who were saying to the host community and its institutions:[15]

> . . . it too late now
> I did warn yu.

12

THE WHEATGERM AGE

Quite suddenly, bigness and blandness were not enough. In the seventies size came to be a disadvantage: the size of families and populations, the spread of urban 'comprehensive redevelopment' and the motorway network, the merged molochs of industry and their green siblings, the prairie farms. For many of the new campaigners, Kipling's Gods of the Market Place had displaced the Gods of the Copybook Headings; it was time for old wisdom to be re-learned. The community should reassert itself against the remote bureaucracy of planning, the small-scale enterprise against the multinational, the wholesome and the natural against the synthetic and the artificial – be it a matter of bread, beer or bleached veal. Above all, the family of man should realise its own interdependence, that there was what one effective tract of the times called 'Only One Earth', to be shared rather than ravaged.

One contributor to the *Scientific American* in September 1970 caught the new mood exactly. G. Evelyn Hutchinson wrote:

'Many people . . . are concluding on the basis of mounting and reasonably objective evidence that the length of life of the biosphere as an inhabitable region for organisms is to be measured in decades rather than hundreds of millions of years. This is entirely the fault of our own species.'

The piece was reprinted, with others, in the portentous Club of Rome publication *The Limits to Growth* in 1972. There were many similar studies reproducing fast in the ecosystem of the radical book-shop, with titles such as *The Population Bomb*, *Blueprint For Survival*, *The Seventh Enemy* and – deservedly the most influential of all – E. F. Schumacher's *Small is Beautiful*. The height of the ecological wave was ridden by the Department of the Environment itself, a super-ministry housed in a new home which did little for the environment and even less for the London landscape. The Secretary of State, Peter Walker, commissioned a number of elegantly written reports for the 1972 UN conference in Stockholm on the Human Environment.

'Pollution: Nuisance or Nemesis?' and 'Sinews for Survival' on natural resources marked a rapid response to the powerful ecology lobby.

This lobby had grown fast, often with American inspiration. Friends of the Earth came to Britain in 1970, to intermingle with the Conservation Society, Save, the Movement for Survival, Transport 2000, the Farming and Wildlife Advisory Group, Planners Against Growth and many more. In 1974 the Ecology Party was formed, five years before the German 'Greens' ran their first slate of candidates in the Euro election. In their study of the movement, Philip Lowe and Jane Goyder point out that concern for the environment moves forward by spasms, not by steady progression – in Britain, often in strong reaction to the excesses of a sustained period of economic expansion.[1] Late Victorian England produced the first interest in urban and rural conservation and the first real anti-pollution lobby. By the 1970s another profound revulsion to the appetites of industrial society was being felt. The young came first. The generation of the flower children sought to re-discover the lost tribe of humankind's beginnings in the hippie commune and the high-school campus alike. They believed in 'the Greening of America', sharing Charles Reich's overblown optimism:[2]

'When, in the fall of 1969, the courtyard of Yale Law School, the Gothic citadel of the elite, became for a few weeks the site of a commune with tents, sleeping bags, and outdoor cooking, who could any longer doubt the cleaning wind was coming?'

Who indeed? Not the radical young who, like Simon and Garfunkel, would 'rather be a forest than a street', and who wanted to oppose the 'consumer fascism' and 'one-dimensional society' which had enslaved their elders. In Britain, as in the USA, they swelled the ranks of the ecology movement, became the militant wing of bodies such as Greenpeace, Friends of the Earth and the League Against Cruel Sports. They ran counter-culture bookshops and health-food co-operatives, organised tenants' resistance to city-centre developers and nuclear power stations. They left a mark, though many moved on.

At this high point, while the demands of the world economy for its natural and non-renewable resources seemed to be growing voraciously year by year, the hype of the ecology lobby found a wide audience across all age groups, though it was (like the students) predominantly middle class. 'Blueprint for Survival', the special report of the *Ecologist* magazine in January 1972, set out the great fear:

'Indefinite growth of whatever type cannot be sustained by finite resources. This is the nub of the environmental predicament.'

The largest audience was reached by the humane, sensible voice of Fritz Schumacher, who sought to reverse the cult of bigness with a new kind of technology, accessible to all, small-scale in application, and 'compatible with man's need for creativity'. He did not hesitate to take issue with the remark of Keynes that the world was not yet ready for a society which preferred the good to the useful, ends more than means. 'Avarice and usury and precaution,' Keynes wrote, 'must be our gods for a little longer. For only they can lead us out of the tunnel of economic necessity into daylight.' Schumacher observed:[3]

'When great and brilliant men talk like this, we cannot be surprised if there arises a certain confusion between fair and foul, which leads to double talk as long as things are quiet, and to crime when they get a bit more lively.'

Schumacher's friendly persuasion, his plea that there had to be something better beyond the economic calculus of modern capitalism 'if people mattered', had a resonance for a world that was to become deindustrialised by neglect and happenstance rather than by design. He wrote:

'Wisdom demands a new orientation of science and technology towards the organic, the gentle, the non-violent, the elegant and the beautiful . . . There is wisdom, if only on account of the smallness and patchiness of human knowledge.'

Many of the co-operative and community groups of the next decade can be accounted Schumacher's children.

Not all prophets spoke so softly. Some eschewed growth except in their own hyperbole, especially in the population lobby. As demand for resources grew, they argued, so did the world's population, and at a crazier pace. Dr Paul Ehrlich, who had had a vasectomy after the birth of his first child, warned that, if the doubling-times of the human population continued on present (1971) figures:[4]

'. . . for about 900 years there would be about 60,000,000,000,000,000 people on the face of the earth. Sixty million billion people. This is about 100 persons for each square yard of the Earth's surface . . .'

(Ehrlich also put his opponents through the numbers game. Of one, a father of ten, he wrote, 'If Barrett's descendants continued his rate of propagation for just ten generations, they would number in the tenth generation ten billion people – three times the entire population of the Earth today.')

There was substantial overkill in campaigning on this level. One of the most effective later campaigners in the ecology movement, Jonathan Porritt, concedes this:

'There was too much emphasis on doom and gloom in the early seventies, and there's a limit to how much people will take of this.'

The credentials of some of those who offered the direst warnings, the starkest predictions, came under counter-attack. The science of ecology became blurred by some 'multi-disciplinary' approaches which projected population growth, resource consumption and pollution in ways which seemed to be of dubious validity. After the oil price hike of 1973–4 and the subsequent recession, it became harder still for the more dramatic predictions of imminent exhaustion of tin, lead and copper within decades, and fossil fuels not so long after, to be taken seriously enough. The doomsters' slips were showing. In the harsh new realities of a collapsed economy, the ecological pressure groups no longer expanded as they had in the early seventies. But they did not vanish either. Concern for resources and the environment permeated much of the new community and single-issue politics of the period.

The combativeness was very much a middle-class phenomenon. Sometimes it put middle-class activists at odds with a locality where their agitation – against mineral extraction, industrial development, or large-scale farming – seemed to put working-class jobs at risk. No one cherishes an unspoiled landscape as much as those for whom it is a new refuge. Tony Crosland, the Secretary of State for the Environment who killed off what he called 'Heathograd' (the Conservatives' plan for a third London airport at Foulness), forfeited environmentalist applause by constantly pointing out that the middle-class campaigners could often afford to ban something which gave the workers an improved life – economic growth. On one notable television programme he appeared to be asleep when a passionate anti-growth film was put on before an approving audience – just resting his weary eyes, he said when he got home.

Elsewhere, the benefits of these campaigns did embrace those who had not been in their forefront. This was notably the case with population limitation. The availability of contraceptives and vasectomy on the NHS in the seventies and the stubborn defence of the reformed abortion laws by women's groups meant that everyone could limit their family size if they so chose. Many did. The birth rate turned down, to no more than replacement levels. The pressure on resources which would have come from an ever-expanding population was therefore eased. In Britain, at least, the population lobby could regard the decade as successful. The problem shifted to one of support for an ageing population by the end of the century.

The environmentalists had their successes in other areas too. The urban planners had bestrode the sixties. Theirs were the inner-city ring roads which often marooned Victorian civic centres in a wasteland of windswept 'precincts' and gaseous tarmac, the ambitious re-developments, the high-rise housing units. If the rewards of the office boom and the dash for growth stuck to them, so did the odium. By the end of the decade, developers were in retreat, and architects an endangered species. They were attacked on both flanks, by the radical young, who sought to save communities from their depredations, and by the middle-aged preservationists, some with near-Betjemania for the Victorian heritage. There was a strong feeling that town and country alike were somehow being concreted over, and the life that could be lived in them eradicated. It was a mood perfectly caught in 1974 by Philip Larkin's 'Going, Going':[5]

> I thought it would last my time —
> The sense that, beyond the town,
> There would always be fields and farms,
> Where the village louts could climb
> Such trees as were not cut down;
> I knew there'd be false alarms.
>
> In the papers about old streets
> And splitlevel shopping, but some
> Had always been left so far;
> And when the old part retreats
> We can always escape in the car.
>
>   *   *   *
>
>   It seems, just now,
> To be happening so very fast;
> Despite all the land left free
> For the first time I feel somehow
> That it isn't going to last,
>
> That before I snuff it, the whole
> Boiling will be bricked in
> Except for the tourist parts —
> First slum of Europe: a role
> It won't be so hard to win,
> With a cast of crooks and tarts.

The alliance of radicals and preservationists fought back. They did not want a world safe for crooks and tarts to live in, especially if they had to share it. Clean-air acts had coaxed the young professionals back into the city centres; many of the rest of the middle class migrated from town and suburb to the country. The earnest newcomers, now immortalised for posterity in the cartoons of Posy Simmonds, commuted or had weekend cottages. They wanted the rural environment to be, well, rural, rather than a series of booming agro-businesses linked by motorways. Yet their own coming changed the environment they often fervently wished to preserve, even fossilise. In the most direct way a powerful and articulate pressure group came face to face with what Fred Hirsch[6] called the social limits to growth. Time and again, both urban and rural community pressure groups called on resident members who were, in their working lives, lawyers, surveyors, teachers, engineers, with the professional skills to confront the planner and the developer on equal terms.

London saw some of the best examples. The developers were much loathed. Harry Hyams, who had commissioned Colonel Seifert to design him a slender, hard-to-let skyscraper at Centre Point, became a favourite quarry of the press. Centre Point was empty for a decade, easier to borrow against than to let to a single tenant. Others of his central London properties also stood idle. (They were advertised by estate agents called Waite and Waite!) Sit-ins, protests, threats of compulsory purchase, hung over the scheme. Other nearby developments, such as the one planned for Tolmers Square in Camden, were stopped. Housing and pubs hung on where the office block was threatened. Then came a battle for Covent Garden, under the shadow of Centre Point itself. The market was moving out to Nine Elms. With land valued at £2 million per acre, there were killings to be made. The GLC believed it had achieved a compromise between conservation and redevelopment. One of its own planners, Brian Anson, who disagreed, helped local residents to set up a Covent Garden Community Association. In its early days it featured many of the Covent Garden working-class community who survived in the area. They gave the hapless Lady Dartmouth, chairwoman of the GLC Historic Buildings Committee, a very hard time. After a noisy public inquiry, the GLC were allowed to enact their compulsory powers over the area, but with near-saturation listing of the buildings and a strong emphasis on conservation.

The buildings were saved. The architect Lionel Esher wrote:[7]

'[It was] a change of consciousness. The epithet "obsolete" was now as indecent for a building as for a person; and within this quite fortuitous square kilometre bounded by six ugly general-purpose streets, the time-honoured notion that knocking down worn-out buildings and replacing them with something better was a useful and often profitable occupation was ruled out. It was no doubt very English that the decision to mothball a particular group of buildings at a particular moment in their history should be made too late for Portland Place or for Smith Square or for Berkeley Square and should now be accorded to this "dear old slum" . . .'

The dear old slum did not retain its old occupation. Anson bitterly commented that, when the community association reported the numbers who had left Covent Garden:[8]

'. . . they omitted to point out that most of those who had left the area were from the traditional working-class community. Nor was it made clear that a steady stream of newcomers – all from the middle class – were moving in.'

The streets where the old community had lived were refurbished for health-food shops, media-facility houses and peddlers of overpriced gewgaws for the tourist.

Other neighbourhoods, less in the public eye, were smashed to fragments without any of the fuss which its media prominence guaranteed for Covent Garden. Central Birmingham, Liverpool around the two cathedrals, and many more, turned to rubble, ring roads and motorway spurs. As in working-class London, the planners knew best. The high-rise, high-energy-consuming boom of the sixties was already over after the ignominious collapse of Ronan Point in 1968 and the discovery of the realities of tower-block life: broken lifts, vandalism and condensation. Population forecasts, as the planners could not have foreseen, pointed downwards. Councillors and planners became contrite about the accommodation units which had replaced homes. The tower blocks remained. Some, such as the notorious 'Piggeries' in Liverpool, became uninhabitable. A whole literature grew up around them, from the graffiti-daubed nightmare future of the novel (and film) *Clockwork Orange* to Mervyn Jones's fine novel *Holding On*, in which the old East End stevedore suffers a stroke in the last undemolished house left among the tower blocks:[9] 'There were eighty-eight families across the street, but no neighbours.'

Not all high-rise was bad, or doomed to degeneration. After its initial redevelopment hubris as 'the Brasilia of the North', Newcastle-on-Tyne won high praise for its Byker tower blocks, maintained with

the same care for community which the city was to put into its new
integrated transport system, the Metro. Elsewhere, some tower blocks
which remained unpopular developed, in the end, their own tenacious
sense of community, even if the caretaker had fled and the lift had
broken down – as Tony Parker discovered during his five-year research into the estate he named 'Providence' south of the Thames.[10]
But the overall conjunction of clearances and redevelopment with
the falling city populations and revenues of the 1970s was often
disastrous. Lionel Esher sums up what they meant for one fine
city:[11]

'Liverpool by the mid-seventies provided the locus classicus of the
collapse of the inner city: the loss of the go-ahead young; the consequent shrinking of the tax base, yet no diminution of the number of
under-privileged needing multiple support, of young children, of the
impoverished old; the loss of jobs within reach of the centre; and
above all the failed, frightening environment.'

Jim Amos, chief executive in the seventies with both Liverpool and
Birmingham, had a taste of the residents' anger when he appeared with
colleagues before a televised public hearing into Liverpool's inner
urban motorway. Rebuilding was, he concedes:

'. . . seen very much as a construction operation. Let's knock down
the old, create something new and then everything's all right . . . There
was little thought to the requirements of society as society.'

To the urban environment, late in the day, there came succour.
General improvement areas, Home Office grants, a fresh impetus
under the Housing Corporation for co-operative schemes, a new wave
of tenants' and community associations: all began to put back into the
blighted urban neighbourhood some of the colour which had been
bleached and leached from it. What these initiatives could not do
was eradicate the blight caused by the incursion of the motorcar, the
flyover, the inner ring road, the urban motorway. Until the late
seventies it was not possible to object to such schemes in terms of
national necessity or priority; objections could only be raised in terms
of whether this or that scheme could be justified on its local merits and
the traffic forecasts upon which the schemes were based. Eventually
the motorway protesters, best financed and best prepared in rural
areas where the middle-class conservationist was often ranged against
cities desperate for traffic relief, changed all that. John Tyme became a
figure of mythic proportions as he roamed the country fighting
set-piece battles against the inspectors at public inquiries marked by

cheerful bourgeois hooliganism. At the Aire valley inquiry in 1975, he proudly narrates the opening exchanges:[12]

Inspector: 'My name . . .'
Uproar.
Inspector: 'But I only want to tell you my name . . .'
John Burnhope: 'Right then, who are you?'
Inspector: 'My name is Ernest Ridge and I am . . .'
Uproar.
John Burnhope: 'Mr Ridge, you have told us your name. That is what you said you wanted to tell us and now you have told it us. We don't want to hear any more. We now wish to hear Mr Tyme.'
Cheers and applause.

Hear him they did. Abundantly. In the end the hearing was abandoned, after heavy press and television publicity. The protesters' 'hooligan' tactics wrung important concessions from the Department of the Environment about the terms of reference of its inquiries. In the following year John Tyme reappeared at Winchester, leading objectors who wished to re-open the Line inquiry into that section of the M3 motorway which would push through the local water-meadows. His 'eyeball-to-eyeball' confrontation with the inspector was abetted by such unlikely rioters as the headmaster of Winchester College and Jennie, Viscountess Enfield. A number of protesters, one dressed as King Alfred, were evicted from the hearing. The inspector, a courteous major general, suffered a heart attack. To some observers this kind of behaviour (taken further at some later inquiries, such as those into the Archway scheme in North London) rarely advanced beyond pure self-interest. Sometimes it was not 'conservationists against mean-minded ministry vandals, but, to some extent, urban conservationists against rural conservationists'.

Mean-minded or not, the road lobby had been riding for a fall. The ambitions of the sixties had built up a considerable self-interest in the Department of the Environment and the road construction units. Too often, planning by attrition had replaced planning by consent. Road plans were not revealed until they had created their own logic: one completed section funnelling traffic into the next district to be softened up until that district begged for relief from the new vehicle pollution. The motorway protesters succeeded, in the teeth of the tradition of secrecy in Britain, in forcing the road planners out into the open and demoralising them once there. In the cuts to capital programmes the road builders therefore became a popular target by the late seventies.

In sharp contrast, another favourite target of the time escaped almost unscathed. Schumacher and other environmentalists had drawn attention to the nuclear power programme. It was taking up more and more of Britain's energy needs, without solving the problem of making safe over many centuries its own waste products. As Britain's own gas-cooled reactors (AGRs) found little favour abroad, there was increasing pressure from the industry and its allies in the Department of Energy for an accelerated programme of orders for pressurised water reactors (PWRs) of the type much used in the United States. This involved a running battle between the Energy Secretary from 1975 to 1979, Tony Benn, and the officials in his own department, much of which never entered the public domain. Concern about dependence on nuclear power, marked by the sun emblem and the slogan 'Nuclear Power – No Thanks', which was one of the most widely displayed badges of the period, centred on the major public inquiry which Benn ordered in 1977.

This was the inquiry into the application of British Nuclear Fuels Ltd to build a reprocessing plant for irradiated oxide fuels at their Windscale plant. It was held from June to November 1977. Three matters were to be decided. Should this reprocessing of spent fuels happen at all? Should it happen at Windscale? And if it did, should it include doubling the plant to handle contracts for foreign waste as well as British? It was conducted by Mr Justice Parker at Whitehaven with elaborate courtesy to the many proponents of alternative energy sources. The Friends of the Earth and associated groups put up a well-marshalled argument ranging from long-term radiation hazards to the danger of plutonium being seized by terrorists to make a nuclear bomb. BNFL's scientists kept rigid upper lips and iron digestions. One said he had eaten a 'beautifully fried' radioactive brill caught near Windscale and had lost half of the ingested radioactivity within two months.

More seriously, the Town and Country Planning Association, in a multifaceted submission over seven days of the inquiry, challenged the whole concept of a future in which society would continue to be run on high-energy lines.[13] In such a society, it argued, the technology took over, creating its own justification for expansion, just as reprocessing would lead to a persuasive case for the fast breeder reactor in 'the plutonium political economy'. The alternative now beckoned:

'If energy is once again going to be scarce and expensive, places are going to be of prime, not secondary, importance. These forms will then have to determine, not be determined by, our life-styles.'

This vision of the alternative life-style did not prevail at the Windscale inquiry. In spite of the fact that the objectors had commanded a sympathetic coverage, in which many thought they had made their case, the findings went against them. But it was not all cost and pain. The inquiry set valuable precedents. Following them, the expansion of the nuclear industry would be approached step by step, in contrast to the onrush that was occurring in, for example, France. In the great array of witnesses there was an impression of many disparate groups who were now prepared to follow the lead of Friends of the Earth, and become active campaigners for a different set of values.

The involvement of large and hitherto 'respectable' organisations in the environmental movement probably counts more to the credit of the direct-action pressure groups who inspired them than the strictly limited results of that action itself. The successful campaigns achieved their aim in publicity. The dumping of non-returnable bottles outside Schweppes depots gave British streets their discreet bottle banks. The Greenpeace voyages to Save the Whales or to stop the dumping of radioactive waste also brought dividends, and, in the 1980s, results. Most spectacular of all were the protests against nuclear tests, which put the Greenpeace mariners at personal hazard, from angry French sailors as much as from radiation.

The radical groups were nervous that they would be 'sucked into the establishment', Jonathan Porritt recalls, and embraced by the seductive processes of 'consultation' rather than remaining their old confrontationist selves. Friends of the Earth won some small successes in Parliament, such as seeing the Endangered Species Act onto the statute book, but their consultative role on bodies like the Waste Management Advisory Council led to constant frustration at being voting down. But Friends of the Earth transformed, by osmosis, the more sedate pressure groups with which they worked; if they were themselves slowed down, others acquired more dynamism from the contact. The process was not always painless. The RSPCA, for example, was torn in the late seventies by a conflict between its traditionalists and younger radicals who were active campaigners against vivisection and hunting. The battle became so fierce that at one stage rival members of the executive were addressing each other through lawyers.

The shock of the new environmentalism was felt in other traditional movements. The Council for the Preservation of Rural England

(CPRE), if it did not move to fresh pastures, at least looked at the old ones with a more eagle eye. Robin Grove-White, the present director, recalls:

'We used to act within a framework of consensus as regards progress and the need for development in terms of growth. What happened in the seventies was that there was much more development thanks to these new bodies.'

The CPRE acquired a harder edge, placed a greater emphasis on matters like resource depletion and population pressure. One of its officials was quoted in a study by Lowe and Goyder as saying:[14]

'We are very media-conscious. This is better suited to the general style of environmental politics which has become much more conflict-oriented. However, unlike some of the more radical groups, we still prefer to clobber a chap in private rather than in public.'

Something of this new mood communicated itself to established bodies like the Nature Conservancy Council, the National Parks and the Countryside Commission as well. Clobbering chaps in private, and in public too, became a style for the times for groups which had previously had the image of rucksack and retreat from the world. The Ramblers Association celebrated the mass trespasses of fifty years earlier with a determined defence of Britain's footpaths, which were disappearing with the hedgerows along which they had run for time immemorial. The Royal Society for the Protection of Birds (RSPB) flung itself into lobbying for the threatened wetlands and estuaries which once teemed with birdlife. It increased its membership sevenfold between 1969 and 1979. In the same period the National Trust's membership rose from 200,000 to one million at the end of the decade. By that time a pressure group within the Trust, organised by a housewife from Hughenden, Audrey Urry, was challenging the Trust's decision to make some of its land available to the Ministry of Defence. The new, vocal middle-class radicals would not go away.

In the literal sense, they had arrived on the scene. The migration back into the countryside was on. Villages within commuting distance of the cities and towns had long been repopulated by the commuters. Professor Howard Newby, who chronicled the changes in the country-side in *Green and Pleasant Land*,[15] analyses how the middle-class incomers soon became a majority in some villages and small towns. They received a shock, though, at the character of their hard-won rural retreat:

'They've found that the reality of the countryside is very different from what they've expected, which tends to be something they've seen in a painting by John Constable, for example. What they find is something very different. They find there are very few animals in the fields in this part of the country [East Anglia]. They find that wildlife in many areas has largely disappeared. They find hazardous chemicals are used over large areas of farmland, and they find that a lot of small woodland and the hedgerows have all been removed. This means that for the first time in the countryside we have an articulate population which knows its way round politically and which is prepared to speak out against the practices of the local farmers and landowners.'

The newcomers flocked to the cause of rural conservation. The areas of beautiful English countryside which were most open to the depredations of the new agribusinesses also had the most rapid rise in protest against them. The south-east had by far the highest membership of nature conservation and local amenity societies in the country. On the downs and the Weald, in the wetlands and estuaries, in the ancient woodlands, the coming of the axe and the plough were marked with alarm. Marion Shoard, a former assistant secretary of the CPRE, sounded the call to resistance in 1980, when she wrote of the 150,000 miles of hedgerow rooted out, the 24 million hedgerow trees gone, along with one third of our woodlands and the meadows, streams and marshes which had nurtured British wildlife. In *Theft of the Countryside* she began:[16]

'The English landscape is under sentence of death. Indeed, the sentence is already being carried out. The executioner is not the industrialist or the property speculator, whose activities have touched only the fringes of our countryside. Instead it is the figure traditionally viewed as the custodian of the rural scene – the farmer.'

This was to mis-state the case somewhat. The point was that farming had become an industry; it was capital intensive, using all the techniques of a successful factory and the newest technology for the longest possible production runs. More and more prosperous farms were owned by pension funds and leased back to farm managers whose job was to get a return on investment. The farmer as husbandman had been replaced by the farmer as factory manager.

So the conservationists in the countryside were taking on a powerful adversary, well equipped with huge implements which could transform the landscape overnight from woodland and meadow to something like the Flanders battlefields of 1916. There was money in it. In Shoard's phrase, 'Every unfelled wood or undrained wetland repre-

sents forfeited profit.' Throughout the 1970s the farmers reaped the
benefits of the EEC intervention payments. In 1980 the direct benefit
to British farmers was in the order of £1500 million. It became
profitable to plough up any remaining piece of downland, to fell any
wood, to drain any wetland, to add a little more to the barley and
wheat mountain. By 1980 Britain was in net surplus in grain production. For a long time the awesome new power of the farmer was looked
on with admiration. 1970s' television programmes abounded with
shots of an armada of huge harvesters or tractors in line abreast,
flanked by Land-Rovers spraying saturation Paraquat into what was
left of the boundary hedgerows. The farmers are indignant that they
were blamed in retrospect for what they did. Oliver Walston, who
farms in Cambridgeshire, puts up a defence:

'Conservationists are right when they say that farmers have drained
land, have pulled out hedges, when they shouldn't have, from a
conservation standpoint. But don't ever forget, the reason a farmer did
it was because the government was asking him to do it, and the
government was paying him to do it.'

If it paid to pull out a hedgerow, or to buy a machine which would
rip an ancient wood to pieces within hours, if you could get a grant or a
tax offset for it, then you did it. And outside the national parks the
conservationists found that local authority planners could not or
would not intervene on their side. Marion Shoard laments the fate of
Graffham Down, Sussex, a medley of marvellous downland and
woods north of Chichester, well known as a haven for plant- and
birdlife, alongside the South Downs Way (which otherwise now has
very little downland to traverse). A Dutch farmer bought it in 1978,
and applied for a grant to clear it. Local protesters were swept aside. A
cosmetic screen of trees had to be retained, to spare the view from the
South Downs Way. The rest vanished beneath the barley. Local
planning authorities did not have the power of intervention given to
their big brothers in the cities. Nor was there such a national spotlight
on what went on in their locality. Notoriety was the lot of those who
destroyed the Euston Arch, and the politicians who let it happen. The
farmer who gouged out the Viking 'Thing-mount' in Little Langdale to
construct a sileage store is already as anonymous as those who once
met there twelve centuries ago. But the rural conservationists began to
construct an early-warning system of their own. They proved adept at
permeating the planning mechanism for the preservation of the rural
villages and small towns where many of them now lived, but in the

set-piece struggles for the environment around them they had less to show. Victories, such as the RSPB and Nature Conservancy Council campaign to save the Ribble Marshes from yet another Dutchman who wished to turn them into polder, were few and expensive. A new phenomenon would appear: the farmer who threatened some rural atrocity in the certain knowledge that he would be bribed not to do it, either by repurchase or compensation. And still the grain mountain grew.

There was one grain mountain much approved by conservationists: the boom in wholemeal products sold by co-operative shops. British diet had diversified throughout the period, become more cosmopolitan as travel became wider. The espresso bar and the Chinese chippy had been followed by the pizza parlour and the takeaway tandoori. Interest in a healthy high-fibre diet had grown too. It proved an ideal outlet for the small co-operative, run by supporters of an 'alternative' style of living. The emphasis switched from the self indulgence of the sixties and the hippy communes to the self-sufficiency of the seventies. Of the three hundred co-operatives flourishing in the late seventies more than half were wholefood retailers, along with bookshops, crafts and design. Some became multimillion-pound businesses, sorely trying the ideals of the founders, as the entrepreneurial spirits chafed at the requirement that all members should be paid the same wage, and were resented in their turn. They found a market quickly, in the middle-class distaste for the processed junk food which dominated the high-street supermarket. They were successful enough to compel imitation as well as admiration. By the eighties many supermarkets included sections given over to homeopathic medicines and health foods. The alternative shopper could hunt for out-of-season delicacies all year round, perhaps pausing to reflect that his aubergine might have come from some Third World country unable to produce the staple diet to feed its own population or basic cash crops to compete with the EEC's own subsidised products.

As for real food, so for 'real ale'. The Campaign for Real Ale (CAMRA), launched in 1971, was a pressure group which did span the classes. Its magazine *What's Brewing* explains why this happened, in the wake of brewery mergers that left an oligopoly of six giant firms with 80% of British beer production:

'It was time to do something about the lacklustre, fizzy apologies for beer that were the only products available in more and more British pubs.'

Within four years CAMRA had built up a membership of 28,000. By 1980 its campaign had forced the hand of the brewers. More than half the pubs in the country were selling real ale. There were also a large number of home breweries. CAMRA meanwhile launched its Pub Preservation Group, catching in its booklet *Pub Preservation* the enthusiasm for the small and the cherished which was at work elsewhere:

'If pubs are taken away then the community is the poorer for it. The buildings themselves often give a sense of security in our changing times. An old town pub is not just an attractive Victorian or Georgian façade, it is a building which is still being used for the purpose for which it was built. The designs of the interiors are as valid – snugs, parlours, each with their own atmosphere . . . Somewhere along the line people have forgotten all this.'

The pub came to be the focal point of redevelopment in the cities. If there was redevelopment, the pub survived, a reminder of times past. If there was an improvement area set up, the pub was refurbished. It was conservationism from an unlikely quarter. CAMRA found imitators quickly. The Vegetarian Society launched a Campaign for Real Bread, which gave a fresh boost to the wholemeal, wheatgerm and muesli market, and the small shops where they flourished.

The Campaign for Real Bread proved to be a nursery for other ideas too. The co-operative idea spread out from bread, beads and book-shops. The proportion of co-ops devoted to wholefood fell from 50% to 2% between 1980 and 1984 as the co-operatives themselves bloomed like Christmas roses in the cold landscape of post-industrial Britain. Ian Brierley of the Co-Operative Development Agency re-marks:

'We've moved out of the candles and sandals era, and are now much nearer to the basic structure of British industry.'

There was an awareness, too, that new initiatives could not and should not be in the form of large-scale aid administered from on high. They had to come from the roots and move upwards. In this, the environmentalism of the seventies played its most formative role. It is easy to laugh at middle-class worthies campaigning to keep the view from their rural retreat intact, to make their urban street a conserva-tion area, or to put a break in the name of amenity on the very economic growth from which they have benefited. It is just as easy to point to their limited success on a national scale. But they did inculcate in the public consciousness an awareness of the limitations of scale, of the exhaustion of resources and the interdependence of humankind. They made it possible for a new kind of countervailing power to be deployed, appropriate for an age of depletion. By the end of the seventies, however, there had been no significant move on the part of the hulks of British manufacturing industry, cut loose in the process of deindustrialisation, to come down to meet the co-ops and the communes which were coming up. There was one attempt of substance. On its shop stewards' instigation, the Lucas Aerospace combine worked through 1974 and 1975 to launch an alternative corporate plan which would both protect them against redundancy and introduce a range of new socially useful products. Neither management nor union hierarchies responded with enthusiasm. Similar hostility has met proposals for alternative technology abroad. The Lucas combine, however, offered a pioneering glimpse of how one alternative to deindustrialisation might be to adapt industry to the environment, instead of the reverse. Without the involvement of industry, the co-operative movement would be doomed to remain on the fringes of British life, with conservation a reactive, defensive process. The coming decade would show if it could be used effectively by the generation who were Schumacher's children.

13

NUDGING THE BANKS

James Callaghan's premiership lasted only three years. So rocky was the first of them that few political observers expected him to complete a second, let alone a third. In that first year he faced the loss of his parliamentary majority, the public discipline of the IMF, and the death of the one senior colleague on whom he could have expected most to rely: Foreign Secretary Anthony Crosland. Although his son-in-law Peter Jay claimed that he saw himself as a Moses leading his people in search of the Promised Land, Callaghan's style was better suited to the close huddle and the well-chosen word than to the wilderness and inspired leadership. The rival whom he had swiftly let go to Brussels, Roy Jenkins, who had described him to Crossman as a unique case 'where a man combined such a powerful political personality with so little intelligence',[1] now sees his period in office more charitably:

'He had a great ability to nudge himself along a channel . . . He navigated not by sitting down in advance and working out his course with instruments but doing it very successfully by instinct.'

This was the only method Callaghan could use in negotiating the uncharted political waters in which he found himself: nudge the banks, and hope to get through. He believed that this caution would win him support when he had to submit himself to the electorate in his own right. One of his youngest cabinet ministers, William Rodgers, remembers that Callaghan used to muse:

'We can win the election if when I go into [it] people will say, "Jim Callaghan is the Prime Minister of this country, he's the able seaman, he's a man who understands the common man."'

Or, as Len Murray describes this common touch:

'He was best when he thought with his stomach. He had every strong intuition about what was possible in the field of politics.'

Such a leader does not put the highest priority on the views of his middle-class activists or their cherished aims. It was later to be a cause of rebuke from them that his government failed to deliver on its manifesto promises. In fact Callaghan's government continued the attempt of the Wilson cabinet to implement further social and employment legislation buttressing the Social Contract, and, in spite of a prolonged procedural rearguard action, nationalised the aircraft and shipbuilding industries. Failures included, in the end: devolution for Scotland and Wales, where the government strove mightily (see chapter 14); and pledges to introduce a wealth tax, reform of Official Secrets, and the reduction of the privileges of private education – in all of which the government strove not at all. Winning time, rather than winning the arguments, sometimes seemed to be its preoccupation. Time for the reduction of inflation to be appreciated. Time for the country to get over the falling sickness of 1976. The key to gaining this time was to win the support, or at least the acceptance, of the major groups in and out of Parliament who held the fate of a minority Labour government in their hands.

The tactic was the same as with the IMF: get what is on offer for the lowest possible price. The trade unions held the line on pay. Callaghan had been their steady ally. His close working relation with his deputy leader, Michael Foot, ensured that whatever the unions wanted in legislation could be delivered (except for the Dock Work Regulation Bill, tailor-made to protect the employment of Jack Jones's TGWU dockers, and destroyed at its last stage by two Labour rebels, John Mackintosh and Brian Walden, soon to be removed by premature death and television presentation respectively). For their part the unions not only contributed an ever more generous proportion of their income to the funding of the Labour Party, but their leaders acquiesced in a second, and nodded at a third, period of pay restraint. By 1977 the purchasing power of the average worker with two children had fallen by 7% since the pay policy had been introduced. Stage 2 of the policy (5% increases with an upper limit of £4) was, wrote Sir Denis Barnes, former Permanent Secretary at the Department of Employment, 'the most severe cut in real wages in twenty years'.[2] All this was done, in Callaghan's first year as Prime Minister, with the lowest figure of industrial disputes recorded for a decade. The accomplishment was against a background of still-rising unemployment, as the impact of deflationary policies worked through.

Inflation was falling rapidly from its 30% peak. It came down to single figures within three years, but by 1977 the hardships of the incomes policy were making it clear that there would not be continued trade union consent. At by-elections in that year, notably in the West Midlands, the angry voices of skilled workers whose differentials had been badly eroded were raised against the government. In November

1976, while the Callaghan cabinet still wrangled over their approach to the IMF, safe seats at Walsall North and Workington had been lost, with swings of 22% and 13%. The Walsall debacle owed something to the departure of the former member, John Stonehouse, to Australia and his subsequent return to face fraud charges, but these were heavy blows. The government had already lost two MPs to the breakaway Scottish Labour Party formed by the maverick Jim Sillars. The overall majority of 3 won in 1974 had melted away. In February 1977 the government was defeated by its own anti-devolutionist backbenchers in a guillotine motion on the legislation (see chapter 14). Unless and until some new bill could be cobbled together, the uncertain support of the Scottish and Welsh Nationalists could not be guaranteed. The government would have to woo the Liberals, and promise to go steady, in both senses of the words.

The Lib–Lab pact

Matters came quickly to a head. Smarting at the IMF cuts, Labour left-wingers threatened to abstain and force the defeat of the March Public Expenditure White Paper when it was debated in the House of Commons. The government squirmed, and dodged away through the device of a vote on the adjournment in which all its supporters abstained. In the arcane procedures of Parliament, such votes are both less and more significant than they seem. This one carried potential dynamite. Had the government's power to command a majority gone for good? Margaret Thatcher thought so, and put down a motion of no confidence. The Scottish Nationalists, riding high in the polls, would support it. They had every expectation of further gains if an election were called. It was the nadir of the government's fortunes. The budget was weeks away. Reports from the by-election campaign in Stechford, caused by the departure of Roy Jenkins to Brussels, were gloomy. The car workers were in revolt. Feelings about the incomes policy and immigration were running high. Jenkins was taking another MP, David Marquand, with him. Crosland was dead. That meant two further by-elections. With a swing like Walsall they would all be lost.

Fortunately for Callaghan, the electoral fortunes of the Liberal Party were in a trough that seemed equally deep after the party's heady days in the political surf in 1974. Throughout the following year the allegations of the egregious male model Norman Scott about Jeremy

Thorpe were poured out to those who would listen. In January 1976, at the same time as further embarrassment was caused for Thorpe by the publication of the official report into the collapse of London and County Securities, Scott made his allegations of 'persecution' in an outburst in open court. In May 1976, after persistent rumour and innuendo had forced Thorpe to allow the *Sunday Times* to publish letters written by him to Scott, the Liberal leader had had to step down. David Steel, a hard-headed Scot who was a premature social democrat in a party of individualists, defeated the combative John Pardoe to take over the leadership. Steel's victory was to be greatly to the Liberals' long-term advantage, but the benefits were slow to appear. The Liberals do not do well during periods of unpopular Labour government. In 1976–7 they did disastrously. The Thorpe allegations continued to reverberate. In Walsall North the Liberal candidate trailed in a bedraggled fifth, well behind the National Front and the leading independent. A general election promised nothing but eclipse.

In the spring of 1977, therefore, the Liberals and Labour needed each other. Steel and Callaghan came from different generations, which made for an easy, avuncular relationship between the veteran Prime Minister and the tyro party leader. The new Liberal Chief Whip, Alan Beith, shared Steel's determination to make a pact work – as his predecessor, the egocentric and easily bruised Cyril Smith, would not have done. Steel and Beith did not push their luck. They asked for nothing from the government which it could not give: a shopping list which included a Liberal bill, two-party consultation, particularly on economic affairs, a fresh start for devolution, the introduction of direct elections for the European Parliament – but without a guarantee that these would be conducted through the Liberals' cherished medium of proportional representation. The 'terms' were heard with some incredulity by the cabinet and the elected liaison committee which represented Labour backbenchers, when they were expounded by Callaghan and Foot. The party had simply undertaken to do what it had anyway intended to do and desist from what it could not do. Although many Labour MPs claimed after the event that they were against the pact but were overruled or not consulted, the general feeling was one of relief. The government's sternest backbench critic, Dennis Skinner, recalls:

'I thought the Lib–Lab pact was just a system of buying time that was typical Callaghan really . . . He'd done it on the National Executive of the Labour Party for donkey's years before he became Prime

Minister, wooing the trade union leaders, and here was a typical Callaghan move in which he called upon the Liberals to bury themselves in this Labour administration without any real power at all, with a little bit of consultation on the side . . . Many of us opposed it, but it all become once again a question of confidence.' The opposition was not vigorous.

Some Liberals were worried. At a crucial stage of the talks John Pardoe left for a BBC television interview, convinced that the party could set tough terms on PR at least. He was to be surprised:

'I went over to Lime Grove and said my piece: "there will be no agreement". I was absolutely sure of that at that stage of the negotiations. I knew what Steel was going to say. He'd agreed with me completely . . . I went back to the House around midnight. Steel was in his room and I said, "What happened?" He said, "Oh, we signed." I said, "You what? You mean he conceded on PR?" – "Well, not exactly, John, but he's done the best he can and really you mustn't expect people to do more than they can deliver." David was determined to do a deal at all costs.'

Steel saw it quite differently. He argues:

'One of the reasons why I was keen to try this experiment was for a purely party reason, that was to get the Liberal Party back into thinking about sharing in power. After all we believe in a proportional election system, so the logic of that means we would have to share power with somebody.'

So he signed up for the voyage. The relationship had its difficulties. There were few on the Labour side; Healey sums them up:

'Well, I think three words, Pardoe, Pardoe and Pardoe. I had to negotiate with John Pardoe, who was the economic spokesman of the Liberal Party . . . and I found him really quite difficult to handle, because in the literal sense he was totally irresponsible.'

Pardoe and Healey, both fond of the Bull Moose approach to politics, never got on. The other Labour ministers quietly swallowed their gratitude at the modesty of Liberal demands. A minor brush between the Treasury ministers and Pardoe over increased petrol tax in the March budget led to its later reduction – too late to save either Labour or the Liberals from humiliation at Stechford. (Labour lost the seat in a final burst of anger at the budget tax rises, and the Liberals again finished behind the National Front.) Thereafter the pact functioned smoothly in general. Steel delivered his errant band in the government's lobby when necessary, and with some courage.

This cool nerve under pressure was needed at the turn of the year. On a free vote, the Commons turned down a PR system for the forthcoming direct elections for the European Parliament. It was one of five occasions in the Callaghan administration when some version of PR was offered in amendments to European and devolution legislation. All were heavily defeated. Although the Prime Minister delivered all but four of his cabinet, the Liberal MPs were indignant. So were the party activists, who insisted on a special conference to discuss the future of the pact. Steel's support for it prevailed. He did not hesitate to make his leadership conditional upon the acceptance of his strategy. The Liberals saw it his way. Steel does not overplay the influence which the Liberals had:

'I think we had a very marginal influence, positively, but we had a lot of negative influence, and we had a lot of stabilising influence.'

The stability was bitterly resented by left-wing ministers like Tony Benn:

'That was a very profound political change, because Jim Callaghan said, "In future, now we have the Liberals in alliance with us, no minister is to bring anything to cabinet that hasn't been cleared in advance with a Liberal spokesman." So that in practice the Liberal Party knew what we wanted to do before it was announced in Parliament.'

Something of Steel's relationship with the Prime Minister emerges in his diary of the time. In February 1978 he wrote of Callaghan:[3]

'He says he wants to play the next election as the leader of a left-wing party heading towards the centre while she is the leader of a right-wing party heading towards the right. He says he needs a good size Liberal vote, and that the next parliament may well be hung.'

Callaghan also told him, he recalls, that the virtue of the fact was that:

'He could say quite openly to the trade union leaders, or to his own left wing or whoever were making demands on the government, that these things couldn't be delivered because he had to keep the Liberals happy. And that was something he told me at the time he had learnt from Chancellor Schmidt in Germany.'

These confidences were unusual between leaders competing for the same voters. The image of a leftish party aimed at the centre was near enough to Steel's view of where the Liberals themselves should be: formative thoughts for a leader who had always been able to find common ground with social democrats.

So the pact bought a respite for the government, during which their electoral fortunes seemed to brighten. Parliament settled again under the yoke of Scottish and Welsh devolution legislation (see chapter 14), which consumed much time and deterred the Nationalists from seeking an early election. Callaghan and Foot had further consolidated their position by an informal deal with the ten Ulster Unionists, who now sat at Westminster under assorted banners varying from plain orange to blood orange. They had come in on a wave of bitterness at the power-sharing executive created by a Conservative government. In their ranks was Powell, who had called on the British electorate to vote Labour, and a new breed of working-class Unionist who had pushed aside the old squires, kindred spirits to the Tory knights of the shires.

The Secretary of State for Northern Ireland, Roy Mason, and his long-serving junior, Don Concannon, an ex-Guardsman, had defence backgrounds and gave what the Unionists saw as a proper priority to security. The new Secretary of State's brusqueness with critics of the security policy – the Republic, the BBC and Amnesty International all felt the weight of his wrath – suited the Unionists, if it further alienated the lone Republican MP, Gerry Fitt. It also enabled Mason to see off another attempt at a Loyalist strike, with a firmness that had been lacking in 1975. The Northern Ireland Development Agency channelled money to the province for economic development. (Its rules were succinctly set out by an aide of the American huckster John De Lorean:[4] 'The worse the area, the more financing they'd give us.') There was no imperative for an early election for the Unionists. They had achieved what they wanted in 1974–5. Now they had to hang on to it, and bargain for the return of Stormont. They knew that the Callaghan government would have to come to them. Harold McCusker, probably the Unionist closest to Labour, says:

'[It was] clear to us that ultimately they would have to choose between getting the support of two Irish Republicans or ten Ulster Unionists . . . When it came to it, the Labour Party had no difficulty in choosing.'

The Unionists knew that they could never get Stormont back from a Labour government. What they did get, 'out of the blue', was the offer of a conference on parliamentary representation. It could only have one outcome: an increase in 'the number of MPs, to bring Northern Ireland, deprived of its parliament, into line with the kind of representation enjoyed' by other parts of the United Kingdom. The Unionists' voice at Westminster would therefore be louder. They could afford to let the government survive, but the price was higher yet. There were other concessions. The pace of comprehensive-school reorganisation was slowed down in the province. Homosexual law reform never arrived at all. Individual Unionists found constituency favours easy to come by. Enoch Powell's refusal to sign the Commons Register of Interest (for reasons of principle that most MPs found perverse, not for reasons of concealment – Powell is proud that he earns every penny he has) came under the protection of Michael Foot. The effectiveness of the register, grudgingly accepted after the Poulson disclosures, perished. But the government lived on.

So did the British economy. It had gone into recession later than other Western economies, and it was slow to pull out. Manufacturing output began a fitful climb back to pre-1976 levels. The pound, boosted as artificially by the oil funds now at Britain's disposal as it had been talked down in the autumn of 1976, rose through the $2 barrier again in 1978, with benign results for the counter-inflation strategy, if not for exporters. Balance of payments deficits were transformed into surpluses. At home, British industry clamoured for economic assistance to help it stagger through. The restraints on public expenditure caused by cash limits and the IMF package curtailed what could be done. The high cost of support for British Leyland and Rolls-Royce inevitably limited what could be done elsewhere. The approach was managerial rather than salvationist. The National Enterprise Board cajoled from within the industrial sector, rather than instructed from without. Its mandate now, the new chairman wrote in his 1977 annual report, was to be as 'a state-owned body operating in the competitive sectors of the economy, and forming a bridge between state ownership and private entrepreneurial activity'. Private industry would be helped back to life by public funds, not taken over wholesale.

Sir Leslie Murphy had replaced Lord Ryder as head of the NEB in 1977. The latter's over-optimistic report on the future prospects of British Leyland had been mocked by events. A new approach was blessed by Downing Street. Murphy offered the British Leyland bed of nails to the South African industrialist, Michael Edwardes. Although the consequences of this appointment for the workforce were to be profound, it was management which trembled first, and rightly. The NEB was determined to improve British management in the sector it could influence. One of the trade union representatives on the Board agrees that:

'[It was a priority] from the beginning [to] grasp the nettle of management. We weren't just concerned to put money in and take up new ventures. We were concerned to put in good management as well.'

This was a condition of assistance for private sector firms which limped into the NEB casualty station, as Ferranti had done. It was also the fact of life that British Leyland had to face. Murphy had few illusions about the firm's problems:

'Almost at the first meeting we had with BL, I said to Alex Park, then chief executive, "Well, Alex, I really don't know an awful lot about the motor industry. Tell me, which models make profits and which make losses?" . . . He said, "I don't know." I was slightly surprised but never mind, it's our first meeting. I said, "We can talk about it next time." "No, no," he said. "That's not what I mean − I can't find out. The accounting system in BL is such as not to produce an answer."'

Michael Edwardes confirms that this obscurity was the norm:

'When I went in in November 1977 we did not know the cost of a Mini. I mean that literally. And in fact we found out quite quickly that we were losing £26 million on the TR7, and £24 million on the MG.'

Within six months of Michael Edwardes's arrival at BL all but two of the board had been purged, two hundred top managers redeployed, and ninety sacked. The trade union general secretaries on the NEB were happy enough with this. BL 'had come to be seen as a lame duck's home', one thought. Another, more brutally, says:

'The left criticised us because we all assented to the view that we had to invest the money in expectation and intention that we would create profitable companies, even if it took some years. We didn't take the view that we were there to help industries with loans of cash if they wouldn't make a profit.'

So strict were the NEB's criteria that it was often unable to spend the money allocated to it. The alternative was sometimes to hold back, deliberately to shrink a company's market share. Under the new terms of reference for the restructured BL, this involved halving it. Michael Edwardes's initial plan proposed the loss of 12,500 jobs and 7 plants. An early casualty of the restructuring was the closure of the Triumph plant at Speke, Liverpool. There was, says Edwardes, 'gross disruption and a structured laziness in the place'. The public got a glimpse of a different view when one worker said on television of the TR7:

'Even I know it's a bad product. If the workforce had any say in the design, that could be a good car [but] a plant of 2500 men doesn't even have a suggestion box.'

The subsequent loss of jobs in an area of high unemployment and precipitate industrial decline, which did not have a tier of small companies to provide economic regeneration, had serious political consequences. Edwardes went to see Callaghan, and explained his free-enterprise approach to what was then an almost wholly state-owned company:

'I ended the meeting by saying to him: you've got to understand, I do not believe in state ownership. I'm determined that whatever we do in BL we should end up where we come out from under government. And he just smiled patiently. Ah, I mean he was concerned with pragmatic day-to-day matters. The fact that my philosophy was different meant nothing to him. And that I think is the sign of a big man.'

Speke was closed. Slowly the message began to get across that Edwardes would not buy a quiet life, and that strikes of the kind which traditionally plagued BL (there were nearly 350 disputes in the first six months of 1978 alone) would be faced down.

The NEB was also beginning to demonstrate that there were areas of entrepreneurial innovation which could be backed, even if the traditional sources of finance were not forthcoming. The launch of IN-MOS, to give Britain a foothold in the new field of microtechnology, was the largest of a number of attempts to get a place in the sunrise industries of the future. As the originator of the NEB concept, Stuart Holland, points out, the Board was able to save the pride of private industry, from the Ferranti rescue to:

'. . . giving a leg up to Sir Clive Sinclair . . . [whose] company has had some £50 million worth of capital wiped off by the National Enterprise Board – which it invested with him in the first place – without which it's quite arguable that Sinclair Electronics itself wouldn't now be in business.'

In its general industrial policy the government was caught between the recession and the orthodox deflationary policies imposed upon it on the one hand, and the impact of high unemployment in its own heartland on the other. The nationalised industries were the last to realise, in their forward planning, that the era of growth was over. British Steel had been built up to serve an expanding industry about to enter Europe like a tidal bore. In the late 1960s there had been heady talk of an industry with a capacity of 37 million tonnes per year. The investment was put in – and it coincided with a world slump. Before 1974 demand had risen by 5% per year since 1951. In the following decade the UK market shrank by 37%. By 1977 BSC was losing £450 million annually, with only 50% of the domestic market. BSC chairman Sir Charles Villiers, confronted with these figures on television, conceded the low productivity:

'Bethlehem Steel in America, a great company, makes about the same amount of steel as we do. They have 85,000 people making steel, and we have 160,000. The cost to Bethlehem per man . . . is about £13.5 thousand per year. And our cost is about £5.5 per man. So this is the target we have to shoot at. Fewer people but much better remuneration.'

There were some closures – including Ebbw Vale, to the personal agony of its constituency MP, Michael Foot – but the government tried to hang on to the bulk of British steel capacity in the anticipation of better times.

Improvement expectations were linked to heavy support for the domestic market and British manufacturing. The subsidy of £28 million to British Shipbuilders to construct ships for the Polish Merchant Marine (which, at best, would enable the Poles to undercut British shipping), and the diversion of British aid projects for India and elsewhere into costly naval contracts never sought by the recipient country, were notable examples of how far the policy went. So was the initial advance of £53 million to John De Lorean to build his gull-winged sports car in Belfast. Like the introduction of a temporary employment subsidy and the pilot youth-employment schemes introduced in 1978–9, these were all determined palliatives, attempts to keep as much of British industry as possible alive on a drip-feed if all else failed. By the end of 1978, they had created a quarter of a million new jobs, in addition to those which were maintained.

Unemployment reached 1.6 million in the autumn of 1977 – 6% of the workforce. The government's critics were not slow to point out that, in addition to the hardship and despair caused, particularly after the short-term earnings-related phase, each person reduced to the dole was costing the state some £4000 in unproductive expenditure. The Chancellor injected £1 billion back into the economy in a mildly reflationary mini budget that October, followed by a further £2.5 billion in April 1978. Unemployment began to turn down. To the surprise of some ministers, however, it was incomes policy rather than unemployment which brought the most trouble from Labour's natural supporters.

Incomes policies are rarely what their name implies, since they are too often no more than means of regulating wages and salaries alone.

In the year 1977–8 real weekly net income was 7% less than in 1973–4. The trade union leaders who had endorsed the £6 pay limit two years before, notably Scanlon and Jones, were in trouble with their membership. For the former the problem was the pressure on the differentials of his craftsmen. Roy Fraser of the BL toolroom workers' committee was much in evidence as the trustee of this view. The visiting *New Statesman* writer Mervyn Jones wrote of him in March 1977:

'He had a pleasant modern house with attractive furniture and array of indoor plants, and offered coffee in cups of stylish design. His way of life is the sort which used to be called middle-class ... The maintenance of these standards has suddenly become difficult.'

Although inflation was coming down, prices were outstripping wages. The workers could do their sums.

The TUC had called for an 'orderly return to free collective bargaining' in the government's third year. Jack Jones went to his last TGWU conference as General Secretary on the Isle of Man. In the words of one industrial correspondent who saw it, he was 'torn to pieces by the shop stewards he helped to create'. Jones summarises his argument to the conference:

'Let's have priorities, let's go for a shorter working week, for example, to ease the unemployment problem rather than just a total free-for-all in wages. But the conference would have none of that, and before I went to the rostrum I knew that the majority was against me.'

He warned his conference that the beneficiaries of their action would be Thatcher, Joseph, Heseltine 'and all the ilk of privilege'. They voted him down. The defeat of the man dubbed 'the Emperor Jones' and 'the most powerful man in Britain' was watched with some awe by his fellow general secretaries. They knew the power he had wielded on the TUC General Council. Now, as that avuncular, moderate postmen's leader Tom Jackson puts it:

'It was a case of "when father turns, we all turn". I mean, when Jack's conference turned, Jack turned, as he had no option ... But when Jack turned, a good many other people turned at the same time.'

There could be no third year of agreement with the government. It says much for Callaghan's persuasive powers, and the loyalty of the unions, that the government's proclaimed third-year target of 10% increases with twelve months between settlements received at least a tacit acquiescence. Wages rose by some 16%. The number of days lost in strikes began to rise rapidly. One dispute, involving the firemen, confronted the government as employer. By the use of troops for eight weeks in their ancient Green Goddess reserve vehicles, the strike was broken. The process was watched by the TUC, who felt unable to intervene. The government could congratulate themselves that their alliance with the unions held, and that they had in effect had a third year of incomes policy. The warning signs were there, however: there was a new militancy in the offing – the more so as the new 10% figure struck at the low paid, who had done well from flat-rate limits.

There was a further disappointment for Jack Jones in his last year of power when the Bullock Committee proposals for industrial democracy were published. Since they favoured the single-channel approach of representation entirely through the trade union structures, they found little favour with industry. Nor were the trade unions themselves prepared to fight very hard for what seemed to some of them an incompatible division of functions. Here, as with the lukewarm response of the hierarchies to proposals from the Lucas Aerospace shop stewards for diversification to socially useful new products, there was little evidence that the Labour movement as a whole had effected a fundamental and irreversible shift in its own attitudes to the challenge of change.

There were other reasons why the government was at odds with its own party supporters. The reductions in the rate of increase in expenditure on the public social services made themselves felt by 1978. The rate of increase for social security in 1975–6 had been 8.3%, for education 1.8%, for health 3.2%, and for the personal social services 6.5%. After the IMF cuts, these figures had slumped for 1976–7 to 2.9%, −0.3%, 0.8% and −1.3% respectively. Worse followed in 1977–8.

Since the Wilson government had begun with a major improvement in the real value of pensions, housing subsidies and the personal social services, the drop subsequently to the lowest rate of increase for many years – and a negative figure for 1977–8 – infuriated Labour activists. Many of them were in the professions now affected. Teachers, social workers, welfare officers, all found both political and career expectations falling far short of the expectations of their formative years of the 1960s. In the field of equality, the government seemed to take one step forward and then step back with the other foot.

Barbara Castle had followed her pensions legislation with action against pay beds (private beds for non-NHS patients) in National

Health Service hospitals, urged on by the increasingly organised and militant NHS unions. The aim was to stop queue jumping and the habit of consultants taking a ride on the NHS for their private patients. The consultants were not amused. In November 1974 in the *Guardian*, the veteran journalist James Cameron, then undergoing heart surgery in the NHS, had poured scorn on:

'. . . public facilities being used for private gain. No union as far as I know demands that bus conductors reserve special seats in the bus for which they charge personal fees . . . Yet a handful of prosperous medicine men (and what a tiny minority of the doctors they are, albeit eminent, articulate and loud) require to earmark little slabs of the NHS facility for their own use, at their own time, and at their own price. You could knock me down with a catheter.'

The doctors wielded heavier weapons than that. If they were to be dislodged from the NHS, they argued, they would build up a bigger private sector. Tackling that was something which divided the DHSS ministers, in a foreshadowing of wider splits in the party to come. Barbara Castle wanted to limit the number of beds licensed in the private sector to the level of those previously allowed in the NHS. Her Minister of State, David Owen, disagreed. Her diary records:[5]

'He gets quite tetchy at the idea of trying to control the quantity of beds in the private hospitals that will undoubtedly spring up everywhere. He is far more reactionary in this than my officials are . . . I am convinced that we have to fight like hell to prevent the building-up of a vast empire of private medicine.'

So it proved. Castle was removed by James Callaghan. Under her successor, David Ennals, only some one thousand pay beds were phased out, and the licensing system for new private schemes proved ineffective. The consultants went on with their private practice – if anything, under more favourable contracts with the NHS than before.

The Health Service was not the only area where the attempt to produce a more egalitarian policy foundered, and actually produced greater inequalities between the state and private sectors. In education Callaghan had launched the 'Great Debate' with his speech at Ruskin College, which is discussed in the context of chapter 10. Among its supporters, the debate was about the government's spending cuts which postponed those improvements, especially in nursery provision, presaged in the early seventies. Worse, the abolition of the direct-grant schools had the unlooked-for effect of swelling the private system. Given the choice between accepting a non-selective intake or losing the grant, many schools opted for the latter. Following its own election manifesto, the government was expected to discourage this by action to end the charitable status, fee support and the other tax advantages of the private schools. The three successive Secretaries of State, Prentice, Mulley and Williams, allowed themselves to be snared in a tangle of civil service obfuscation. The tone of this is well caught in a memorandum from the Permanent Secretary at the DES, Sir William Pile, to the minister, Fred Mulley:[6]

'First, the term "public schools" has no definable meaning . . . There are substantial problems of definition involved in discriminating between one kind of school and another. Secondly, there is at the root of the matter the problem that charitable status is not enjoyed by the schools as such but by the institutions which provide them . . . Thirdly, any progress in relation to the withdrawal of tax reliefs is critically dependent upon finding ways of re-defining charities or discriminating between charities . . . [Thus] I do not think there is anything we ourselves can usefully do in the interim.'

The proposals died in the dark. As with the NHS, Labour hopes of greater equality of treatment within the nation rather than merely within the state sector were not fulfilled.

Sometimes the fact that the policy arguments were carried out far from the public arena enabled the government to escape the wrath of its own left wing, in the short term. For example, in defence expenditure, the extension of the life of the British nuclear deterrent at substantial cost was effected without public debate. Knowing that his predecessor Heath had been rebuffed by the Americans when he had asked for the Poseidon missile to replace Polaris, Harold Wilson had brought up the Chevaline project (to upgrade Polaris) once only. Castle's diary recalls the occasion – 20 November 1974:[7]

'Harold prepared the way carefully by saying that, though we would keep Polaris and carry out certain improvements at a cost of £24 million, there would be no Poseidonisation and no MIRV. The nuclear element represented less than 2% of the defence budget but it gave us a "unique entrée to US thinking" and it was important for our diplomatic influence for us to remain a nuclear power.'

Around the table, Foot's comments were 'so muted as to be almost token'. And 'Wedgie said nothing.' The real cost even then was estimated at almost £350 million, later rising with inflation to £1 billion. The matter never returned to cabinet. A small group – the Prime Minister, the Chancellor, the Foreign Secretary, the Defence

Secretary – reviewed it from time to time. It was not subject to cash limits. Nor did it appear in the successive defence reviews. Instead, other substantial expenditure was loaded onto its budget by the navy.

By 1977, when the inner group was Callaghan, Healey, Owen and Mulley, the cost had already risen to £700 million. Owen, who believes with hindsight that the project should have been cancelled in 1974, once an international treaty on anti-ballistic missiles had been signed by the superpowers, reflects on the decision taken when these costs were known:

'It was more than double what had been believed, nearly treble what the cabinet had believed in '74. Probably it ought to have gone back to the cabinet, at that time, but the history of private decisions and private monitoring had been well established, and it was a secret decision. I mean, there's no doubt about it, it was something we didn't want the Russians to know in its full detail ... I think perhaps we should have been opener and I think perhaps it ought to have been more openly discussed.'

The former Minister of State at Defence, William Rodgers, also feels free now to express regret at the lack of openness:

'I think if the argument on Chevaline had been openly conducted there would have been a majority for it. It could even have been taken to the Labour Party conference. But everybody ducked away from it. In this respect Callaghan later, no more than Harold Wilson earlier [felt] that because defence was sensitive there should be a minimum row.'

Unlike the increase in NATO expenditure, to which Britain was asked to contribute its share in 1978, the secret Chevaline programme could not inflame the Labour left at the time. It was only after the programme was deliberately revealed by the incoming Conservative government that the Labour leadership suffered from its obsessive secrecy.

There had been examples enough of secrecy during the lifetime of the government. In 1976 the proposed introduction of child benefits paid directly to the mother was delayed. An article in June in the magazine *New Society* by Frank Field of the Child Poverty Action Group revealed that the cabinet had panicked at the thought that any switch away from child tax allowances (CTAs) to child benefit would reduce take-home pay and imperil the incomes policy. Clearly using leaked cabinet papers, the author showed how this desertion of a policy commitment had been sold to the unions by stressing what a blow child benefit would be to their members. This was the reverse of what had been expected of the cabinet: 'a clear example of a radical government becoming managers rather than reformers'. The row which followed helped to push a reluctant Chancellor into the introduction of child benefits in his April 1978 budget. But it also increased the ire of the Prime Minister about leaks and Official Secrets. (The child benefits' mole was never found.)

Reform of the Official Secrets Act, and especially its notorious 'catch-all' Section 2, had been long mooted. The Franks Report of 1972 had proposed that Section 2 be cleaned up , and reduced to easily defined categories of confidential information. It proclaimed that:

'A government which pursues secret aims or which operates in greater secrecy than the effective conduct of its proper functions requires, or which turns information services into propaganda agencies, will lose the trust of the people.'

The sentiment was bold, though the Franks proposals hardly added up to a charter for freedom of information, being concerned to define what should still properly be protected. An undertaking to replace the Official Secrets Act appeared in the October 1974 Labour manifesto. 'Proposals' were promised in the 1975 Queen's Speech, after Roy Jenkins had visited the USA to study its Freedom of Information Act. They were not forthcoming, and Jenkins went on his travels again, this time to a new job in Brussels. The new Home Secretary, Merlyn Rees, came from the Northern Ireland Office, where security preoccupations had not predisposed him to open government. He repeated the commitment to do something about Section 2, to make it, in a chilling metaphor, less of a blunderbuss and more of an Armalite rifle.

But the blunderbuss kept going off. In November 1976 two dissimilar Americans, the writer and ex-CIA agent Philip Agee and the journalist Mark Hosenball, were told that they were to be deported from Britain. Agee had infuriated the US and British intelligence services by writing about his former CIA colleagues and 'exposing' their worldwide activities. Agee was told that he was disseminating information harmful to the UK and that he had contacts harmful to its security. Hosenball was a more curious case, a young journalist with no more than conventionally radical views who wrote for *Time Out*, sometimes about British information-gathering through SIGINT at Cheltenham. He had a girlfriend with an Irish name, had occasionally touched wings with other birds of passage on the radical left. Curious as to why he, out of hundreds like him, was marked for deportation, he told the panel of 'three wise men' appointed to hear his defence (made without the opportunity to hear such evidence as there was against him) that some of his articles had relied on information from a British journalist, Duncan Campbell.

Campbell was under surveillance already, as an active member of the Agee–Hosenball Defence Committee. He was soon arrested with another journalist, Crispin Aubrey, while they were hearing an account from a young ex-soldier called John Berry of his experiences in signals intelligence in Cyprus. All three were charged under the Official Secrets Act, Sections 1 and 2. So wide was Section 2 that Berry was bound to be technically guilty. The subsequent 'ABC Trial' roared on for many months. Unnamed witnesses were named under parliamentary privilege, in the press, and on the seashore sand at the NUJ conference. The Section 1 charges were dropped. Clumsy jury vetting was disclosed and the whole trial had to start again. The final suspended sentence for Berry and conditional discharges for the two journalists were secured at a heavy price for the government in credibility. Agee and Hosenball did not remain to see it. Both were deported, their appeals rejected without their knowing why ... Merlyn Rees takes full responsibility for it: 'I looked at the papers and decided to do it. It was my decision completely, it is not a matter for the cabinet.'

The cases did not endear the government to civil libertarians in the Labour Party. Nor did its inability thereafter to make another effort at reform of Official Secrets law itself, one area where the support of the Liberals would have guaranteed a parliamentary majority. (A bill from the Liberal Clement Freud was before Parliament at the dissolution.)

The failure to expand the public services, the secrecy and illiberalism were not excused as the necessity of difficult times. The reduction of real public expenditure by 4% through the period of the cuts was seen as a dress rehearsal for a further Tory attack. The Labour left agreed with – and hated – Walter Eltis's prediction in the *Sunday Times* in 1978 that:

'Public spending was 4% less in 1977–78 than in 1976–77, and if the Conservatives win the election they can now cut public spending further by using precisely the methods which Mr Healey has pioneered.'

The cautious approach of James Callaghan, steering with the right hand down, never picking up speed, might have been understood by that older Labour Party from which he himself had sprung. But things were different now. The impatient generation of the sixties had rejoined the party, and was finding little difficulty in moving through the shrunken caucus which was sometimes all that remained of an inner-city Labour Party. A series of by-elections, from Govan to Ladywood, exposed the fragments of the old-time machines for the rusting relics they were. The fiasco in Newham of Reg Prentice – whom 180 Labour MPs had been persuaded to support with an open letter pleading for tolerance to the disaffected constituency – moving from a Labour cabinet to the Conservative whip inside two years seemed to cast a lurid light on Labour ministers. So did the anonymous revelation of another to the media that he went to his constituency once a year. The Campaign for Labour Party Democracy, a child of the Wilson years, found a happy playground in scenes like these (see chapter 18). Labour conferences became the scene of acrimonious debates about mandatory reselection of MPs and an electoral college to perform the same service for the party leader. Mandatory reselection was defeated at the 1978 conference, thanks to a disputed vote cast by Hugh Scanlon on his last outing as president of the engineers. The nature of the defeat simply reinforced the CLPD determination to bring back reselection with a vengeance in 1979. For some, the vengeance was not so long delayed. Ian Mikardo was voted off the NEC in an act of petty retribution by the constituency delegates, because he had proposed a compromise arrangement which would have allowed local parties to avoid going through a full reselection if they retained confidence in their MPs. Compromise was now anathema to the reformers.

One who joined the Callaghan Labour Party, up from Young Liberalism, was Peter Hain, who did not like what he found:

'They seemed increasingly to be offering an authoritarian image in terms of their prosecutions of people like the ABC individuals or the deportations of Agee and Hosenball, the failure to repeal the 1971 Immigration Act, and so on. Above all they were not, I think, seen by party members such as myself as really seriously putting forward a socialist economic strategy. They were seeking to manage capitalism in crises . . . So I think there was tremendous disillusionment, and a feeling of betrayal. That was a word often used – that lots of these Labour leaders actually didn't believe in the policies upon which they'd been elected.'

Hain and many others came together in the Labour Co-ordinating Committee (LCC) in 1978 to press for these policies to be honoured. Measures, not men, were their target.

Throughout his administration James Callaghan had greater difficulty with the National Executive Committee than his predecessors had done. Whereas Wilson had often treated it with cavalier disregard, Callaghan, the punctilious attender, the supreme fixer, suffered more. He could not command a majority on the NEC. Tony Benn, his chief critic, presided over the Home Policy Committee, from which flowed a series of new initiatives and policy formulations. Liaison with Labour cabinet ministers was not always easy. Gerald Kaufman has produced a memoir of one such meeting in the Department of Industry:[8]

'The ministers at the Department, in company with the Secretary of State for Employment and Civil Service officials, awaited the large and formidable contingent from the National Executive who had communicated their intention of turning up. But only three, one of whom was the youthful representative of the Young Socialists, actually arrived; one of these three was very late and another left early.'

Such scenes led to much mutual suspicion. So did the NEC's apparent reluctance to take up, or even publish, the report of its own national agent, Reg Underhill, into the entryist tactics of the Revolutionary Socialist League (RSL), better known in the seventies as Militant Tendency. (Technically, the Tendency comprised readers of the weekly newspaper *Militant*, and referred to itself, following an old Labour tradition, without the definitive article.) There was a deep aversion on Labour's National Executive to the old proscribed list, a feeling that Militant, although often tiresome and intolerant, represented no real danger, and should not be banned. The gap between what James Callaghan's generation stood for and the new young activists was widening dangerously. And there was to be a problem of communication on another front.

The election that never was

Despite its difficulties and disappointments, the government had gone into 1978 on a wild surmise. Things might come right. It had survived longer than had been thought possible. The economy seemed to be on the mend, albeit from an abysmally low take-off point. Callaghan felt he had a sense of what the country wanted. The problem was that, as Bernard Donoughue of the Downing Street Policy Unit saw it:

'While public opinion appeared to be drifting to the right, the Labour Party was drifting to the left, and so you had a situation in which the Labour Party was getting more and more adrift from the electorate's views.'

The public backed incomes policy, at least in opinion polls; the Labour left opposed it. Callaghan decided to go for more, and his boldest gamble yet.

In a radio interview on New Year's Day he floated the idea of a 5% pay norm; wages should be kept in line with inflation now inflation was down:

'30% wage increases, roughly 30% price increases; 5% wage increases, roughly 5% price increases. 10% wage increases, roughly 10% price increases . . . 1979 is the year I am looking to . . . I want to see 5% price increases.'

If the figure was not entirely plucked from the air, it was perhaps plucked from the Treasury computer. This would give not just single-figure inflation, but low single-figure inflation. Even the Treasury hardly dared believe that he could get away with it, in the circumstances of 1978. The union old guard was changing. New figures had emerged, unwilling to play drill sergeant for any incomes policy. By the time the 5% policy was formally put to the TUC General Council in July, it was clear that there could be no deal, certainly nothing on the lines of the proposals now so closely identified with the Prime Minister. The TGWU, under the flaccid leadership of the new General Secretary Moss Evans, was firmly behind a full return to free collective bargaining. The burgeoning public sector union NUPE had already announced its intention to take industrial action the following winter should its claim not be met. Reg Race, then one of the NUPE research officers charged with co-ordinating such a strategy, explains why it was designed to take the government to, but not over, the brink:

'We reasoned that it was a good time to do it, first of all because the economy was relatively buoyant at that time . . . second because we knew that the government was coming up to a general election and we said to ourselves, "Well, the government will not risk the possibility of a confrontation with the trade unions over an issue of this kind" . . . And we therefore went deliberately out of our way to publish in advance documents which described the justice of the claims of the workers concerned.'

Battle lines were being drawn up, but at the time they involved phantom armies in a phoney war. The government believed that, if it could get away with grudging acquiescence once, it could do so again. Living standards were rising. The inflation rate had fallen. The causal connection between low wage settlements and a low inflation rate would persuade the unions to be moderate in practice. Denis Healey now recalls advice which he and his colleagues then chose to ignore.

'I remember very well in my own area, one of the wisest and most moderate of all trade union leaders, the regional organiser of the Transport and General, Ernie Hayhurst, saying to me, "Denis, it will not work another time; you'll have to find some other way." But we didn't listen to this advice; we were carried away by the degree of success we'd already had.'

There was another reason why the government thought it was shadow boxing with the TUC: the prospect of an imminent election. Cabinet discussions throughout July were preoccupied by it. The Liberals had served notice that the pact would not be renewed for a third session. Without it, the government would have to survive from day to day. The House of Commons broke up for the long recess with MPs convinced that they had two months to prepare for an election. The Prime Minister brooded on the polls taken for his party. Labour's recovery seemed shallow, especially in the marginal seats. The Conservatives had launched their 'Labour Isn't Working' pre-emptive advertising campaign, which looked as though it would peak to coincide with an October election. The last two Prime Ministers who had gone to the country early had suffered for it. Unlike them, this one would have no second chance. The Liberals had cut themselves loose, after a brief dalliance with the Conservatives, to force extra tax cuts out of the Chancellor, but there was no reason to believe they were in shape to fight an election. The spectral figure of Thorpe haunted the Liberal leadership. On 4 August 1978 he and three other men were charged with conspiracy to murder Norman Scott.* Thorpe protested his innocence, and believed he was right to contest the next election. He appeared at the Liberal conference, breaking a promise not to come, striding in purposefully past the aghast dignitaries. 'I don't think my feelings were printable at that point,' David Steel remembers, 'I knew the whole thing would be dominated by him.'

Even before this it was clear that the Liberals would think thrice about precipitating an election. It would be 'like turkeys voting for Christmas', said David Penhaligon.

---

* He was later acquitted.

A week before the TUC conference, Callaghan entertained the six senior trade unionists who sat on NEDC, the 'Neddy Six', to dinner at his Sussex farmhouse. All but one of them urged him to go to the country sooner rather than later. He heard them out, but was noncommittal. They came away believing that there would be an election. At the conference itself, in the atmosphere of a pre-election rally, insofar as the modest hype which the GMWU's David Basnett permitted himself could produce such a mood, the Prime Minister spoke. He even sang, a song from Vesta Victoria – 'There was I, waiting at the church . . .' – teasing his audience and the watching nation. Most of his listeners took his assurance that he had 'promised nobody that he would be at the altar in October' as part of the tease. Two days later, on 7 September, it was the TUC leaders who were all dressed up with nowhere to go. Mr Callaghan appeared on television to say there would be no autumn election. Basnett and the TUC were made to look foolish. The cabinet were stunned when they were told earlier that day. 'There was a moment's silence,' Bill Rodgers remembers, 'then every cabinet minister fell off his chair.'

Why had he done it? The polls conducted for the party by its genial American soothsayer, Bob Worcester of MORI, had suggested another hung parliament. Foot and the older men in the government had shared Callaghan's thoughts, and shaped his conclusion. Denis Healey's memory is:

'The decisive thing to him was that he didn't want another five miserable years of internal manoeuvring to keep these factitious majorities in Parliament. He wanted to either go down or win with an absolute majority.'

What the Prime Minister got was another five miserable months of internal manoeuvring, but he held on to high hopes. He told his aide Tom NcNally that his fear of a hung verdict concerned the deal with the unions over the autumn pay round:

'We'll not get any agreement out of them after a general election. But with a general election imminent we might get them to go along with it . . . The gun was there, the gun was loaded, and in those circumstances the trade unions surely wouldn't pull the trigger and let in a Tory government.'

Hindsight plays the hanging judge. In the light of what happened subsequently, Callaghan's decision can be interpreted as the caution of age getting its deserts. His former economic adviser Thomas Balogh had telephoned him to say of the 1979 position, 'Look, it's a peak. A submerged peak, maybe. But a peak.' Nevertheless Callaghan wanted to get clear of the water. He thought he knew the trade unions. He had many old debts to call in. In his recent political memory governments which had played it long had done better for it. But he was now at the mercy of his trade union allies. The handling of the election decision had not made them more kindly disposed to talk of 5% limits. 5%, Denis Healey now thinks, was a terrible figure to be stuck with:

'I'm convinced now that if we had said we want settlements in single figures, we'd have come out with probably something like 12% overall and retained the support of the unions, avoided the Winter of Discontent, and won the election. But hubris tends to affect all governments after a period of success, and by golly it hit us.'

The winter of discontent

Any hope which the government had that continued political uncertainty would act as a constraint on its union allies was swiftly dispelled. First the annual party conference, then the biggest union, and finally the Labour left in Parliament: all played their part before Christmas. At the conference a resolution from Liverpool Wavertree demanded that the government: '. . . immediately cease intervening in wage negotiations, and recognise the right of trade unions to negotiate on behalf of their members.'

It was supported by the low-paid workers as well as by those with industrial muscle. Alan Fisher of NUPE spoke with great emotional force about the 5% limit: 'You know what percentages do for the lower paid. It gives least to those who need it most and most to those who need it least.'

Following him, Sid Weighell of the NUR looked ahead to the winter pay round:

'Look what is lining up ahead. 20%, 35-hour week, a month's holiday for Ford's. Alan [Fisher] wants 40%. This is what they call responsible collective bargaining. Responsible. Really? . . . My union helped to create this party. The union that sponsored the conference that created the Labour Party. I am not going to stand here and destroy it. But if you want the call to go out at this conference that the new philosophy of the Labour Party is that you believe in the philosophy of the pig trough – those with the biggest snout get the biggest share – I reject it.'

The emotional tide however ran strongly with Fisher's attack on the problem of low pay – where he was in effect asking the government as public sector employer to do more – and with those who wanted the government to keep out of collective bargaining, after the years of pay restraint. The Wavertree resolution was carried by a vote of more than 2 to 1.

The gap between the government and the TUC was not concealed by the document 'Collective Bargaining, Costs and Prices', which mentioned neither 5% nor any other figure. Apart from some fudged pledges to persuade unions not to make claims that would feed price inflation, the General Council could not help. It stated that it would not '"vet" claims, act as watchdogs in the process of negotiations, or scrutinise settlements'. This document had been drawn up by the 'Neddy Six' in close consultation with the government – which, for its part, promised to look into the problem of low pay and comparability. The mood of NUPE members, expressed by Fisher at the conference, had registered in Downing Street. The union leaders had said there would be no problem, Bernard Donoughue remembers: 'We were told, [give us] something on low pay, something on the public sector, and then we'll deliver it.'

But they didn't. Tom Jackson chaired the TUC General Council meeting on 14 November:

'. . . I was right on the point of saying, "Well, that's agreed then," when Bill Sirs, of all people – as right-wing a member of the General Council as you'll meet in a day's march – stands up and says he's against it. Now if Bill Sirs says he's against it, what about the left-wing members of the General Council?'

The vote tied at 14–14. Jackson did not believe that he should use his casting vote. The document was not ratified. Cosmetic it may have been, but without it the features of whatever social contract survived between government and TUC looked raddled indeed.

The confrontations were not long in the making. A strike at Ford's led to the company's deciding to settle at 15%. When the government hauled out its last rusty weapon of proposed sanctions against Ford – boycotting the firm's cars, and denying it grants – it crashed to a humiliating defeat at Westminster on the issue. Labour abstentions allowed the united opposition parties to vote the policy down. Although it won the usual ritual vote of confidence, the government's moral authority in the matter of pay limits was gone. What the press rapidly dubbed the Winter of Discontent had begun. Some ministers argued that the right course was for the government to reformulate its policy on prices and pay as a White Paper, take it to Parliament as a matter of confidence, and if the vote was lost, go to the country. This did not happen. The cabinet inched forward into the winter wastes.

Moss Evans, one of the Neddy Six, had been inadvertently absent from the TUC General Council when the document agreed with the government had been voted down. He returned to find the TGWU tanker drivers next in line to burst through the Callaghan limits. A bitter road-haulage dispute rapidly followed the settlement with the tanker drivers, involving secondary picketing and the disruption of supplies. The press weighed in with graphic descriptions and photographs of deprivation. As with the public sector disputes which followed, it was neither the extent of the strikes nor the economic damage caused by them which made an impact. The strikes were effective because they were visible and they hurt the public directly. The harshest winter for some years added to the misery. The government did little for itself by agreeing to a BBC wage settlement which exceeded its own guidelines, to avoid a blackout of the nation's screens over the Christmas holidays. By then, others, with claims they believed to be far more justifiable, were pushing into the queue. By early January the government seemed to be at war with its own ally, the TGWU. The major docks were reported closed on 8 January, with serious disruption to supplies of food and animal foodstuffs. The *Guardian* quoted one TGWU pickets' leader in the north-west as saying, 'If I can't afford to buy food, why should anyone else have it?' The cabinet clung together for mutual support, shaken by the difference between what the TGWU leadership told them about the codes of conduct for the dispute and the apparent reality on their television screens. In *Inside the Treasury*, Joel Barnett wrote:[9]

'The most alarming information was available on television where we saw strict picketing by lorry drivers who were deciding which firms should get through. This was despite the fact that often neither the lorries nor the depots were actually involved in the dispute. It was secondary picketing at its worst, and much of the public was outraged. The pressure for government action was becoming stronger all the time. But what action?'

The Prime Minister had no heart for it. He was demoralised by the press he received from a summit meeting in Guadeloupe on 10 January. He was tired. He was irritated that the press had ignored the big subjects covered at Guadeloupe with Schmidt and Carter, and that they had tried hard to get a snap of him frolicking in the sun while

Britain shivered. On the plane back his aides had differed in their advice. McCaffrey said: say nothing. McNally said: show them you're in charge – this isn't the end of the world. The Prime Minister would have been wise to follow McCaffrey; his airport press conference was a disaster, as his watching colleagues realised. Calmness came over as complacency. Healey remembers:

'He didn't actually say. "Crisis, what crisis?" But he said something tantamount to that, and it struck the country as extraordinarily inappropriate, and also untypical of him. He was normally extremely sensitive to public feeling.'

What Callaghan had in fact said in reply to questions about 'mounting chaos' was:

'I promise you that if you look at it from outside, and perhaps you're taking a rather parochial view at the moment, I don't think that other people in the world would share the view that there is mounting chaos.' But the *Sun* used the headline 'Crisis – What Crisis?' and the phrase stuck.

The next few weeks saw the lowest point of Callaghan's premiership. The Conservatives, and Margaret Thatcher personally, soared ahead in the polls. Bernard Donoughue observed the Prime Minister's near despair:

'For some time ahead Mr Callaghan appeared depressed and almost paralysed into inactivity, and he became very tired. I think his basic problem was that, having grown up as a politician working with the trade unions, he didn't know what you did when you were fighting the trade unions, and he was very reluctant to take [them] on.'

Eventually he had to. Before the lorry drivers' dispute was settled, the water workers were joined by a broad front of local government and public sector employees. The TGWU, GMWU, NUPE and COHSE brought out 1.5 million people in a nationwide day of action. It was the most severe disruption the public had yet experienced. Roads went ungritted, rubbish uncollected, and in one macabre twist the dead on Merseyside were left unburied. Unlike the tabloid press, with their screaming headlines – 'Has Everyone Gone Mad?', 'No Mercy', 'The Road to Ruin', 'Pickets Rule!' television gave some coverage to the views of the strikers themselves: standing by refuse lorries, hospitals, or unoccupied graves half filled with rainwater, they told a story of wretched conditions and poor pay. But the pictures counted against them.

The picketing of hospitals aroused particular outrage. At its height it was the perfect television story: accessible, emotional and easily stereotyped. 'Target for Today – Sick Children' said the *Daily Mail* and the cameras showed distraught mothers at the bedsides of children smitten with cancer. The strikers' leaders seemed as indifferent to their public image as to those in their care. When the leader of the London ambulancemen said, 'If it means lives must be lost, that is how it must be,' or the NUPE branch secretary at the Westminster Hospital, Jamie Morris, described the ailing Secretary of State for Social Services, David Ennals, as 'a legitimate target for industrial action', they seemed to confirm what the pictures showed – for the pictures were strong. Men waiting for postponed heart pacemaker operations, young nurses who had torn up their NUPE cards rather than strike, disabled patients picketing the pickets: all denounced the strike. Few cameras looked beyond the self-assured, often arrogant young radicals who were the union spokesmen and women to the workers who carried the banners calling for a £60 basic wage: unskilled, badly paid, often from the many immigrant communities, they caught the full blast of public fury. Jamie Morris himself, looking back on the dispute at the Westminster Hospital, says:

'We were beginning to frighten society. There was the small person, actually beginning to climb out of the mire and say. "Hold up, I'm part of society and I've got rights."'

Why did NUPE go over the top in this way, more than any other union? It was ideally placed to do so. It had expanded rapidly in the seventies, from a membership of a quarter of a million to 600,000, in areas which had not previously been unionised and which benefited from the growth of the public sector. In Alan Fisher it had a General Secretary who combined a gift for easy left-wing rhetoric with a real commitment to eliminate the low pay and bad conditions from which many of his members suffered. Around him were others who believed in the use of the union to radicalise both the Labour Party and society. The campaign for an extension of the public sector suited the union, which would gain more members, and brought socialism closer. Research officer Reg Race remembers:

'It was an exciting time to be part of NUPE. We were attacking first of all the chronic low pay of workers in the public sector ... and second the change in the public sector itself.'

The young radicals looked at the recently revealed overestimate of the public borrowing requirements and reasoned that there was more

room for real expenditure, on higher pay, on new jobs, than the
Labour government would allow. So they felt no compunction in
attacking it. Already, in organisations such as the Campaign for
Labour Party Democracy, activists were looking well beyond the
survival or otherwise of the Callaghan government. Reg Race, himself selected to fight the next election as a Labour candidate, argues
that:

'The Labour government of Harold Wilson and James Callaghan
was destroyed by its own actions. It was destroyed by its action in
increasing unemployment. It was destroyed by its actions in attacking
public expenditure. It was destroyed by its relationship with the
Labour movement, which deteriorated very markedly . . . To blame
trade unionists is therefore looking at the symptoms rather than the
causes . . . for what subsequently happened.'

The Prime Minister was in deep despair. 'We are prostrate before
you,' he told the TUC. A new concordat between the government and
the TUC was put together, full of good intentions about the progressive reduction of inflation over the next three years and the guidelines
for orderly conduct of industrial disputes. The government undertook
to set up an 'independent commission' to look at public and private
sector pay comparability. This bastard son of Solomon Binding
pleased neither the supporters of incomes policy nor those of free
collective bargaining. But it was all the government had. The NUPE
strike dragged on through March, leaving some cabinet ministers with
a deep sense of foreboding. Peter Shore says:

'We were engaging in what I called occupational tribal warfare, as
though every separate group in the country had no feeling and no sense
of being part of a community, but was simply out to get for itself what
it could, and I thought that was terribly damaging to the Labour
movement, and the whole long tradition of solidarity, of socialist
commitment.'

When the civil servants joined in on 22 February, Callaghan stirred
himself to denounce them at once. His Foreign Secretary ostentatiously crossed a Whitehall picket line 'with great pleasure'. Government
advisers were horrified to find that well-paid senior civil servants were
slapping in huge claims. The men and women who had drafted the pay
code put in claims for 26% increases, with up to 49% at some senior
levels. Bernard Donoughue remembers one meeting of these men of
principle:

'. . . where it was decided that perhaps they shouldn't include the numbers [in the claim] . . . such as the cost, which was many hundreds of millions. Nor the percentages. As one person said. "Those kind of percentages will bias ministers."'

Such gestures increased the Prime Minister's fatalism. They were never made the subject of tabloid headlines or press abuse.

It was the collapse of the government's other, tacit, coalition with the minority parties which brought about the election. The devolution bills had gone through. But their fate hung on popular consultation through referenda, imposed on the government by its backbench rebels. In these referenda Wales voted emphatically against devolution, and the Scots for it in so lacklustre a manner that they fell far short of the affirmation of 40% of the total electorate specified in the Cunningham amendment (see page 298). The SNP felt compelled to withdraw their support from the government, even though the polls indicated that an early election would catch them with their credibility down. The Liberals were also obliged now to vote for Christmas after all. Jeremy Thorpe's full trial was due shortly. The committal had been bad enough. An early election in high national drama would spare the party adverse publicity.

A No Confidence vote was put down for 28 March. At the beginning of the month a Labour veteran who had seemed indestructible, Tom Swain, had been killed in a car crash. Another, Sir Alfred Broughton, was known to be dying.

In its last days the government struggled to draw breath. The Welsh Nationalists were won over. So were two Ulster Unionists. The others might have been acquired, though there would be a new price to pay. Enoch Powell remembers the talks, and the sense of the Prime Minister's growing frustration:

'Watching Callaghan in that last eighteen months I couldn't help saying to myself, "There's a man who's fed up" . . . If he hadn't been fed up he wouldn't have lost the vote of confidence . . . He could certainly for a ha'porth of tar or a whiff of gas have had the two or three votes which were necessary.'

The whiff of gas would have been the installation of a pipeline to Northern Ireland. More had been given earlier to the Ulstermen. This time the Prime Minister baulked. The hardest blow of all was Gerry Fitt's announced decision to abstain: he could not bring himself to support a government which had already given so much to the Unionists.

The debate was tense, the result always in doubt. The Tory historian

Robert Rhodes James, writing in the *Listener*, caught well the frantic chatter in the Whips' office:

'Fitt was going to abstain, but would Maguire? No one had seen Clement Freud. Was Broughton coming? If he was voting, then it must be a tie and the Government saved . . .'

When Michael Foot sat down on the stroke of ten after one of those rasping extempore speeches at which he excelled, but never more so than in his first and last speeches as a minister, the division seemed to take an eternity. Fitt – who, as promised, abstained – had poured scorn on his rival, the rubicund Republican from Fermanagh Frank Maguire, who had flown in he said 'to abstain in person': Labour MPs told him he would never forgive himself for what he was about to do, but Maguire stayed out of the lobbies. When the tiny Labour whip Jimmy Hamilton appeared from the scrummage in the lobbies like a terrier from a foxhole, flushed with apparent triumph, it seemed that Labour had tied. There was a roar of premature triumph. Then the Tory whip Sir Anthony Berry, languid but beaming, gave the figure from the other lobby to Mrs Thatcher. The counter-cheers reached their crescendo. For the first time in fifty years a government had fallen on a vote of confidence.

The Prime Minister announced an immediate election and went to his room. There his aide, Tom McNally, joined him: 'He was writing a letter to Broughton telling him not to worry.'

14

THE SCOTTISH CROWBAR

Great Britain is a unitary state taken for granted by its majority population group, the English. It comes as a surprise to the English to find that they share the country with other nations, and that they do things differently in those unforeign climes. George Orwell, at the end of his life, when he was living on the Isle of Jura, wrote:[1]

'In this country I don't think it is enough realised – I myself had no idea of it until a few years ago – that Scotland has a case against England. On economic grounds it may not be a very strong case . . . The point is that many Scottish people, often quite moderate in outlook, are beginning to think about autonomy, and to feel that they are pushed into an inferior position.'

In 1945, for a brief six weeks, a Scottish Nationalist had been elected to Parliament. In 1949 two million people signed the Covenant of the Scottish Convention. But separatism remained on the fringes of Scottish politics, never central to it. In Wales the separatist movement centred on the struggle to preserve the Welsh language, and the rich culture which that language nourished, while the tradition of political and cultural dissent found its home in the Labour Party.

By the mid-sixties Labour was dominant in British politics as it had not been for a generation, and there seemed no great change for the better in the Celtic heartlands it often took for granted. Disillusion took a political form, and turned not, as in England, to the Conservatives, but to the Liberals and the still-small nationalist parties as well. Both Scotland and Wales bore the marks of economic decline. In Wales the slow shrinkage of the coal industry brought emigration from the valleys and a search for new manufacturing to supplement the steel-making that remained. In Scotland the collapse of heavy industry was dramatic. The country that had built 12% of the world's ships in 1954 was down to a 1% share by 1968. The railway engineering industry vanished. Textiles were fading out, coal not in demand. John Davidson, now head of the Scottish CBI, says:

'We had a situation where people woke up one morning and

discovered that the world wanted something else and Scotland was not geared to provide that.'

Unemployment rates in both Scotland and Wales were well above the British average. In Scotland the rate was 50% higher through the period 1952–70.

The Welsh Nationalists, Plaid Cymru, were inextricably identified with the language they struggled to preserve and to maintain at least at parity with the invading English tongue. The identification was both a strength and a weakness. It gave them a base in the Welsh-speaking heartlands and an appeal to all who wanted to preserve the national distinction. But at the same time it made them seem a threat rather than a promise to the English-speaking Welsh, who outnumbered them four to one, who were used to the conventions of Wales and England being administered together. It was one thing to have a timely means to chastise the 'Taffia' of local Labour politicians when they monopolised power; quite another to move towards separatism. Booing the English at Cardiff Arms Park if they 'scored more points' was very different from painting out road signs the English could understand, or trying to paint Wales out of Britain. So the majority thought.

If Wales was, in Eric Hobsbawm's phrase, a typical 'non-historic nation', Scotland was in the same terms 'historic'. It had its own legal system, with the professional middle class of advocates and solicitors who served it. It had a distinctive system of education, with some of the most ancient universities in Europe. It had its own banking and investment sector, and with them in Edinburgh – that city which John Betjeman had called one of the only two true capital cities left in Europe – it had had, since 1939, a Scottish Office first set up in 1885, whose Secretary of State had progressively acquired new powers. Under Wilson the Secretary of State was William Ross, a sharp-tongued proconsul who ruled a small empire of civil servants and planners from St Andrew's House, adding to them new bodies such as the Highlands and Islands Development Board in an attempt to reverse the decline and depopulation which had overrun much of the country. All of Scotland except Edinburgh became a development area. Additional economic intervention seemed promised through a Plan for Scotland, within the centralised national planning of the Labour government. On a different scale the model was transposed to Wales, when a Welsh Office was set up in 1964.

When, after July 1966, the graph of rising expectations crossed that of declining fulfilment, Scotland and Wales suffered severely. The more planning was seen in the context of the national regions, the easier it was to think in terms of more devolved power for those regions, particularly when hopes were dashed or implemented by unimaginative hierarchies. The need for reform seemed especially true of the Labour Party in Scotland, with its fiefs in the rotten burghs of West Central Scotland, its second-rate candidates progressing dourly from one plateau of union or local government activity to the next, finally to wash up in the debates of the Scottish Grand Committee at Westminster. Professor Henry Drucker of Edinburgh University watched the party's cautious progress:

'It was a very old-fashioned Labour Party. It was more like the Labour Party in London ... of Herbert Morrison ... It was based solidly on the trade unions; it had a very heavy component of support from the Roman Catholic Church. It was not adventuresome. It certainly was not revolutionary... It moved slowly. It had the support of a substantial block of Scottish people – more than any other party – and it had the advantage therefore, or the disadvantage in some respects, of being the established party in Scotland. It was a bit like the Church of Scotland. It predominated without actually doing anything.'

Since in Scotland the Communist Party, on the industrial front, offered an alternative on the left, there was even less of a challenge to the 'toon cooncillor' domination within the Labour Party than in England.

The Scottish National Party (SNP) seemed different. It drew its early strength from the leadership of the professional middle class, and the support of the upwardly mobile young voters. Both groups had in common a discontent with what modern Scotland had to offer them. Drucker identifies the new ground which the SNP was able temporarily to occupy between Labour's base in industrial manufacturing and that of the rural Scottish Tories:

'It was your new town voter, the two-income family, people who were substantially better off than their parents but who had not yet arrived, who were voting for the SNP.'

The National Party was to hand, ready to be transformed from its romantic past:

'It had nationalist fervour, yes. It had Burns suppers. But it was really about a frustrated kind of managerialism, a group of people who felt that what Wilson was trying to do was in effect the right thing but he hadn't done it with enough flair or in the right context.'

Such a party stood to gain from Scotland's increasing dependence on multinational firms, and from its movement out of traditional industries altogether into white-collar service jobs. Between 1952 and 1970 mining, shipbuilding and textiles between them had lost 117,000 jobs. Professional and other services had gained 166,000 in the same period. The six new towns attracted many Scots who might have otherwise joined the exodus of over a million of their kin since the war. This expanding sector was fertile ground for an exciting and less class-based party. The SNP's leaders in the sixties, the accountant William Wolfe and the solicitors Winnie Ewing and Gordon Wilson, were articulate and personable, with a dash of the romantic about them.

That romance might become reality for the nationalists was first signalled from Wales, rather than Scotland, with the victory of Gwynfor Evans in the July 1966 Camarthen by-election. The Plaid Cymru market gardener, elected to Parliament at his eighth attempt, began to build a nationalist redoubt in North Wales which has lasted, there or in adjoining constituencies, ever since. His victory brought great encouragement to the SNP. After good results in by- and local elections, accompanied by much razzmatazz of a kind new to the Scottish political scene, they were presented with an opportunity at the moment of Labour's maximum weakness. Winnie Ewing captured Labour's second safest seat, Hamilton, from a tired old party wheelhorse. Helen Liddell, now Labour's Scottish Secretary, who was then in Labour student politics, remembers:

'I looked like the original fuddy-duddy, because all the fun was happening in the SNP, all the excitement, all the exuberance was in the SNP. Whereas the Labour Party looked terribly dated. We spent our time worrying about local government and what kind of stoppers people got for their sinks, and how the direct labour department was doing, when the Scottish Nationalists were talking about these great issues of national importance.'

Reeling from the blow of Hamilton, Labour did not know how to hit back. The MPs feared being undercut by any Scottish assembly. The 'toon co\u200bncillors' feared being overcut in the same way. A Royal Commission on Local Government in Scotland recommended in 1969 the creation of seven new regions, with the largest surrounding Glasgow, to contain over half the population of Scotland. This rich prize made a devolved assembly in Edinburgh less attractive still to the Labour Party. Much scorn was poured on the SNP. The title stood for

Still No Policies, Scottish Narks, or even Scottish Nazi Party to some of their more strident critics. Many left-wing intellectuals who later embraced the case for devolution were then bitterly hostile to the nationalists, none more so than Jim Sillars, co-author of *Don't Butcher Scotland's Future*. The tract argued for regionalisation within the UK rather than any Scottish parliament which would encourage the English to shrug Scotland off. In 1969, as Labour candidate in the South Ayrshire by-election, Sillars said:

'Economic dismemberment would be disastrous for Scotland and – socially and politically – a tragedy for the whole United Kingdom.'

Sillars beat the SNP into third place. The nationalist tide was receding. Back in London Harold Wilson, watching the auguries for a 1970 election, took great comfort from the result. But he had characteristically taken other steps to ward off the threat. Yet another Royal Commission was set up to take minutes and spend years examining the constitution. Perhaps the problem would go away. In his different style, the Conservative leader Edward Heath went north in 1968, and in the grandiosely titled Declaration of Perth committed his party to a devolved assembly in Scotland. Devolution, which the Scots rhymed with revolution, the English with evolution, meant many different things even then. To Heath it meant a directly elected assembly, but with the Scottish executive still responsible to Westminster. The proposal was not carried through in practice. Once in government, the Conservatives implemented the Wheatley Plan for new Scottish regions and sat back, like Labour, to wait for the leisurely deliberations of the Royal Commission. The SNP had fallen back in the 1970 election, and made no initial impact afterwards. On issues such as the Upper Clyde Shipbuilders' work-in they were unable or unwilling to compete with Labour for the support of those antagonised by Heath's industrial policies.

'It's Scotland's Oil'

There matters might have rested, but for the exceptional conjunction of events in 1973–4. In rapid succession the nationalists deployed the oil weapon, the Royal Commission reported, and there was a dramatic change in electoral fortune. The main argument against the SNP's avowed separatism had been that it made economic nonsense. Scotland commanded between a third and a quarter of all regional aid funds, although it accounted for only a tenth of the British population.

It covered 35% of the UK land mass. Its planned infrastructure investment, airports, bridges, motorways, was a visible reminder that it received some 20% more than its strict per capita share of public spending. Whatever the despoliation of the past, the British connection was a benefit not to be gainsaid. Separation would mean not greater economic independence but less.

All these arguments were turned on their head by North Sea oil. North Sea gas had been brought ashore since the early sixties. In 1969 the first prospecting companies struck oil, and from 1970 onwards it was clear that a major source of wealth lay off the east coast of Scotland, in the Forties field. Granite cities began to adjust to plastic credit cards and the pleasures of prosperity. The SNP put this moment to brilliant use, adapting their thistle/saltire logo to a new slogan: 'England Expects – Scotland's Oil'. Or, simply and crudely, the posters claimed 'It's Scotland's Oil'. The nationalists pointed to Britain in decline and asked: rich Scots or poor Britons, which is it to be?

The campaign was launched in March 1973. One of the men behind it was the SNP's press chief and theorist Stephen Maxwell:

'It had always been possible for the opponents of nationalism to say that it was all very well for the middle class . . . to favour independence because they would benefit through getting increased public appointments and increased job opportunities. But they would benefit at the expense of the working class, who would lose job opportunities because Scotland couldn't stand on her own feet economically. Once the oil was discovered, the economic tables were turned . . . the discovery of oil helped to persuade the Scots, for a while anyway, that they could get lucky.'

This luck, as filtered through some SNP propaganda, would extend to a stable level of services for much lower taxation. The 1973 oil crisis, which resulted in a huge increase in the price of oil, made the new-found wealth seem still more alluring. The campaign also had resonance for both the working class and the political left, for behind the clammy hands of the English the multinationals could be seen at work. John McGrath and his 7:84 Theatre Company turned up at the 1973 SNP conference for one of the early presentations of *The Cheviot, the Stag and the Black, Black Oil*, lampooning past and present exploitation. Now the exploitation came from Whitehall and Texas, singing together:[2]

'As the rain on the hillside comes in from the sea
All the blessings of life fall in showers from me
So if you'd abandon your old misery
Then you'll open your doors to the oil industry.

CHORUS: 'Conoco, Amoco, Shell–Esso, Texaco, British
   Petroleum, Yum Yum Yum.

'There's many a barrel of oil in the sea
All waiting for drilling and piping to me
I'll refine it in Texas, you'll get it you'll see
At four times the price that you sold it to me.'

The SNP audience listened to the magnificent Elizabeth MacLennan declaim when the performance was over, 'Nationalism is not enough.' For most of them it was. The banks and businesses were keen to make overtures to them. (Sir Hugh Fraser of Harrods' fame, and later notoriety, joined the SNP in 1974 – their most publicised recruit.) They were further strengthened by another piece of happy timing. The Royal Commission at last reported, two years late, in October 1973. (Its first chairman had died; his replacement was the eminent Scottish judge Lord Kilbrandon.) It backed devolution to the 'historic nationalities' of Scotland and Wales. In Scotland this would mean an elected assembly, the abolition of the office of Secretary of State, and a reduction in the number of Westminster MPs. Among the several dissenters on the commission, two, Norman Hunt and Professor Peacock, wanted uniform regional executive councils throughout Britain, anticipating the English backlash that would otherwise come. One day earlier Labour's Scottish Executive had put out a statement rejecting the idea of an assembly out of hand.

This line was soon tested. In a by-election in Labour's Glasgow stronghold the moribund Govan constituency Labour Party and its diminutive candidate were swept aside by the SNP's Margot MacDonald, who could speak with, and in the accents of, the West of Scotland working class, but with a captivating self-confidence and charm. Although MacDonald was defeated at the surprise general election of February 1974, the SNP had striking success in that election, sending its 'magnificent seven' newly elected MPs to Westminster. Most of these victories had been in Conservative territory; only two seats had been captured from Labour. But the threat to Labour's West of Scotland base was there for all to see. Once more Wilson moved to secure his rear. It was announced on 12 March that legislation on devolution would be drawn up. There was now a strong devolution lobby among the younger Scots Labour MPs, around John P. Mackintosh, who maintained that Britishness and Scottish devolution could and should go together. This duality was not strained, but natural, Mackintosh argued, quoting Burns to his purpose:[3]

> 'Be Britain still to Britain true
> Amang oorsels united,
> For never but by British hands
> Maun British wrong be righted.'

Unfortunately for them, the least united body in Scotland at that moment was the Scottish Labour Party. Its executive committee met to consider the various devolution options put up by the Wilson government in a White Paper. Only eleven of the twenty-nine members could spare the time for this matter. There was an important World Cup football match to distract them. Those who did turn up voted 6 to 5 against all the proposals, as 'constitutional tinkering' – to the rage of the Labour Party in London. Union heavyweights were shown a MORI poll indicating that without devolution Labour could lose another 13 seats to the SNP. The Scottish Party was abruptly told to reconvene. Helen Liddell remembers being 'verbally beaten up' by anti-devolutionists in the bitter arguments at the Dalintober Street conference:

'We were really at that time taken by the scruff of the neck by the National Executive Committee and by people, particularly in the trade union movement, who espoused devolution.'

Union powerbrokers such as Alex Kitson and Alec Donnett swung the block vote to good effect. They wanted another Labour government. To get it, Drucker comments:

'You had the ironic and really humiliating picture of the Labour Party in London forcing the Labour Party in Scotland to demand more power for Scotland against London.'

The new line was at least entrusted to people who believed in it. In a clumsily staged but candid election broadcast John P. Mackintosh appeared with three young candidates, Sillars (now the most committed devolutionist of all), Liddell and George Foulkes. The aim, he said, was to have 'a directly elected group of Members of Parliament sitting in Edinburgh . . . with certain powers of revenue and taxation allocated to them so they can choose what to spend our money on.'

And, said Liddell, 'They'll have control of the Scottish Development Agency,' which Labour planned to set up, using the funds of North Sea oil for the people of Scotland. The theme was to be 'Powerhouse Scotland'.

Up to a point this new strategy worked. Scottish Secretary William Ross held his tongue, then embraced devolution. The SNP won four further seats – but not from Labour – with 30% of the total vote. Given the Labour government's slender overall majority, their leverage in London remained. So devolution was coming. But in what form? The 1975 White Paper 'Our Changing Democracy' proposed elected assemblies for Scotland and Wales. The assembly in Scotland was not to have the power to raise revenue, determine economic policy or control the Scottish Development Agency. It was unpalatable equally to the SNP, who thought it toothless, and to northern Labour MPs, who saw it as a dangerous threat to their own claims for regional assistance. The Conservative opposition adopted the line they had bitterly resented when it was used by Harold Wilson over the EEC: they were in favour of the principle, but the terms were wrong. A year later Sillars, with heady thoughts of a major role for himself in a Scotland now confirmed through the referendum as a member of the EEC, quit the Labour Party to form his own short-lived party, much puffed by political journalists.

The battle in Scotland persisted between the Labour Party in its second-hand devolutionist clothes and the SNP, unsure whether it should continue to wear its old garb of separatism. Gavin Kennedy, who later chaired the SNP's Defence Committee, has no doubt that a chance was missed:

'I have to say in all honesty we had our chance – we flunked it. I doubt if we'll ever get another . . . We missed our opportunity by a combination of: one, political immaturity . . . secondly, because we didn't grow fast enough in the period when we were the leading party in Scotland, the leading edge; and thirdly, we were totally out-manoeuvred by the Labour Party.'

Douglas Henderson, one of the 'magnificent seven' MPs, agrees that it was wrong to give support to half-baked devolution: 'The party ought to have stood for its principles and ought to have denounced it.'

The SNP group at Westminster carried no big guns. There was often ill will between those who had been elected and those in the titular leadership of the SNP who had not. At first these things barely mattered, because Labour was in trouble enough of its own.

In a tactical blunder, despite the differences between the two countries and what was proposed for them, Scottish and Welsh devolution was lumped together in the Devolution Bill. This helped to maximise opposition in the Commons, where Michael Foot and John Smith were taking the bill slowly and painfully on the floor of the House. Labour MPs from the north-east and north-west of England, the forceful Anglophone anti-devolutionists from Wales such as the rising Neil Kinnock and the hard core of Scots dissenters barred the way. Tam Dalyell of West Lothian, most pertinacious opponent of all, organised 70 of his colleagues in a declaration that they could not support a timetable motion to guillotine the debates. In the event, 22 did so refuse, and voted with the opposition. The motion was lost, and with it the bill. Dalyell put then, and continued with unwearying zeal to put for the next two years, what he called the West Lothian Question. Why should he, as a Scots MP, have the right to vote on English matters in West Bromwich or Westhoughton, along with 70 other Scots, while the Members for those areas had no say in what happened in West Lothian? Labour would keep a British majority thanks to the Scots and Welsh contingents, and there would be no assembly for England. Douglas Henderson thinks that:

'Tam Dalyell was quite right to point out these inconsistencies, and I don't disagree with them or dispute them. And I think we should have come out much more strongly and said yes, he's absolutely right. It's independence we need.'

The magic moment for the nationalists was the spring of 1977. Perfidious London had failed to deliver its compromise. Labour was torn, and the Conservatives under Margaret Thatcher were swinging strongly against devolution – much though this distressed some Scots Tories. The opinion polls showed the SNP in the lead in Scotland with 36% of the vote. James Naughtie, then a young Scots journalist, remembers:

'. . . a heady sense of self-importance, an almost incestuous interest in all our institutions which were being re-examined . . . I think some people in Edinburgh used to look forward to Embassy Row springing up somewhere in the terraces of Edinburgh . . . There was a sense of great excitement about the future, and in the arts and politics . . . of a rebirth coming.'

In this climate of ferment the nationalists took themselves more seriously than most. The SNP Defence Committee proposed a defence budget for Scotland nine times that of Eire. As chairman Gavin Kennedy recalls, they were heady days:

'We spent hours and hours in endless meetings, policy meetings, discussing everything, right down to the titles of district officers and the size of farms that would be permitted . . . On the Defence Committee at the time I joined it they were actually designing epaulettes and badges for the regiments that would be taken out of the British army.'

That spring, while Callaghan tried to put together his Lib–Lab Pact at Westminster, the SNP made a breakthrough in local government. Even Glasgow slipped from Labour's grasp. 'It was my darkest hour,' remembers Helen Liddell, just appointed Secretary of the Scottish Labour Party, but she counts the blessings that came under this heavy disguise. Once they were in local power, the contradictions in the SNP left/right coalition became apparent. It had all happened too soon for the talent available. Gavin Kennedy was on the selection panel considering applicants:

'Quite often, our members in this committee would say. "Well this person's not really suitable, but they're never going to get elected, so why have a hassle of rejecting them?" And some of them did get elected, and they were absolutely appalling.'

The SNP was also hamstrung by the nature of its support. The polls showed a large majority of Scots, and even half of SNP supporters, to be against independence. It was devolution of power the Scots appeared to want. They veered towards the SNP when Labour appeared unable to deliver, then back to Labour when it proposed to do so. The SNP had to hang on to its devolutionist support, knowing that only if this 'halfway house' was never reached could it play for the journey to a separate destination and independence. The SNP in conference, under banners proclaiming 'Scotland a Nation Once Again', may have looked like a party expecting 37 seats at the next election, and then secession. In practice it had to deny that that was the aim, to the dismay of Gavin Kennedy:

'The mistake we made when the separatist charge came up was to try to deny it. And by denying it you made it worse . . . We said, "We're not *really* separatists." Well, we *are* separatists. We wished to separate Scottish government from English government.'

Unwilling to distance themselves from a further attempt at devolution, the Nationalists were trapped. They had to support the two separate Scotland and Wales bills brought forward in 1977. The government used their new Liberal allies to press for wider devolution, then sold out to the recalcitrant Labour backbenchers on what their business managers called 'the revolving door' strategy. What might have come out to please the rebels had to be popped back to sweeten the Liberals. The bills went through with some dispatch, because their opponents knew that this time the last word might be with them. There were to be separate referenda in Scotland and Wales to approve the form of devolution agreed by Parliament. The expatriate Scot George Cunningham, who was throughout the seventies one of the half-dozen most effective backbenchers, knew that he had no chance of persuading the Labour leadership of his fears:

'They were committed to go on marching into the sea, deeper and deeper, until their hats floated. It was necessary for someone else to call halt, and that's what we did.'

Cunningham moved an amendment which made the establishment of the two devolved assemblies dependent on 40% of all those entitled to vote declaring in the affirmative. Cunningham says that the original idea came from his younger colleague Robin Cook, an able Scot who had always been troubled about the costs and benefits of devolution. Cook had wanted a 33% vote. Fanatical anti-devolutionists wanted 50%. They split the difference at 40%. (At the time of the amendment 40% looked well within reach.) 'What the amendment did,' Cunningham argues, 'was to make it credible that this juggernaut was going to be stopped.' Only then would those with doubts see that they had a genuine choice in the exercise. Cunningham did not stop the juggernaut, but he attached a limpet mine to it.

The amendment enraged the nationalists. Douglas Henderson says:

'We've always had the feeling in Scotland that when the English start losing they change the rules of the game. If they're losing at football, they tell you it's cricket they're playing . . . Forty per cent of the electorate, not just the people voting . . . If that was applied to parliamentary elections, Britain would not have had a government this century.'

But a majority of the SNP had to stick with the bill; it was not the summit of their ambitions, but it was a base camp. They wanted to avoid the odium that would result from their destroying the bill by bringing the government down before the March 1979 referendum.

Their quandary was that they could not attack Labour, but Labour could attack them.

The government could display a concern for Scotland. Chrysler had been rescued, and Linwood with it. The Scottish Development Agency was in business, with a wider remit than the NEB in England, and the possibility of backing winners rather than helping losers. The Agency was also involved in the transformation of the grimmest parts of Glasgow with the GEAR urban renewal programme which began in 1976. The British National Oil Corporation (BNOC) was set up, with its headquarters in Glasgow and a distinctively Scottish flavour. There were comforting Scots accents in the ministerial team at the Department of Energy. The coming of the oilmen stimulated Scotland's banking and legal services, already second only to London in expertise, and second to none in their sense of their own locality, and their responsibilities to it. Scotland is small enough to be a community. Its major centres flourish as networks, where paths continually cross, at university, in politics, in business, where the question 'Who was on the plane today?' is as naturally asked at the Glasgow end of the shuttle as it would be absurd in London. The SNP had helped to put the Scottish community in the spotlight, which made it easier to use what one leading banker calls 'the Scottish crowbar' to prise more money out of central government. But the Scots also used the crowbar on themselves, on their reserves of money and talent. And they were asking about separation: what would they get out of it?

Labour had been lucky too. When the Nationalists had been riding high, there had been no by-elections. In 1978 there were three, all won handsomely by typical products of the new-style party: Donald Dewar, John Home Robertson and George Robertson. The latter defeated the SNP's most glamorous campaigner, Margot MacDonald – at Hamilton. ('Make Sure of Your Assembly', her election address had said, but for that the voters turned to Labour, which appeared to be genuinely committed to it.) Fear of rising unemployment, plus a sense that the Labour Party had somehow come back to them, swayed the electorate. The breakaway Sillars Party was disintegrating in rancorous feuds. (Sillars was later to marry Margot MacDonald, and embrace the SNP too.) By contrast, Professor Drucker observes:

'The fact that the Labour Party now stood on constitutional ground which proposed important improvements for Scotland but was not in any way extreme or worrying or frightening came together to make the nationalist position impossible.'

There remained the referendum to win. In Wales, where opposition had always commanded a majority, the devolutionists had no chance. Wales was to vote by 4 to 1 against a Welsh assembly. In Scotland the assumption throughout 1978 had been that devolution would be carried; all the political parties were committed to it, or at least could not afford to be seen to be hostile to it. In March 1979 this was not so. The figure of 40% necessary to activate the devolution legislation suddenly began to look distant. This referendum was not to follow the pattern of that on the Common Market, with impressive lists of cross-party speakers on each side. The SNP and Labour saw themselves as rivals in the coming general election; neither wished to be seen to be playing the other's game. Therefore they did not co-operate. This did not prevent some of their respective activists sitting out the campaign. Any identification with what was thought to be the chauvinism of the SNP was avoided with superstitious dread by Labour leaders. (There had even been some private signs of relief at the ignominious collapse of 'Ally's Army' – the Scotland team in the World Cup – in the summer of 1978: victory might have swept the SNP onwards.) So although the younger generation of Scots Labour MPs fought hard for a yes vote, though sadly deprived by his early death of the advocacy of John P. Mackintosh, the loudest Labour voice which the electorate heard was that of the irrepressible Tam Dalyell. Dalyell took to the courts to get parity in television time between the pro- and anti-devolutionist campaigns, which forced the referendum broadcasts off the air. He debated the defector Sillars up and down Scotland, further confusing Labour voters about the party's position.

There should have been no doubt about that. The party in Scotland, anxious not to widen its differences, settled on a personality campaign. Helen Liddell says:

'We decided to use the establishment figure of Jim Callaghan, which would help allay people's fears about devolution, and we went through a very expensive and very extensive poster campaign that featured Jim Callaghan just with the word 'Yes' on it. We hadn't banked on the Winter of Discontent . . .'

Callaghan's popularity in Scotland had been high in 1978. In the winter of 1979 it was not. The 'Yes' posters may have garnered some no votes, and more abstentions.

The Conservatives, for their part, sought to use the referendum as a dress rehearsal for an anti-Labour vote at the coming general election. Margaret Thatcher was notoriously cool on devolution. She did not have her predecessor's faith in constitutional reform. But some Tories were ardent devolutionists. The strategy was to attack the Scotland Act, but not the principle of devolution. Lord Home, who in other days had backed the Declaration of Perth, now reappeared to advise a no vote. He said in Edinburgh:

'I should hesitate to vote no if I did not think the parties would keep the devolution issue at the top of their priorities.'

His opponents found this approach deceitful. Home argues today that the Tories' view changed because behind devolution was the separatism of the SNP:

'That frightened the majority of Scotsmen out of their lives, because if a Scotsman knows anything he knows which way his belly's buttoned, but it also made no sense whatsoever, and until we got that out of the picture we thought we'd better go slow on devolution.'

The argument worked for most Scottish Conservatives. They were further influenced by the presence of the Scottish industrialists in the well-financed no campaign, 'Scotland is British', who were fearful of a separate economic policy. 'At the moment,' said John Davidson of the Scottish CBI, 'there's a border between Scotland and England, and all it is is a notice on the A74.' If devolution led to another layer of bureaucracy, and additional taxes, 'Industry felt that would be very destructive.' So the CBI said no.

In the event, Scotland did say yes to devolution – narrowly. Of those voting 51.6% were in favour. More significant, though, was the fact that 36.4% of the electorate did not vote at all. 32.9% voted yes, 30.8% voted no. The yes figure came nowhere near the stipulation of the Cunningham amendment. Even without it, the figures would have represented a singularly lukewarm endorsement of an idea which two years before seemed to have taken Scotland by storm. The sad, inevitable sequel was that the SNP had to punish the Labour government by rejecting offers of further talks and opting for a no confidence vote in the knowledge that the party was likely to be decimated in an early election. (It was reduced to two MPs in the May election.) The failure rankles, but Stephen Maxwell does not think that the five years in which devolution dominated the national debate were wasted:

'They . . . undoubtedly increased the political awareness of Scottish opinion as a whole. Second, and this may be more critical, it tutored a new young generation of Labour Party members in the national question.'

The SNP had not set out to achieve the rejuvenation of the Scottish

Labour Party but to advocate the potential of a separate Scotland. The
increased interest in all things Scottish meant that the distant threat of
such a separation was taken seriously in the south. The Scots could
turn this to their purpose, greatly strengthening the Scottish Development Agency when the political climate became icy for such bodies.
The Agency contrived to become within a very few years a force in
urban renewal and factory leasing, as well as in the promotion of
industry. Oil became a less powerful political weapon, but it produced
some 60,000 related jobs and the wealth generated in the North Sea
trickled down to those industries and services canny enough to exploit
it. Electronics began to boom, though with a disappointingly small
impact on unemployment. A relatively small society where those on
both sides of industry know that 'if you don't know somebody, you
know somebody who does' can use this shared sense of identity.

'Imagine the guffaws in the City,' wrote a visiting *Economist*
correspondent up to see the effect of the Scottish crowbar for himself,
'if you went to it for funds arguing that yours is an English company
creating prosperity and jobs for England. You will not hear them in
Edinburgh.'[4] For the first time since the Act of Union the English came
north to see if they could learn from Scotland's more flexible system of
higher education, from features of Scottish law such as the office of the
Procurator Fiscal. The national debate has had its impact, and this
gives both the SNP and those younger politicians in other parties who
were forced into dialogue with it some sense of achievement. Gavin
Kennedy sees this as the main vindication of the long argument about
identity:

'You began to see Scottish all over the world – the word Scottish. I
don't just mean kilts and tartan and all that rubbish . . . Scotland
became a place, not a backwater north of Watford. Became a place in
its own right . . . These don't really amount to much, but they're the
remnants, if you like, the vapour trails of a great event that took place.'

15

JUBILEE!

1977 will be remembered for many things. Britain had a coalition government by another name, in the Lib–Lab pact, and a Prime Minister who in his first broadcast after taking office asked Britain whether it felt, like him, that standards were slipping. Violence on the picket line in pursuit of trade union recognition at Grunwick and the first successful prosecution for half a century for blasphemous libel, of *Gay News*, provided evidence of a kind for both left and right that Callaghan had a point. With Scottish and Welsh nationalism rampant, with Northern Ireland still caught between rival pieties and terrors, most symbols of the British nation seemed at a discount. The celebration of Elizabeth II's Silver Jubilee as Queen of the United Kingdom of Great Britain and Northern Ireland seemed a chancy affair at such a time.

In the event the British, and two-thirds of the Northern Irish, decided that one way to confront a future that might not work was with the trappings of a past which had worked. Their affection for the monarchy sprang in part from the fact that it had come through the quarter-century apparently undiminished, in sharp contrast to everything else. The second Elizabethan age, of superpower status on vanished means, of brave new ventures from the Comet to the conquest of Everest, had not turned out as planned. Empire had been transmuted into a somewhat seedy Commonwealth. Britain's first colony, and her last, witnessed bloodshed verging on civil war. At home we were a pawn of the international bankers. It seemed a long time since the pound had been worth a pound. *The Times* lamented:

'The everyday symbol of that decline is the common token of exchange, the pound note, bearing the Queen's image, and now having a value one quarter of the value it had when the Queen came to the throne.'

That value had vanished along with the pre-decimal coinage, the old, solid, massively obsolete pounds, shillings and pence, the familiar jingle of half-crowns and bobs and tanners, phased out in 1971. The general suspicion had been that decimalisation was all due to official Europhilia, as well as a convenient excuse to level up prices.

In fact the British had something to celebrate. They had survived without major wars or disasters, in a continent incomparably more prosperous than it had been in 1952. The standard of living was twice as high, as R. A. Butler had promised back in 1951. Four out of five British households now lived in a home with a garden. Well over half had the mobility of car ownership. The telephone, the television set and the refrigerator were commonplace where they had been middle-class luxuries in 1952. British eating habits had been revolutionised, not least by successive generations of immigrants, Italian, Hungarian and Indian, all of whose influence yielded pride of place to Britain's 2000 Chinese restaurants, which enabled a grateful nation to watch the Jubilee junkets on television over a plateful of takeaway chow mein. British holidays had improved too. There were now 1200 miles of motorway linking Britain's cities and countryside for the new generation of motorists. Real poverty remained; in some areas it had intensified relative to the raised standards overall. Unemployment stood at a record postwar level of 6.2%. But for the 90% in work, whose rising real incomes had no more than faltered occasionally in the decade, there had been an advance on the material conditions of their parents. For them the Jubilee was more a national house-warming party than an orgy of nostalgia for the white-washed cottages of yesteryear.

The Jubilee had political significance too. The government was grateful for it, for it added to the balm of reassurance that was spread over the Callaghan era. On one famous occasion the political aspect assumed greater importance. On 4 May, the day after the SNP had scored a resounding success in the Scottish district elections, with Labour's devolution strategy gone awry, Queen Elizabeth II came to Westminster Hall to tell the assembled Lords and Commons, in exchange for a Loyal Address, that she could never forget that she had been crowned Queen of the United Kingdom of Great Britain and Northern Ireland. It was not quite George III on the American colonies, but the message to separatists was very clear.

The Queen began her Jubilee tour in Scotland, where there was no noticeable resentment at her rebuff of the separatist wing of the SNP. The general enthusiasm for the visits took opinion-formers by surprise. The plentiful supply of royal personages to open every known British institution does not diminish the appetite for more. The press

devoted many columns to the fortitude of otherwise sane members of
the general public who slept all night in plastic rubbish sacks on the
pavement in order to get a glimpse of the Queen passing. Everywhere
street parties were held, on a scale not seen since the end of the war.
They were small-scale carnivals in their own right – 4000 in London
alone – which conjured up the old sense of community, and sometimes
regenerated it. The most bizarre street party was held in Queen Street,
Rugeley. The street no longer existed. It had been demolished and built
over by the planners. For the Jubilee, however, its former residents
came together on the site. For them, the past really had been better
than the present.

There was bell-ringing. There were bonfires – a chain of them all
round the country were set ablaze on 6 June, the first by the Queen at
Windsor. There was bunting with flags and rosettes on many houses
from gutter to grate. Various individuals made brief headlines by
turning themselves into walking flags. A Leamington art teacher
turned his house front into a gigantic version of the Annigoni portrait
of the Queen. Others had their hair, their bodies or their poodles dyed
in red, white and blue. Nothing could match the vulgarity of the
souvenir industry, which turned out eveything from scarves and scent
to buttons and bras with patriotic gall. The Portmeirion Jubilee potty
was vetoed by the Lord Chamberlain, and triumphantly relaunched as
a 'planter' with the addition of a second handle. The sex magazines
Penthouse, Forum and *Mayfair* all produced Jubilee editions – without official approval.

There was no official blessing either for the Sex Pistols pop group,
whose new lyric opened bluntly:

> God save the Queen,
> A fascist regime
> Made you a moron,
> A potential H-bomb
>
> God save the Queen,
> She ain't no human being
> There ain't no future in
> England's dream.

The gusts of official disapproval propelled the single up the charts
like a hot-air balloon. The *Sunday Mirror* spluttered in the week after
the Jubilee:

'Top chain stores are refusing to stock the record. Concert promoters have cancelled Sex Pistols' appearances. But such is the new-found and disturbing power of punk that nothing can stop the disc's runaway success.'

Vivienne Westwood reported more indulgently:[1]

'Little boys come running into my shop and say, "Do you really think the Queen is a moron?" ... If you took away the Queen, the army and all those people wouldn't have this figurehead to look up to that smiles at them and pretends everything's all right. Maybe though, she doesn't know what's going on, the old burke.'

Johnny Rotten of the Sex Pistols was attacked and razor-slashed by an anonymous loyalist in a pub.

The Jubilee was a bad time for more orthodox republicans, heirs to a long tradition, who were painfully reminded that in Britain they were thin on the ground. The red flag was hoisted at Ruskin College, Oxford. A decent profit was earned by the manufacturers of 'Stuff the Jubilee' badges. The *New Statesman* self-consciously produced an anti-Jubilee edition with a hostile profile of the consort and a collection of rude essays about the monarch by North London schoolchildren. One wrote, 'She doesn't care for any babye and shes got a big mouth like Jaws and shes an old bag shes only wants money and to be rich.'

Nothing by the paper's adult contributors matched this for invective. The anti-Jubilee issue was a firecracker that failed to fizz. The *Morning Star* tried harder, concentrating on the social divisions which the celebrations obscured. Its efforts to show the seamy side of the royal racket did not get beyond pictures of the flunkeys whose job it was to walk along behind and sweep up after the royal horses. A People's Jubilee at Alexandra Palace on 19 June, featuring the veteran Spanish Communist Santiago Carrillo, did not cover its costs. But it was a bumper success compared to the demonstration called on Blackheath by the Libertarian Communists' 1649 Committee, which attracted only five people and was rained off. The causes for which a king's head had been cut off in 1649 seemed obscure in 1977. The cruellest cut for a showbiz monarchy would have been indifference. That was a fate suffered by its critics. Apart from one scorcher from the *Sun* _ 'Out of the woodwork they crawl, the Termites of the Left' – the anti-Jubilee demonstrators were cruelly ignored.

In Northern Ireland it was different. The Queen came late to the province. Sectarian bitterness had already marred the thanksgiving service in Belfast, boycotted by Presbyterian fanatics because a Catholic was to take part. The proximity of the royal visit on 11 August to the Apprentice Boys' parades unsettled the Catholic community, who saw the British crown as a symbol of their alienation, Queen Elizabeth as the heir of William III. So, while there were bonfires and dancing in the Shankhill, the Catholic enclaves stayed quiet and undecorated. It was difficult to get things right. Some were offended because the Queen wore a green dress; their opponents because she visited sites, such as Coleraine University, which were held to be the product of favours to the Protestant community. The image of the visit in the media – in sharp contrast to the way the rest of the royal tours that summer were portrayed – was of a disunited kingdom.

Mr Peregrine Worsthorne took it upon himself to make a progress around Jubilee Britain, patronised the Scots and was pleasantly surprised by some northern towns. His hosts included his brother, 'who lives a few miles outside Burnley', a magnifico otherwise known as the Custos Rotularum of Lancashire, and Mike Yarwood. Worsthorne reported Yarwood's problem in catching the tone of the royals for his imitations:[2]

'Mike Yarwood has spent a frustrating day trying to write a take-off of the Prince of Wales, whose character and way of talking are terribly difficult for him to catch. The trouble, he says, is Charles's superior education, which places him outside Yarwood's secondary-modern range.'

Elsewhere Worsthorne found Jubilee Britain in good heart, still living it up in spite of the ravages of the socialists, although one of his hosts had had to economise by switching off the heating in the swimming pool.

Did the Jubilee add up to more than a pleasant day out in the sun for most people? Was it true, as the Labour Lord Chancellor said in the radical spirit of the administration, that 'amid the debris of political controversy we yearn for the symbols of national unity'? There were many ready to add to a contemporary myth of monarchy the view that the cynicism and levity of the pranksters, satirists and liberal trendies since the early sixties had obscured the real affection and loyalty with which the Queen's subjects regarded her, as she presided stoically over Britain's national decline. To read Mr Ronald Butt's panegyrics to the hereditary principle in The Times, or the hopes of Mr Hugh Montgomery-Massingberd that the Queen should now extend her kingdom to embrace a federal Europe, was to see that this was not a time for a proper debate about the subtle advantages of monarchy or its limitations. The British were invited to contemplate an institution *sans pareil*, whose virtues had continued unchanged down the ages. In fact, modern monarchy and the rituals which accompany it are relatively modern inventions, like the stately Royal Progress through London devised by Lord Esher for Edward VII. Popular esteem was for the person at the centre of it all, as mediated by the press and television. Through the mediators the British saw the Queen as they would have liked to see themselves: she had her family troubles, was still respected in the neighbourhood, had managed to hang on to the family property – above all, she was a survivor. As the small lady with the slow smile travelled round the British Isles, myth and person fused. She was there. She had come through. There was a flash of sentiment, and plentiful affection. Then, like the Jubilee crowns, they were put away among the national souvenirs.

16

THE WOMEN'S HOUR

In 1960 the only woman in Britain who was the head of her profession was the Queen. Some rose high, as some always had, but they rose in a man's world, making the sacrifices necessary to accommodate to its assumptions. In terms of a surface prominence, women shared in the expansive optimism of the sixties, but they learned with some pain that greater visibility was not the same as greater viability for the lives they wished to lead. They were told it was an age of liberation. In some genuine respects it was. The 1967 Abortion Act was the first real blow for a generation to the tyranny of the back-street quack for the poor and the flash privateer for the wealthy and discreet. Cheap and reliable contraception opened up the possibility of wider and less guilt-ridden sexuality. Divorce was stripped of some of its archaic humiliations. The pop festival, the flower culture, and the soaring mini-skirt: all carried the expectations of sexual freedom. The advertising world spoke its language, sometimes to the exclusion of all others. Women's bodies became the most potent selling image of the time. As Professor Stuart Hall says:

'Sex moves from a topic you can't speak about to the bonnet of the next car you want to sell . . . and something has been missed in that jump from sexual prudery into sexual permissiveness, and that's the real sexual revolution.'

The permissive revolution made big gains in a certain kind of freedom. The new generation were much envied by those who felt, with Philip Larkin, that this new sexuality was:[1]

> . . . everyone young going down the long slide
> To happiness, endlessly . . .

It was only later that young women found that the new permissiveness was something less than freedom. They were still exploited, expected to be subordinate. Few men are as candid about the way in which the sixties were turned to male advantage as the present GLC leader Ken Livingstone, when he says:

'There was all this supposed liberation, but it was more a greater ease by which men got to go to bed with women. There's no real change in the relationship, it's still dreadfully exploited. I think women were under this incredible pressure not to complain, because this was progress and it was change and it was good. And I think they went away thinking: why am I not enjoying this?'

Sex was the way men wanted it to be – just as so much of the structure of work, family and leisure were organised in the way they wanted it to be. The writer Beatrix Campbell reflects that:

'The sexual revolution barely touched women's pleasure. It may have expanded women's access to sex but it was the same old kind of sex.'

In all the snapshots of that upbeat decade women are there. They were desired, by the man and the camera of the moment; they were scolded by the moralists. In fiction and film, from *The Collector* to *Blow-Up*, they never fluttered free. Even the most effective representations of working-class struggle in fiction had embedded in them 'the tragedy of the man's resistance being at the expense of the woman'.[2] The writer Lynne Segal remembers the realisation at the time that:

'Much of what had been happening in the sixties was a continuation of the way in which women in society generally were subordinate to men. So while women were active in all the campaigns that were going on, they were active in a subordinate way. So they were the ones licking the envelopes and making the cups of tea. They were the ones doing the background work while the men were in the foreground.'

A revolution within the revolution was required. In everything from the sexual act to the wage packet, the necessary satisfaction of men remained paramount while women were relegated to a secondary role.

This was a source of bitter disillusion, not only to the young middle-class women beginning to gain access to the higher education or freewheeling lifestyle previously the prerogative of their brothers, but also on the shopfloor. In the world of Rosie the Riveter and her British counterparts there was no equality with men. Women sewing-machinists at Ford's Dagenham plant had struck in 1968 for re grading, in protest at having to do the same job as men for less money. The strike threw down the gauntlet to the TUC and the Labour Party, which had paid lip service to the principle of equal pay for a decade, and intermittently for eighty years. They found that men saw this as a 'divisive' claim. Madge Crooks was one of the machinists' spokeswomen. She remembers:

'The men would not come out, although we asked them to come out with us, and fight for us . . . They thought we were working for pin money. Women's work is always pin money, if you're married . . . If they'd come out with us, it would have been over in days.'

The dispute was resolved after Barbara Castle, the Employment Secretary, had a much publicised tea party with 'the girls' (see chapter 1). The women went back, but to be paid only 95% of the men's rate, and remained in the unskilled grade. At the moment of writing full parity has still not been achieved. What the strike did achieve was a signal to other women to intensify the pressure for equal pay in law. A National Joint Action Campaign for Women's Equal Rights was formed among trade unionists and other sympathisers to press for equal pay and equal opportunity to be more than the empty platitudes of government and TUC. A major demonstration in 1969 helped to force the cause back on the political agenda. The Equal Pay Act was passed at the beginning of the new decade, in May 1970. But it was so hopelessly hedged around with qualifications, with delicate ambiguities about what constituted 'equal pay for work of equal value', that it scarcely looked like a historic turning point – especially as it was not to come into force for five years.

At the same time, another group of campaigners against work to role were preparing a wider assault. By the end of the sixties women in Britain were beginning to feel that 'strange stirring, a sense of dissatisfaction' which Betty Friedan in the United States had called 'the problem that has no name'.[3] It was a sense of alienation from a world that seemed to be full of concern for civil rights – except theirs; keen for liberation – except theirs. As Beatrix Campbell recalls:

'To move from the sixties where there were all these explosions, a feeling that things were on the move; and to come out of that feeling that women were still nowhere, still zilch really, was excruciating. And I imagine that for some women that was experienced as an implosion, quite a self-destructive thing. And for others it produced feminism.'

So women began first to talk and then to organise. 'Consciousness-raising' groups grew up around the country, exploring the disparity between the expectations put upon women as wives, mothers, lovers, consumers, and their real needs and aspirations as individuals. Slowly, a different reality unfolded. It happened to Audrey Battersby, with a broken marriage and three small children, one disabled, at a course run in 1969 by Juliet Mitchell:[4]

'Then the bells rang and the connections were made and there was the feeling of militancy that I'd never experienced before, despite involvement in various left-wing groups. I was no longer alone, but part of a movement which was primarily political but could be personal to me.'

There were many like her. By the time of the first Women's Liberation conference at Ruskin College in 1970, a political agenda was formulated to address those inequalities which limited women's lives. In the analysis of the role which women had been compelled to act out according to male expectations, the conventional barriers between the personal and the 'political' were erased. One of the organisers wrote:[5]

'We thought perhaps a hundred women would come. In fact more than five hundred people turned up, four hundred women, sixty children and forty men, and we had to go into the Oxford Union buildings because Ruskin was too small. I'd never seen so many women looking so confident in my life before.'

The women's movement did not rely on charismatics, or on a central organisation or secretariat. It was about attitudes as well as Acts of Parliament. Because of the lurid and distorted press tales from the 1968 disruption of the Miss America contest, feminists had been caricatured as bra-burning harpies intent on phallic destruction. For some time the conventional power structures ignored the women's movement in Britain altogether. Collectively, women do not get a single mention in the index of Anthony Sampson's compendious *New Anatomy of Britain*, published in 1971.[6] In that year, marches were held in Liverpool and London on International Women's Day, under the banner of the four basic demands of the movement: equal pay now, equal education and job opportunity, free contraception and abortion on demand, and twenty-four-hour nurseries. Far from the old Beveridge assumptions of the 1940s on which welfare provision for women as housewives was based, it was a programme addressed to the realities of the 1970s, when women worked not for pin money but to keep families above the poverty line, either through multiple household earnings, or as the single parent and sole breadwinner. Women needed equal access to what education offered. (Sampson's 1971 survey noted that only five of all Britain's universities had as many as 45% women students; none had more than half.) And they needed equality at work, with the facilities to make true equality possible.

It was clear that the Equal Pay Act would be meaningless unless it was accompanied by the statutory right to equal opportunity. The nature of women's work was (and largely still is) in an employment ghetto. By 1980 57% of working women were in only four service industries. The majority of jobs in those industries were all-women in practice. The Equal Pay Act would have very little effect in these segregated workplaces, unless 'women's work' could be revalued. In the five years they had to prepare for the coming of the Act, employers were carefully preparing to sidetrack it by regrading and resegregating jobs. Sometimes this was done with the tacit connivance of the trade unions, where cherished differentials seemed threatened. The campaign for an Anti-Discrimination Bill was begun by Joyce Butler MP in 1967. Her bill fell at its first parliamentary hurdle. The Liberal Lady Seear managed to get a Lords bill referred to a select committee. In the Commons Willie Hamilton set off on the same route, and with the same destination. Despite intense lobbying, torchlight processions and press support, the bills were lost in favour of an ineffectual Green Paper from the Heath government. Hopes that there would at least be forceful proposals from the cabinet's only woman member were disappointed. Margaret Thatcher saw no reason to set an example in education and training.

Nothing seemed lost, however, when the Labour government returned precariously to power in 1974. It introduced the 1975 Sex Discrimination Act, which came into force at the same time as the Equal Pay Act, in an acknowledgement that the two had to work together. Sex discrimination was taken to include education, training, housing, employment and the provision of goods and services. An Equal Opportunities Commission (EOC), based in Manchester, was set up to enforce the Acts. In that same year – International Women's Year – the government embellished its Social Contract with the Social Security (Pensions) Act to help women whose working lives had been disrupted by home responsibilities, and the Employment Protection Act, with its provisions for paid maternity leave, protection from unfair dismissal, and a right of return to the same job for up to twenty-nine weeks after the birth.

This was no mean package, in principle. How would it work in practice? The greatest disappointment was the EOC. It gave assistance to many of the cases which went before employment tribunals – over 200 by 1981. But in that same period it initiated only six formal investigations of its own. The charge against it by feminists was that it had the power, but not the will. The commissioners argued that they had to proceed with circumspection, building up a body of research and guidelines, rather than winning publicity for major cases of law enforcement. Dipak Nandy, EOC deputy chief executive, argues that quangoes like the CRE and EOC are hobbled by the very fact of their dual function:

'On the one hand they're asked to eliminate unlawful discrimination ... and that requires a certain steel of nerve and purpose, a willingness to be unfriendly and to encourage unpopularity. The second task was ... of promoting equality of opportunity between men and women generally, and that seems to me to be a recipe for paralysis.'

Had the EOC concentrated on its first task, it would have done better with those whom it was intended to protect. There were some cases which came before the industrial tribunals which showed just what a handful of vigorous judgements could have done. Belinda Price, who won her case against the Civil Service when she claimed that a maximum entry age of twenty-eight discriminated against women who had born children in their twenties, burst the entry requirements wide open. The case served to remind public opinion that it had to look behind the spate of 'firsts' among women in employment – first newsreader, judge, airline pilot, taxi driver – to see not the first but the few. In too many professions the line taken was that of Sir Humphrey Appleby in *Yes, Minister*, when asked why none of the forty-one Permanent Secretaries was female:[7]

'If women were able to be good Permanent Secretaries there would be more of them, wouldn't there? Stands to reason.'

The October 1974 Parliament itself had only twenty-seven women MPs and reacted with huffy disdain when its youngest Member, Helene Hayman, asked for a crèche for her infant child.

The bulk of women in employment were, and remain, in the lowest paid sections of the workforce. With the implementation of the Equal Pay Act there was a temporary narrowing of the differential between men's and women's wages; by 1977, women were receiving 75.5% of men's wages. After that, the gap widened again, and by the early eighties women's pay was back to 70% of men's. When equal pay cases were taken to the tribunals, there was no guarantee that the judgement could be made to apply to other workers in the same factory. In the most notorious long-running case, that at Electrolux, management made haste slowly in acting on the decision of courts. The Electrolux workers made an attractive and articulate presentation of their grievances about the better-paid men on the night-shift – men whom in some cases, they themselves had trained, as they were not slow to point out. One of the most striking images of the time was the smoke-filled room in which the women confronted a platform of exclusively male trade union representatives resentful that they were pushing this sectional cause. Prodded by the courts, the EOC embarked on an investigation of Electrolux. Four years later it had still not been fully completed. Nor had any way been worked out of preventing managements who had to concede equality in one grade moving women employees to other grades later. Not surprisingly, the number of applications to tribunals under both Acts fell steadily between 1976 and 1979.

It was clear that the best protection for women, given the vulnerability of their working conditions, was to be active in trade unions themselves. The number of women trade unionists rose substantially in the 1970s. From 1968 to 1978 NUPE increased its female membership from 130,000 to 457,000, a leap of 236%; ASTMS from 9400 to 77,000; and the AUEW from 97,400 to 148,300. Feminists within the unions began to press for greater representation at executive level, and to set up their own equal opportunities' committees. The Working Women's Charter, set up in 1974, was used to push for changes in life at work. It originated with women in the London Trades Council, and was adopted by a number of unions and political bodies. It set out a number of demands which, taken together, would have allowed women genuine equality in the workplace: eighteen weeks' paid maternity leave, free contraception, abortion on demand, day nurseries, an increase in family allowances, a national minimum wage, and an end to discrimination in tax and social security. The TUC was pushed into adopting a similar list of demands in 1975, partly to head off the more left-wing groups behind the Charter.

The demands were not met, except in a partial and piecemeal way in individual union agreements. But they gave the women's movement, with its broad front and (for men) baffling combination of diverse aims and intense sorority, a chance to make some new gains, and protect some old ones, in the more restrictive climate of the seventies. Free contraception on the NHS was incorporated into the 1974 NHS (Reorganisation) Act; this now includes vasectomy for men as well as the provision of appliances. Since 1974 saw the height of the population lobby in Britain, in this respect women campaigned in accordance with the wisdom of the times. In the struggle to prevent the curtailment of abortion law reform, however, they had to combat a powerful new

pressure group. The great increase in the number of abortions performed annually affronted the Catholic Church. Others were alarmed
by the private traffickers' huge profits. In November 1972 the *Guardian* reported one clinic owner, who had a capacity for 11,000
abortions a year at £200 a time, as saying. 'I did not grapple with my
conscience but with commercial viability.'

The pressure groups Life and the Society for the Protection of the
Unborn Child (SPUC) harnessed concerns about the spiralling abortion rate into a powerful campaign to restrict the terms of the 1967
Act. Outside Westminster they had formidable polemicists. Inside they
had the Catholics and a substantial number of MPs worried either by
the number of abortions or the number of constituents who lobbied
them on the subject. Anyone who took up this standard would have
the support of the mercurial Leo Abse MP, who combined unique
expertise in private members' legislation with a low view of the
motivation of his women colleagues. (He wrote of them, 'They are
endowed with high intelligence but are fated by constitution or
upbringing never to acquire a full creative femininity; that requires the
full travail of working through the little girl's genital trauma when
suddenly she comprehends that she has not and never will have a penis.
Many of our women politicians have not reconciled themselves to that
loss and move in perpetual and unworked-through bereavement.'[8]) In
the seventies three MPs, James White, William Benyon and John
Corrie, introduced restrictive bills. Each was defeated. Women MPs
were not too traumatised to lead the opposition, together with the
Abortion Law Reform Association (ALRA).

Outside Westminster there was a crucial counter-pressure. Here
was an issue on which the trade unionists could be asked to deliver, as
Tess Woodcraft of NALGO explains:

'Abortion was one of those issues that had come up from the
women's movement . . . The new trade union feminists were saying.
"Come on, this is the sort of thing that our unions should be looking
at, this issue has a big effect on our lives." Something like abortion
which is supposed to be private is actually a very public issue . . . a
trade union issue, it affected women's working lives.'

The climax came when 80,000 trade unionists marched through
London in October 1979 to protest at the Corrie Bill, which had had
the fair wind of a newly elected right-wing parliamentary majority
behind it. The march did not stop Corrie – parliamentary attrition did
that – but it demonstrated how widespread opposition was. Corrie's

became, after that of George Davis, the best-known graffito in London: 'Women Will Not Obey Corrie' slogans remain to this day. Corrie and his supporters were deeply shaken. No one was willing to take up where he had left off, and the abortion controversy resolved itself into restrictions on the private sector and on abortions after the first twenty-four weeks of pregnancy.

The abortion issue was only one of the areas where the assumptions of the sixties were now under challenge. Feminism was held to threaten the old notion of the family as much as was the new sexual ethic. It advocated a different way of organising social life; particularly that section of the movement which favoured sexual separatism – doing without men in respect of bed as well as board. Mary Whitehouse, already by the seventies a veteran morality crusader, was one of those who lumped the agencies of the new permissiveness together. In one bravura passage she wrote of:[9]

'. . . the in-breeding which characterises organisations like the NCCL, the BHA, ALRA, the "Gay Liberation" movement, the Campaign for Homosexual Equality (CHE), the Euthanasia Society, the Paedophile movement . . . shows a training in ideological warfare which should alert Christians to the fact that "being good" is not an adequate programme for living in the seventies.'

All these diverse organisations, she believed, had their allies in the mass media, in publishing, and in the theatre. And they had a target for disruption:

'All the power of the permissive lobby in the sixties was aimed – deliberately or otherwise – at the heart of the family, removing from parents responsibility and caring . . . feeding young people still in adolescence, still growing in their own emotional development, with hard trendy ideas.'

The Whitehouse line became a central part of the rhetoric of the seventies, as it merged with other anxieties. In Stuart Hall's view:

'There's always been a commonsense view that, if the family holds, the rest of society holds. It's the kind of image of what social order is all about . . . It can transmit traditional values to the next generation, and it can uphold a kind of image of authority – the father figure, as it were – and it can regulate sexuality by keeping it within the bounds of monogamy. So . . . women becoming more liberated and a kind of libertarian attitude towards traditional authority [are] felt to be undermining the very basis of stability of the family itself.'

The feminists, lumped together with other 'subversives', gave as good as they got. Beatrix Campbell argues that what women's liberation was trying to do was:

'. . . to say: if we can assume that this is some natural order of domestic organisation, there's a terrible problem in it. Women go potty. Women are poor. Women are often beaten up in this haven. So its inner life has to be examined, and we all have to take responsibility politically for what goes on in it.'

One thing that went on, ignored by men, nodded at by the law, was domestic violence. It was only after Erin Pizzey set up the Chiswick Women's Refuge in 1972 that the unmentionable subject of male brutality to women within marriage was analysed and treated. By 1980 the Women's Aid Federation covered ninety-nine groups, two hundred refuges, and enjoyed government support. The Domestic Violence Act of 1976 gave women threatened by their partners the proper protection of the law for the first time. Rape Crisis Centres manned by women gave additional support to the victims of violence on the streets, which was sometimes made worse by the conduct of the police. Even the judges often seemed convinced that the woman concerned had 'asked for it' simply by being a woman at that place and moment.

The image of the traditional family – male breadwinner, housewife at home, and several children – was in reality very far from the norm. Most working women worked because they had to. According to DHSS statistics, the number of two-parent families living below the poverty line would have trebled if the women had stopped working. One in ten households, containing over a million children, were then what the contemporary jargon styled one-parent families. In most of them the head of the household was a woman. As a result, Lynne Segal recollects:

'Feminists were able to point out that the traditional family ideal covered less than 30% of families. In fact only 5% of families relied on a single male breadwinner . . . Unless we looked at what was really going on, we were keeping hidden what the very real needs of many people in society were.'

Even where the family was a unit with two adults and the woman at home, motherhood in a tower block or a new estate was often a sentence to an isolation ward. There was a high incidence of women with small children taking drugs to counter depression and anxiety. In 1974 CIS Report No. 15, 'Women Under Attack', showed that 70% of

Born British: Lewisham teenagers in 1979

Police defend National Front marchers against counter-demonstrators in Lewisham, 1979

The winter of discontent: the strike by refuse collectors

Conservatives press home unemployment figures,
1978. The dole queue were Young Conservatives

'We have rights too.' Nurses on picket duty, 1979

Left: A broken career: Jeremy Thorpe at the Old Bailey to answer charges of conspiracy and incitement to murder. He was acquitted

Below left: A new style of politics: Margaret Thatcher shows her solidarity with British troops after twelve of them had been murdered by the IRA at Warrenpoint

Below: The ones they left behind: Labour's National Executive sing 'The Red Flag' after the Wembley special conference had heralded the breakaway of the Social Democrats

Above: '£20 million worth of television coverage': The Gang of Four launch the SDP in March 1981

'I was outmanoeuvred': Jim Prior operating on the hard left of the Tory Wets. Conservative Women's conference in May 1981

Photo call for a new Alliance: David Steel and Shirley Williams
announce a pact between their parties in June 1981

Toxteth burns during the riots in July 1981

the users of anti-depressant drugs were women, who were actually targeted in medical advertising for these products:

'Struggling against impossible odds ... surrounded by children, with poor housing facilities and little money ... these neuroses usually respond best to therapy with Triptafen.'

Some of the worst horrors of the period came from the side effects of drugs taken during pregnancy.

So it could be argued that for many women family life was no big deal. Nevertheless the advent of the first woman to lead a British political party in 1975 marked a new emphasis on 'family policy'. Margaret Thatcher had never expressed sympathy with feminism: 'What has it ever done for me?' she snapped at her first press conference as leader.[10] She had come through with a blend of masculine toughness and feminine intuition which allowed her first to win, and then to dominate, the Conservative Party. The Conservatives set out in opposition to champion the traditional family and the traditional role of the woman within it. In 1977 Patrick Jenkin, Tory spokesman on Social Services, proclaimed:

'Parenthood is a very skilled task indeed. It must be our aim to restore it to the place of honour it deserves ... Perhaps the most important social work of all is motherhood.'

Margaret Thatcher's appeal to those who championed the family was instantaneous. Mary Whitehouse expresses it:

'She understands the importance of the family, and perish the day when we in this country don't realise the significance and importance of the family. That's absolutely central if you're going to have a democratic society. Smash the family and you get a disintegrated society.'

The new emphasis soon became clear. Women repatriated to the home would be able to do those tasks which formed a large part of the financial cost of the social services. Jenkin believed the woman's role had been changed enough:

'There is now an elaborate machinery to allow her equal opportunity, equal pay and equal rights; but I think we ought to stop and ask, where does this leave the family?'

In this, as in other areas of social policy, Prime Minister Callaghan discovered that there was tactical ground to be regained which fitted his own instincts. He announced:

'We have to pay much more attention than we have in the past as to how industry organises woman's role at work, so that her influence as the centre of the family . . . is not weakened.'

A series of speeches followed, which extolled 'women who choose their families as their life's work', but there were no proposals about how a system of financial support and back-up, building on the single great advance of child benefits, might help these heroines of the home front to do their life's work without trauma. By the time of the 1979 election, an auction in family values, which in their different ways Callaghan, Thatcher and Steel all represented, was under way. The ineffable Jenkin, who had already booked a place among the sayings of the decade, had his last word on the TV programme *Man Alive*:

'If the good Lord had intended us all having equal rights to go out to work and to behave equally, you know he really wouldn't have created man and woman.'

Victorian values were back. The cuts in social welfare acceptable in such a scheme of things were to follow.

In June 1978, at the height of the family auction, Melanie Phillips pointed out in *New Society* that the DHSS's own submission to the Royal Commission on Income and Wealth revealed that family support had dropped considerably between 1946 and 1976, while family householders had suffered, from 1969 onwards, a disproportionate increase in their tax burden, compared to the single earner. By the end of the decade, when the first breaches were made in the Employment Protection Act, it was possible to think that working women were now a political target. Zoë Fairbairns's novel of a decrepit future, *Benefits*, in which a new political party called Family advocated a single payment to mothers 'so long as they stayed at home and looked after children under 16', to provide 'an explosion of job opportunities for men', seemed less like fantasy.[11]

In terms of tangible gains for all their sex, the feminists of the seventies had a very limited success, rolled back before it had had time to consolidate. The increase in women going out to work also peaked in 1979. If women had any security in employment, it was precisely because they were often in the lowest paid, least unionised, and therefore most pliant, sections of the workforce. Middle-aged women returnees, in the eyes of the employer, were tractable as highly organised male workers were not. The bulk of that mysterious reserve army of labour who do not show up in the unemployment statistics, who are in and out of part-time work, are women. Does that show that the 'consciousness-raising' of the women's movement was a failure? Not for the women whose lives were transformed by it – for whom its narrow platform of political gains were never more than a ledge with a view. Tess Woodcraft thinks that:

'It had really given a whole new way of looking at the world . . . It had made it quite clear that women would have to be equal partners in any organisation in which they were involved and their needs would have to be integrally part of the agenda, not just added on at the end.'

A rough equality – even if in the eighties it was often manifested as an equality of misery – had been hewn out.

One of the major changes, which has established itself without fanfares, because that was its style, has been the networking movement. Loose, non-hierarchic groups of women have come together, in the unions, in the professions, inside pressure groups, and in the churches, swapping help, advice and information, coping with the pressures of the recession. These women thought differently. The politically active argued that:[12]

'. . . it is up to us to dismantle and overtake power and transform the organisation of society.'

And what they said and did inspired the actions of others, who came to see that they could begin by transforming the organisation of their own lives.

There was more. Changes in lifestyle, once recognised, were absorbed into the overground culture. It became a commonplace to talk of the success of *Spare Rib* and Virago Books. Less often noticed was that such ventures were discussed as though they sprang from some small but promising ethnic minority. The age of male patronage was not yet over. But it had been made to feel uneasy, in the space of a decade. As a participant and historian in that decade, Beatrix Campbell can say:

'The seventies were a women's decade, and there have been mighty changes in women's lives – not least because women found each other, personally and politically. There have been real changes in women's expectation at work, in their personal lives, that can't really be recorded and measured statistically . . . the way that women walk down the street, the way that women have insisted on certain things now being part of their working lives.'

It is true. The changes will not be reversed. But few of those who set out on the road in 1970 would have predicted that, a decade on, their way would be blocked by Britain's first woman Prime Minister.

17

THE ONLY MAN ON THE FRONT BENCH

The late political commentator and psephologist Robert Mackenzie once enunciated to perfection the old principle of leadership and its constraints in the Conservative Party when he wrote: [1]

'When appointed, the Leader leads, and the party follows, except when the party decides not to follow; then the Leader ceases to be Leader.'

That was written of the old days when leaders emerged, rather than were elected. Edward Heath was the first elected leader. The procedures provided for selection, but not reselection. In the autumn of 1974, when Heath had lost three elections – more than any leader of his party since Balfour – there were plentiful warning signs that the party was no longer prepared to follow.

Such was Heath's pre-eminence in a notably integrated cabinet that only one of his colleagues had broken ranks during the edgy period between the two 1974 elections. Sir Keith Joseph had let it be known that if and when a contest could be arranged he would be a candidate. He had gained Heath's agreement to set up what became the Centre for Policy Studies (CPS), whose purpose was to study why Britain's economic performance was so relatively poor and what lessons could be learned from abroad. Funds were raised, its scope was broadened. Keith Joseph regarded this period as one of intense self-questioning. He was to write of it later:

'In 1959 I was given my first ministerial post. But it was only in April 1974 that I was converted to Conservatism. (I had thought that I was a Conservative but I can see now that I was not really one at all.)'

A lively controversialist, Alfred Sherman, whose own intellectual conversion had led him from the further shores of Marxism to the political right, was brought in to help. The CPS began to fizz. Within months it was throwing out a golden rain of Josephite speeches.

The most notable of these was delivered at Preston, the most notorious at Edgbaston. Joseph first staked out a new territory for his party, and then abdicated any reversionary rights he might have had to take possession of it. The Preston speech was to be one of the most influential of the decade. At one bound, it put monetarism high on the political agenda. Joseph identified inflation as 'the most important issue before the country', which was 'largely a self-inflicted wound'. He went on to diagnose what he saw as its cause:

'Our inflation has been the result of the creation of new money . . . when the money supply grows too quickly, inflation results. This has been known for centuries.'

He proceeded to undermine the Conservative leadership's late conversion to incomes policy as the main counter-inflationary weapon:

'Incomes policy alone as a way to abate inflation caused by excessive money supply is like trying to stop water coming out of a leaky hose without turning off the tap; if you stop one hole, it will find two others.'

Joseph then turned to the postwar attitude to unemployment, in a manner which his shadow cabinet colleagues thought reckless, coming as it did just before a second general election when the party would be on the defensive. In a remarkable passage, he proclaimed that fear of unemployment had made the concept of sound money seem outdated:

'It was this which made us turn back against our own better judgement and try to spend our way out of unemployment, while relying on incomes policy to damp down the inflationary effects. It is perhaps easy to understand; our postwar boom began under the shadow of the 1930s. We were haunted by the fear of long-term mass unemployment, the grim hopeless dole queues and towns which died. So we talked ourselves into believing that these giant tight-lipped men in caps and mufflers were round the corner, and tailored our policy to match these imaginary conditions.'

Joseph was asserting that traditional demand management had, in his view, increased unemployment and not diminished it. He also said that he thought that full employment was compatible with stable prices, collective bargaining and a sound balance of payments. The impact, though, was of his apparent unconcern about unemployment and its consequences. His colleagues were not pleased. Robert Carr, the shadow Chancellor, was dismayed by this ostentatious invasion of his own territory:

'I think some of us found it very difficult to understand, because Keith Joseph as a man, as a person, didn't seem to be the sort who would run that kind of campaign deliberately. It seemed to some of us that Keith Joseph had allowed his brain activity to run ahead – a little bit – of his political sense. Perhaps we didn't take them [the speeches] as seriously as we should have done. We found them embarrassing, but not, if I may use the phrase, in leadership terms, disloyal.'

Heath and his circle had received little advance warning of the speech, which was not what they had thought the CPS would be all about. Jim Prior says:

'We felt that if that speech was delivered it could only do us great harm . . . I think the speech was written mostly by Alfred Sherman and we tried to persuade Keith – in fact, we got hold of Margaret Thatcher and tried to persuade her to persuade Keith – to make changes in the speech. And I think she did speak to Keith, but I don't think that she spoke to him very strongly because I have a feeling she really rather believed what Keith was saying.'

Margaret Thatcher was a vice chairman of the CPS, and one observer there describes them as already a political pair: '. . . like William and Mary . . . she was always the more militant of the two'. The party leader, openly contemptuous of Joseph's born-again brand of Toryism, saw no danger in the promotion of his disciple. When the election came it was she, now shadow spokeswoman on Environment, who was able to model the Conservatives' new clothes – 9% mortgages and the abolition of rates – which helped to keep Labour's majority well below the expected level. After the October 1974 election, perhaps now forewarned, Heath shifted Mrs Thatcher again, this time to be second opposition Treasury spokeswoman under the trusted Robert Carr. But there too she shone among the complexities of the Finance Bill, the morning star of the committee corridor. It was not only Carr who was outshone, but often the Treasury team of Healey and Barnett as well.

Heath had fought a good, dogged, election in October, the more so since he was suffering from a then undiagnosed thyroid complaint. Labour's tiny overall majority might well mean that the parliament could not run its full term. He saw no reason why he should not stay on as leader, for a final round with Harold Wilson. The party thought differently. There had been mutterings in the constituencies. (Some Ashton-under-Lyme Tories had said darkly on television that, whereas they believed that if Wilson took them on a bus ride to Victoria they would end up at Waterloo, with Heath they would not even get out of the garage.) Heath's two closest advisers went to him to spell out how precarious his tenure now was. Francis Pym told him, with all the shrewd knowledge of an ex-Chief Whip, that he ought to:

'. . . put his leadership on the line at once . . . But he seemed very, very reluctant to do that and thought he had the right and the position to go on, and I thought that a very great mistake.'

Heath's former PPS and old friend Jim Prior recalls:

'I'm afraid that after the October '74 election I gave Mr Heath pretty unpalatable advice. I've always been a fairly candid friend, I think, and I told him that I thought it was very unlikely he could go on as leader, but there was just a chance if he submitted himself to an early election through the 1922 Committee . . . I thought he ought to have said early, right at the start, the day after the election if you like. "Look, I've now lost a second election and obviously the party will need an opportunity to decide whether I'm to remain leader or not." If he'd done that straight away, there was a chance that he could have stayed on. But I rather doubt it. The animosities were too great.'

These animosities were not confined to the right-wing Conservatives now excitedly caballing in their London homes. Heath had made many enemies. He had been disdainful of the traditional emollient of failure, honours, whereby a man who could not become a minister quickly could at least look forward to becoming a knight slowly. His rudeness was legend, his humour uncertain. 'When Mr Heath makes a joke,' the columnist Edward Pearce has written, 'it is no laughing matter.' MPs who shared Heath's social and economic views did not find it easy to socialise with him. Norman St John-Stevas recalls what happened when one Conservative worthy who was desperate to make small talk with the leader remarked that he was a home-loving man:

'Heath replied, "Well, why don't you go home then?" Well, that's an interesting style, but it's not calculated to win the devoted support of those who are exposed to it.'

In the autumn of 1974 these things mattered. Julian Critchley MP was dining with two other backbenchers and James Prior immediately after the election when Heath appeared, engaged Prior in earnest conversation, and then marched off:

'Not by one word or gesture did he acknowledge those of us who had just fought an election under his banner. And as he walked away Jim Prior said, "What can I do with him?"'

There were many similar cases of men on the left of the party who, like St John-Stevas and Critchley, were to vote against Heath when the moment came. That moment could not be long delayed. But the delay until the new year which Heath's obduracy imposed had unforeseen consequences: the two extra spins of the roulette wheel which made Margaret Thatcher, a wholly unconsidered outsider in October, party leader in February. The first was a change in the rules of election. The second was the spectacular auto-destruction of Keith Joseph.

On 14 October the executive of the 1922 Committee met at the home of its long-serving chairman Edward Du Cann, amid much press attention. After a more public meeting at the Milk Street offices of Du Cann's firm Keyser Ullman, it was dubbed the Milk Street Mafia by the Fleet Street sub-editors. The group decided to press for a leadership election. Heath demurred, rashly, for any leader ignores the voice of the Tory backbenchers at his peril. When the parliamentary party met, Heath was again asked, in pointed terms, whether he saw his leadership as a freehold or a leasehold. The message was plain. Heath agreed to set up a review committee under his predecessor Lord Home to look at the procedures. He could hardly have predicted the outcome. Home reported back in December that there should be a provision for annual elections in the parliamentary party. In a contested election the winner would have to have a margin of at least 15% of the entire electorate over the nearest challenger. If there was a second ballot, new candidates could enter the lists at that stage. This bizarre 'coward's charter' was seen to be – and was – an ingenious way of smoking out an unpopular leader. Heath's challengers would have an opportunity to hold back from an initial challenge and move in for the kill on the second ballot. But who would they be? Apart from Joseph, Du Cann was thought to be interested, although his motives were often as obscure as his utterances were delphic.

The position changed after the fall-out from Keith Joseph's Edgbaston speech on 19 October, on Conservative social policy. The speech included a passage about social classes 4 and 5 being least able to bring up children without resort to the state, and seemed to suggest that they should be encouraged through birth control to have fewer. His advisers report him as 'mesmerised' at that time by the poverty of single mothers and divorcées in the lower social groupings. The speech lost a key paragraph from its conclusions, which qualified the remarks on contraception. To Joseph's unconcealed chagrin, the press seized on the speech as evidence that he wished to stop the lower classes breeding, and that he was some crazed advocate of Social Darwinism. *Private Eye* dubbed him Sir Sheath, and lampooned him saying, 'If the cap fits, wear it!' All this was agony for a sensitive man, whose tormented self-questioning now took in his own fitness for leadership. His marriage was rocky, his family edgy; he flinched from the exposure of which this was a foretaste.

Looking back on the disaster of the Edgbaston speech, Joseph sees it as a blessing in disguise:

'I was trying, and I did it very clumsily, to say that the permissive ethos was cruel, and cruellest to the least loved, least educated, poorest section of our society. That's what I was trying to say. But I said it clumsily. I blame no one else, it was my own fault. I got hold of some research which I'd misinterpreted. I was trying to say something rather sympathetic . . . But I did it wrong. Just as well I did, because it killed off any idea that I might be a suitable leader of the Conservative Party, let alone the country, and that was a valid perception. So it led to my precipitate withdrawal from any pretensions and made way for Margaret Thatcher with her infinitely larger political capacities.'

So, on 21 November, Joseph went to see his confidante, Margaret Thatcher. On the tenth anniversary of her subsequent election she recalled the moment:

'I thought, in particular, that Keith Joseph would stand. He came along one day to tell me that he wouldn't and I knew then that I must stand. It had not been a preconceived ambition but I just knew I had to and so I did. I hadn't sat and thought about it and had a great ambition . . . Keith Joseph and I were holding very similar views . . . and I thought that view would be represented in any election for the leadership. If it was not going to be represented by Keith, then someone had to do it; I had to.'

There is no reason to believe that this view was disingenuous. In June of that year, Mrs Thatcher had told the *Liverpool Daily Post*:

'It will be years before a woman either leads the party or becomes Prime Minister. I don't see it happening in my time.'

It was to happen in less than one year, but at the moment of her declaration she did not look a strong candidate, rather a stalking horse. So thought Heath, whose reply to her privately conveyed message that she would be a candidate was Coolidge-like in its brevity: 'You'll lose.'

But Margaret Thatcher's good fortune was only beginning. Du Cann decided not to run. The banking boom had collapsed. His firm Keyser Ullman was affected. He knew his own vulnerability. This released key support for Thatcher, whose initial campaign team had been composed of obscure and bumbling backbenchers. The rest of the cabinet had stayed loyal to Heath. If he was a candidate, they would not be – neither Whitelaw, nor Prior, nor the rest. Mrs Thatcher was out on her own. But not quite alone. Her campaign team was joined by Airey Neave, legendary escaper of the Second World War, left to rust by Heath. Neave's natural bent was for intelligence-gathering and undercover work. He had tried to persuade others to stand. Now he surfaced as Thatcher's campaign manager. Heath's own organisers poured scorn on him: 'That man has crawled out of half the prisons of Europe,' said one. But in the subterranean passages of the parliamentary party Neave was supreme. His information was accurate, because people were honest with him. Heath's managers were less effective. There was no central direction. Those involved (Peter Walker, his PPSs Tim Kitson and Kenneth Baker, Bernard Weatherill, the Deputy Chief Whip) could not conduct an accurate canvass. No one wishes to tell the man with the patronage that his time is up. Attempts to dine and wine the backbenchers who had been snubbed for years proved an embarrassing failure. The Heath campaign was dead in the water.

Margaret Thatcher's style was different. One backbencher who was later to join her cabinet sums up her successful overtures:

'Thatcher was immensely courteous in listening to everybody, and that hadn't been a characteristic of Heath's style . . . I think there's no doubt Thatcher had an immense advantage in seeming to be a more sympathetic and receptive person. I don't think that many people thought in starkly ideological terms. Her overwhelming advantage was that she garnered an enormous number of votes of people who certainly didn't want Heath, and the only way they could make sure of that was to ensure there was a second ballot. And the only way to ensure a second ballot was to vote for Thatcher.'

There was to be a third candidate, the engaging but light-weight maverick Hugh Fraser, but in the absence of any candidate from the left and centre of the party Thatcher was in a stronger position than she can have dreamed of when she declared her candidacy. In the week before the poll she set out her critique of Heath's failures in the *Daily Telegraph*:

'To deny that we failed the people is futile, as well as arrogant. Successful governments win elections. So do parties with broadly acceptable policies. We lost . . . Indeed one of the reasons for our electoral failure is that people believe that too many Conservatives have become socialists already.'

Her response was to be a positive defence of 'middle-class values'. She went on to write that:

'My kind of Tory Party would make no secret of its belief in individual freedom and individual prosperity, in the maintenance of law and order, in the wide distribution of private property, in rewards for energy, skill and thrift, in diversity of choice, in the preservation of local rights in local communities.'

This had a wide appeal in the Tory ranks. It enabled Thatcher to beat off suggestions that if she were elected the party would, in Ian Gilmour's phrase, 'retreat behind a privet hedge' in its suburban strongholds. The Heathmen continued to exude public confidence that this was, indeed, the future that the challenger represented. Heath was told by his canvassers that he would get at least 120 votes (out of 277) but they were privately uneasy. Tim Kitson did a final tally on the eve of poll:

'I had a feeling that it was slipping away, and I did actually say on the day of the election – because I went up to be his teller at the count – that I didn't think he was going to win.'

This mood was the precise opposite of that of the cunning Neave. Privately optimistic, he mooched round the lobbies on the eve of poll saying dolefully that, while Margaret was doing well, Heath's final surge might put him so far ahead that there would be no second ballot. As he intended, this panicked many intending abstainers with no love for his candidate to vote for her in order that the second ballot should take place.

The tactic was brilliantly successful. A good result was transformed into an outstanding one: Margaret Thatcher – 130 votes; Edward Heath – 119 votes; Hugh Fraser – 16 votes.

Heath resigned at once, with bleak dignity. Fraser dropped out. There was a rush of new candidates, led by the heir apparent William Whitelaw, whose reputation was based on his achievements in Northern Ireland and his popularity in the Commons. Jim Prior, Geoffrey Howe and John Peyton, all put down their markers without much hope of success. All now shared a disadvantage against the heroine of the hour. Their colleague Geoffrey Rippon summarises the strength of the new front runner:

'First of all I think it was because she had the courage to declare herself in time. I think people respected that. That gave her the edge over those who said, "Oh well, we'll support Mr Heath on the first round, but if he doesn't do well in the first round, then we'll come in afterwards." Well now, that doesn't present a picture, you know, of extremely loyal lieutenants, determined to stand by their leader.'

The challengers were seen off easily. 'Willie's glass jaw', much feared by his minders, was much in evidence that week. While Mrs Thatcher flew the flag in the Finance Bill Committee, and ostentatiously stayed away from a *Panorama* television programme featuring her rivals (to appear, solo, on the rival channel), Whitelaw seemed bumbling and uncertain, his natural dignity and presence reduced, rather than enhanced, by his new status. On the second ballot Thatcher secured 146 votes to his 79. Prior and Howe (19 each) and Peyton (11) trailed in nowhere. She had won, by an emphatic overall majority. The Conservative Party had taken its biggest gamble since the emergence of Benjamin Disraeli.

The new leadership

Margaret Thatcher had played her luck. Enoch Powell, the man who might have been in her place, had he not thrown over the party in 1974, sums up what happened:

'She didn't rise to power. She was opposite the spot on the roulette wheel at the right time, and didn't funk it.'

The last Conservative leader but one, Lord Home, who had backed Heath, was not surprised at the result, recalling:

'After the first day I saw her in cabinet, in Mr Heath's government, I came back to my wife and said, "Whether you like it or not, here is a woman who has got more brains than most of us put together . . . and what's more she'll probably go right to the top." And this was early on. So, no, I wasn't surprised.'

The views of the outgoing leader were not put on record at the time. Thatcher called on him at his house in Wilton Street. They talked briefly among the pianos, prints and yachting trophies. Heath denies that any offer was made to him to stay on the front bench. The Thatcher circle say that it was, in general terms. The conversation terminated so quickly that the new leader had to be ensnared by Tim Kitson with small talk in the hall afterwards, so that the press would not be able to write about a meeting over almost before it had begun. There began a period of mutual ill-will between the two which continues to this day, and has left Edward Heath so bruised that his recollection of the whole contest and its aftermath has clearly been transformed into a nightmare.

So there would be no Heath in the shadow cabinet. But it was still a stronghold of the Heathites. Only Keith Joseph had supported Thatcher on the first ballot. Only St John-Stevas had come over on the second. The previous shadow cabinet, essentially the loyal Heath team from government, was attached to, and shared the philosophy of, her predecessor. There could be no wholesale purge. Carr, Rippon and the young Heath galloper Peter Walker were dropped, along with a few other lesser lights. That was all. Gradually more sympathetic figures whom Thatcher respected were brought into the inner circle, John Nott and John Biffen among them. Whitelaw was offered the post for which she saw him to be ideally (and perennially) suited: deputy leader. Keith Joseph was ranked third, and appropriately garlanded as the new guru of policy formulation. Maudling was called back to shadow the Foreign Office, a veteran to the left of her on economics but believed to share her lukewarm view of the EEC in the year of the referendum. Due balance was preserved. The new team would be given its chance. Some of them may not have realised then how acutely their performance would be watched by the leader.

What did they think of her? They knew they had taken a gamble, but they took comfort from their numbers, and her inexperience. They 'feared for the worst but hoped for the best', as one of them put it. Some of those who had entered Parliament when she did knew that her instincts lay to the right of the party. She was known not to travel in the realm of doubt, or, if she did, always to look as though she had a return ticket. The mutual respect between her and Institute of Economic Affairs' luminaries such as Ralph Harris was growing. Its depth was not understood. Professor Milton Friedman first met her at a dinner party before her election as leader. He recalls:

'I was enormously impressed with her understanding of the economic situation, and the extent to which she recognised very clearly the relationship between monetary policy on the one hand and inflation on the other . . . It was clear that she recognised the extreme importance of having a detailed programme to put into effect before she got into power.'

This emphasis was soon evident to Thatcher's colleagues. Francis Pym accepts that:

'It was quite clear from the outset that Mrs Thatcher's intention and objective was to introduce and have as part of the party's platform a very precise and clear economic policy designed . . . quite correctly, to deal with the problems of inflation which were incipient and fatal . . .

The centrepiece of the discussions of the shadow cabinet throughout its period of existence was all the argument surrounding the economic policy.'

Sir Keith Joseph had blazed the way, throwing open to question many of the assumptions of the postwar consensus. The young guard who rallied to the new leader, however, saw themselves as atoning for the U-turns of the Heath government, which they regarded as disastrous. Some, such as John Nott, look back to the Selsdon Park conference ideas (see pages 39–41), and see Edward Heath's pragmatism as a form of backsliding:

'I think I see the origins of the Thatcher economic policies as lying much earlier, with the aberration of the Heath government, and when we were in opposition again, following the loss of the election in '74, we merely continued the discussions and the ideas that we'd been developing earlier.'

Others disagree. One influential policy adviser says:

'While it may be possible to characterise, interpret, and describe what happened between '74 and '79 in terms of a quest for the original holy grail, the original truth for consistency with past principles, I don't think that's really what it was . . . The one thing you didn't do was to say: is this holy writ?'

The Heathites were uneasy at the new attempts to explain inflation as a monetary phenomenon, especially when these were linked with a complete rejection of incomes policy on the grounds that it was the money supply which caused inflation, not wages. James Prior argued tenaciously in the shadow cabinet against any such blanket rejection, saying that 'no government, like any other employer, could avoid having a policy with regard to its own employees'. Prior and his colleagues comforted themselves with the thought that they had seen all this before. The extremities of opposition are embarrassments to be discarded after an election has been won. The new enthusiasts, the monetarists and the born-again economic liberals, could be tolerated for the moment. One well-placed moderate remembers that:

'Keith was always dashing off into the woods and coming back with a new stick between his teeth, but I don't think he had any practical effect on what went into documents or became party policy, except that he kept pushing back the shrubbery . . . I and others thought it was a little like the '65, '66 to '70 period. The Conservative Party was sort of rushing around and producing all these slightly barmy ideas, but oppositions were always more extreme than governments, and that when we got into government it would all be civilised very rapidly by events. Well, as we know, because of the condition of the Labour Party and a few other factors, that didn't actually happen. I think it's one of the few examples of a government being more extreme than the opposition which bred it.'

This miscalculation about the shadow cabinet's direction had several causes, besides the one already hinted at. The Conservative establishment of the Heath years did not understand the depth of their new leader's convictions, that she was, in Milton Friedman's description after meeting her:

'. . . not a typical, classical Tory. She really is the closest thing there is equivalent to a nineteenth-century liberal in British political terms, a Whig . . . What you had [in Britain] is an alternation between groups that wanted to construct different aristocracies. In the one case it would be an aristocracy of labour, in the other case it would be an aristocracy of the wise, the well born, the meritocratic. So Mrs Thatcher's ideas and approach represent a sharp break.'

The break was easier for her to effect for two further reasons: the misfortunes of the British economy in 1976, and her own shrewd and populist approach to non-economic issues – often over the heads of her shadow cabinet and advisers.

The years 1973–6 had made their mark on many senior Tories. The collapse of incomes policy and its shotgun revival, the escalating growth of public expenditure and government borrowing with monetary profligacy, the onset of very high inflation accompanied by political instability and no small establishment panic that Britain's institutions were threatened: all sent politicians back to the ideological drawing board. The crises of Denis Healey's first two years as Chancellor seemed to provide empirical support for a counter-revolution in economics. Healey's application to the IMF, his acquiescence to money supply targets and his cuts in planned public expenditure eased the task of Mrs Thatcher's allies in the Conservative Party. Nigel Lawson wrote later of the point when:

'. . . the IMF had to be called in, humiliatingly, to bale us out and impose its de facto monetarist terms . . . It was this experience that, more than any other, shifted the economic consensus which the new Conservatism had earlier influenced and has now inherited.'

In a world which had been in flux since the instability caused by the Americans' financing of the Vietnam War, the collapse of fixed exchange rates and the consequences of the fourfold increase in oil prices, the West seemed caught in a crisis of inflationary expectations. Peter Jay in *The Times*, Sam Brittan and other writers were emphasising in their columns the role which excessive monetary growth played in the promotion of inflation. When James Callaghan chose to make his first conference speech as Prime Minister a challenge to the old orthodoxies, believers in monetarism such as Friedman hailed the conversion:

'It was a speech in which he said, "We used to think we could spend our way out of recession – we know now that that only works for a little time and it ends up with higher inflation, higher unemployment, instead of the reverse." That, I think, was a very significant turning point, because from then on nobody could talk about inflation without at least having to say something about monetary aggregates.'

All this helped Thatcher's cause. That Healey and Callaghan were doing what they were delivered her Conservative opponents to her; how could they object to a real dose of monetarism, when the Labour government had already been impelled so far? A senior cabinet minister in the later Conservative government acknowledges the method by which the monetarists' arguments gained common acceptance:

'They originate in heavy tomes, then they get popularised and put in more digestible form by an IEA pamphlet, and then a *Daily Telegraph* article, chat, etc. And it permeates in that way.'

Mrs Thatcher's advent also coincided with a period of prolonged scrutiny of the public sector, on both economic and philosophic grounds. It was being argued that public expenditure 'crowded out' private sector investment and thus damaged the wealth-creating part of the economy. Two Oxford economists, Walter Eltis and Robert Bacon, had had a great success with a series of articles in the *Sunday Times* in which they claimed to show that the increasing proportion of resources devoted to unmarketed goods and services was seriously damaging the nation's economic health. Thatcher's economic adviser, Sir Adam Ridley, has written that:

'. . . their articles struck an immediate chord everywhere in public opinion . . . and it is impossible to think of any other case in which the effect on public opinion was so swift and electrifying. From then on the level of public spending became a major public issue.'

Linked as it was in the mind of the electorate to the power of the burgeoning public sector unions, this critique was perfectly suited to the strong anti-collectivist line of the Thatcherites.

Economic policy in opposition was thrashed out by an Economic Reconstruction Group chaired by the shadow Chancellor, Geoffrey Howe. It included the paladins of both wings of the party: Joseph, Nott and Biffen on the right; Prior and Gilmour on the left; David Howell in sinuous movement between them. The Prior group thought that they were strong enough to hold their ground, although they came slowly to see that Geoffrey Howe was not a neutral arbiter between the factions. The monetarists however were convinced that they were winning, for they had changed the terrain, as their economic adviser Professor Brian Griffiths explains:

'You had . . . a much greater emphasis on the supply side of the economy, on the efficiency of markets, and on the argument that full employment without inflation could only be assured with really flexible labour markets. And that was a fundamental change, and really broke with the whole of postwar Keynesian thinking.'

The policy document 'The Right Approach to the Economy', published in 1977 over the signatures of Howe, Joseph, Prior and Howell, was a truce. Prior had fought hard to limit the document's section on trade union reform to the general assurance that something could be done about 'labour laws aimed at protecting employees and jobs [which] may actually be acting as a deterrent to the creation and maintenance of employment opportunities'. There was no commitment to another Industrial Relations Act. Here too Prior was to be undone by subsequent events. Prior admits that he should have been warned when Thatcher refused to allow the document to go out as a shadow cabinet paper at all, since there were major disagreements about it:

'One should have seen the writing on the wall a bit more at that time – that she was going to pursue a very different policy.'

Policy in those years was often the by-blow of style, of catching a mood and holding it, until the policy somehow caught up. As soon as she became leader, Margaret Thatcher threw herself energetically into the presentation of a new style. This was manifest not just in the grooming picked up in tedious detail by the press, nor in the voice dropping through a coached octave to a husky, confidential pitch – no longer 'fluting across the room', as Simon Hoggart had described it during the Finance Bill debates. It was in what she chose to emphasise. There is nothing new in the knowledge that opinion surveys have consistently shown a majority in the country leaning to the right of both Labour and the liberal consensus on foreign affairs, defence, law and order, and immigration. Mrs Thatcher, unlike her predecessor, actively sought out this constituency and addressed it. Her speeches, when published, carry the credits of those who influenced her: F. A. Hayek, Keith Joseph, Arthur Seldon, Paul Johnson, Robert Conquest. Her achievement was to use the words which brought these thinkers the mass audience they would not otherwise have enjoyed. Keith Joseph believes that:

'She has an almost magic combination of ideas, drive, resolution and moral courage. And this was a very convincing combination. And she has a populist touch because she chimes with the aspirations and the problems of a large majority of the population; she chimes instinctively.'

In her first conference speech as leader, Thatcher tore into the 'deliberate attack on our heritage and our great past' by 'those who gnaw away at our national self-respect, rewriting British history as centuries of gloom, oppression and failure'. In the United States she cried:

'Let our children grow tall, and some grow taller than others.'

Opportunity, she said, meant nothing unless it included the right to be unequal. The levelling, over-mighty state must be held at bay. So should the mightiest threat of all, the Soviet Union. Against the grain of the policies of detente pursued by the last three Prime Ministers, Mrs Thatcher contrasted the Helsinki accords with the reality of Russian power. She claimed in 1976 that:

'The Russians are bent on world domination, and they are rapidly acquiring the means to be the most powerful imperial nation the world has seen.'

This speech brought down on her the wrath of the Soviet media, with additional domestic dividends in her new soubriquet, 'the Iron Lady'. It also enraged her Foreign Secretary. Maudling did not see the world in terms of red and white. He wrote to her when he saw the draft speech to protest that:

'No doubt a violent and sustained attack upon the Soviet government may have some political advantage within our own ranks, but I am doubtful as to what long-term purpose it is intended to serve, not only in opposition, but more important, in government.'

If she meant massive rearmament, he said, surely the shadow cabinet should be consulted. Maudling was later dropped from the shadow cabinet, lamenting to his cronies in the Smoking Room, 'Appointed by Winston Churchill. Sacked by Margaret Thatcher.'

The tough line, and the response it evoked, produced political dividends. It was particularly valuable for a woman leading the Conservative Party to be seen to be tough, an Iron Lady. When the Labour Party mocked her unnerved colleagues, and dubbed her 'the only man on the Front Bench', she took that title too, and brandished it at her opponents. By 1978 she was confident enough to 'produce policy from her handbag', as one rueful adviser put it, on the delicate subject of immigration. The brief heyday of the National Front in 1976–7 had worried all political parties, and Thatcher had been overruled by the party when she opposed Conservative participation in the Joint Committee Against Racialism set up in 1977. Her television interview (see page 235) surprised some of her colleagues. Her motives were clear to shadow cabinet critics such as Prior:

'Because she didn't find it easy to get her own way round the shadow cabinet table, she would tend to make policy on television, and certainly she made a great deal of immigration policy on television, in the knowledge that once she had said it on television it was quite difficult for the party to get out of the commitment that had been made.'

Whitelaw, like Maudling before him, was left floundering, but chose to make the best he could of what had happened. Thatcher collected fan mail on a scale not seen since Enoch Powell's Wolverhampton speech.

Events played into Margaret Thatcher's hands once more. In 1978 the Callaghan minority government seemed to have recovered much of its ground. It had reduced inflation. Callaghan's public avuncularity was popular. Throughout the summer the Conservative poster and cinema-ad campaign, on the theme 'Labour Isn't Working', got under way. If the desired effect was to head off an election, as some have suggested, it was a singular success. Callaghan astonished the nation by postponing the election, and went on to his nemesis in the winter of discontent and defeat in the Commons. The bitter clashes and unattractive scenes of that winter stripped the government of their claim that they could work with the unions while the Tories could not. Opinion in the shadow cabinet swung behind tougher legislation against trade union power. The 1979 manifesto promised changes in the law on picketing, the closed shop and secret ballots. A new influence at the CPS, John Hoskyns, an army officer turned businessman, came to the leader's attention with pleas for a 'big bang' approach to fundamental trade union reform. If Prior would not do it

– well, find someone who would. Hoskyns did not get his way, but after the election moved into a key job, running the No. 10 Policy Unit.

Margaret Thatcher now seemed booked for Downing Street. She made a notably successful broadcast, drafted by the most luminous intelligence in her team of advisers, Chris Patten, a former head of the Research Department, and the playwright in residence, Ronald Miller. With the government in disarray, she was able to project herself, in a low-key way, as a national leader in waiting. Her manifesto could be vaguer now, since victory seemed more certain. (It was less specific than the draft which was being proofread when Callaghan dropped his bombshell the previous autumn, telling the Tories they did not have to fight an election they feared they might lose.) Her kindred spirits, not yet numerous, were tactically placed for power and influence in the new administration. The assiduous cultivation of her backbenchers, always one of her strengths, meant that she would not lack for new recruits to her cause. The old Tory paternalists waited to see if her populist approach in the social field would outweigh what they saw as the bleakness of her economic philosophy. Heath's legacy had been wound up, although Thatcher still felt herself to be the prisoner of the Heathmen. Callaghan's remained. All that was left now was the winning of the election. Then she would be prisoner of none. What Enoch Powell calls 'the grim two-handed engine at the door', the power of the axe, would be hers to wield.

18

BREAKAWAY: THE SPLIT IN THE LABOUR PARTY

The split in the Labour Party had been a long time coming. Historic-
ally, from its beginnings in 1900, the party was a coalition between
socialism and labourism, between those who yearned to see socialism
realised and those who were happy to see labour gain a share of power,
between gradualist and revolutionary impulses. The postwar party had
had a mass base, powerful trade union sustenance and the assurance
that came from being one of the two great parties of the state, sharing
95% of the vote and most of the political spoils between them. In such
a party sat, more or less happily, many who would have been (and
some who had been) equally content with the Liberal Party of the
twenties before it ran out of the loaves and fishes of political patronage. With them were a smaller number who had been in the Communist Party of Great Britain, but had left it between 1939 and 1956, when
they found themselves dubbed premature anti-fascists, Titoists, or
could not swallow the King Street line on Hungary. Both groups, and
others from a variety of origins, were absorbed into the broad mass of
the Labour Party, most of whose members were not, and had never
wished to be, anything else.

By the seventies Labour Party membership was neither so broad nor
so massive. The secular decline in the party's vote since 1951 was
obscured both by the 1966 upward blip and the memory of the solid
votes won in good times and bad by the Attlee administration. Within
the party tensions were growing. There had never been a formal
'historic compromise' between the left and right. Attempts to dictate
one on the right's terms, with the rewriting of Clause 4 of the
constitution (pledging common ownership of the means of production, distribution and exchange), had backfired on Hugh Gaitskell,
the one party leader who came from, and led from, a position right of
centre. There was no British Bad Godesberg. By the 1970s it was the
left's turn. Enraged by the compromises and betrayals, as they saw it,
of the two Wilson governments, they set out to bind his successors

with constitutional chains, so that such things could never happen again.

The spectre of the constituency activists raised up against them was an old nightmare of the Labour right. Richard Crossman's diary for 1953 records Roy Jenkins as saying:[1]

'We on the Right feel that every force of demagogy and every emotion is against us. In the constituency parties, which are now Opposition-minded, the Bevanites have it all their own way. I suppose one must wait for the tide to turn, as it did in the 1930s, from the Opposition-mindedness of 1931 to constructive policies.'

In the late seventies Jenkins and a number of others came to doubt that the tide would ever turn again, in the face of a surge of constituency feeling as strong as Bevanism had been, and proportionally more powerful in a shrunken party. The left, for their part, came to see the 'broad church' formulations of Harold Wilson as just another tiresome obstruction to the kind of change they were determined to achieve. If the broad church had to be demolished so that socialism might advance, so be it. Instead of the historic compromise, there would be the historic quarrel, in which each side saw only the cloven feet of the other.

Most of the participants see the long row over British membership of the EEC as the start of the fundamental split. It did not begin that way. The argument produced some strange allies. Among the 69 rebel MPs who voted in favour of the principle of entry on 28 October 1971 were old left-wing heroes such as Hugh Delargy and Bob Edwards. Voting against were right-wingers such as Douglas Jay and Reg Prentice, and subsequent founder members of the SDP such as John Horam. It might have remained no more than an honest division of opinion between those on the one hand who saw the choice as one between internationalism and insularity, and those on the other who saw it as between the Third World and a selfish rich nations' club. But that would be to ignore the personalities involved, as well as the depth of personal commitment which the struggle was to evoke. The leader of the party stayed with what clearly came to be the majority party view. The deputy leader, Roy Jenkins, stuck to his long-held convictions in favour of entry. Jenkins, who had seemed the heir apparent in 1970, a minister who emerged from the Wilson government with an enhanced reputation from all three offices which he had held, was progressively alienated from the other members of that government in turn, as each peeled away from the European cause, first Callaghan, then Wilson, finally even Healey and Crosland. For the first time in a generation the right was split. At the same time a persuasive voice was heard in the constituencies: Tony Benn, embarking on his hyperactive year as chairman of the party.

1971–2 was therefore a time when many of the pro-Europeans felt an emotional coming-together. They believed the cause was fundamental to Britain's future, somehow above the opportunism and manoeuvres of party politics, in the best tradition of European social democracy. The fact that their opponents in the party accused them of gross betrayal only heightened the emotional experience. As Shirley Williams describes it:

'There was a feeling of tremendous dedication in the air, a feeling that we didn't care what happened, this is the way we were going to vote, we were going to put our names on the line . . . I think it was the beginning of the ultimate split in the Labour Party into an SDP and a Labour Party, and that was, when I look back on it, really where it all began.'

The pro-Europeans' loss of influence in the Labour Party after 1971 was precipitate. Jenkins resigned the deputy leadership in 1972 over the adoption of Benn's proposal for a Common Market referendum. He lost at once both his place on Labour's National Executive and the post of shadow Chancellor. With him into the wilderness, for a crucial period, went a number of others: Lever, Thomson, Owen and Taverne. (Neither Roy Hattersley nor Shirley Williams resigned, the former incurring much odium from the Jenkinsites, the latter none at all.) As the party moved left in the debates which led up to the formulation of the 1973 programme, Jenkins and his allies seemed even more isolated, although it was plain that Harold Wilson had preserved the opportunity for their return – by ensuring that the Labour policy on Europe remained opposition to the terms negotiated, not to the principle of entry.

Jenkins himself acknowledges the doubts which plagued his supporters when he resigned the deputy leadership:

'If I'd had an absolute determination to be leader of the Labour Party in any circumstances, any conditions, then of course it was a hideous error. If I hadn't resigned, if I'd rolled with these various punches, the overwhelming likelihood is that I would have become leader . . . [But] rightly or wrongly I don't think it was in my temperament to go along more than a certain distance with things, on major issues, which I didn't believe in.'

Some of his close allies urged him to go further, faster. Dick Taverne
had been a passionate critic of the compromises which the pro-
Europeans had accepted, in particular voting against the Second
Reading of the European Communities Bill. He had been made to 'eat
dirt', he told the parliamentary party. Under intense pressure in his
Lincoln constituency from left-wingers who believed that at his original selection he had been foisted on them by the Gaitskellite organisation and by his support for the Wilson government in which he had
been a junior minister, Taverne took the offensive. He agreed to
appear on a television programme, in which the row boiled over in
public. The viewers saw twenty-five minutes of raw emotion as
Taverne and his principal critic, Leo Beckett, exchanged verbal blows.
In the short run this episode brought Taverne much public support.
Beckett found himself being personally abused in the street. As often
happens, such a public statement of opposed views made any subsequent reconciliation impossible. Each side was caught in its public
posture. The result was a by-election, when Taverne resigned in March
1973 in response to being disowned by his constituency party.
He knew that if he waited until the next general election he would
simply drown in the national tide, whichever way it flowed. He also
hoped that the resignation would flush out the Jenkinsites in his
support.

Taverne sees the Lincoln Labour Party of that time as a prototype of
a wider transformation that was taking place nationally, in its asser-
tion of the rights of the activists and the delegate role of MPs and
councillors:

'They were determined to see the grassroots, by which they didn't
mean the ordinary Labour Party member, but the activist Labour
Party member, control the party more effectively. I saw this happening
at Lincoln. I could see the way they were extending their influence
elsewhere, and I personally came to the conclusion that there was no
hope for the moderates, or social democrats as I prefer to call them,
inside the Labour Party.'

Taverne, running as 'Democratic Labour', found himself a premature anti-leftist. Most of the pro-European rebels had made their
peace with their constituencies. Some had had the active sustenance of
Michael Foot and other respected anti-marketeers, who came down to
speak for them in a public gesture of conciliation. Taverne hoped that
Roy Jenkins might break ranks and support him:

'If you resign, you resign to fight. Now he didn't really want to promote a split so he resigned and conformed. But if you're going to conform you don't resign, and I think that he then entered into a period of political life which was relatively ineffectual.'

He tried to persuade Jenkins to speak for him. 'I said to him, "Roy, if you come and speak for me, you will undoubtedly get kicked out of the Labour Party . . ." Were there others who would also leave the party if Jenkins did? "And he said, 'Yes, I think we might get about a dozen.'"' Jenkins argued that a dozen was not enough, that grassroots moderates, many with their own seats in local government about to be contested, would not join in. He kept away from Lincoln. Those pro-Europeans who went to the by-election, including Crosland, did so to speak for the Labour candidate. Taverne had the consolation of a sweeping victory, polling 58% of the vote compared to 23% for Labour's John Dilks and 18% for the eccentric Conservative Jonathan Guinness. Taverne had an overwhelmingly favourable press for his campaign on the Burkian principle that an MP was a representative and not a delegate and the support of the sharpest scribbler of the day, *Times* columnist Bernard Levin, who posed the choice as 'between a Dick Taverne and a Dictaphone'. The Labour Party headquarters, Grafton House, came to resemble a beleaguered fortress. Taverne's own memoir of the by-election invokes the shade of non-doctrinaire radicalism on the American model – Eugene McCarthy riding again:[2]

'Supporters came flooding to us, of all ages (though mainly young), of all parties and none, and nearly all full of enthusiasm . . . The *Economist* remarked on the way in which Conservative matrons worked side by side with shop stewards, whom they would have regarded as dangerous subversives only a few months before.'

They had made history of a kind, Taverne told them after the poll. So they had. In the following year Taverne's Democratic Labour Party swept to power in the local elections in Lincoln, from its new headquarters, Taverne House. Taverne himself held on in the first general election of 1974, and ran four candidates against Labour left-wingers without any success. He took up one of the nominated seats in the European Parliament which the Labour Party was then boycotting. All to no avail. The matrons and the shop stewards were returning to their old alliances. In the second election of 1974 Taverne was defeated by the Labour candidate Margaret Jackson (who was later to marry Leo Beckett). The Democratic Labour Party also began to fade, all the faster when it appeared that Taverne's connection with Lincoln was now at an end. It seemed that the Taverne 'phenomenon' was no different in kind from that of other MPs, like Eddie Milne, who were able to run against and beat their constituency party – once. Taverne remains convinced that a split in 1972–3 led by the Jenkinsites would have been more successful than that which occurred in 1981. This is to misunderstand Jenkins. Unlike Taverne, Jenkins was not searching for a white horse. His instincts were not those of a natural rebel.

So Jenkins soldiered on, returned after an absence to the shadow cabinet. All the Jenkinsite ex-ministers held office in the 1974 government, and their leader was perhaps the only one whose career had slipped back, conspicuously. He returned to the scene of former successes at the Home Office. Second time around it was not the same. He showed his old resolution in firm but sensitive handling of the Price sisters' hunger strike, and by his insistence that the police should help to put their own house in order over the matter of complaints against them. New legislation on race relations and sex discrimination resulted in those quintessentially Jenkinsite bodies, the Race Relations Commission and the Equal Opportunities Commission. Otherwise there were few opportunities to shine, and those which came his way widened the gulf with the left of his own party, now increasingly in the ascendant. He refused to release the 'Shrewsbury Two', Des Warren and Ricky Tomlinson, who had been jailed for alleged violent incidents during pickets of building sites. (Some of the offences had taken place on a site at Telford called Brookside; curiously Tomlinson was later to win a different kind of celebrity when he starred in a Channel 4 soap opera of the same name.)

'No one,' Jenkins said in a speech at Haverfordwest in 1974, 'is entitled to be above the law.' It was an implied reproof to his erstwhile friend Anthony Crosland – who had lifted the penalties on the rebel Clay Cross councillors, imposed on them for their defiance of the Conservatives' Housing Finance Act – as well as to the Labour left. In the same speech he argued that Labour could only find fresh support to break the stalemate in British politics by looking to the middle ground:

'There is in Britain a great body of moderate, rather uncommitted opinion, and unless substantial sectors of such opinion can feel happy in supporting one or other of the major parties the result will be intolerable strain upon the traditional pattern of politics.'

His own appetite for cross-party politics was increased by his role in the Britain in Europe Campaign, when he was able to use the referendum against its onlie begetter – to Benn's discomfort. His party loyalty had been based on the belief that:

'Within the party you belonged to, even though there were deep schisms, nonetheless you were all part of the same happy tabernacle; and I think the referendum did perform a releasing function . . .'

Schisms in the tabernacle became harder to ignore for other reasons. Just after the referendum the troubles of the beleaguered Reg Prentice boiled over in his Newham constituency. Prentice held cabinet office. He had once been the darling of the anti-marketeers: the only Labour MP to take the trouble to go to Norway to speak in the referendum there against the EEC. Now he had lost the support of his party activists, and of trade unions who found his blunt contempt for the Shrewsbury Two and other cherished causes hard to bear. 180 Labour MPs were prevailed upon to sign a letter in his support which was sent to his constituency. Jenkins, with Shirley Williams and Tom Jackson, went further, braving flour bombs and verbal abuse at a meeting there. Jenkins said that the new zealots wanted only MPs who were of their own kind or trimmers who would agree with them:

'Either would make a mockery of parliamentary democracy. The first would reduce . . . the House of Commons [to] become an assembly of craven spirits and crooked tongues. The second would, quite simply, divorce the Labour Party from the people.'

In the event it was Prentice who divorced himself from the Labour Party, ironically just as a couple of undergraduates arrived in Newham to prove that 'bed-sit politics', which combined maximum infiltration with minimum qualification, could be organised from the right on his behalf. After a brief sojourn as an independent, he joined the Conservatives and secured a Northamptonshire benefice, to set a bizarre record by holding office in successive administrations of different parties.

The defection of Prentice delighted the Labour left. Chris Mullin, already prominent in the Campaign for Labour Party Democracy, relishes the moment:

'Reg Prentice kicked them all in the teeth, this was the beauty of it. He kicked them all in the teeth by announcing that not only was he not a socialist, he wasn't a Liberal, he was a Conservative! And he went one better than that, he said that he'd been a Conservative for the last four or five years whilst he had enjoyed the support of all these Labour MPs . . . That was the biggest fillip the Campaign for Labour Party

Democracy ever had, and so I felt justified in dedicating my pamphlet on "How to Re-select Your MP" to Reg Prentice and the 180 Labour MPs who supported him.'

The Prentice affair made suspicion of parliamentary Labour Party 'traitors' more plausible. No other MP went all the way along that road, but the acrimony over Prentice concentrated the minds of others who were already at odds with their parties.

By January 1976 Jenkins was publicly questioning the wisdom of further increases in the proportion of gross domestic product taken by public expenditure. 'I do not think you can push public expenditure significantly above 60%,' he said at Anglesey, 'and maintain the values of a plural society and freedom of choice. We are here close to one of the frontiers of social democracy.'

This was a view not accepted by all on the right. To the left it was anathema. To the Crosland faction in the party it marked a point of departure, a time to drop the pilot. It was not, Jenkins concedes, 'a very wise preparation for a leadership contest' two months later. Jenkins had already been offered, through Wilson, the presidency of the EEC, which would involve breaking his links with British politics. Only afterwards did he learn, with his surprised colleagues, that Wilson was resigning. He had to stand in the contest, at the worst of times, and for a proud man who had known great days in the Labour Party the result was a bitter blow. While Foot got 90 and Callaghan 84 on the first ballot, Jenkins polled fewer votes (56) than any of his supporters had predicted. He made a hurried farewell, quoting Robert E. Lee at Appomattox, and dropped out at once. The eventual success of James Callaghan, a man with no love for the rival who had outshone him in two offices of state, also blocked his hopes of the Foreign Office. That went to Crosland. Jenkins went to Brussels in the autumn, little thinking that within a few months of his taking up European office Crosland would be dead. Some of his close advisers went with him, among them David Marquand, who, like him, left a safe Labour seat to be lost at a subsequent by-election. At Westminster those of Jenkins's old persuasion clustered together for comfort in a cold climate in the Manifesto Group of Labour MPs. The Jenkinsite chapter seemed over.

The three demands: Labour's constitutional clash

The four years in which James Callaghan led the Labour Party climaxed with a clamour for constitutional reform, whose champions transformed the face of the party, and of British politics – in ways they had not entirely intended. The greater the momentum for change the more others, worn out, disenchanted or just keen to jump before they were pushed, began to leave. The new activists, some freshly arrived from the proliferation of Marxist sects incubated in the heated atmosphere of the sixties, found the going good. Labour had been complacent in its city fiefs, which were often run by tiny caucuses of councillors from the old urban working class. The middle-class newcomers colonised the inner-city parties triumphantly. One Labour MP who regretted it, Austin Mitchell described what happened:[4]

'All this made the left stronger because less diluted, as well as less representative of the Labour vote for, with an average Labour vote of 20,000 per constituency in 1979, the average membership was only 2% of it and the average GMC only fifty strong. The old working-class membership drifted away; new, better-educated, more articulate and more middle-class groups, many of them from the public sector, came in, making the departures worse because the older generation often felt inadequate at dealing with them . . . An instrument of advancement was becoming one for protecting an entrenched vested interest.'

On that view, what happened in the party in the late seventies was a class upheaval not envisaged by Marx, in which the polytariat ousted the proletariat, and client-style relationships developed between the new activists and the unions which represented their white-collar public-sector jobs. There was another view: that Labour governments had promised much, delivered little; that too many MPs had used their constituencies as a freehold base for touting and tripping around the world. There were other cases similar to that of Prentice. Militant Liverpool was unhappy with Sir Arthur Irvine's sparse visits (he was rumoured to keep a taxi with its engine running outside his surgeries, to whisk him back to the station). If the leaving of Liverpool so cheered him each month, his activists said, why did he not leave it for good? But Sir Arthur hung on, like some ancient bird of prey. There were others like him. So there came a movement for change, from the bottom up.

The Campaign for Labour Party Democracy (CLPD) had been launched in 1973 by a handful of grassroots activists, initially to compel the parliamentary Labour Party to treat annual conference resolutions with due respect, after Harold Wilson's less than reverential approach to the proposal to nationalise twenty-five leading companies. This objective came to be part of a triple demand: for the mandatory reselection of MPs, for the election of the leader by the whole party, and for the control of the manifesto by the National Executive. CLPD soon picked up a wide range of active supporters. Among MPs the young Neil Kinnock joined in 1974. Labour pressure groups, to succeed, need an organiser of obsessive application, and tactical skill, with no ice pick to grind. CLPD found such a figure from its earliest days in Vladimir Derer. Wholly unknown in the party at large, Derer, with the aid of a battered duplicating machine, put his model resolutions into every constituency in the land. They began to come through in increasing numbers for debate, finding their hour in the activists' disillusion with the Labour government. To the embarrassment of some of their parliamentary allies, CLPD insisted on keeping mandatory reselection at the top of their agenda. Chris Mullin is frank about the reason why:

'They'd begun to realise that it was a waste of time passing resolutions at party conferences. What you had to do was to render Members of Parliament accountable, and you could only do that by making it clear to them that something seriously to their disadvantage would happen if they continued to treat the membership of the party with contempt.'

Derer and his allies in the party insisted that it was the principle that counted: 'that MPs could be displaced, not that they should be'.

By 1977 the National Executive had undertaken to look at reselection. It already had a working party to consider alternative ways of electing the party leader. When in 1978 Ian Mikardo, speaking for the NEC, proposed the compromise which came to carry his name (that there must be a vote of no confidence in an MP before an open selection procedure could get under way), CLPD supporters opposed it, and proposed mandatory reselection in the course of each parliament instead. This was voted down only because the retiring President of the AUEW, Hugh Scanlon, 'forgot' to cast his vote for it, having said to those who sought to remind him, 'You mind your business and I'll mind mine.' The consequent resentment caused festered throughout the year – a year which also saw the Winter of Discontent, and Callaghan's veto of cherished policy nostrums in the 1979 manifesto – particularly the abolition of the House of Lords. In the eyes of the constituency activists the Labour government's whole incomes policy had been drawn up in flat disregard of the expressed views of the TUC and Labour conferences. Mullin's view of the time was widely shared:

'By the end of the 1970s the Labour Party was no longer the party of change; that was the Conservative Party. The Labour Party was the party of the Establishment, the party of steady-as-we-go, leave it to Jim.'

The 1979 annual conference at Brighton gave Callaghan a rough ride. There was no mercy for the fallen. The chairman of the party, Frank Allaun, made his fraternal contribution: all would have been well if the grassroots had been tended rather than ignored. The general secretary, Ron Hayward, agreed. The mood was best caught by a defeated MP, Tom Litterick, whose Selly Oak party was typical of the new middle-class radicals incensed by Callaghan's caution. Waving a clutch of policy papers at Callaghan, Litterick cried:[5]

'It was these documents which your NEC sought to incorporate in our election manifesto this year. Then one day in April of this year, Jim Callaghan turned up, and that is what he did to your policies. The end result was the fatuous, vacuous document called the Labour Party election manifesto of 1979. "Jim will fix it," they said. Ay, he fixed it. He fixed all of us. He fixed me in particular.'

The three constitutional proposals were all up for debate again. Normally there was a delay of three years before proposals could be brought back, but this provision was suspended by the NEC. Mandatory reselection was carried. The election of the leader by an electoral college (whether this would be the conference or some other body was not always clear) was defeated, but only on the basis that the post was now to be that of leader of the whole party, rather than, technically, of the PLP. The reformers knew well that this alteration would make the continued control of the franchise by MPs alone look even less supportable. They could bide their time. Control of the manifesto by the NEC alone, a proposition which in the atmosphere of the time MPs jostled to support, was postponed. The NEC was instructed to bring proposals to the 1980 conference. On the surface, it looked like a draw, with a replay on the manifesto to be held on the left's own ground. In fact, the sense of profound change hung in the Brighton air. It had been a remarkable week for the CLPD, which at that time had only 450 individual supporters and the affiliation of one-ninth of the constituency parties.

The rancour of the debates and the derision heaped on the PLP and the fallen Labour government left some of the pillars of those bodies very shaken. Not all of them were old Gaitskellites mourning vanished supremacy. One was Peter Shore:

'Within weeks of the coming to power of the most virulently right-wing, class-oriented government that we've had in Britain since before the war, [Labour] was assaulting itself and continuing to rake over the alleged failures of the previous periods . . . tearing itself apart in the frantic search for scapegoats. And in my view there was almost a release of paranoia in the party, that it wasn't just a matter that circumstances had been difficult or particular individuals had made the wrong decisions, but as though there was a kind of organised system of betrayal built into the Labour Party's parliamentary representation.'

Some of the parliamentary left were also uneasy at what was boiling up. Joan Lestor then sat on the National Executive. She recalls:

'I became frightened because I could see people that had stayed with that government right through suddenly coming out as arch critics . . . whereby they were going to be seen to be as it were messiahs and campaigning for change.'

Searches for scapegoats are often accompanied by searches for solutions, for high priests of the faith. Such a figure now appeared in the shape of the party's most gifted communicator, Tony Benn. He says that he had already decided in the 1979 election, 'having served uneasily in the cabinet', that, win or lose, he would resign and 'would devote myself thereafter for a period to rebuilding the strength of the Labour Party'. Though spared the ordeal of renouncing office, he did not shirk his new task. From his base in the Home Policy Committee flowed the lava of new commitments. Each policy change pushed back the Labour right wing towards the beach.

Under the banner of 'Peace, Jobs and Freedom' the National Executive now launched a policy statement anticipating unilateral nuclear disarmament. It was endorsed at a special conference at Wembley in May 1980. Uneasy right-wingers thought they felt the ground moving under their feet. If they checked out their position on the sliding scale of socialist virtue prepared by Chris Mullin's *How to Re-Select Your MP* they could tell it was poor, and worsening. They feared that the coming reselections would be a purge on policy, rather than assiduity in the constituency. 'If you can chant EEC, AES, CND, you'll be all right,' one Tribunite member of the NEC sarcastically assured his colleagues. But supposing you could not, did not have the correct line on the Common Market, or the alternative economic strategy, or defence? At the May special conference David Owen, until recently Foreign Secretary, went to the rostrum to argue with the unilaterialists. His own thinking about the possible strategic use of cruise missiles was directly challenged by the new policy. He was, he said, 'telling you as someone who has dealt with these negotiations'. The remark was greeted with whistles and jeers. It sounded patronising, and in 1980 ex-ministers made such remarks at their peril. He returned to his seat shaken by the experience. For the first time Owen, who had previously had hopes of the Labour leadership himself, found himself doubting his place in it.

The Labour right were outnumbered and out-gunned in the conflict now joined. The Campaign for Labour Victory (CLV), set up in 1977 by Labour and union moderates to rally the constituency moderate, had only limited success. It was not the re-run of the old Campaign for Democratic Socialism which they had intended. The party leader, though of their persuasion, was unhappy about open factions. The unions saw nothing wrong with most of the policy and constitutional changes now being pushed through. One of the CLV rank and file complains plaintively that:

'We always thought that the unions would come to the rescue; but part of CLPD's key to success was organising the left in the unions.'

CLV looked like a clutch of worried loyalists. The unions were moving with the party tide. One reason for this was another new umbrella organisation, set up in June 1980: the Rank and File Mobilising Committee.

In all the alphabet soup that was the Labour left at this time the Rank and File Mobilising Committee (RFMC) was the richest mix. It brought together every organisation on the left that could squeeze into affiliation, including several Trotskyite groups. Militant Tendency, the political wing of the submerged Revolutionary Socialist League, and the Young Socialists, whom it controlled, linked up with old enemies in the National Organisation of Labour Students (NOLS) and the Labour Co-Ordinating Committee (LCC). For a single year these organisations were to hunt as a pack. And it was open season. The new grouping concentrated on a blitz of union delegations and conferences to swing the block vote their way. Their first target was to influence the commission of inquiry set up at the 1979 conference to bring forward proposals for a new method of electing the leader. Their second was the 1980 annual conference at which all the constitutional proposals –

now referred to in shorthand as 'the five demands' – would be resolved. Their eventual successes were due as much to luck as to skill and persistence. The first happened before a single vote was taken or resolution called. Quite simply, they frightened their opponents to the point of political death. A united left was a spectre which demoralised the right.

One observer of the jitters of the Labour right was not displeased. Roy Jenkins was coming to the end of what had not been a particularly happy spell as President of the EEC. He had home thoughts from abroad. In one of his elegant and elaborate metaphors at a Press Gallery lunch in 1980, he likened his dream to an aeroplane which might never be able to take off from the runway. The dream was of a new political party. In fact, for much of 1979–80 Jenkins himself had resembled an aeroplane trying to land. In November 1979 he had taken up the BBC's invitation to deliver the Dimbleby lecture. He chose to speak of domestic politics, of proportional representation as a precursor of coalition government. Better external coalitions between identified groupings, he suggested, than the internalised coalition between incompatibles which the Labour Party had become. The pattern of politics had been frozen because:

'. . . everyone believes that if a party splits it will electorally be slaughtered. They may be right. They may be wrong. I am not so sure. I believe the electorate can tell a hawk from a handsaw, and that if it saw a new grouping with cohesion and relevant policies it might be more attracted by this new reality than by old labels which had become increasingly irrelevant.'

But the wind was not yet southerly. Jenkins had his circle of advisers, all working for the return of the Old Pretender. Former aides stood ready to brief a sympathetic press. A Radical Centre for Democratic Studies was set up. One small group of zealots had already set up a Social Democratic Alliance to run candidates in local elections. But the Labour right were different. They had a lot to lose. Jenkins had been out of their circle. Three years is a long time in political loyalties. Of the Jenkinsites, Dick Taverne puts his leader's dilemma with candour:

'Unless he got leading parliamentarians it wasn't likely to be a very successful break if he was the person leading it. After all he was the President of Europe; he looked like a fat cat from Brussels, and wasn't ideally qualified to start a new sort of popular movement.'

The Labour right seemed to agree. 'We will not be tempted by siren voices from outside, from those who have given up the fight from within,' announced David Owen magisterially after the Dimbleby lecture. A senior colleague remembers Owen at the time as 'terribly anti-Jenkins; violently so. I think it came from when they clashed when he was Foreign Secretary.' Owen was absolutely clear that the one thing he would not back was a Jenkins-led movement. At meetings of the CLV, Owen had openly clashed with Rodgers and Williams, who were already announcing limits of time and faith to what they would give the Labour Party, if it changed further. They had both seen Jenkins, and talked over possibilities, but their public line was still that they would stay the course, while issuing their warnings about the drift leftwards. As late as June 1980 Shirley Williams dismissed all the Jenkinsite talk of broken moulds and new models with a brutal (for her) rejection of the concept of a centre party, which she said would have 'no roots, no principles, no philosophy, and no values'. She says:

'It was necessary to make it absolutely clear to my fellow moderates that I was not playing games with Roy Jenkins's suggestion for a realignment of British politics at that time.'

Jenkins's overtures had found a significant response in one quarter. David Steel, the Liberal leader, had had an easy relationship with Jenkins since, as Home Secretary and freshman backbencher, they had collaborated on the Abortion Act. Jenkins indeed carried something of the air of the old Asquithian Liberal Party – reforming, meritocratic, but leisurely and patrician as well. He had invited Steel to dine with him in Brussels before the Dimbleby lecture. The young Liberal leader was surprised to discover that the tête-à-tête was not to be about the future of the European Commission but about the future of Roy Jenkins. There were later meetings with Jenkins and some of his supporters, including Labour MPs who were already in touch with the Liberals. They agreed that what Steel calls 'a cataclysmic effect on the shape of British politics' could only be achieved by a new party tailored to entice Labour moderates. It was to be subordinate to the Liberals:

'To be blunt, at that particular time, I don't think either of us was thinking in terms of a new party which would be equal in status to the Liberal Party . . . [but] a party which might . . . conceivably get up to maybe 100 candidates . . . working right from the beginning clearly with the Liberal Party and frankly rather under its umbrella.'

So at this time the Liberals were prepared to wait; they knew there were advantages in welcoming a separate Jenkinsite faction rather than Jenkins himself as a member, but were still doubtful about what kind of faction it would be. In that summer of 1980 few predicted the pace of events, or the extent to which Labour's internal groupings would eagerly play out their surgical role in dismembering the Labour coalition.

Bishop's Stortford to Blackpool: Labour on the brink

For the left it was like a cavalry charge, exhilarating, sweeping aside one defensive position after another with no need to regroup. For their targets it seemed a Calvary, or so they said in moments of despair. The commission charged to examine a fresh method of election for the leader met at Bishop's Stortford, guests of the shrewd and manipulative General Secretary of ASTMS, Clive Jenkins. The union leaders wanted to be helpful. They pressed a proposal on Callaghan which would give the parliamentary party 50% of the votes in an electoral college, with 25% for the unions, 20% for the constituencies, and 5% for the affiliated socialist societies. The same college would be asked to ratify a manifesto drafted by the NEC. Moss Evans and David Basnett of the GMWU were pressing as well as helpful. A weary Callaghan gave way. The details were not what the Labour left wanted. The principle was. It did matter thereafter whether the proposals received general assent or not. The door was open, and the majority of the PLP, which had tried to mandate Callaghan against such proposals, was furious.

No one was more furious than David Owen, his plumage already ruffled by his treatment at Wembley. He recalls:

'Jim was not entitled on behalf of the shadow cabinet to make the deal that he did at Bishop's Stortford. He felt guilty about it and it was a great mistake. He fell for David Basnett's soft soap and the belief that you could go on and on compromising.'

Like the left, Owen understood that the college was not about constitutional niceties but about power over policy:

'We thought that if we got the electoral college, you would close down any possibility of the PLP asserting its sovereignty over the rest of the party on some crucial issues of policy. So effectively you would be saddled with all the nonsense of coming out of the European Community, of unilateral disarmament, and all the rag tag and bobtail of nonsense that we weren't going to put up with, because we just genuinely didn't believe it was in the country's interests.'

Owen was now prepared to make common cause with Williams and Rodgers. More impetuous, less deeply rooted in a Labour background, he would be their pacemaker, running in months a course that had taken them more than a year. He contacted Rodgers, with whom he was not personally on close terms. The three drafted a statement for the press which began with the words 'The Labour Party is facing the gravest crisis in its history', and concluded that, although they wished to work within it for democratic socialism, support would grow for a new 'party of conscience and reform' if Labour continued on its present course. Sub-editors played on the recent trial of Madame Mao and her confederates in China to dub the trio the Gang of Three. For the left, reading their statement in the *Guardian*, the Gang had put themselves in the dock. The response was not to ease off, but to press home the indictment.

The 1980 conference at Blackpool was not a wholesale rout of the Labour right: they succeeded in keeping control of the manifesto from the sole charge of the NEC – a reversal of what had happened the previous year. Mandatory reselection was ratified. On the election of the leader confusion reigned. The NEC could get the principle of an electoral college through, although the precise formulations of Bishop's Stortford had been abandoned. No set of voting proportions found favour with the delegates; the issue was postponed to yet another special conference. At one point the NEC left-wingers were prepared to accept a college in which 40% of the vote went to the PLP. It was typical of the time that they were lobbied out of this position within hours by a handful of RFMC activists who flitted around the bars and cloakrooms of the Imperial Hotel. Meanwhile the conference carried votes calling for the removal of all nuclear bases, British as well as American, from Britain, and for withdrawal from the EEC – without a referendum. For the Gang of Three, in urgent and much-photographed conclave on the conference floor, these votes seemed like a deportation order.

Mood matters as much as motions. This was above all the conference of Tony Benn. He seemed to be everywhere, addressing fringe meetings three at a time, if the agenda was to be believed, and mixing a potent brew of instant socialism on the platform. On the first day of the conference he had set the tone. The next Labour government, he said, would have an Industry Act extending common ownership and industrial democracy and controlling capital movements 'within a matter of days'. Such a government would be out of the Common Market 'within a matter of weeks', and in the same time span abolish the Lords 'by creating a thousand peers and then abolishing the peerage as well at the time that the bill goes through'.[6] This was heady stuff. The constituency delegates broke into spontaneous applause. Many of his parliamentary colleagues, horrified at the expectations thus stoked up, sat in silence and rage at what they saw as the demagoguery of a leadership candidate. (One, Andrew Faulds, the macho thespian from Stratford and Smethwick, later devoted a whole speech to Benn's motives – until cut off by the chair.) The 'Thousand Peers' speech was only the beginning. Two days later Benn was back; arguing for the NEC that they should take charge of the manifesto, he made a clear charge of betrayal against the party leader who sat alongside him:

'I have seen policies develop in the sub-committees, come to the executive, go to the unions for consultation, be discussed in the Liaison Committee with the unions, come to conference, be endorsed; then I have seen them cast aside in secret by those who are not accountable to this movement.'

All the bitterness of Benn's isolation as a cabinet minister came out in this speech, for which he was shortly to pay a further price by being voted off the shadow cabinet.

In the context of Blackpool, what was now called 'Bennery' seemed irresistible. His near contemporary Peter Shore offers an explanation of why his influence was so crucial:

'He was in these Labour governments which he so savagely attacked longer than anyone else except Denis Healey . . . He therefore speaks with great authority about what actually happened. He's an insider, he was there, he knew. Secondly because he has a tremendous gift for communication, and thirdly because he has this capacity for self-deception which is absolutely essential if you're going to persuade others that you're right.'

1980, not 1981, marked Benn's high point: he was the right man with the right message for that audience. By contrast, James Callaghan, whose touch had once been as sure as Benn's now was, seemed a lame duck leader at that conference, unable even to say if he would be a candidate for the leadership in November, either under the old rules, or in the New Year, after the proportions of the electoral college had been agreed.

The Labour right wingers, unhappy and disoriented, spent their last night in Blackpool arguing passionately in Shirley Williams's room about what they should do. Owen was now the hawk. Looking back, he regrets that they did not take flight:

'On that Thursday, we might well have broken and formed the new party, and in many ways it would have been a lot simpler and a lot clearer as a Social Democratic Party if we had . . .'

Shirley Williams spoke equally vehemently at the meeting. If the present trend in the Labour Party continued, she said, it (and perhaps Britain) would be in the East European mould within ten years. At the time she saw no haven:

'We had no consciousness of anywhere to go to at the time, absolutely none; we just saw ourselves as unable to continue.'

In the event the meeting broke up without agreement. They would wait on Callaghan's intentions. Meanwhile most, whether their minds turned to staying or leaving, kept their thoughts to themselves.

Benn himself sees the moment as one where the Labour Party had a chance to show that it was in earnest, and did not flinch:

'What frightened people was the thought that the Labour Party might be being serious. And if I were to sum up the real critique of what we were doing, it wasn't that we were hard left, or extreme, or revolutionary, it was that we were serious. In the heart of the analysis of the role of the Labour Party has been the understanding that, however revolutionary a speech may sound at conference, you go and have a chat with the lobby afterwards, and laugh about it, and it doesn't mean anything. And I think the thing that really made the Labour Party alarming to the British establishment was that they realised that we were a serious left, and we weren't playing games.'

The Labour right took Benn at face value too. Shirley Williams called for 'the good men and women who have remained silent' to come out over the parapet:

'If you don't start fighting, you won't have a Labour Party worthy of the name.'

The road to Limehouse

James Callaghan did not linger after the Blackpool conference, although some in his party believed he had lingered too long already. His deputy, Michael Foot, was not one of them. Foot pleaded with him to stay on:

'I urged him to stay because I believed it would be best for the Labour Party if he'd stayed and seen us through some of these difficulties . . . But he'd had a hard time and he wanted to make way.'

To the supporters of the constitutional changes Callaghan's resignation seemed an attempt to outmanoeuvre them. Benn could hardly run (and would not do well) in a contest they regarded as illegitimate. The front runners were therefore Healey and Shore. Healey was assumed to have the Labour right sewn up. Shore still had some credit with the left, for his passionate hostility to the EEC and known opposition to the IMF cuts. But he could not hide his ardent opposition to unilateralism, or to the entryism which he believed was ravaging the party. At the outset he had the goodwill, and was assumed to have the declared support, of Michael Foot. Some early head-counts of the PLP put him a good half-dozen votes ahead of Healey.

That was not what the Labour left wanted. A frantic move was launched to draft in the elderly Foot, not so much as a favourite son as a favourite caretaker. Chris Mullin and Stuart Holland drew up a list of MPs who would (they claimed) vote for Foot but not Shore. Having failed to send a telegram, they drove round to stuff it through Foot's Hampstead letterbox, to join a barrage of mail from other quarters. More influential were Neil Kinnock, Clive Jenkins and Foot's wife, Jill Craigie. Over the weekend Foot came round to the idea: he would run. He says now:

'Peter had taken a number of steps which injured his possibility of being elected. And I don't believe that he would have beaten Denis Healey . . . Somebody had to do his very best to hold the Labour Party together. And I thought I could do that better than other people. That's why I stood.'

Shore's candidacy sank without trace. He was eliminated, with 32 votes; as was John Silkin, with 38. Healey led Foot by 112 to 83, but the two eliminated candidates both urged a vote for Foot, and actively canvassed for him. Shore's action was based on optimism and friendship:

'There is a wisdom about Michael which curiously enough has never been publicly communicated . . . I had come to recognise that he had also great talent in government, as well as his older and more famous talents as an orator . . . So I had a very strong belief in his character, and in the virtues that he had, and that they would be revealed. They were not.'

The leaders of the right now looked to Healey. The Gang of Three urged him to come out fighting; he had nothing to lose. His problem was that, while they had by this time no objection to increasing the rifts in the party, his premiss was that it could still be held together. This made for an impossible tangle:

'We were hit as much by the image of division as by the image of extremism, and it was very difficult to fight the extremists without increasing the image of division.'

On the second ballot both candidates knew that the result would be close. Healey was still favourite, and as he entered Committee Room 10 on the evening of 10 November after being told the result he still had the favourite's mien: jovial, floridly self-confident, relaxed. Foot, by contrast, was deathly pale, tense, and leaning on his stick. The spectators were fooled. Foot had won, by 139 to 129. His pallor reflected his anticipation of the task which lay ahead, for which his great gifts were unsuited. Among those who loitered in the committee corridor was Edward Du Cann. chairman of the Conservative 1922 Committee. He was observed to leave with a smile of benign satisfaction. Why did Healey lose? He attributes it to a mixture of cowardice and sabotage among the normal right-wing majority in the PLP:

'I think there were some people who decided to join the SDP, who wanted Foot to win because that would provide a better background to their decision to defect from the Labour Party. Then there were quite a number of MPs who thought that Michael would give them a quiet life and I would give them a more turbulent life.'

Eight future founder members of the SDP, determined on a Pyrrhic defeat, had indeed voted for Foot. Two, Neville Sandelson and Tom Ellis, have subsequently admitted to it. Healey's brusque style, his tenure of the office which the Labour Party loves least, and the real terror now rife in the PLP as reselection loomed, also played their part.

Foot was now leader, with a special conference to face within two months. He knew of the hopes vested in him. The majority of his support had come from the left. Some used him cynically. Most had dual expectations of him, as expressed by Michael Meacher:

'I regarded Michael Foot as the great conciliator. There was clearly a factional left/right problem within the Labour Party, and most of us felt that if anyone could hold the party together it was Michael Foot . . . Secondly, we did after the experience of the 1970s want to have a more leftward direction . . . articulated with greater genuineness because here was a man who had been in the wilderness over twenty or thirty years.'

But were both these aims achievable, not in years but in weeks? Foot had to hold the party together, in Parliament and at the special conference. He never looked likely to succeed.

Harold Wilson in these circumstances would have scurried to conciliate the Gaitskellites. Foot tried, lamely. (With a kind of awful symbolism he broke his ankle on the morrow of his election.) Owen declined to stand for the shadow cabinet, because, he says, 'I didn't believe Michael Foot was fit to be Prime Minister.' Shirley Williams cut her links with her former constituency, but still dutifully carried out her functions as a member of Labour's NEC and chairwoman of the Fabian Society. William Rodgers, little known to the public but respected as a sinewy organiser within the PLP, became the pressure point. He had sounded out his friends for months past, had discovered that some of them, such as John Horam, were intent upon leaving, whatever he did. Nevertheless, Rodgers had run for the shadow cabinet, and been elected. Now he was laid up with back trouble, perhaps psychosomatic. To his house in Kentish Town came Foot, to talk terms. The heir of Bevan and the organising secretary of the Gaitskellite campaign for Democratic Socialism had little in common. Rodgers might have taken the Industry portfolio – but it was promised to Foot's old ally Stan Orme. The meeting simply left both men despairing of agreement. Rodgers took no post:

'I'd reached a crisis which was a crisis that nobody could resolve but myself,' he remembers. He stayed abed, thinking that if there was a split it would not be for another year. At Westminster the dissidents grouped themselves around the more impetuous David Owen.

Owen did not waste time. He went to see Jenkins at his country house in East Hendred in late November. '[He] suggested that really it was silly for us all to go off on different routes and that we ought to link up.'

For a man who had been openly contemptuous of Jenkins's earlier solo flight, this was a major switch of direction. His one condition was that Jenkins would not automatically assume the leadership of the new party. It was accepted. The new duo turned to their colleagues, for whom the pains of withdrawal were much more drawn out. Shirley Williams, whom Michael Foot and others now begged to stay in the Labour ranks, was the most hesitant:

'Bill and I were much more of the Labour ethos than probably David or Roy were . . . It seemed much more a whole life that was going and I guess that we were more reluctant to face the fact that probably the Labour Party was by that time irrecoverable.'

Over the first weeks of 1981 that is what they came to believe. Rodgers shook off his trauma: 'I rose from my bed and I was on the way to becoming a Social Democrat.' At his house, with the press in attendance, there gathered what could now be called with the certainty of cliché the Gang of Four. The Labour leaders were seen to be consorting with Jenkins, who arrived in a shapeless overcoat, urbanely brushing off suggestions from the others that he had leaked the meeting to the press. One of those there, Roger Liddle, remembers:

'Jenkins was smoking one of those great big cigars and he said, "A tragedy that our great enterprise should have started off in the atmosphere of the worst of a Wilson cabinet." He was magnificent.'

The Four decided that they would wait for the Wembley conference. There they would argue for the principle of one member, one vote, if the Labour Party was to change its method of choosing the leader – in the certain knowledge that they would lose. The Labour right had never previously shown any interest in wider franchises. It was unlikely to prevail now, when the new method it advocated would take power away from both the activists and the unions before they had tasted it. Owen's last appearance at the Manifesto Group was valedictory in tone. He left no one present in much doubt that a parting was imminent.

The Wembley conference decided on the form of the electoral college by a shambolic procedure. Two alternatives had been canvassed. One, favoured by the PLP and some of the big unions, kept 50% of the electoral college for the PLP, 25% each for unions and constituencies. The other, favoured by the NEC, was for an equal three-way split, plus 1% for the socialist societies. The unions could have outvoted the constituencies, but they were disorganised and uncertain. (The long-running inter-union dispute on the Isle of Grain at this time meant that some unions normally in alliance on the right of the party were not speaking to each other.) The young activists of CLPD knew exactly what they wanted. They swung enough support behind a third motion, from the moderate union USDAW, which proposed 40% for the trades unions, 30% each for PLP and constituencies, to ensure that it survived early balloting, though it was the first choice of very few. Its survival prevented USDAW from switching to the union's own second preference, which was the 50% for the PLP option. In a run-off with the latter, the USDAW motion won – for a bizarre reason. The second largest block vote, that of the AUEW, had been locked up for any solution which gave the PLP more than 50% of the college (90% was its own favoured figure!). A more subtle figure than the slow-moving AUEW President, Terry Duffy (whom, the wags said, wanted a 50–50–50 split), would have unlocked his delegation. Instead, the AUEW sat and watched a system voted in which gave the largest choice in the selection of a potential prime minister to the unions.

It fell to Michael Foot to speak after the vote. His speech, whimsical, redolent with gentle reminders that everyone – leader, MPs, conference – could be wrong, was not intended as a rallying point. In a deliberate disavowal of another speech after a famous defeat, he said he had heard that he should fight, fight and fight again. But he didn't want to fight anybody. He accepted the vote. He didn't want anyone to leave the party either. A few hours later he got his answer. The Gang of Four walked out of David Owen's house in Narrow Street, Limehouse, to face the world's press. They issued what became known as the Limehouse Declaration. A Council of Social Democracy was set up. The declaration had no memorable prose, but its conclusion would not be easily forgotten:

'We recognise that for those people who have given much of their lives to the Labour Party, the choice that lies ahead will be deeply painful. But we believe that the need for a realignment of British politics must now be faced.'

It was faced elsewhere. When Tony Benn seemed to be pressing home his advantage in the PLP by seeking an oath of loyalty to conference policies, Michael Foot replied with a furious defence of liberty of conscience, condemning those who wanted to 'open a window into men's minds'. Once more he pleaded with the dissidents, one of whom still sat on his front bench. It was too late. On 5 February the *Guardian* carried a list of 100 notables described as supporters of the Council for Social Democracy and an appeal for support. The list could have been headed the Friends of Shirley Williams: many on it were drawn from her vast acquaintance. A handful were later to remain in the Labour Party, but this was a dry run for a new party, and seen as such. Early in February Shirley Williams resigned from the NEC amid much acrimony. Any delay now in launching a new party would depend on propitious timing, not on personal doubt.

The Labour Party saw the defectors' departure with mixed feelings. On the hard left, especially in London, there was jubilation. GLC Councillor Val Wise was quoted as saying of the right wingers still in the party, such as Healey and Hattersley:

'The sooner they go the better because the trouble with these people is that they are very much identified with the last Labour government and with previous Labour governments who betrayed the working people of this country.'

Others were more publicly circumspect. The defectors, for their part, like those who rejoiced at their going, rationalise the process in retrospect. As in most divorces, the two parties cannot see any good in each other, despising the hundred small arrangements and understandings which had allowed them to go on living together for so long. With hindsight, Benn believes that nothing could have kept the defectors in, without transforming Labour to something 'to the right of even the American Democratic Party'. (The spectre of such a party was a recurrent nightmare of the left. In Trevor Griffiths's television series *Bill Brand*, about a leadership contest actually won by the Jenkins-figure, the winner is seen declaiming quotations from Roosevelt's first inaugural speech after his election.) Benn's amanuensis Chris Mullin sees the defection as 'long overdue . . . my real question would've been what stopped them going ten years earlier'. Michael Meacher, however, speaks for others on the Labour left when he says:

'I didn't anticipate the degree of the divide in British politics which has since developed, which has proved to be extremely damaging. Had I realised that it was going to be as damaging as that, perhaps we would have made more effort at the time to prevent it occurring.'

Could it have been prevented? No single event of the terminal year was in itself crucial, unlike some of the political cataclysms of the past. There had been previous swings to the left after an unsatisfactory period of minority government. There had been complaints from the right, as Austin Mitchell puts it about this period of time, that 'the language of socialism is about priorities; the trouble is no one in the Labour Party speaks it'. There had been complaints from the left about parliamentary grandees who seemed to forget the people who had toiled to put them where they were. But the particular conjunction of the rise of Tony Benn in the Labour movement and the polar star of Roy Jenkins outside it – two men from similar backgrounds who now articulated opposed views of the pace and direction of change – provided a personal focus for a political quarrel. Add to this the impetuous haste of David Owen, always willing to discard unwanted baggage (as exemplified by the excisions he made between the first and second editions in 1981 of his book *Face the Future*[7]) and the eagerness of the Labour left to press on and consolidate their gains, and sufficient stress factors were in place to break open the old coalition. The new pattern of British politics was quilted, the conventions which had kept Labour an internal coalition in a 'two-party system' casualties of the times.

19

DRYING OUT THE WETS

Margaret Thatcher came into office as a self-styled 'conviction politician'. In a famous pre-election interview in the *Observer* in February 1979 she had said that 'as Prime Minister I could not waste time having any internal arguments'. In time she was able to make the world of Tory politics fit in with this attitude. It is an attitude which reflects how her administration, and what has come to be called Thatcherism, now tends to be seen – the first question always: is he one of us? Her dominance was not easily or quickly won. At times she must have asked herself, in relation to her cabinet colleagues: am I one of them? The years 1979–81 are only now seen as an epilogue for the seventies and the old tradition of Tory paternalism. At the time many observers would have agreed with the assessment of Hugh Stephenson, current editor of the *New Statesman*, of her first year:[1]

'Her rhetoric is radical, even reckless. But from the start her deeds have shown a politician's instinctive caution.'

It was the caution of a leader who knew that she could not command a majority in her party's ruling circle, but was biding her time until she could summon up the party in the country, whose instincts and values she believed she shared.

The Conservatives' 1979 election platform had five main planks: the control of inflation and union power; the restoration of incentives; the upholding of parliamentary sovereignty and the rule of law; the support of family life and a more efficient welfare system; and the strengthening of defence. That meant a high profile for tax cuts, cuts in public expenditure and in the role of the NEB, the sale of recently nationalised assets, and of council houses to their tenants, and legislation to curb the unions. The manifesto was short: a skilful compromise among the party factions. Over the next four years, the party was taken well beyond it.

The manifesto was carefully tailored to the public rating of issues of importance. This put prices first, unemployment second, taxes and strikes equal third, and law and order fifth. Surveys showed that, on the first two issues, the electorate put Labour ahead, but the new prominence given to the others greatly favoured the Conservatives. The Conservatives were able to reap an electoral harvest from the concerns about ungovernability which had taken root in the seventies, and had grown again in 1979. Callaghan's reassuring and unradical mien kept him personally in greater public esteem than Thatcher throughout the campaign, and there were moments, as those in her circle recall, when she suspected that her senior colleagues believed that she might throw the election away. In fact the result was never in doubt. 'There's a sea change in politics,' Callaghan mused to Bernard Donoughue, just before polling day. 'Whatever we do, this election is all about Mrs Thatcher.' Whether because of, or in spite of, being perceived as the more radical party, the Conservatives won an overall majority of 43 with the largest swing since the war.

The victory was more emphatic than that of 1970, but it did not leave Margaret Thatcher in as strong a personal position as Edward Heath had then enjoyed. She was surrounded by the cabinet colleagues she had inherited from him. Her own closest adviser, Airey Neave, had been assassinated in New Palace Yard by the self-styled Irish National Liberation Army just before the election. The moderates were not purged or slighted. With Carrington at the Foreign Office, Whitelaw at the Home Office, Pym at Defence, and Prior at Employment, they could feel that the old dispensation had not been changed. They missed the significance of other moves. First, quite deliberately, there was no cabinet place for Heath himself. Julian Critchley, later a vigorous critic of Thatcher, admits the importance of the move for the future:

'The real success, from Margaret's point of view, was her refusal to offer Heath a job in 1979. Had she done the decent thing and offered a former Prime Minister that he become Foreign Secretary, Heath would have been in the cabinet. There would have been a focus, a major figure, around whom others like-minded might have gathered. But she didn't, and Heath was exiled to the backbenches. Now that should have been signal enough, because the rest of them in fact were no match for her, either man to woman or collectively.'

The second march stolen on the moderates was the overnight occupation of the key economic posts by men who could be trusted to be true believers in the new Conservatism. Geoffrey Howe became Chancellor of the Exchequer. Under him was the former Powellite John Biffen, Chief Secretary with a place in the cabinet, and Nigel Lawson. Keith Joseph went to Industry – a department which, he believed, should perhaps not even exist – there to distribute a monetarist reading list to his bemused civil servants. (Nineteen of the twenty-nine works came from either the IEA or the Centre for Policy Studies, eight written by Joseph himself.) John Nott went to Trade, David Howell (a convert to the new ideology) to Energy. Once this latter group asserted its more rigorous view of public spending cuts, the moderates, who in fluctuating groups and unco-ordinated fashion opposed them, came to be dubbed 'wets'. The description was Thatcher's; they adopted it for themselves with a dash of pride, as the old contemptibles of 'One Nation' Conservatism. The monetarists were known as the 'dries' in contrast. The story of the next two years is in part of the struggle between the two factions, and how the 'wets' came to live up to their name.

The wets' initial problem was that they did not grasp the extent to which they were excluded from the thrust of policy-making. John Biffen observes that:

'The 1979 government contained quite a number of people who had a clear commitment to the concept of controlled public spending, reform in taxation, a greater role for the private sector, and borrowing restrained in such a way as to minimise the likelihood of inflation. [That gave] a cohesion which quite often governments don't possess, being drawn from large political parties that are themselves a coalition of interests.'

In fact, one part of the coalition, sometimes a minority in cabinet, reinforced this cohesion by gathering together as an inner group. The senior Thatcherites met secretly, to bolster their sense of common purpose. John Nott recalls:

'We met, informally, outside cabinet committees, and we, I think, gave moral support to Mrs Thatcher that the policies we believed in were right. And so to some extent those who didn't agree with us in the cabinet were put rather on one side . . . We met sometimes at No. 10, sometimes over a meal, occasionally over breakfast.'

The fruits of this collaboration were soon noted in cabinet. Norman St John-Stevas, Leader of the House of Commons and a confirmed wet, says:

'I realised very soon . . . that although the people supporting the traditionalist view were in fact the majority, the weight of the cabinet was not with them.'

Jim Prior, looking at the composition of the teams at the Treasury, Trade and Industry, sensed his isolation without needing to know of their informal links:

'[It] obviously showed she was going to go her own way as far as she could. I think I was the only minister in the economic team with whom there were likely to be difficulties from her point of view. So the writing was on the wall.'

There was a third area in which the new Prime Minister rapidly strengthened her position. The comfortable assumption of the wets among the back-room policy-makers had been that, once the election was won, things would settle down, the government would be tempered by events and would certainly not go beyond the manifesto. Then, says one disgruntled former aide, 'All the loonies came out of the woodwork, and assumed great positions in No. 10.' The Prime Minister's circle of advisers was hawkish, encouraging her natural tendency towards impatience with the old establishment, in whatever form it appeared. Bright sparks from outside were brought in to ignite the damp mass of the civil service. Terry Burns, a thirty-five-year-old, non-Oxbridge economist from the London Business School, became chief economic adviser. John Hoskyns, a career soldier who had been blooded in Dick Taverne's skirmishes in the early seventies, came via the CPS to run the Downing Street Policy Unit. There would be no excessive deference to consensus politics from them.

The first problem was the economic situation. The Conservatives inherited an economy which had been managed on a mixture of incomes policy, employment promotion and monetary constraints through cash limits on public expenditure. The latter, from the year of the IMF onwards, had already been a central enough concern to justify Peter Riddell's comment that 'if there has been a Thatcher experiment, it was launched by Denis Healey'.[2] By May 1979 there was a £1000 million balance of payments surplus, with oil coming ashore in quantity. Unemployment had fallen from its peak under Labour of one and a half million to 1,238,000. The index of industrial production was mounting again and the Bank of England's minimum lending rate (MLR) had come down to 5% in 1977. Inflation, however, having been reduced to single figures, was back above 10%. In the Conservative analysis, inflation was the real enemy; they believed that much of Labour's job-support mechanism had been the cosseting inefficient industry which would be best helped by an incentive society rather than infusions of public money. They wished to be bold but, as Terry Burns later said regretfully, the summer of 1979 'was not a good place to start'.

There were two reasons for this which the government overlooked:

a second 'oil shock' in the wake of the fall of the Shah of Iran, and the wage explosion in Britain which had been building since the settlements of the Winter of Discontent. The pound was now a petrocurrency, responsive to a new rise in oil prices. The economy was sensitive to a rise in costs. David Howell, the Energy Secretary, found it 'difficult to get through to other people, in Parliament and in the government, the enormity of what was happening'. He recalls the argument of the government's economic theoreticians:

' "Well, if the price of oil goes up, the price of something else will come down and we must just hang on to our targets." But of course this was for an ideal world; in the real world it was hopelessly unrealistic because the price of oil was very important to the price of a vast range of goods and rapidly began to push up the retail price index [RPI].'

The RPI in turn began to affect wage increases. So did the last legacy of the Labour government, the Clegg awards, which proved to have a delayed fuse for the Conservatives similar to that which Heath's threshold payments had had for Labour in 1974. Professor Clegg had been charged with ending unrest on the pay front through a Comparability Commission, which would recommend public sector pay increases justified by discrepancies between public and private sectors. Labour's policy adviser Bernard Donoughue had had his misgivings about Clegg:

'We didn't believe there was a comparability of input in the public sector and a superiority . . . in terms of job security and in terms of pension [so] it couldn't be justified in terms of equity, and [this] was fatal economically.'

In the election the Tories committed themselves to accepting Clegg's recommendations, and found that in the wage inflation of 1979 this meant 20% increases. Ministers were divided. John Biffen believes it would have been 'unthinkable . . . to cast aside . . . that which you had underwritten for the purpose of winning votes'. Cecil Parkinson, however, concludes that:

'It was a mistake to endorse Clegg in the run-up to the election . . . There's always this pressure to recognise the problems of the special interest group, and we did, and we gave that commitment which turned out to be a very, very expensive one.'

Geoffrey Howe's first budget remained true to its ambitions, rather than to the reality of new inflationary pressures. The manifesto had pledged him to 'cut income tax at all levels to reward hard work, responsibility and success'. The basic tax rate was cut from 33% to 30%, the top marginal rate of tax on earned income from 83% to 60%. The well-off became much better off overnight, and had cause to rejoice at Howe's 'opportunity budget'. He says now that his priorities were right:

'We had the highest direct tax rates on high earnings of any country in the world except, I think, Albania . . . Two, we'd got a very high direct tax rate applicable to everyone. And, three, we'd got tax thresholds that were absurdly low.'

The price for this spectacular reward to the people the government wished to encourage was elsewhere – indirect tax. VAT was raised from 8% to 15%, across the board. There had been rumours that this would happen. (It was one of the 'twelve Labour lies' savaged in the *Daily Mail* during the election.) The CBI lobbied Prior, who argued to no avail with the Prime Minister. The VAT increase was inevitably passed on in higher retail prices. Pay, price and dividend controls were scrapped. Exchange controls were to go the same way. The combination of extra inflationary pressures and those in the pipeline and the psychological sense of a coming free-for-all combined to stoke inflation. It rose from 10.3% to 21.9% in the Conservatives' first full year. Prior thought the budget 'a mistake':

'We did increase the rate of inflation and the cost of living very considerably indeed.'

The monetarists, for their part, argued that the clearest possible signal had to be given at once to supporters and opponents alike that the government meant business.

The second phase of such a strategy would be the curbing of the unions. The opportunity budget would be coupled with an enterprise economy, with legal disincentives to strikes and restrictive practices. Howe, who had drafted the ill-fated Heath legislation, now accepted a gradualist approach. But the aim was the same as before: seek out and break the unions' monopolistic powers. The Thatcher circle had urged her not to appoint Prior as Employment Secretary. Some of them were almost hysterical about him. Those intent on 'bashing the unions into the middle distance' believed him constrained by his good relations with union leaders, and disdainful of employers of the George Ward type. John Hoskyns makes no secret of his own tough line on the unions:

'The whole question of reducing trade union power . . . was absolutely central to the government's strategy.'

There were three reasons which Hoskyns advanced: the unions impeded the government's plans to cut public sector spending; they helped to swell its losses; and they affected the competitiveness of the private sector. The argument found ready listeners. Keith Joseph in particular wanted urgent action, which would help to make industry more competitive.

Prior, who knew something about both industry and the unions, was determined to move cautiously, but realised that the national mood had changed in 1979:

'It's almost inconceivable to someone like me who did actually see the passage of the Industrial Relations Act and all that happened subsequently in '71 to '74 to recognise the difference [in] mood. It was really the case that the union leaders had, I think, vastly exceeded their own authority in the eyes not only of the public generally but also of their own members. And therefore the mood was right for rather more legislation, and . . . more union bashing than I ever thought would be justified or politically acceptable.'

The unions picked up the changed mood, not from Prior but from a visit to Downing Street, when, as Tom Jackson remembers, they ran into a sustained hectoring:

'It was a bad meeting, but it was quite different, and there was a coldness there which I've seen since but which I hadn't seen before when the TUC had gone to Downing Street. Now there'll be those who say that that was a good thing, but in fact it was the start of a real divorce between the government and the trade union movement.'

Len Murray had not met anyone like this Prime Minister before:

'She rejected the idea of unions as valid institutions within society, and as organisations which, even if you didn't like 'em, you were stuck with and had to come to some sort of agreement [with].'

In spite of this, the initial legislation was in the Prior mould: changes in the law on secondary picketing, compensation for workers at odds with the closed shop, and the assistance for union ballots – all of which had been promised in the manifesto.

Prior could believe that he had got away with that decent minimum which could actually help to improve industrial relations. He had reckoned without the 1980 steel strike. Some of the employers in the small private sector of the steel industry, faced with secondary picketing from the Iron and Steel Trades Confederation, went directly to the Prime Minister. She had lost the argument in cabinet for a short bill purely to deal with secondary picketing, and for opening union funds to legal claims for damages. This did not stop her trailing the ideas again, both in the Commons and on the BBC's *Panorama* programme. Not for the first time Prior discovered that, while the government could have one policy, its leader would be foraging ahead in search of something nearer to her instincts. To make matters worse, she went out of her way to humiliate him on the *Panorama* programme. His poor opinion of the British Steel chairman Sir Charles Villiers's handling of the strike had been leaked to the press. Robin Day asked if Prior had been scolded. 'I think it was a mistake,' the Prime Minister told the nation. 'And Jim Prior was very, very sorry indeed for it; very apologetic. But you don't just sack a chap for one mistake.' Jim was very sorry – but about the broadcast. He continued to defend his bill as it went through Parliament, but there was little doubt that his party would be back for more.

In that area of the ideological battlefield the wets still believed that they were holding their own. Elsewhere they could point to real influence, sometimes persuasion. Margaret Thatcher had come to power knowing little of foreign affairs. Rhodesia had been for a generation a graveyard of British political reputations, as successive administrations tested the water for a settlement with the Smith regime, only to stub their foot against the immovable rock of African opposition. That opposition had sent the Pearce Commission packing in 1972. It had forced Smith into an 'internal settlement' with a black Prime Minister, Bishop Abel Muzorewa, but all the levers of power remained in the hands of the whites. There Margaret Thatcher found it, and her first instinct, expressed in some impromptu remarks at a press conference in Australia, was to recognise Muzorewa and drop economic sanctions, as the vociferous 'Rhodesia lobby' in the Tory Party urged. The Foreign Secretary differed. Lord Carrington knew that Britain would be isolated if it backed a minority regime while a bitter guerrilla war continued against it. He persuaded Thatcher that she was wrong, and within a matter of months she had come to terms with the African states backing the nationalist Patriotic Front and set in motion the Lancaster House conference. Once again a British government was offering a settlement of the Rhodesia imbroglio – but this time to the majority. Unlike Smith, the Patriotic Front leaders grasped the chance, and returned home from Lancaster House to win elections supervised by the British, under the rococo figure of Lord Soames as interim Governor, a position he filled with great skill. Lords Carrington and Soames could feel with some justice after her conversion that the Prime Minister was a pragmatist before all else.

Other wet ministers found they had considerable freedom of action during the first Thatcher year, which in some cases diverted them from the absence of discussion about the central thrust of the government's economic policies. Whitelaw, ever the loyal deputy, was busy putting money into law and order. A week after the election the police were given a 20% pay rise without having had the benefit of Clegg. (The next day the armed forces were given 32% – a massive increase in defence costs.) The new 'short sharp shock' treatment for young offenders was phased in, but the Commons voted conclusively against a restoration of the death penalty, which had been much trailed in the press during the election as a consequence of a Thatcher victory. In the free vote the Home Secretary was in the anti-hanging lobby, Margaret Thatcher with the hangers. Francis Pym, Michael Heseltine and Mark Carlisle settled down to the defence of their departments. Pym at Defence had the luxury at first of being a minister whose increased public expenditure was smiled upon. He was able to increase defence spending to the highest level as a percentage of GDP it had enjoyed since Wilson's East of Suez commitments were scrapped. Among his decisions was that to purchase the multiple-warhead Trident missile system from the United States, revealing in the process Labour's support in office for the Chevaline. This, together with the endorsement of the 1979 NATO decision to site Cruise missiles in Britain, had the effect almost overnight of rejuvenating the Campaign for Nuclear Disarmament, with a new generation joining the veterans of Ban-the-Bomb days.

At the Department of the Environment the flamboyant Michael Heseltine could put an appealing face on the 'roll-back' of the local government empires by squeezing public sector house-building, and using the carrot and stick approach to break up the council estates. The carrot was the right for tenants to buy, sometimes at no more than half the market price; it was not extended to private tenants. The stick was the forcing up of council rents, to remove subsidy; again, no similar action was taken to remove the subsidy enjoyed by mortgage-holders. The policy was bitterly attacked by Labour, because of its effect on the housing stock and the council house waiting list; to their chagrin, it proved to be enormously popular with those who acquired a capital asset at a bargain price.

Norman St John-Stevas had no full department to defend, but he ensured himself a place in parliamentary history by setting up inves-

tigative select committees to shadow the departments of his colleagues. His colleagues were not delighted. Some of the resultant
investigations – of the Home Affairs and Education Committees, in
particular – left civil servants suspicious and angry about this new
predator. Those backbenchers who wanted a proper function separate
from the executive were given it, a second ladder among the snakes of
the Westminster life.

The battle over economic policy

By early 1980 it was obvious that things were going badly wrong with
the government's economic strategy: the policy area reserved to
ministers of the Prime Minister's persuasion. The expansion of the
money supply, both in bank lending and the finance of the public
sector, led the government hastily to raise minimum lending rate to a
record 17%. The pound was soaring already, in its new role as a
petro-currency. It rose to a high point of $2.45 in November 1980. In
the midst of a deepening world recession British industry was in
serious trouble. As one critic succinctly puts it:[3]

'Industry found its labour costs raised by one third in two years, its
interest costs doubled, its export earnings slashed, domestic demand
cut, and import competition generously increased . . . about as subtle
in conception, and salutary in effect, as if one had driven a bulldozer
into a symphony orchestra.'

As industrial output fell, unemployment began to climb rapidly.
From the winter of 1979 it was increasing by 100,000 per month,
passing the two million mark for the first time in August 1980.

Some of those in the cabinet at the time acknowledge surprise at the
rate of increase. David Howell admits that:

'What was not thought about was the combination of circumstances. With recession, the gigantic siphoning of purchasing power to
the Arab countries from Europe, plus the de-manning that we wanted
to see, plus the tight public expenditure which we wanted to see as
well: it wasn't conceived that all these would coincide and produce
unemployment in the low millions.'

A former economic minister accepts that 'we were neither intellec-
tually nor emotionally prepared for increases of this magnitude'. The
Treasury ministers and their allies believed that they should not be
panicked, as they thought Heath had been, into reaching for the tools
of demand management. The rising Thatcher protégé Cecil Parkinson
puts their case:

'We believed that the only way you're really going to tackle the problem of the unemployed is to free up the system, and that the jobs will be generated not by sudden splurges of public expenditure but by continued improved economic performance. It isn't that you're saying: we don't care about the unemployed; they are a central preoccupation of the government . . . but the answers are, to use the jargon, more on the supply side – government reducing its burdens on industry, and reducing some of the restrictions.'

With the publication of its medium-term financial strategy in the spring of 1980 it was clear that the government meant to keep as a virtue what others had had to embrace as an odious necessity. Its budget day memorandum, the 'Red Book', said:

'[The government has] deliberately not set its targets in terms of the ultimate objectives of price stability and high output and employment because these are not within its direct control. It has instead set a target for the growth of money supply, which is more directly under its influence, and has stated that it will frame its policies for taxation and public expenditure to secure a deceleration of money supply without excessive reliance on interest rates.'

This was, as a supporter of the policy and subsequent Treasury minister Jock Bruce-Gardyne has written, a 'different concept' of the role of government:[4]

'It formally abandoned the pretence that full employment and economic growth were in the gift of government.'

Public spending was cut in the budget by a further £680 million, and indirect taxes raised again. Unemployment was bound to rise – but by how much?

There was already disquiet in the cabinet at the repercussions of such a policy. It focused first on the consequences of sterling appreciation. The average worth of the pound in 1978 had been $1.92. In 1979 it was $2.12. In 1980 it was still rising, towards its November peak. (The average for the year was $2.32.) Dr Otmar Emminger, ex-president of the Federal German Central Bank, described this to the new Commons Treasury Select Committee as 'by far the most excessive over-valuation which any currency has experienced in recent monetary history'. The government's monetary policies and pronouncements were helping to boost the rise. The government was not averse to this. The London Business School's economic forecasters had argued in the seventies that a tough anti-inflationary policy would strengthen the exchange rate, which would then itself act more harshly on inflation than on output. *The Right Approach to the Economy* had echoed this when it said:

'Internal inflation is the real enemy of successful competition. A falling exchange rate makes internal inflation worse. Short-lived gains in price competition are too rapidly eroded for them to bring lasting benefit to the balance of trade.'

When Terry Burns took up his post as chief economic adviser in January 1980, the LBS gained a powerful advocate at the heart of policy-making, who did not flinch from the unfolding consequences of the high pound for manufacturing industry.

It was soon clear that these consequences were catastrophic. The high pound reduced import prices, which put the British manufacturer under further pressure from import substitution in the home market, while abroad he found it almost impossible to sell. Birmingham and the West Midlands, the workshop of Britain, found that their order books had 'fallen off a cliff'. One of the most forceful local industrialists, Reg Parkes, spoke for many when he said:

'There is much talk about industry rising like a phoenix from the ashes. But what if we are just left with the ashes?'

As wage claims passed on the pressures of the existing (and still rising) inflation, labour costs further squeezed what margins remained. The output of British manufacturing production fell by 20% in the years 1979–81, with what came to be known as 'deindustrialisation' blighting old and new areas of mass unemployment. A series of industries in public ownership were forced to go to the Department of Industry for further financial help in order to survive. To the anguish of Keith Joseph, the help was given where state or local political considerations were overriding: British Leyland, Rolls-Royce, British Steel, Harland and Wolff. At the CBI conference, its Director General, Sir Terence Beckett, said he would be involved in a 'bare-knuckle fight' with the government:

'We've got to have a lower pound . . . We've got to have lower interest rates.'

The argument was put in cabinet. Prior remembers the debate:

'There were a number of ministers who took the view that there was nothing we could do about the currency. I never took that view myself. I think that the currency was kept high, partly by having high exchange rates, which was all part of the monetary policy . . . They were almost the same ministers who said, "Well actually, it's what British industry needs, it's going to sort out those who are good from those who are bad." I personally thought that the policy at that time was much too severe.'

The Trade Secretary, John Nott, was one of those who thought the shakeout would have a salutary effect:

'It was hastening a fundamental change in the structure of British industry which, in my judgement, was going to happen in any event. But of course it did intensify the social pressures because everything was happening faster . . . but we knew that there was no way we could sell sterling in the way which would have been necessary to hold its value down. We just simply wouldn't have been able to do it, and therefore we didn't attempt it.'

The Prime Minister remained firm. Interviewed on the day that unemployment passed the two million mark, she said:

'I've been trying to say to people for a very long time: if you pay yourself more for producing less, you'll be in trouble. They will . . . There are some people who are going out of business because of the world recession, and that's very, very tough on them. In this government we must fight inflation, that is absolutely critical, and we must go on fighting.'

Would there be a change in the policies? she was asked: 'No change, because the policies are right.' She was known in her party, not altogether affectionately, as Tina, from the reiterated message that 'there is no alternative'. When Michael Edwardes of British Leyland went to talk to her about the 'incredible heights' reached by the pound, he found:

'She was absolutely impervious to the argument that this would bring about deindustrialisation, it would bring about a structural change. I realised we were dealing with a fairly tough philosophy. And of course great damage was done in early 1980.'

In the cabinet there were still many who believed that there should be an alternative, but they could not always agree what form it should take or how they might combine to achieve it. Prior, Walker, Pym, Gilmour and St John-Stevas expressed related anxieties; Carrington and Whitelaw listened as friends, but were too loyal to be allies. Back in February 1980 Ian Gilmour had said:

'The Welfare State and the interventionist state are not going to go away . . . Those who believe otherwise have, in my view, fallen into the trap of ideology and dogma, which is, or should be to Conservatives, the unpardonable sin.'

Shortly afterwards a backbench colleague committed another unpardonable sin: writing anonymously in the *Observer* to attack the 'A Level economics' of Thatcherism which 'have elevated economics above politics in an almost Marxist fashion'. Swiftly exposed, Julian Critchley's tactical error detracted from what he had to say. His reception discouraged other dissidents. In any event, backbenchers seemed to prefer giggling dissent over dinner to speaking out in public. The burgeoning number of nicknames and jokes about the Prime Minister marked her strength, and their weakness. Cabinet dissidents declined to cabal, as Prior admits:

'I can't say we ever got together to discuss our concerns. . . . We did have desultory and periodic meetings between a few of us when we got more than usually het up.'

As Peter Riddell remarks, 'It was sometimes difficult to know who the "wets" were.'

Desultory meetings did not get far. The other senior wets resented, as one puts it, 'being made to take responsibility for a policy one regarded as wholly damaging' and about which they were not consulted. But, by the same token, they found it difficult to speak out in areas which were not their departmental responsibility. They watched glumly as the government pressed on with the reduction of the public sector borrowing requirement (PSBR), reflecting that, in their youth, the new monetarism had been called deflation.

The government's resolution was fortified by the comparative ineffectiveness of opposition outside its own ranks. Although the polls had rapidly turned against it, there had been no great reverses. A strong supporter of the tough line, Teddy Taylor, who had lost his Scottish seat in 1979, was scathed in the Southend by-election, but survived a strong challenge from the Labour candidate. Labour's own internal arguments were beginning, in the autumn of 1980, to distract it from a full-scale attack on Thatcherism. For the rest of the parliament it never did as well again as it had at Southend. The TUC's Day of Action in protest at government policies had flopped, and the stupendous rise in the number of unemployed rapidly inhibited trade union response. Those on the left who had been impatient at Len Murray's attempt to get on terms with the new government felt that the optimum moment for action had slipped past. Dennis Skinner says:

'They missed the boat, because there's a time when unemployment is rising when the unions are strong and when they can actually take action. In my view they failed to understand that, and so by the time the TUC wanted to look strong and take action there were too many workers who were feeling insecure.'

The 1980 Conservative conference met at Brighton, immediately after a deeply divided Labour Party had been on show at Blackpool. There was a heavy police presence as Right to Work demonstrators converged on the town, but the main criticism of the government came in one of those coded addresses in which Conservatives specialise. Norman St John-Stevas launched a criticism of the 'high priests' of monetarism of the Lawson sect who believed that the quantity of money controlled inflation, and therefore that what mattered was for governments to use their power to control the quantity of money. The wets, he says, wanted to assert a higher priority for:

'. . . preserving the social fabric, keeping the One Nation tradition, believing that the government had an overriding social duty which took precedence over all economic considerations.'

Margaret Thatcher found this view exasperating: it had led to all the policy somersaults of the Heath era. She was in robust form at the conclusion of the conference, saying to the demonstrators outside (and to one who briefly got in to heckle), 'This government is pursuing the only policy which gives any hope of bringing our people back to real and lasting employment.' Then a well-crafted joke sounded a warning to her critics:

'We shall not be diverted from our course. For those waiting with bated breath for that favourite media catchphrase, the U-Turn, I have only one thing to say. You turn if you want to. The lady's not for turning.'

Among those whom the television showed smiling – if not exactly convulsed – at this quip was Francis Pym. Privately he was dismayed:

'I thought it was a very great mistake to say the lady's not for turning – clearly indicating that, whatever the circumstances were, it didn't matter what the conditions were or how things altered, everything else as far as she was concerned was going to go on the same. Well, I don't view life like that. Politics isn't like that. Circumstances alter cases . . . The Prime Minister has a style [where] there's never any flexibility, never any compromise, never any change.'

For those now working closely with her, this was precisely the exhilarating attraction of Thatcher. As the criticisms of the economic policy and its consequences in unemployment and social distress mounted, they knew she would not flinch. John Hoskyns speaks of her in almost military terms:

'She doesn't say: well, I'd rather survive, so I'll fudge and compromise. She'd say: on that basis, I'd rather not survive. And that was very clearly understood by everybody who worked with her, and of course that did make the thinking so much easier. I mean, people knew, you know, that the lines of retreat had been cut off.'

When the Treasury demanded more savings in November, totalling £2000 million, there were pockets of resistance throughout Whitehall. Pym was asked for £500 million from defence; he and his service chiefs succeeded in cutting the demand by almost two-thirds. Other departments were encouraged in their own resistance. The Treasury men fell back. There was disarray too among the Prime Minister's own advisers. One of the 'high priests' of monetarism, Professor Alan Walters, had been coaxed back from an American university to be her personal economic adviser. Established at No. 10, he expressed concern to others in the charmed circle such as Hoskyns and Alfred Sherman that the monetary policy was too tight. The Treasury had believed that their control was still not tight enough. Sterling M3 was growing too fast. Walters looked at the high exchange rate, the level of bankruptcies and unemployment, and suggested that the clue lay in the slow growth of the narrower monetary aggregates, Mo and M1. A Swiss monetary economist, Professor Jürgen Niehans, was brought in by the Centre for Policy Studies to adjudicate. His report concluded that 'the appreciation of sterling in the last two years is largely a monetary phenomenon', and contained an indictment of the whole basis of Thatcher's economics:

'UK monetary policy not only seems to have rejected any concession to "gradualism" but also refused to make any allowance for real growth. It thus appears to have been more abrupt than even the most ardent monetarists ever advocated. This was a policy shift with few historic precedents.'

The report was not published in Britain. One of the inner caucus who saw it accepts its conclusions but says:

'Perhaps that gave the real economy, particularly the private sector, the shock that it needed . . . There must have been firms that failed that might not have failed. I don't think there's any doubt that it made unemployment higher than it otherwise would have been.'

Throughout the winter of 1980–1 the government was told by its critics that, with the economy in deep recession, and manufacturing industry blighted, measures to encourage and sustain economic growth were needed. The CBI called for a lower exchange rate, lower interest rates, the continuation of public sector capital spending, and a cut in the National Insurance surcharge. Unemployment had continued to rise, to 2.75 million, with all its attendant social discontents. Company liquidations were running at twice the level of 1979, about 130 per week. But the Prime Minister was not for turning. In January 1981 she removed one wet critic from the cabinet and took another away from his departmental base. St John-Stevas was the cabinet victim. The press was told that he had made one joke too many about the Blessed Margaret and immaculate misconceptions. He had also found, as he remarks lugubriously in his memoirs, that his 'contributions in cabinet on economics were clearly not welcome'.[5] Francis Pym was brought from Defence to replace him, and was replaced in turn by one of the trusties on economic policy, John Nott. Leon Brittan, until then thought of as brother of the more famous Sam, but with an acute mind at his and the Prime Minister's disposal, came into the cabinet as Chief Secretary.

The Treasury had not accepted the theory that it was pursuing the wrong monetary indicator. The Chancellor believed that he had to continue a tough policy, but the Downing Street advisers argued that such a policy should be based on tighter fiscal measures – raising taxes – rather than on reducing the PSBR in accordance with Treasury forecasts. At a strategy meeting at Chequers early in 1981, Terry Burns had noted the increases in the level of both public expenditure and the borrowing requirement. The deficit for 1980–1 had turned out to be 60% above forecasts. Given the unprecedented depths of the recession and the consequent public expenditure necessary (£5000 per unemployed person in lost tax revenue and benefits paid out, as a beginning), this was not surprising. Fiscal policy could be tightened, to guard against the Treasury's estimates being inaccurate yet again. The Prime Minister's advisers were active in all the pre-budget discussions where the rival cases were thrashed out. Those who wanted a tougher fiscal policy thought the whole credibility of the government's counter-inflation strategy was at stake. The PSBR targets had proved to be so wildly unreliable that they were in danger of being wholly disbelieved. Fiscal policy would have to be tightened to allow for a loosening of the monetary targets, they argued. 'It all fitted together as a sort of grand arch, like Verdi's *Otello*,' says one. Until a fortnight before the budget, Walters thought that he had lost the argument. But he had the Prime Minister's backing. Influential Treasury men such as the fast-rising Peter Middleton moved over to the No. 10 position.

Howe's budget, which froze tax thresholds and allowances, and thus in effect raised direct taxes as well as indirect, was, one of its architects says, 'the most spectacular contrast to what Keynesian prescriptions would have been that we've seen in our economic history'.

By increasing taxes at the bottom of the recession the Chancellor served notice that, for this government at least, Keynesian reflation was dead. The necessity of controlling the budget deficit, and thus inflation, was pre-eminent.

There were still Keynesians in the cabinet. Nobody had told them that all the arguments had been between two 'dry' factions. The cabinet had not been consulted about the broad economic strategy or the details of the Chancellor's package. Prior had proposed a strategy meeting at one point but been slapped down. The wets were hoping for tax cuts and expenditure increases in counter-cyclical reflation of the economy. They were not expecting tax increases, and did not hide their dismay that Tuesday morning. One of the supporters of the budget remembers that Prior in particular 'made a great fuss that morning . . . [and] was very intemperate, which wasn't helpful'. Prior's anger was shared, The Times reported, by 'a strong and influential minority', in the cabinet: Gilmour, Walker, Carrington, Soames, Pym and Carlisle were singled out. Time has not blunted Prior's anger:

'I thought the 1981 budget was a shocker. I thought it was a deflationary budget at a time of very considerable recession throughout the world. With the British economy pretty much on its knees, I felt this was really pushing further into the ground an economy, and particularly industry, which was already suffering a good deal.'

Prior, Gilmour and Walker, identified as the leaders of the revolt, now considered resignation. In the end they did not take that step, which Gilmour at least now regrets. Prior offers an explanation:

'The reason I didn't resign was because the government was at a very low ebb. I was elected and wished to support a Conservative government. I'd been through all the traumas of changes of government, and I didn't want to be responsible for causing that sort of thing at that time. And I thought that once I had resigned I would have been pretty ineffective in opposition.'

For these jumbled reasons, the standard of the wets faltered and fell, giving the victors in the cabinet an enhanced sense of their own rectitude. They had come through. Geoffrey Howe maintains that:

'The 1981 budget was crucial to the continued success, the strengthened credibility and effectiveness of the Thatcher government. It would have been a watershed of a different kind if we hadn't had it.'

The budget's supporters point to its success in bringing down interest rates, and demonstrating that the government meant to stick to its targets by 'screwing the medium-term financial strategy into place'. Inflation did thereafter fall throughout 1981–2, and productivity rose, but the budget's critics point to the massive increase in unemployment as its most important and most unacceptable consequence. Unemployment was rising twice as fast as the average of the big seven countries that formed the Organisation for Economic Co-operation and Development (OECD). The UK had become, in Peter Riddell's phrase, 'the least Keynesian of all major industrial countries'. In a letter to *The Times* 364 economists attacked the budget. One wet MP defected to the newly formed Social Democrats, with a pointed if stagey crossing of the floor. The Thatcher circle remained serene. They know how big a victory had been won in the defeat of the wets. Sir John Hoskyns sees it this way:

'What I think it did do, which was psychologically very, very important – almost regardless of the merits of the budget – it was such a courageous, some might say foolhardy thing to do, that it enormously strengthened the moral ascendancy, the position and power and authority of the Prime Minister and the Chancellor.'

The Prime Minister demonstrated her own sense of her new strength in cabinet in an extraordinary outburst at the *Guardian* Young Businessman of the Year lunch on the day after the budget. There was no doubt that her targets were the cabinet rebels. While the CBI leadership listened glumly, she pitched into the wets in uninhibited style:

'Now what really gets me is this. It's very ironic that those who are most critical of the extra tax are those who were most vociferous in demanding the extra expenditure. And what gets me even more is that, having demanded that extra expenditure, they're not prepared to face the consequences of their own action and stand by the necessity to get some of the tax to pay for it. And I wish some of them had a bit more guts and courage than they have. I'll tell you what they really mean. They mean: we don't like the expenditure we've agreed, we're unwilling to raise the tax to pay for it. *Let us print the money instead.* The most immoral path of all. What they are saying is: let's go and put a pair of bellows onto the rate of inflation we have now, and make it a really big raging furnace!'

This was the voice of Alderman Roberts, betraying the deep hatred of borrowing which had, according to your point of view, kept him solvent or kept him small. Alderman Roberts's embattled daughter now found herself engaged in conflict on all sides. There was a prolonged civil service strike over pay, temporarily uniting the nine unions, and ended only after the setting up of another independent inquiry. The main image of conflict which settled on the government, though, came in the two most disaffected parts of the population of the United Kingdom. In Northern Ireland the Conservative Secretary of State, Humphrey Atkins, had been welcomed to office by the IRA in their own special way by the blowing up of Lord Mountbatten and his holiday companions and the murder of eighteen soldiers at Warrenpoint, County Down. Atkins's attempts to move beyond the tough but unimaginative security-first approach of Roy Mason got nowhere. Nor, after a first exchange of civilities, did discussions between Margaret Thatcher and the Irish Taoiseach, Charles J. Haughey. IRA prisoners had been 'on the blanket', protesting at the loss of 'political status' in 1976. Since these protests, for all their discomfort, left the British unmoved, there had been a hunger strike in 1980 to which Atkins made some concessions, although these fell far short of the prisoners' five demands. In March 1981 a second hunger strike was begun by Bobby Sands, a leading Provisional in the Maze. It was to have profound consequences.

The Provisionals now deployed their ultimate weapon: their ability to kill themselves, slowly, agonisingly, to the grief of the community from which they came in the waxen glow of publicity around the death bed. The British, after previous experiences, did not know whether this was a fast to death. Before the matter could be proved, the IRA received an uncovenanted bonus. Frank Maguire, MP for Fermanagh and South Tyrone, died suddenly. The seat had a Catholic majority. The IRA nominated Sands as an 'Anti H-Block' candidate. The SDLP were nudged or coerced into leaving him with a clear run against the Unionists. Some Catholics stayed away from the poll – not least influenced by a recent IRA murder of exceptional vileness even by the IRA's standards. But enough of them voted for Sands to win by 1446 votes. No British party on the mainland wished to concede political status to the Maze prisoners. Most were aware that the situation was changed by Sands's victory. After that, writes Padraig O'Malley:[6]

'The IRA could only have lost on the hunger strike issue if Mrs Thatcher had acceded to their demands before Sands died.'

That she could not do, as the IRA were well aware. Sands died on 5 May. Nine other men of the IRA and the INLA followed him to the grave, recruiting as they went. It gave the terrorists a powerful emotional hold in their own community. Few will identify with murder, many with sacrifice. It also taught the IRA of the valuable extra status that came from election; the strategy was first outlined in 1981 as 'a ballot paper in one hand and an Armalite in the other'. Throughout the summer of 1981 the continuing deaths of the hunger strikers in ghastly progression dogged the British government. The ghost of 'Bobby Sands MP' was everywhere at its elbow.

So was the image of urban riot in the cities of the mainland. Discontent had boiled over before, in Southall in 1979, in the St Paul's district of Bristol in 1980. In 1981 resentment at policing methods combined with the frustrations of high unemployment, which struck disproportionately hard at the young and less skilled in inner-city areas, led to widespread rioting. Brixton, London, came first, with three days of rioting after a sustained saturation exercise by the police, codenamed Exercise Swamp '81 – a phrase with many resonances. Resentment at police harassment and the widespread use of 'sus' (see page 228) fuelled the anger of the black community, who comprised 77% of the arrests under the law in the Lambeth area. For a period the police lost control. Buildings were fired, and there was widespread looting by black and white alike. The riots were a mile away from Parliament. They had political as well as televisual immediacy. The government brought in Lord Scarman to head an inquiry. While the inquiry sat, further riots broke out in early July in many British cities – in Southall, in Liverpool's Toxteth, in Manchester's Moss Side, and others, in imitation, elsewhere. The riots in Liverpool were accompanied by ferocious violence and the burning of the racquets club and other apparent symbols of privilege throughout the Liverpool 8 district. The police used CS gas in reply, in breach of Home Office guidelines. In Manchester 'swoop' tactics with police snatch squads – also familiar in Northern Ireland – were employed.

For some days the riots and the tough responses to them from a number of high-profile chief constables – McNee in London, Kenneth Oxford on Merseyside, and the loquacious moralist James Anderton in Manchester – seemed to indicate a nation transfixed in confrontation. Television showed vivid images of burning and gutted buildings,

and of phalanxes of riot shields illuminated by the flames. The Prime
Minister visited some of the disturbed areas. Her instinct was to see
what happened as an extreme example of criminal behaviour. One
former senior civil servant says that 'she just felt very sorry for all
the shopkeepers who'd had their windows broken'. After the Toxteth
riots she inserted into a party political broadcast a statement which
concentrated entirely on the violence:

'Nothing can justify, nothing can excuse, and no one can condone,
the appalling violence we've all seen on television, which some of
our people have experienced, and so many fear. Each one of us,
parents, grandparents, teachers, whether we have a job or not,
whether we are black or white, whatever else we may argue about,
we have this in common: we know that violence will destroy everything we value.'

Other analysts of the riots, from the opposite angle to hers, agree
that excessive and insensitive policing was the prime cause. Unemployment and urban decay were contributory, but the spark was that
'people witnessed specific acts of street injustice which no longer
seemed tolerable'.[7]

The public, in opinion polls, named unemployment as the main
cause (though blacks put racialism high among the causes). The
cabinet critics of Thatcher's economic policy agreed. So did their old
mentor Heath, who said, 'Of course you will get racial tension when
you have young blacks with less chance of getting jobs.'

Prior believes now that the link with economic policy was there:

'I simply don't believe that the problems of the inner cities . . . were
simply law and order matters. I think they went deeper than that. They
were a symptom of the decline of inner-city life and unemployment
and a number of other factors as well.'

Looking back, no one in the Prime Minister's inner circle will
concede that the riots made the slightest difference to the government's
no-alternative economic strategy. As the riots have not (so far) been
repeated, memories of that tense summer have now faded. Their
repercussions at the time were great. When its critics asserted that
monetarism had put the social fabric under a 'test to destruction',
answers did not come easily. Lord Bruce-Gardyne, who has mounted
an eloquent defence of the Thatcher administration, concedes
that:

'For once the Prime Minister's nerve seemed momentarily to falter;
it seems conceivable that, had the critics round the cabinet table

mounted a united campaign for a change of course, their demands might at this moment have prevailed. But they never did.'

Prior agrees that: 'It was a deeply worrying time for the government – I would have thought the most worrying time really that this government has faced.'

To cap their worries, there was an outbreak of trenchant moderation to their rear. The new SDP was soaring in the polls. One Tory defector had joined them. The press buzzed with rumours of three others who planned to do so. And in the Warrington by-election in July, Roy Jenkins not merely ran the Labour candidate close in a Labour stronghold but mopped up the Tory vote.

The defeat of the wets

The wets now had their chance. They would never have a better one. The cabinet agreed to send Michael Heseltine to spread a little glamour and extra cash around Merseyside. The youth training schemes and the burgeoning empire of the Manpower Services Commission were expanded. When the Chancellor came to cabinet to propose yet more public expenditure cuts – 3–5% all round – some of the dries switched sides. Biffen and Nott both thought that the cuts had gone far enough. Nott was now head of Defence; in a Tory cabinet, the strongest spending ministry of all. He has no illusions about the consequences of what the Prime Minister saw as apostasy:

'When I joined with the economic wets, not being considered one myself, and said that I thought we could not go through another short-term public expenditure cut in the summer of 1981, it was, I'm sure, regarded by my boss, Mrs Thatcher, as a great act of treachery, and I have subsequently heard from a number of sources . . . that Mrs Thatcher never ever forgave me for that.'

Nott's chance of the Exchequer disappeared from that moment. The then Chancellor says now that the demand for further cuts was necessary:

'It was not possible to sustain the overall control of public expenditure and the overall control of economic policy . . . without addressing ourselves at the same time to the question of how to balance the books.'

Of the spending ministers only Sir Keith Joseph supported the Prime Minister and the Treasury. The cuts were rejected. The government plumbed new depths of unpopularity in the polls. Unemployment was plainly heading for the unprecedented three million mark. The only lightening of the public mood came from the marriage of the Prince of Wales to Lady Diana Spencer, who got the only job for life secured in that year by (as her contemporary Julie Burchill cruelly described her) 'a teenage school-leaver from a one-parent family with not one CSE to her name'.[8] For her there was general goodwill.

If at this time the wets had brought a united and credible case to the cabinet they might now have prevailed. But they were disunited. The Thatcher group was not. Some thought that a change of mood by the government was inevitable; they forgot that those who wait upon events have a habit of missing them. Party chairman Lord Thorney-croft said he detected 'rising damp'. Others were too gentlemanly to engage in a brutal conflict to turn the lady. Those who tried met what one critic describes as 'a will of iron and the physical stamina of a long-distance runner, making her nearly impossible to "manage"'[9] Indeed, she managed them. She had control of the cabinet agendas. She had the safe haven of the Long Recess, which Tories use for its original purpose – no SDP seminars or Young Socialist summer camps for them. The Prime Minister brooded on the events of July. Cecil Parkinson, much in her confidence, describes her mood:

'The Prime Minister had discovered that she was in a minority in the economic policy which she regarded as central and which she regarded herself as having been elected to implement . . . She'd been the leader since early 1975. It was then mid-1981 and she was still in a minority in her own cabinet, which, whatever else it proves, doesn't prove she was an intolerant person . . . I think she probably decided then that it was time to bring more like-minded people who shared her commitment to the economic policy into the cabinet.'

There were leaks throughout the recess that this was to happen. The wets had been warned. They appear to have done nothing collectively to try to sustain their position. In particular there was speculation that Prior would be prised out of the economic responsibilities of government and exiled to Northern Ireland. He allowed it to be put about by his PPS that he would not go. 'I will resign, Prior warns,' the *Observer* reported, in a story which accurately named all the other wets in danger. But when Prior was called to Downing Street, even when he knew that his successor at Employment was to be the government's ultimate hit-man, Norman Tebbit, he tamely acquiesced in a transfer to Northern Ireland. There he remained for the rest of the parliament, with younger men of his own persuasion sharing his self-exile. 'We're all Keynesians here,' he was wont to tell visitors. In Northern Ireland he was allowed to be; there the Westminster spending rules did not apply. The cabinet's rising damp was now countered by a new course of bricks more to the Prime Minister's liking: Nigel Lawson, Norman Tebbit and Parkinson. Soames, Carlisle and Gilmour received the quittance they had read about for weeks in the press. So did Lord Thorneycroft. The surviving wets were bound over without term to be of good behaviour. The battle of wills with Prior was seen as a crucial test. The wets were bitterly disappointed. St John-Stevas says:

'Having said in public, and let it be known, that he would not take a position, then in fact by actually accepting it, he did give the Prime Minister a very great prestige victory. I don't mind that, but he did deal the cause with which all of us were identified a very heavy blow, because he deprived us, I think, in many people's eyes of that moral basis which was our greatest strength.'

Prior knows this, and admits to it with candour:

'I think I got it wrong, and if I had my time over again I would play it differently. But it was just one of those things that happened. I was outmanoeuvred by the Prime Minister – probably the reason why she's Prime Minister and I'm not.'

This new cabinet was prepared to move at the Prime Minister's pace, in economic policy, in union legislation, and in the pursuit of a full market economy and a shrunken state sector. As a result, the government's programme was to accelerate well beyond its manifesto commitments over the next two years – the first postwar example of an administration exceeding its own promises. The Tory establishment of the sixties and seventies had been put aside. The new men clustered in delight around the strong woman. It was, says Sir John Hoskyns 'probably the most critical point of the first term', in which, '[Thatcher] felt for the first time she had to a man really a team who were broadly with her in what she was trying to do.'

Another confidant says shrewdly that from now on 'she came to identify with the government instead of criticising it'. She could recognise it as a Thatcher government at last. Harold Macmillan had once told the 1922 Committee that he had watched his predecessor lose first the country, then the party, and last the cabinet, which he would win back in reverse order. Margaret Thatcher had stormed her own cabinet. At the Conservative conference she was unchallenged in the party, ostentatiously applauding the law and order lobby to the public dismay and private fury of William Whitelaw. When Edward

Heath, who had hailed his 'Quiet Revolution' from the platform eleven years earlier, came to lament this unquiet alternative, he was booed for overrunning his time. 'Please don't applaud,' he said. 'It may annoy your neighbour.' He pleaded that 'This is still our party, all of us, all over the country.' As he was led off to a few pockets of ovation, the signs were that he was wrong. The wets sent off their coded messages around the fringe. But few who watched Margaret Thatcher at the Young Conservatives' Ball, pushing the lanky Ian Gilmour, whom she had just sacked, around the dance floor in a cloud of green tulle could be in any doubt about who called the tune. She had, in Hoskyns's words:

'. . . changed the agenda for debate, both for people in her party and for people in other parties. There was simply a different point of departure.'

To the disconsolate wets, who saw it rather less grandly, she had, in Critchley's phrase, 'locked up the party and thrown away the key'.

There was still the country to win. At the mid-point of her administration *The Times* described her on 9 October as 'the most unpopular Prime Minister since records began'. The Conservatives lost Croydon to a Liberal who had insisted on being the by-election candidate in spite of his leader's desperate attempts to ditch him for Shirley Williams in order to consummate the alliance with the new SDP. In spite of this, and of a campaign style that was less than the promise of his name, William Pitt won Croydon. If Pitt could win, said the wiseacres, the Liberals could win anywhere. Shirley Williams rapidly made up for earlier hesitations by winning the Crosby by-election.

No one paid much attention to the obscure general with the Italian name who was sworn in as the third leader of the military junta in Argentina in December. Yet he, more than anyone in British politics, was to influence the fate of the new style in British politics, and how it was evaluated in popular judgement. Without him it still might be said, as John Biffen does, that 'the Thatcher government like the Attlee government . . . stamps its character on succeeding parliaments'. The polls were turning back before Galtieri invaded the Falklands. But no external test could have been devised more suited to the Thatcher style, and therefore more likely to postpone judgement, for a parliament, on the Thatcher substance.

20

WINNERS AND LOSERS

The seventies was a time when economic reality seemed a sudden solvent to the optimism of the previous decade. The middle class felt that the certainty of betterment had gone. They blamed the corporate rich, but they blamed the unions more. The working class, confused and worried, were told that, when it came to responsibility, they had the broadest backs. Two British novelists, among the few who chose to address reality, caught the anxiety of the times. In *The Ice Age* Margaret Drabble described the moment at which, for the middle class, the optimism ended:[1]

'All over the country people blamed other people for all the things that were going wrong – the trades unions, the present government, the miners, the car workers, the seamen, the Arabs, the Irish, their own husbands, their own wives, their own idle good-for-nothing offspring, comprehensive education. Nobody knew whose fault it really was, but most people managed to complain fairly forcefully about somebody: only a few were stunned into honourable silence . . .

'Expansionist plans were, it is true, here and there being checked: for a second holiday, a three-piece suite, a new car. But very few people were having to work out how to do without what they had already got, though they were puzzled by the way their hard-won wage increases had got them nowhere at all. The old headline phrases of freeze and squeeze had for the first time become for everyone – not merely for the old and unemployed – a living image, a reality: millions who had groaned over them in steadily increasing prosperity were now obliged to think again. A huge icy fist, with large cold fingers, was squeezing and chilling the people of Britain.'

The industrial workers were the recipients of much blame. In *Looks and Smiles* Barry Hines recounted the response of a young unemployed worker when he heard that yet another engineering factory was sacking half its workforce:[2]

'It would probably be the fault of the union that the men were being sacked. It usually was. According to the papers the unions were responsible for all the economic ills of the country. They were too greedy (i.e., tried to keep up with rising prices), too strong (i.e., organised), always on strike (i.e., only as a last resort), and communist-inspired (i.e., disagreed with management policies). They were criticised for over-manning (i.e., looking after jobs), underproduction (i.e., ancient plant), working to rule (i.e., eight hours a day) and wanting too much overtime (i.e., poor basic rates). All of which reduced profits, which discouraged investment and led to redundancies. Which was all the fault of the unions . . .'

How fair was the picture of the United Kingdom as a society of doubt, decline and mutual recrimination, more deeply divided by class politics than it had been for forty years? Much of the comment centred on such a view: Britain in Agony, Alas, Alas for England, Britain Against Itself – the titles proliferated. In fact, as it always had been, it was a society of winners and losers. Some of the gains and losses were predictable; others were not. Over the fifteen years since Wilson's July 1966 crisis all manner of change had come over his 'natural governing party' and the country it had administered.

First, there had been a remarkable shift in the geographical divide. Mainland Britain tilted eastward. The changing pattern of British trade, beginning before but intensified by British membership of the EEC, was one reason. The EEC's effect on agriculture was another. The discovery of gas and oil in the North Sea was a third. Some of the costly investments in infrastructure begun in the sixties had become major assets by the end of the seventies. East–West motorways exerted a pull of their own: the M4 corridor and Heathrow west of London; the M11 to the science park and new industries of Cambridge and the new ports of East Anglia; the M62 trans-Pennine route to Europe via Hull. Between 1971 and 1981 the population rose sharply in East Anglia, the home counties around London, and in the Grampian and Shetland regions of Scotland. In the years of recession after the oil crisis, as manufacturing industry was blighted, the balance of prosperity began to shift too. In 1973–4 the regions which had the highest average weekly household income were the South-east, Greater London, the West Midlands, the East Midlands, the South-west and Scotland. Northern Ireland came bottom of the list of twelve regions. By 1981–2 Greater London and the South-east were still substantially ahead, followed by the South-west, the North-west and East Anglia. Northern Ireland was still last. So great was the imbalance between the rich, populous South-east, including London, and the rest that all the other regions were below the average.

The transformation of East Anglia from backwater to business hub was remarkable. A string of ports from Wivenhoe to Boston sprang into rejuvenated life, nurtured on European trade, less unionised, less wedded to old practices. The most sensational success story was Felixstowe, the booming container port. In 1972 it employed 800 people and handled 100,000 containers annually. By 1981 the workforce had risen to 1300 – many of them recruited from the local agricultural community rather than (as the union would have preferred) from existing dockworkers – handling 250,000 containers each year. The tonnage of cargo going through the port more than doubled in the decade. It was easy to keep harmonious labour relations when jobs and traffic were expanding. The bitter labour disputes which were killing ports such as Liverpool, where containerisation had led to the 1972 Heaton's dispute, sprang partly from the realisation that to accept change meant accepting fewer jobs. These legitimate fears fuelled the engrained conservatism reflected by such as Jack Dash who, when taken by the BBC to see the port of Rotterdam, proclaimed that this was a future he did not want to work. The London docks are no more. The traffic has moved downstream to Tilbury.

A new generation of traders and entrepreneurs saw the shifting pattern of things, and took advantage of it. They set up business on the pattern of the eighteenth-century merchants and chandlers. For example, one of the early traders in British cereals, John Waring, had spotted that the British arable farmers were going places. From old mills and a derelict deep river wharf at Boston he expanded trade in the new agricultural surpluses, moving from scratch to a turnover of £35 million inside the decade. A million tonnes of British cereals went for export through Boston. How had Britain been so transformed in agriculture? The farmers who sold their crops to Waring provide the answer.

Securely based in East Anglia, the new 'prairie' farming grew fat on the Common Agricultural Policy. The whole of East Anglia as far as Humberside had more than three-quarters of its agricultural land under the plough. Similar methods were employed to achieve similar results over much of eastern England and Scotland, as far north as Nigg, where the American-style farming of the 'barley barons' caught the headlines. Barley acreage doubled. With the CAP intervention payments it was almost impossible to go wrong – a stark contrast to what was happening to the unfortunate hill farmers of Wales and the west. The farm lobby successfully protected itself from any real move by governments of either party to interfere with the mesh of subsidies within which it operated, in effect as a subsidised industry. In 1980 one irreverent Tory MP made a pointed reference to this state of affairs in a letter to *The Times*. Matthew Parris wrote:

'Is it only to me that the solution to British Leyland's problems has occurred? The government should lay down a minimum selling price for Leyland motor cars, pitched to ensure a profitable return on the capital invested in the industry. Should the company prove unable to dispose of all their motor cars at this price, the European Commission should intervene to purchase the unsold stock. These unsold vehicles would be stored at Canvey Island or sold to our enemies at half price. I hope nobody thinks this is a ludicrous way of dealing with the marketing of a commodity?'

The farmers were indignant at such attacks. Oliver Walston, Cambridgeshire farmer and famine aid organiser, concedes the scale of the success:

'In the 1970s farming did better than it has ever done before in the history of agriculture . . . Going into the Common Market in general and the CAP in particular . . . meant that we were told by Brussels to produce regardless of cost and regardless of quantity, because Brussels, God bless them, thought that self-sufficiency was the name of the game . . . We went into surplus in this country around 1980, for the first time since the Middle Ages.'

The CAP intervention payments were repeatedly raised through the seventies. Their original purpose has been lost, Walston admits:

'Far from stopping me going bankrupt if I sell to the government, I can now make a large amount of money selling . . . and this is crazy. When the safety net under the acrobat starts becoming the ceiling of the tent, then it's made.'

Mad or not, the CAP payments made the farmers the outstanding winners of the seventies, as they turned the countryside April-yellow with oilseed-rape and grew sugar beet where grass had grown before.

The farmers regarded themselves, with some justice, as an efficient industry, using their large profits to invest in capital-intensive machinery and research into new crops with heavier yields. They drew a moral too. Walston, harvesting sugar beet with 220 h.p. machines which cut six rows at a time, says:

'None of these machines are English. We have to go to France to buy that [harvester] because the British agricultural engineering industry just about died on its feet in the seventies. Those tractors are made in Germany. The trailers are made in France. Only the plough is made in England.'

British manufacturers, it seemed, could not pick up on the one domestic growth market under their own noses.

The recessionary blow fell hardest in the West Midlands, which were in steep decline, losing 100,000 manufacturing jobs between 1970 and 1979. British industry, peculiarly open to foreign competition, inefficient and riven by differences of class and practice, did not benefit from entry to the EEC. It caught pneumonia from the 'bracing shower' which Westminster had prescribed for it. All the numerous attempts to intervene with support through the agencies and funding of the state had only limited success in the seventies. When support was withdrawn after 1979, leaving industry at the mercy of a high pound, inflated labour costs, and the withdrawal of capital for investment overseas, one-fifth of Britain's total manufacturing capacity was lost within two years. The weakness of industry, the major loser of the seventies, is illustrated by the case of the West Midlands.

Bad industrial relations and nervous managements unwilling to risk investment combined to pull the region down. Unions blamed management for weakness and indecision. 'It suited me to the hilt to be able to push them around,' one veteran shop steward reflects on his long reign at the Rubery Owen factory at Darlaston. Management found unions obstructive. One strike over piecework rates brought Rubery Owen to the brink of closure in the mid seventies. But this was not all attributable to bloody-minded trade unionism. *Time* magazine profiled Rubery Owen in 1975, when the two grandsons of the founder, 'Mr David and Mr John', and their management consultants seemed to be in permanent conflict with the shop floor. 'There has always got to be us and them,' the works convenor was quoted as saying. But the Americans went on to look in wonder at the social divide. The convenor's grandfather had worked at the factory in the time of the first Owen. And still, *Time* noted:

'John Owen and Doug Peach begin their day in ways which are closer to their fathers' and grandfathers' than to each other.'

The plant was a battleground. The unions resisted change; management could not understand the effect of archaic working conditions. One executive commented:

'Sophisticated equipment wouldn't necessarily go well here ... Black country labourers prefer physical effort, and if they're dirty, sweating and completely knocked out at the end of the day, they feel satisfied.'

It took the rest of the decade for the two sides to get themselves together, reduce the different ways of calculating piecework rates from 180 to three, and tone down the aggression. After that the plant closed, crippled by the deep recession of 1979–81. At that time the surviving workforce had not had a pay rise for eighteen months, in the hope of preserving their plant and jobs. It was all to no avail.

For component firms the recession was compounded by the troubles of the car giants, British Leyland, Chrysler and Vauxhall. Matters eventually came to a head at BL with the much publicised sacking of the Communist shop steward Derek Robinson – an attractive prize to lay before a government which had been asked for £300 million in rescue capital. Robinson, too slow-moving and unsubtle to be quite the militant mole he was painted, was one of the losers. The taunts of 'On yer bike, Robbo' which followed him were a clear sign that, in recession, shop stewards' powers of persuasion over their workforce were greatly curtailed.

Richard Clutterbuck has analysed the decline during the decade of the international tractor firm Massey Ferguson, thinly disguised in his account as the 'Atlantic Plant Corporation'.[3] A twelve-week strike over productivity, when the management sought a rate of six tractors per hour on a new production line, and the unions would only accept four, hit the company hard. Its output fell from 85,000 tractors per annum in 1976 to 45,000 in 1981, by which time the company had switched its disputed production line to its French subsidiary. Incomprehension throughout between a multinational management and British unions led to mutual disaster. No Massey Ferguson tractors found their way to Oliver Walston's farm.

Back in 1971 Anthony Sampson had perceptively lamented that:[4]

'Comparing the British industrial atmosphere with that of the continent, it is hard to avoid the impression that the British zeal for industrial organisation has somehow exhausted itself. At the root of the lack of productivity and exports there is often, I suspect, the basic difficulty that both workers and managers are bored with their jobs.'

Sampson thought that the EEC might do for Britain what it had done for Belgium. It did not. Bad timing was only half the problem. There was also the difficulty of persuading the British elite that making things could be fun, rather than done out of an obligation to prop up your father's firm for another generation. The British, Sampson thought, were reverting to their pre-industrial expertise:

'Banking, insurance, farming, entertainment were activities which the British were envied for in the eighteenth century.'

Such pursuits were still extremely agreeable in the twentieth. The first three remained, in substance, the purlieu of those who had the necessary capital and the background. As the distribution of opportunities did not change to any marked degree, neither did those who benefited from them. Such people increasingly came to favour a career in the fourth activity, entertainment, as well – in television especially. Winners they were, winners they remained. Bankers or television men, they had a poor view of the prospects of their kin who were trapped in industry.

This was less true in Scotland. During the seventies that country knew both success and failure in full measure. There was success in the drip-down of the oil wealth. (The oil reserves, variously estimated as giving self-sufficiency for between 16 and 120 years, yielded revenue which not only eliminated the old balance of payments crises and allowed Britain to forget how near to deficit on manufactures it had come; but also allowed London to indulge the political need to hear Scottish pleas.) The population of the Grampian region around Aberdeen grew as rapidly as the number of flights into the airport of the granite city. There and in the Shetlands, new jobs sprang up. But, at the height of the North Sea boom, oil provided only about 6% of Scottish employment.

The Scottish new towns proved another powerful counterweight to Scots emigration, especially Glenrothes, now associated with the micro-electronics boom of 'Silicon Glen'. The new towns had a diverse industrial base, a sense of starting afresh, which proved attractive to American and other multinational industry. Helped by government grants, and the Scottish Development Agency in its role of pilot fish for private industry, new jobs were created. The Scottish banking system, a boon not available to other regions which had fallen on hard times, had a greater sense of responsibility for its local economy. 'We're amongst people and industry in a way the English are not,' says one leading Scottish banker. 'In the seventies we saw the whole thing crumbling about our ears and we decided that something had to be done.' In 1971 Scotland's unemployment level had been the second highest in the United Kingdom, almost twice the UK average. By the 1980s, although the level had grown hugely, in percentage terms it was lower than that of Wales, the North, the North-west, and even the West Midlands.

The Scots would not have numbered themselves among the winners of the seventies, but in psychological terms they were. The 'vapour trail' of national awakening was still in the sky. The excitement rubbed off on projects which were daunting in their scale, such as the GEAR project for the renewal of East Glasgow. The city, in Ian Jack's phrase in the *Sunday Times*, 'decided to invent a future for itself', with ambitious, grant-aided urban renewal. Scots could make common cause. John Davidson maintains:

'If the Secretary of State, the CBI, the STUC, the Scottish Council, the local authorities, the SDA, decide that something is worth going out to get for Scotland, they're a pretty formidable force.'

No English region had such a force. Nor, for different reasons, did the Welsh, who proved better able to preserve their cultural than their economic heritage through political pressure, as the pits and steelworks closed, and the miners' clubs sold sold off their libraries. Resentment in Wales and the remoter English regions focused on this lack, and on the sense that in everything, from the extension of communications from outside to investment within, they were suffering.

Only Northern Ireland seemed a loser by any count. Always at the top of the unemployment ratings, it lost one third of its industrial jobs in a decade. In a despondent summary Padraig O'Malley notes:[5]

'Higher energy and transportation costs, higher wage-per-unit-of-output costs and lower overall levels of productivity have taken their toll. In one five-year period in the early 1970s, for example, industrial costs were 20% more than the price of the goods sold . . . British companies have given up. They invested a meagre £1.3 million in the North between 1976 and 1981, compared to £57 million in the Republic. One after another they are disappearing . . .'

Even the British subvention, which increased in the period under discussion by 1500% to over £1 billion annually, could make little impact on the chronic unemployment of the province. As O'Malley suggests, that in turn incubated the next clutch of recruits for the terror gangs:

'The more deprived communities there are, the more successful the paramilitaries; the more successful the paramilitaries, the more deprived communities there are.'

By the late seventies there was one soldier in Northern Ireland for

every forty-five civilians, without a single paramilitary on either side of
the tribal divide abandoning his hopes of salvation through conflict –
for a new Ireland or the old Ulster. Meanwhile others went their way,
lived as best they could, kept their views to themselves at the road-
block or in the bar. Seamus Heaney has caught the mood in this poem
from his collection *North*:[6]

> Is there a life before death? That's chalked up
> In Ballymurphy. Competence with pain,
> Coherent miseries, a bite and sup,
> We hug our little destiny again.'

The problems of social class on the mainland seem small stuff
compared to the pressures suffered by embattled communities. But
this subject remained a preoccupation of the English, even if they
appeared less concerned with the inequalities that follow in the wake
of class discrimination. John Cleese's superb comic creation Basil
Fawlty, hero of one of the best television series of the decade, *Fawlty
Towers*, was always a cocktail of social anxiety and seething resentment about status. Although Britain had had governments of the left,
which had occasionally thundered about taxing the rich until the pips
squeaked, and promised to deal with the stage props of privilege such
as the private schools, not much was done. Well before the fall of the
Callaghan government it was clear that the distribution of wealth had
been little changed. Writing in 1981, in a postscript to his *Change in
British Society*, A. H. Halsey remarked that:[7]

'Class-based inequality persists, the top half of the population
receiving three quarters of all personal income, the bottom half one
quarter. Wealth also, despite some equalisation between the very top
and the top, remains concentrated to the remarkable degree that the
richest 20% own three quarters of all personal wealth.'

The richest 1% had a take-home pay twenty times that of the
poorest 20%. It had always been the case, Halsey remarked, that:

'. . . three-quarters of the British have been virtually propertyless in
that area which covers the central part of life and occupations.'

By the end of the seventies it was clear that the well-to-do had run
out winners once more. In part it was a question of style. It was no
longer chic to be an egalitarian. While the middle-class panic of the
mid-seventies was in full swing, smart young trend-setters swung in
another direction. Sloane Rangers and Mayfair Mercenaries popula-

rised once more the world of what Edwardian euphemism called the 'comfortably off'. Their observer, Peter York, explains why this 'reactionary chic' was a consequence of the end of sixties' optimism. It was about:

'. . . the end of the belief that we were all in it together, a belief which prevailed as long as people believed in the future. In the seventies things actually continued to get better, the belief that there was a clear common future for everyone evaporated. And people started thinking about "my future", an individual future. It got privatised.'

This phenomenon had occurred before the election of Margaret Thatcher. That victory, and the immediate tax cuts for the well-off which followed, only confirmed the new belief in an initiative society. Lady Hartwell remarked, as reported by Tina Brown, ' "At last we live in a world where it will be possible to sack servants again." '[8]

G. M. Young wrote of the year 1902 that England was a very good country for gentlemen. It still was.

The distribution of opportunities remained unequal too. In the professions there was not, indeed never had been, an exclusive caste system. The exceptionally talented had always moved between the classes. Each additional opportunity created, however, seemed to be disproportionately taken up by the relatively privileged rather than the relatively deprived. This included the expansion of higher education, with entry as of right to those qualified. A. H. Halsey and his co-authors showed in their 1980 study *Origins and Destinations* that working-class boys had to score significantly more on the scale of measured IQ than their service-class contemporaries to get through to university education.[9] For working-class girls the handicap would have been greater. The authors were at pains to say that those who dropped out of contention did so largely before university selection itself. Yet somehow contacts still helped. In 1978, Polly Toynbee of the *Guardian* sat in on interviews for medical school – notoriously difficult to enter. She recorded that the highest entry qualifications were set for the fluent state-school applicant, the greatest tolerance shown to an amiable public-school hedonist with mediocre 'A' Levels but a place already at his father's old hospital. At the end of the latter's interview:

'[The Dean said,] "Give my best to your father. You're very like he used to be. Tell him that if I take you I will do my best to improve you, just as I improved him." The boy smiled and shambled out of the room. "What do you think?" the Dean asked the surgeon. "I knew his

father and he was just the same, but he's a very good doctor now."
The surgeon laughed. "I would say that under no circumstances
whatever would I admit him, if it wasn't that you knew his father and
you say he was the same." The Dean said, "Well, I'm happy to have
him."'

And have him they did. Both in embracing new opportunities as they
came along, and in using old ones to prevent downward mobility, the
middle class came through the seventies unscathed.

The working class, hitherto tenacious in its loyalties and its collective values, began to subdivide. Early studies of the 'affluent worker'
looked at 'privatisation' in a different sense from that in use today; this
was more a home-oriented individual with less time for club, pub and
union. There was less of a homogeneous proletariat, clearer divisions
between unskilled, semi-skilled, skilled and 'staff' jobs. The movement
of women back to work provided both a new source of unionisation
and began the trend to the multi-income household. For such households, as long as their members remained among the 90% of the
working population still with jobs by the beginning of the 1980s, life
had improved. Nine out of ten households had a fridge, a television set,
three-quarters a telephone, more than half a car and central heating.
The home became a leisure centre, a retreat for DIY and gardening. So
great were its comforts, in fact, that some studies showed it acting as
an insulation against despair or political action if personal circumstances were drastically changed through redundancy. Howard
Newby's research leads him to suggest that:

'People have reacted to economic recession not by going out onto
the streets and organising themselves politically but rather by with-
drawing into their own private world inside the home, over which they
do feel they have some control.'

The political climate 'out there' was, like the weather, something
over which individuals had no direct control. Redundancy payments
further cushioned this retreat. Lord Bruce-Gardyne remarks that:[10]

'The producer lobbies regarded it as axiomatic that the citizen
offered a choice between a job and the ability to afford an Italian
washing-machine would choose a job. Perhaps the outcome of the
1983 election proved them wrong.'

Some people in this position were all the more likely to be home-
oriented if they had recently embarked upon the purchase of a house
from the local authority. This transfer from the collective stock to
individual ownership brought a legion of new recruits to the ranks of

the owner-occupiers, now rising towards 60% of the population. The rapid increase in house prices gave all those who were borrowing to buy the largest asset, against which further borrowing could be made, that most of them had ever had. In the degree of tax relief which all mortgage-holders up to £25,000 received lay an advantage that qualified them, in this area at least, as winners. The total cost to the Treasury was £2 billion per annum. These advantages were no less sweet for their conferral by a government which lost no opportunity to inveigh against the evils of borrowing.

Others, just as clearly, lost out over the period. Unemployment reached deep into some social groups: the young, the late middle-aged, the disabled, women and new immigrants taken on when times were good and an expanding and more flexible labour force had been required. Real poverty was no less of a problem than it had been twenty years before. A. B. Atkinson's survey concluded that by the end of the seventies 22% of the population were living in or near poverty:[11]

'The official estimates show that in 1979 there were two million people living in families with incomes below the supplementary benefits level (and not receiving benefit). There were a further five and a half million living within 40% of the scale, and some four million in receipt of supplementary benefit.'

More people were dependent on means-tested benefits at the end of the 1974–9 Labour administration than at the beginning. Their position was not improved by the coming of the Thatcher government.

It is difficult to look at the position of the black and brown communities at the end of the period without despondency. Despite the Race Relations Acts, there remained discrimination against the newcomers both socially and in the labour market. Most observers of the period tend to echo A. H. Halsey's judgement that, without positive discrimination, 'the position of the second and third generation of coloured people is likely to worsen'.[12] They lived in the worst housing. They were the principal victims of that 'black crime rate' with which the press collectively tarnished them. West Indian children suffered from severe under-achievement in the schools, as they tried to cope with the inner-city environment, their frequent lack of fluency in the language of instruction, and the spasmodic racism of some of those who taught them. For the brown community of the inner cities there was an additional difficulty – the constant danger of attack. The stabbings and arson attacks on Bengalis in the East End of London showed no sign of diminishing in the eighties. All over Britain, Asians walked with fear. The sharp increase over the decade in the proportion of immigrants from the Asian subcontinent who were employers or supervisors, and similarly of West Indians transferring from the unskilled to the skilled category, offered the best hope that their perceived status would change too, if the economy emerged from recession.

The contribution of the successive waves of immigrants to the enrichment of British life was seldom considered by the host community. The corner shop open at all hours, the nurse on the night shift, the kebab house and Chinese take away: all added something welcome to the land of the permanently closed tea shop. They allowed Britain, in Arthur Marwick's phrase, 'to acquire a new cosmopolitanism without shedding its old xenophobia'. There was enough need of such variety. The quality of British public services was in decline. The arrival of a Prime Minister determined to cut public expenditure, who never travelled by train, indicated that things were unlikely to improve. Whereas, twenty-five years earlier, travellers had come back from France regretting what they had experienced in the way of shabby streets, late trains, graffiti in the subway and nauseous public lavatories, it was now the French who went home from Britain with the same impression. Football violence worsened the image. In the mid-sixties, studies of the British football scene had been able to make only a short reference to hooliganism. Now it was a central preoccupation: a cult to the participants, a puzzle to the rest. In other ways, too, the quality of basic services, private as well as public, declined to the disadvantage of those most dependent on them. Tabloid newspapers, growing closer together in stridency and viewpoint, made little attempt seriously to inform; by the end of the seventies they were a shabby parody of the newspaper of an advanced and free society. A Royal Commission hemmed and hawed, but baulked at radical solutions which would have given the British a greater diversity of views and proprietorial ownership. The Annan Committee on the future of broadcasting made a number of proposals for greater plurality. Of these the proposal for an Open Broadcasting Authority survived, though with a more ingenious system of finance than had originally been envisaged, as Channel 4. 'Have You Ever Wished You Were Better Informed?' *Times* advertisements asked the passerby. If the public's answer was yes, for many months in 1978–9 *The Times* could not help: both it and the *Sunday Times* were off the stands as the result of a bitter industrial dispute.

By a curious quirk, the British did not consider themselves among the losers. When polled in 1977, they confounded the doomsters by appearing to be happier with their lot than most other people in the world. They left the politicians to diagnose their discontents.

On the political front, Labour had lost the 1979 election because the Conservatives had made deep inroads into the working-class vote, with an 11% swing among skilled workers and 9% among the unskilled. These far outweighed Labour's growing (but minority) support among the middle class. Some analysts, notably Ivor Crewe, rapidly came to the conclusion that 'in the 1980s the Labour Party faces a working class electorate with only a minimal sense of class interest'[13] though group solidarity might still be strong and, on occasion, militant. On this view, too many Labour policies ran against the grain of working-class sentiment, and the suspicion of middle-class activists (fanned by a hostile press) carried the party away from its traditional bedrock. To make matters worse, with the deracination of the old proletariat, the natural support from this quarter was anyway a diminishing factor. The left would have to make allies where it could, some argued, though this view could be aired among respectable socialists only after it had first been launched by the veteran Marxist historian Eric Hobsbawm in a 1978 lecture entitled *The Forward March of Labour Halted?*[14] In the short term, in the internal politics of the Labour Party, it was the left who carried the day. In 1981, determined to build upon their successes within the party, and test the constitutional processes which they had set up, the group around Tony Benn challenged Denis Healey for the deputy leadership. Benn put in his nomination at four in the morning, determined to avoid his erstwhile supporters Jack Straw and Robin Cook, who had been searching Westminster to beg him to desist. To these pleas was added that of Michael Foot, but the Benn group felt they had to go on. Ken Livingstone argued that the deputy leadership contest '. . . crystallised in one simple issue all the debate about policy, all the debate over betrayal, and all the desire for change.'

When asked about his campaign by reporters, Benn energetically distanced it from himself:

'Honestly, brother, it's not about [personalities]. And you corrupt this if you make it that. What we're talking about today is the rebirth of hope for people. If this country wants to change, no power on earth will stop it.'

Benn's campaign brought together all those who believed that the change of which he spoke needed the symbolic cleansing which Healey's defeat would provide. The failure to confront the institutions in all the key policy areas under the Callaghan government, and in the election manifesto on which Labour had fought in 1979, must be made good. Healey's head would be the bounty hunter's prize. Not generally taken into account, although the 'inside left' appreciated it early on, was that the image of division created in the deputy leadership election would be so profound as to make the contest itself a struggle over the ruins. When Roy Jenkins contested Warrington in July 1981, not a seat he was expected to find congenial, the good result for the SDP (though Jenkins did not win) should have warned Labour strategists that the divisions were playing into the hands of the newly formed party. When working-class women told the press and TV that they were voting for Jenkins – 'I'll back him every inch of the way if he'll get rid of half the communist Labour Party. It isn't Labour any more, it's communism' – it was obvious that what Chris Mullin calls 'the unprecedented levels of hatred and hysteria' produced in attacks on Benn were having their effect; as was the spectacle of Healey being shouted down at rallies, while Michael Foot appealed vainly for him to be heard.

In the event Benn was defeated in a desperately close race – so close that a few extra MPs voting for Benn rather than abstaining after the third candidate, John Silkin, had dropped out, or a different result in NUPE (whose members opted for Healey, to the surprise of their leadership), would have turned the contest. Neil Kinnock's support for second-ballot abstention in *Tribune*, just before the Labour conference, fortified many of his parliamentary colleagues. Privately he had said for months of Benn, 'He's created the SDP single-handed.' Publicly his intervention was skilfully timed. The Benn camp read more into it. Dennis Skinner reflects:

'You couldn't divorce the fact that Kinnock was going to be a potential runner at some stage from the fact that he abstained ... People were forecasting that this little ginger-headed whizzkid who used to appear on our television screens ... would one day be some kind of a contender in the leadership stakes.'

Denis Healey, winner by an eyebrow with 50.448% of the electoral college, reflects that in the end Labour had voted to be a party rather than a sect:

'I think if Tony had won there would have been a great movement to get Michael to go early so that he could take over as leader. But I think most of all the country would have seen it as a definitive sign that we were turning into what they regard as a Marxist party. (Mind you, they don't know much about Marx either.) And I think a lot of Labour Members of Parliament would have joined the Social Democrats, and the party structure would have disintegrated. Myself – I could be quite wrong about that.'

Divided and torn, the Labour Party ended 1981 in poor shape, as Michael Meacher agrees:

'The degree of bitterness which developed was certainly very unfortunate, very regrettable, for which I think ultimately at the 1983 general election we paid a terrible price . . . We started off in January 1981 with 46% of the poll. We ended 1981 with exactly half that, 23% of the poll . . . That is the biggest drop of any political party in the course of one year.'

The sharpest comment on this expulsion from the political Eden came from what, in the spectacular shifts of the British left, now seemed to be a new revisionist voice in the Labour movement: the Eurocommunist wing of the British Communist Party. Writing on the debate which had been started by his 1978 lecture, Eric Hobsbawm commented in 1981 that there was 'a confused and divided Labour movement, torn by splits and internal squabble, and isolated from many of its old supporters'. He argued that neither the enthusiasm of the activists who 'believed that organisation could replace politics', nor the trade union militancy of the seventies was enough. The former was too narrowly based, the latter too often sectional, advancing group economic interests rather than political class ones. Labour needed to remember that it had lost 'a significant part of the left-of-centre middle class, which long looked to Labour, and in many cases actually worked for Labour rather than some other party'. In addition it needed to exert a general appeal on working people, in advance of, not because of, their personal radicalisation, thus 'mobilising people who remember the date of the Beatles' break-up and not the date of the Saltley pickets . . .'

There were then, however, and will be in the future, many who believed that a unique moment to turn the Labour Party into a socialist movement with mass appeal, harnessing popular views – against Europe, against American bases and multinationals, against the arrogance of wealth and power – as effectively as Margaret Thatcher had done in another direction, came and went with the failure of the Benn campaign. There were gains for the left in any event. The movement towards greater democracy in the party was not to be undone. Indeed it continued, with each new undemocratic attempt to hold onto power which could be more widely shared coming under scrutiny in its turn. So the party had a chance to rebuild, considering how policy was created and tested, how votes were weighed and cast, as it had not done before the Campaign for Labour Party Democracy had opened up the debate. Only then could the long trail of defections, remarkable even in a decade of defections, be stopped. But in 1981 Labour had lost not merely a caucus of ex-cabinet ministers and MPs worried about their personal reselection, but many who saw themselves as natural social democrats in a broad coalition of the left.

What was remarkable, in contrast, was the way in which propositions at least as controversial as those at the centre of the Benn campaign were accepted and merged into the theology of the Conservative Party in the same period. Here again a populist leader with strong views, will, and an unflinching sense of self-rightness, challenged a party whose moderate wing held to other beliefs about what the country needed and would take. The party they were happy with was, in Julian Critchley's phrase:

'. . . not very interested in politics. It flew by the seat of its pants, it wanted to do the best by the country, it was not a party of doctrine or ideology.'

On this view, given a seat on the Board of Great Britain Ltd, you adjusted to events. If pressed for a rationale, you could always quote Disraeli. In the seventies it was not just the force of Margaret Thatcher's conviction politics which resisted and eventually broke with this approach. The real winners within the factional struggle were the monetarists – or rather that group among them who believed in the control of the money supply as the solution to the overriding problem of inflation. They had not been taken seriously under Heath, either by him or his civil servants. Lord Harris of High Cross notes that the Institute of Economic Affairs (IEA) had been cold-shouldered throughout that period:

'One of the most disappointing experiences we had was that we couldn't reach civil servants. [They] regarded the IEA throughout the early seventies as a crank or fringe institution to which no attention need be paid.'

During the first Thatcher government, however, the regard in which the IEA was held could not have been more different. When the new Conservative administration took office in 1979 many of those who had been entrenched in the traditional hierarchies of the party's research and organisation were dismissive of the new influences. 'We thought people like us were indispensable,' one remembers. 'After all the party had always relied on people like us.' By 1981 it no longer did. The monetarists in the new government left some ideologues on the left open-mouthed at their success in propounding a view which was nothing if not ideological. The proposition that the money supply was under the control of government, that it had a direct causal relationship with prices, or that there was some kind of natural rate for unemployment and output to which the economy would quickly adjust, was challenged in the party, but prevailed. The more their party appeared able to drive on without them, the more the wets were losers – although at the low point of October 1981 most of them thought that even a deeply divided opposition could not save Thatcher from electoral defeat next time. What form that defeat would take was not yet clear. The split in the Labour Party vastly complicated any result in a first-past-the-post electoral system.

What was clear already was that the Liberal Party, in its own terms, had emerged as a winner from the decade, despite having failed to make a mass breakthrough and having had to endure the long-drawn-out destruction of one of its most charismatic leaders in the events which led to Jeremy Thorpe's being charged with conspiracy to murder. The party had slowly increased its share of the vote throughout the sixties and seventies. It had been able to come through each slump in its vote with a higher baseline than before. In 1979 – Thorpe, and the raw attraction of the Thatcher alternative notwithstanding – the Liberals secured almost twice their 1970 share of the poll – 13.8% against 7.5%. Their new leader, David Steel, was shrewd enough to see that the effect of a Labour breakaway would be maximised by the creation of a new party, rather than by asking the defectors to join the Liberal Party – as, in similar situations, others had done before. It had to be a particular kind of new party, however, linked from the start to the Liberals.

In this, Steel was lucky. The fact that Roy Jenkins based his by-election campaign at Warrington on the principle of co-operation, with the Liberals working for him on the stump, gave him leverage over others in the new SDP who saw it as a mark two Labour Party. On record and outlook Jenkins was congenial to the Liberals. When he and his colleagues appeared at the 1981 Liberal Assembly at Llandudno, speaking at a packed fringe meeting, they heard the new alliance supported by the veteran Jo Grimmond. Grimmond's appeal to the

Liberals was pitched according to a delicately calculated blend of tactics and whimsy:

'I beg of you to seize this chance. Do not get bogged down in the niceties of innumerable policies. I have spent my life fighting against too much policy in the Liberal Party!'

The alliance was endorsed. Three of the Gang of Four were there to hear David Steel tell his party to 'go back to your constituencies and prepare for government'. David Owen, who had a different view of the destiny of the SDP, was absent. The new Alliance was crafted for the media. It was new. It was 'reasonable', and it was well packaged. In 1981, it seemed to soar from one triumph to another, the respectable result of Warrington being followed by the election of the Liberal William Pitt and the Social Democrat Shirley Williams in Tory strongholds. Steel's optimism at Llandudno seemed justified by these events. He says now that, at that moment:

'I still believed that it was possible for us to go straight in and confront the Conservative government with an alternative prospectus. I was wrong in that, but I was right in the sense that we were able to inflict grievous bodily harm on the Labour Party.'

The measure of that harm was that Britain now had something close to a three-party system, but with electoral procedures likely to squeeze out a third party, as they had in the past, and artificially to boost any party which secured more than 40% of the electoral vote. Labour, with a vote in secular decline for thirty years, and the number of electors who naturally identified with it falling proportionately, was vulnerable – more vulnerable than some of its leadership, who seemed to think that if the party got out of touch with the people it was time to change the people, understood. While Margaret Thatcher aimed for a majority of the majority – white, employed, property-owning; Labour was in danger of representing minorities of the minority which was its legitimate concern, championing unemployed against employed, North against South, non-white against white. Only in Scotland, where it remained a broadly-based national party, learning the lessons of the nationalist challenge in order to defeat it, did it look like the party of confident, majority reform that it had been in the age of Attlee.

The eclipse of the nationalist parties was one of the surprises of the late seventies. Plaid Cymru did not become the dominant voice of North Wales, in spite of the personal attractiveness of its leaders. The establishment of the Welsh language's parity with English remained its achievement, but it had little success in persuading the Welsh that their destiny could be separate from that of England. The SNP's decline in Scotland was, as its leaders realised, the consequence of their shocking the other parties into action. Britain did not break up, as eloquent commentators such as Tom Nairn had persuasively argued it would. Only in the unity of Britain and Northern Ireland were there signs of terminal stress. The attempt to build a constitutional nationalist party, the SDLP, to win the minority community to a gradual and non-violent evolution towards an Irish unity that was not based on the suppression of one national tradition by the other, was fatally stricken by the hunger strikes and the success of Sinn Fein at the 1981 Fermanagh by-elections. The British had gambled on the belief that, if the IRA's 'political wing' were able to run candidates as a legitimate party, it might be weaned from violence; while, if Sinn Fein rejected that approach, it would itself be rejected in the Catholic community. In 1981 that assumption began to be disproved. Sinn Fein gloried in violence, but paraded its sacrifices. The SDLP, which tried vainly to put a rational case in an irrational environment of paranoia and killing, began to lose ground.

The violence of language in Northern Ireland was matched by violence in deed. In that, what happened in the province was excep-tional. But the stridency of political utterance in the seventies, an assumption that politics had to come down to fundamentals long undisturbed, was not so confined. Corporatism, meshing the great interests of the realm, was discredited. So was the 'crisis avoidance' which, some argued, had been a characteristic of British politics for fifty years. By 1981 the civil service knew that, for once, it faced a government which would not accommodate to its instincts and re-straints. The British had found it hard to shed illusions about them-selves without creating new ones. Having led the world into the industrial age, they were uneasily aware that if they led it out again few would follow. Like their entertainment media, they took refuge in the hope of re-creating the past golden age of their choice: Victorian England and Coketown values for Margaret Thatcher, the 1940s for the Labour Party, the days when they had been the brightest and the best for the Social Democrats. The problem was that such a road led, for Thatcher, through the 1930s; for Labour, through the 1960s; and for the SDP, through half the political spectrum.

The corporatists, who had believed that in the end different kinds of British conservatism could be accommodated, had lost out. Their views had not been replaced by an agreement that unemployment on the one hand and rapid inflation on the other were equally the concerns of the community as a whole. The belief that majorities were comprised of overlapping minorities had been another casualty. Sometimes the minorities – working women, pensioners, blacks, community associations – were able to rally in defence of hard-won gains. Often they were overborne. A new interdependence would have to come from the bottom up.

A last look back

Looking back from the present to Britain in 1981, the view is complex, contradictory, not yet in the pattern of things. So the last glimpse must be of one small part of the mosaic which will one day blend with the rest, a personal impression of a town in the English Midlands as it was. According to the census, it has a profile close to the natural average, for owner-occupiers, and 'A' levels, and unemployed.

It stands on one of the tributaries of the Trent, that Offa's Dyke of psephologists, to the north rather than the south. It has sent two representatives to every parliament since the first, and always had a slight inferiority complex about its larger neighbour, twelve miles to the east. It has a church promoted to cathedral status, and able to dominate more than many grander piles because there are no high-rise buildings around it. In the sixties the civic fathers were cautious and old. ('Of the six councillors selected to receive me,' wrote Richard Crossman, 'two were over eighty and all were over sixty-two.'[15] There were no Dan Smiths, no soaring hopes that this would be the Athens of the north Midlands. There were no tower blocks either. Slums were flattened to make way for new council houses on the surrounding hills.

On arrival by train, on a line which has still not been electrified, you will find a line of waiting taxis where in the sixties there would have been a couple at most. The drivers are mostly immigrants from India and Pakistan. As you leave, you may see that in the rearmost taxis the Muslims among them are squatting in their rear seats facing Mecca, and at prayer. The taxi will take you through the inner city. There is some urban blight. Ancient terraces stand disembowelled. The graffiti of visiting football teams are all around. If you are there for a midweek or evening match, featuring the team with the famous name whose stadium stands isolated among the city clearances, you will see every remaining house shuttered against the endemic violence. The double

file of police, with horses and dogs, contains the visiting fans. You
hope you will survive the sudden eddies among the scarved samurai
on the terraces, where when you were a boy, thousands of men, with
caps and pipes and trilbies, stood silent and rapt.

You will pass the Sikh temple with its incongruous flag, you will
notice the bright flash of saris in the grey streets and young black
teenagers waiting for the drop-in centre to open. Unemployment here
was 2.9% in 1970. It is over 9% in 1981. A former nonconformist
church now taken over by the Serbians, a POW camp converted into a
Ukrainian holiday camp, where they dream of anti-Bolshevik cru-
sades, two Polish clubs, a West Indian centre, a half-finished Mosque:
the signs of a multiracial community abound. The new shopping
centre, financed by the Coal Board, dominates the town's redevelopment. It incorporates a new theatre. The old one has become an Indian
cinema.

At the edges of the dereliction, where planning blight and the
never-finished inner-ring road stop, there is a busy pace of conversion.
Housing improvement grants are rejuvenating the three-bedroom
terrace houses with their long gardens full of ancient roses. Ten
thousand like them have gone already, many of which were beyond
repair, some not. Housing charities slowly gain a firm hold among the
conversions, putting the disabled, the elderly and the troubled back
into the kind of dwellings they can manage.

Out on the estates another kind of conversion is under way. Council
tenants, young and middle-aged alike, have bought their houses at a
favoured price, and are decorating these new assets with Georgian
front doors, brass knockers, bow windows. Beyond stretch the sub-
urbs, villages once, now crowded havens where each new intake of
owner–occupiers laments the next influx to follow it, crowding
schools, spoiling the view. There are other streets where the adrenalin
of ownership does not flow, where no one can or would want to buy,
where the public housing stock may soon be concentrated. The social
workers and housing visitors who mark the rise in applications for
supplementary benefit, free school meals, family income supplement
hardly have time to reflect that, to those in office, they too are regarded
as claimants, importuning the public purse. They welcome, perhaps
more than once they did, the volunteers who have emerged to run
bands, football teams, lunch clubs for pensioners, and win all the other
battle honours of the streets.

You see the great industries where once they made the thingummyjigs that won the war. The biggest and best have survived bankruptcy and reconstruction to stay in the world league. But most of the machines stand idle, and the talk is of low order books and voluntary redundancy. Among the youngest workers, though, as they joke in the canteen over the *Sun* and the *Mirror*, the belief is still that if you have a time-served skill it will see you through life, as it saw your father before you. Many of them have voted Tory: a first-time vote for chance and change; stick or twist after that. In the smaller factories and foundries there is a quiet desperation. The PAYE is six months late, the Revenue are pressing, the prices cannot compete with components from Italy, Japan and Taiwan. Short-time working postpones the day of reckoning, but for many of these men and women this will be the year they walked out of the factory their fathers worked in, for the last time.

In the main street and around the old marketplace you hear the tramp of displaced traders. Some are throwing it in because they are trapped between the more labour-intensive Asian family businesses below and the multinational superstores above. When their shops reopen, it will be as branches of the building societies which now dominate the old shopping centres, as licensed bookmakers, or to cater for the new craze of video hire. The cinemas have closed, giving to bingo what was meant for a great popular art. Only local enthusiasts, with a grant from the British Film Institute, still provide the magic of the movies. Here, as in a dozen different activities around the town, voluntarism is in vogue once more. If seven just men and women were needed to save the city, you could find them here. They are the people whom J. B. Priestley found, and *Mass Observation* documented. They are a long way from the great ones mentioned in this book, but in the end it will be their hands that will fashion a tolerant and productive society from the detritus of 'deindustrialisation'. They do not remember the seventies as 'the devil's decade', but their memories hold little enthusiasm. They have an uneasy sense that changes outside their personal world will not match the comforts within it. Will they be able to cope, when the bill comes in? I am as sure that they can as my father was that they could build the Merlin engine in time, when a different danger threatened.

CHAPTER NOTES

Introduction and acknowledgements (pages xiii–xvii)
1. Günter Grass, *From the Diary of a Snail*. Secker and Warburg, 1974.

1: The End of Some Illusions (pages 1–28)
1. Richard H. S. Crossman, *The Diaries of a Cabinet Minister*, Vol. 1, p. 71. Hamish Hamilton/Jonathan Cape, 1975.
2. *Diaries of a Cabinet Minister*, Vol. 1, p. 321.
3. Harold Wilson, *The Labour Government – A Personal Record*, p. 257. Weidenfeld and Nicolson/Michael Joseph, 1971.
4. Barbara Castle, *The Castle Diaries 1964–70*, p. 148. Weidenfeld and Nicolson, 1984.
5. Cecil Harmsworth King, *Diary 1965–70*, p. 78. Jonathan Cape, 1972.
6. *Diaries of a Cabinet Minister*, Vol. 2, p. 156, 1976.
7. *Diaries of a Cabinet Minister*, Vol. 2, p. 158.
8. *Diaries of a Cabinet Minister*, Vol. 2, p. 159.
9. Peter Jay, *The Times*, 23 November 1967.
10. *Castle Diaries 1964–70*, p. 325.
11. Susan Crosland, *Tony Crosland*, p. 201. Jonathan Cape, 1982.
12. Hugh Cudlipp, *Walking on the Water*, p. 326. Bodley Head, 1976.
13. *Diaries of a Cabinet Minister*, Vol. 3, p. 31. 1977.
14. *Castle Diaries 1964–70*, p. 551.
15. *Castle Diaries 1964–70*, p. 660.
16. *Tony Crosland*, p. 148.

2: A Man with a Pipe . . . (pages 29–50)
1. Robert Rhodes James, *Ambitions and Realities*, p. 133. Weidenfeld and Nicolson, 1972.
2. John Ramsden, *The Making of Conservative Policy*, p. 249. Longman, 1980.
3. Enoch Powell, *The Limits of Laissez-Faire*, Crossbow, 1960.
4. *Ambitions and Realities*, p. 158.
5. D. Butler and M. Pinto-Duschinsky, *The British General Election of 1970*, p. 92. Macmillan, 1971.
6. Andrew Alexander and Alan Watkins, *The Making of the Prime Minister*, p. 112. Macdonald, 1970.
7. Richard H. S. Crossman, *The Diaries of a Cabinet Minister*, Vol. 3, p. 725. Hamish Hamilton/Jonathan Cape, 1977.
8. Barbara Castle, *The Castle Diaries 1964–70*, p. 799. Weidenfeld and Nicolson, 1984.
9. Marcia Williams, *Inside No. 10*, p. 264. Weidenfeld and Nicolson, 1972.

10. Ed. John Woods, *Powell and the 1970 Election*, p. 119. Paperfront Books, 1971.
11. Jim Slater, *Return to Go*, p. 97. Futura, 1978.
12. Ed. Raymond Williams, *The May Day Manifesto*. Penguin, 1968.
13. Figures taken from: Eds. P. Townsend and Nicholas Bosanquet, *Labour and Inequality*. Fabian Society, 1972.
14. *British General Election of 1970*, p. 346.

3: *Preparing for Europe (pages 51–69)*
1. Douglas Hurd, *An End to Promises*, p. 72. Collins, 1979.
2. Uwe Kitzinger, *Diplomacy and Persuasion*, p. 74. Thames and Hudson, 1973.
3. *Diplomacy and Persuasion*, p. 114.
4. *An End to Promises*, p. 62.

4: *Heath and the Search for Solutions (pages 70–98)*
1. Eric Heffer, *The Class Struggle in Parliament*, p. 231. Gollancz, 1973.
2. Michael Crick, *Scargill and the Miners*, p. 58. Penguin, 1984.
3. Douglas Hurd, *An End to Promises*, p. 103. 1979.
4. Quoted in: Ed. Richard Ritchie, *A Nation or No Nation*, Batsford, 1978.
5. Quoted in *A Nation or No Nation*, p. 23.
6. Cecil Harmsworth King, *Diary 1970–74*, pp. 202 and 267. Jonathan Cape, 1975.
7. Anthony Sampson, *A New Anatomy of Britain*, p. 501. Hodder and Stoughton, 1971.
8. Jim Slater, *Return to Go*, p. 155. Futura, 1978.
9. Nigel Broakes, *A Growing Concern*, p. 178. Weidenfeld and Nicolson, 1979.
10. John Plender, *That's the Way the Money Goes*, p. 92. André Deutsch, 1982.
11. Margaret Reid, *The Secondary Banking Crisis 1973–75*, p. 64. Macmillan, 1982.
12. Joseph Jackson and K. L. Young; Ferguson and General Investments Ltd, A Department of Trade Inquiry, 1979.

5: *The Oil Burn (pages 99–115)*
1. Douglas Hurd, *An End to Promises*, p. 108. Collins, 1979.
2. *An End to Promises*, p. 114.
3. Joe Gormley, *A Battered Cherub*, p. 127. Hamish Hamilton, 1982.
4. *An End to Promises*, p. 121.
5. *An End to Promises*, p. 125.
6. *An End to Promises*, p. 133.
7. Cecil Harmsworth King, *Diary 1970–74*, p. 348. Jonathan Cape, 1975.

6: *The Social Contract (pages 116–33)*
1. Ed. Dennis Kavanagh, *The Politics of the Labour Party*, p. 181. Allen and Unwin, 1982.
2. Barbara Castle, *The Castle Diaries 1970–74*, p. 10. Weidenfeld and Nicolson, 1980.
3. Michael Hatfield, *The House the Left Built*, p. 79. Gollancz, 1975.
4. Quoted in *The House the Left Built*.

5. Joel Barnett, *Inside the Treasury*, p. 24. André Deutsch, 1952.
6. Harold Wilson, *Final Term: The Labour Government 1974–1976*, p. 33. Weidenfeld and Nicolson/Michael Joseph, 1979.
7. Terry Coleman, *The Scented Brawl*, p. 840. Elm Tree Books, 1976.
8. *Final Term*, p. 84.
9. D. E. Butler and Dennis Kavanagh, *The British General Election, October 1974*, Macmillan, 1975.
10. Gerald Kaufman, *How to be a Minister*, p. 17. Sidgwick and Jackson.

7: *The Party's Over (pages 134–55)*
1. Harold Wilson, *Final Term; The Labour Government 1974–1976*, p. 108. Weidenfeld and Nicolson/Michael Joseph, 1979.
2. Barbara Castle, *The Castle Diaries 1974–76*, p. 357. Weidenfeld and Nicolson, 1980.
3. Quoted in Philip Goodhart, *Full-hearted Consent*, p. 173. Davis-Poynter, 1976.
4. *Castle Diaries 1974–76*, p. 406.
5. Gerald Kaufman, *How to be a Minister*, p. 53. Sidgwick and Jackson.
6. *Castle Diaries 1974–76*, p. 393.
7. *Castle Diaries 1974–76*, p. 410.
8. *Castle Diaries 1974–76*, p. 415.
9. Michael Stewart, *The Jekyll and Hyde Years*, p. 201. Dent, 1977.
10. *Castle Diaries 1974–76*, p. 396.

8: *The Other Island (pages 156–80)*
1. Rex Cathcart, *The Most Contrary Region*, p. 193. The Blackstaff Press, 1984.
2. Brian Faulkner, *Memoirs of a Statesman*, p. 50. Weidenfeld and Nicolson, 1978.
3. Sarah Nelson, *Ulster's Uncertain Defenders*, p. 118. Appletree Press, 1984.
4. *Memoirs of a Statesman*, p. 191.
5. Conor Cruise O'Brien, *States of Ireland*, p. 299. Hutchinson, 1974.
6. *Ulster's Uncertain Defenders*.
7. Peter Taylor, *Beating the Terrorists?*, p. 339. Penguin, 1980.
8. Padraig O'Malley, *Uncivil Wars*, p. 306. The Blackstaff Press, 1983.

9: *The Road to the IMF (pages 181–201)*
1. Leo Pliatzky, *Getting and Spending*, p. 137. Blackwell, 1982.
2. Susan Crosland, *Tony Crosland*, p. 355. Jonathan Cape, 1982.
3. *Tony Crosland*, pp. 377–8.

10: *Progress Denied (pages 202–20)*
1. Eds. Alexander Cockburn and Robin Blackburn, *Student Power*, p. 101. Penguin, 1969.
2. Eds. C. B. Cox and A. E. Dyson, *Black Paper 2*, p. 108. 1969.
3. Terry Ellis *et al.*, *William Tyndale – The Teachers' Story*, p. 43. Writers and Readers Publishing Co-Op, 1976.
4. *Black Paper 2*, p. 133.
5. Stuart Hall *et al.*, *Policing the Crisis*. Macmillan, 1978.
6. Ed. Philip Norton, *Law and Order in British Politics*, p. 39. Gower, 1984.

7. Michael Tracy, *A Variety of Lives*, p. 313. Bodley Head, 1983.
8. Peregrine Worsthorne, *Peregrinations*, p. 5. Weidenfeld and Nicolson, 1980.
9. Malcolm Bradbury, *The History Man*. Secker and Warburg, 1975.
10. Kingsley Amis, *The Alteration*. Jonathan Cape, 1976.
11. Patrick Hutber, *The Decline and Fall of the Middle Class – And How It Can Fight Back*, p. 54. Penguin, 1977.
12. Arthur Seldon, *Charge*. Temple Smith, 1977.
13. Robert Moss, *The Collapse of Democracy*. Temple Smith, 1975.
14. *Decline and Fall of the Middle Class*, p. 12.
15. Ed. R. King and Neill Nugent, *Respectable Rebels*, p. 82. Hodder and Stoughton, 1979.
16. Joe Rogaly, *Grunwick*, p. 149. Penguin, 1977.
17. Richard Clutterbuck, *Britain in Agony*, p. 209. Faber and Faber, 1978.
18. *Conservative Monthly News*, August 1977.

11: Black British (pages 221–38)
1. John Rex, *Race, Community and Conflict: A Study of Sparkbrook*. OUP, 1969.
2. A. Sivanandan, *A Different Hunger*, p. 24. Pluto Press, 1982.
3. Philip Mason, *A Thread of Silk*, p. 185. Michael Russell, 1984.
4. *Thread of Silk*, p. 182.
5. Stuart Hall in *Racism and Reaction*, p. 25: 'Five Views of Multi-Racial Britain'. CRE, 1978.
6. Stuart Hall in *Racism and Reaction*, p. 30.
7. Linton Kwesi Johnson, 'Inglan is a Bitch', p. 26. Race Today Publications, 1980.
8. Stuart Hall *et al.*, *Policing the Crisis*, p. 81 *et seq.* Macmillan, 1978.
9. Paul Gordon, *White Law*, p. 51. Pluto Press, 1983.
10. Martin Walker, *The National Front*, p. 224. Fontana/Collins, 1977.
11. Nicholas Wapshott and George Brock, *Thatcher*, p. 156. Futura, 1983.
12. *Southall, 23 April 1979*, p. 12. NCCL, 1980.
13. Muhammed Anwar, *Votes and Policies*, p. 38. CRE, 1980.
14. *Civil Disorder and Civil Liberties*, p. 14. NCCL, 1981.
15. Linton Kwesi Johnson, 'Time Come' in *Dread Beat and Blood*. Bogle-L'Ouverture Publications, 1975.

12: The Wheatgerm Age (pages 239–55)
1. Philip Lowe and Jane Goyder, *Environmental Groups in Politics*. Allen and Unwin, 1983.
2. Charles Reich, *The Greening of America*, Allen Lane, 1971. *and see:* Francis Sandbach, *Environment, Ideology and Policy*, p. 27. Blackwell, 1980.
3. E. F. Schumacher, *Small is Beautiful*, p. 82. Blond and Briggs, 1973.
4. Paul Ehrlich, *The Population Bomb*, p. 89. Pan/FOE, 1971.
5. Philip Larkin, in *High Windows*. Faber and Faber, 1974.
6. Fred Hirsch, *Social Limits to Growth*. Routledge and Kegan Paul, 1977.
7. Lionel Esher, *A Broken Wave*, p. 143. Pelican, 1983.
8. Brian Anson, *I'll Fight You For It*, p. 169. Jonathan Cape, 1981.
9. Mervyn Jones, *Holding On*, p. 301. Quartet, 1973.
10. Tony Parker, *The People of Providence*. Hutchinson, 1983.

11. *Broken Wave*, p. 239.
12. John Tyme, *Motorways versus Democracy*, p. 23.
13. *Planning and Plutonium*, Town and Country Planning Association, 1978.
14. *Environmental Groups in Politics*, p. 75.
15. Howard Newby, *Green and Pleasant Land*. Hutchinson, 1979.
16. Marion Shoard, *Theft of the Countryside*, p. 9. Temple Smith, 1980.

13: Nudging the Banks (pages 256–86)
1. Richard H. S. Crossman, *The Diaries of a Cabinet Minister*, Vol. 1, p. 69. Hamish Hamilton/Jonathan Cape, 1975.
2. Denis Barnes and Eileen Reed, *Government and the Trade Unions*, p. 212. Heinemann Educational, 1980.
3. David Steel, *A House Divided*, p. 125. Weidenfeld and Nicolson, 1980.
4. Hillel Levin *John De Lorean*, p. 155. Orbis, 1983.
5. Barbara Castle, *The Castle Diaries 1974–76*. Weidenfeld and Nicolson, 1980.
6. Peter Kellner and Lord Crowther-Hunt, *The Civil Servants*, p. 279. Macdonald, 1980.
7. *Castle Diaries 1974–76*, pp. 227–8.
8. Gerald Kaufman, *How to be a Minister*, p. 112. Sidgwick and Jackson.
9. Joel Barnett, *Inside the Treasury*. Deutsch, 1982.

14: The Scottish Crowbar (pages 287–302)
1. George Orwell, *Collected Letters*, Vol. 4. Secker and Warburg, 1968.
2. J. McGrath, *The Cheviot, the Stag and the Black, Black Oil*, p. 63. Methuen, 1981.
3. John P. Mackintosh, *Mackintosh on Scotland*, ed. H. M. Drucker, p. 148. Longman, 1982.
4. Stephen Hugh-Jones, 10 September 1983

15: Jubilee! (pages 303–8)
1. F. and J. Vermorel, *The Sex Pistols*, p. 97.
2. Peregrine Worsthorne, *Peregrinations*. Weidenfeld and Nicolson, 1980.

16: The Women's Hour (pages 309–21)
1. Philip Larkin, *High Windows*. Faber and Faber, 1974.
2. Sheila Rowbotham, 'Working Class Heroes'. *Spare Rib* 21, 1974.
3. Betty Friedan, *The Feminine Mystique*. Penguin, 1976.
4. Anna Coote and Beatrix Campbell, *Sweet Freedom*, p. 17. Picador, 1983.
5. Sheila Rowbotham, *Dreams and Dilemmas*, p. 39. Virago, 1983.
6. Anthony Sampson, *A New Anatomy of Britain*, p. 174. Hodder and Stoughton, 1971.
7. Jonathan Lynn and Antony Jay, *The Complete Yes Minister*, p. 360. BBC Publications, 1984.
8. Leo Abse, *Private Member*. Macdonald, 1973.
9. Mary Whitehouse, *Whatever Happened to Sex?*, p. 17. Hodder and Stoughton, 1977.
10. Patrick Cosgrave, *Margaret Thatcher*, p. 14. Hutchinson, 1978.

11. Zoë Fairbairns, *Benefits*, p. 56. Virago, 1979.
12. *Dreams and Dilemmas*, p. 313.

17: The Only Man on the Front Bench (pages 322–38)
1. R. T. Mackenzie, *British Political Parties*, p. 145. Mercury Books, 2nd edition, 1963.

18: Breakaway (pages 339–64)
1. Richard Crossman, *Backbench Diaries*, p. 280. Hamish Hamilton and Jonathan Cape, 1981.
2. Dick Taverne, *The Future of the Left*, p. 40. Jonathan Cape, 1974.
3. Quoted in John Campbell, *Roy Jenkins*, p. 167. Weidenfeld and Nicolson, 1983.
4. Austin Mitchell, *Four Years in the Death of the Labour Party*, p. 24. Methuen, 1983.
5. *Report of the Seventy-Eighth Annual Conference*, p. 186. The Labour Party, 1979.
6. *Report of the Seventy-Ninth Annual Conference*, p. 31. The Labour Party, 1980.
7. David Owen, *Face the Future*. 1st ed., Jonathan Cape, 1981; 2nd ed., OUP, 1981.

19: Drying Out the Wets (pages 365–90)
1. Hugh Stephenson, *Mrs Thatcher's First Year*, p. 9. Jill Norman, 1980.
2. Peter Riddell, *The Thatcher Government*, p. 59. Martin Robertson, 1983.
3. Douglas Jay, *Sterling – A Plan for Moderation*, p. 164. Sidgwick and Jackson, 1985.
4. Jock Bruce-Gardyne, *Mrs Thatcher's First Administration*, p. 59. Macmillan, 1984.
5. Norman St John-Stevas, *The Two Cities*, p. 43. Faber and Faber, 1984.
6. Padraig O'Malley, *Uncivil Wars*, p. 272. Blackstaff Press, 1983.
7. Martin Kettle and Lucy Hodges, *Uprising*, p. 250. Pan, 1982.
8. Julie Burchill, *Love It Or Shove It*, p. 8. Century, 1985.
9. Julian Critchley, *Westminster Blues*, p. 123. Elm Tree/Hamish Hamilton, 1985.

20: Winners and Losers (pages 391–413)
1. Margaret Drabble, *The Ice Age*. Weidenfeld and Nicolson, 1977.
2. Barry Hines, *Looks and Smiles*. Michael Joseph, 1981.
3. Richard Clutterbuck, *Industrial Conflict and Democracy*, p. 174. Macmillan, 1984.
4. Anthony Sampson, *A New Anatomy of Britain*, p. 669. Hodder and Stoughton, 1971.
5. Padraig O'Malley, *Uncivil Wars*, p. 245. The Blackstaff Press, 1983.
6. Seamus Heaney, *North*. Faber and Faber, 1975.
7. A. H. Halsey, *Change in British Society* p. 174. Oxford University Press, 1978.
8. Tina Brown, *Life as a Party*. Deutsch, 1983.
9. A. H. Halsey *et al.*, *Origins and Destinations*, p. 186. Oxford University Press, 1980.
10. Jock Bruce-Gardyne, *Mrs Thatcher's First Administration*, p. 168. Macmillan, 1984.
11. A. B. Atkinson, *A Study of Inequality*.

12. *Change in British Society.*
13. Ed. D. Kavanagh, *The Politics of the Labour Party*, p. 23. Allen and Unwin, 1982.
14. Eric Hobsbawm, *The Forward March of Labour Halted?* (eds. Martin Jacques and Francis Mulhern), p. 168. Verso, 1981.
15. Richard H. S. Crossman, *The Diaries of a Cabinet Minister*, Vol. 1, p. 254. Hamish Hamilton/Jonathan Cape, 1975.

NOTE ON CONTRIBUTORS

For their contributions, during personal interviews, both on and off the record, to the television series and book of *The Writing on the Wall*, I am glad to be able to record our indebtedness to:

Professor Brian Abel-Smith, Jack Adams, Sir Campbell Adamson, James Airlie, Rt Hon. Lord Aldington, John Amos, Keith Andrews, Brian Anson, Rt Hon. Sir Humphrey Atkins MP, Dr Robert Bacon, Lord Bancroft, Rt Hon. Lord Barber, Paul Barker, Sir Denis Barnes, Rt Hon. Lord Barnett, David Basnett, Betty Bawden, Bill Beattie, Anthony Beaumont-Dark MP, David Beavis, Rt Hon. Tony Benn MP, Sir Kenneth Berrill, Rt Hon. John Biffen MP, Professor Tessa Blackstone, Lord Boardman, Dr Rhodes Boyson MP, Arthur Brannigan, Ian Brierley, Rt Hon. Leon Brittan, OG, MP, Sam Brittan, Lord Bruce-Gardyne, Sir Terry Burns, John Cameron, Beatrix Campbell, Bert Carless, Rt Hon. Lord Carr, Ray Carter, John Carty, Rt Hon. Barbara Castle MEP, Ray Chambers, Lord Chapple, Rt Hon. Christopher Chataway, Tony Churchman, Dave Clark, Dr Richard Clutterbuck, Jim Colgan, Ian and Nancy Connell, Sir Fred Corfield, Lady Cox, Malcolm Crawford, Francis Cripps, Lord Croham, Madge Crooks, Susan Crosland, Lord Crowther-Hunt, George Cunningham, Lawrence Daly, John Davidson, Gavyn Davies, John Davis, Professor Nicholas Deakin, Rt Hon. Edmund Dell, Rt Hon. Lord Denning, Vladimir Derer, Chief Constable W. Donaldson, Professor Henry Drucker, Rt Hon. Lord Eden, David Edgar, Sir Michael Edwardes, Dr Walder Eltis, Lord Esher, Mostyn Evans, Lord Ezra, Michael Farrell, Lady Faulkner, Frank Field MP, Sir Monty Finniston, John Firn, Alan Fisher, Lord Fitt, Rt Hon. Michael Foot MP, Paul Foot, Lord Fraser of Kilmorack, Professor Milton Friedman, Anthony Frodsham, Andrew Gamble, John Garnett, Lord George-Brown, Rt Hon. Sir Ian Gilmour MP, Paul Gilroy, Professor Wyn Godley, John Golding MP, Geoffrey Goodman, John Gorst MP, John Gouriet, Alan Gower, Richard Graham, William Gregson, Professor Brian Griffiths, Angus Grossart, Robin Grove-White, Sir Douglas Hague, Nigel Haigh, Peter Hain, Joe Haines, Lord Harris of High Cross, Dame Judith Hart MP, Rt Hon.

Denis Healey MP, Rt Hon. Edward Heath MP, Eric Heffer MP, Douglas Henderson, Paul Holborow, Dr Stuart Holland MP, Lord Home of the Hirsel, Sir Brian Hopkin, Peter Houghton, Rt Hon. Sir Geoffrey Howe QC, MP, Rt Hon. David Howell MP, Lord Hunt of Tanworth, Rt Hon. Douglas Hurd MP, Thelma Hyacinth, Tom Jackson, Jim Jardine, Derek Jarman, Sir Alex Jarratt, Rt Hon. Douglas Jay, Peter Jay, Rt Hon. Roy Jenkins MP, Jack Jones CH, Professor Lord Kaldor, Rt Hon. Gerald Kaufman MP, Lord Kearton, William Keegan, David Keene, Billy Kelly, Michael Kelly, Dr Gavin Kennedy, Alex Kitson, Sir Timothy Kitson, Gavin Laird, Jack Lally, Brendan Lamb, Alan Law, David Lea, Joan Lestor, Rt Hon. Lord Lever, Helen Liddell, Ken Livingstone, Rt Hon. Earl of Longford KG, Alan Lord, John Lyons, Bernadette McAliskey, Duncan McClennan, Dr Gavin McCrone, Harold McCusker MP, Peter Macgregor, Sir Ronald McIntosh, Kit McMahon, Tom McNally, Norris McWhirter, Margaret Maden, Euclid Mahon, Sir Donald Maitland, Sir Robert Mark, John Marks, Rt Hon. Lord Marsh, Sir Robert Marshall, Ian Martin, Stephen Maxwell, Michael Meacher MP, Ian Mikardo MP, Sir Derek Mitchell, Jamie Morris, Hon. Sara Morrison, Jim Mortimer, Chris Mullin, Sir Leslie Murphy, Lord Murray, Dipak Nandy, James Naughtie, Dr Howard Newby, Eyre Norville, Rt Hon. Sir John Nott, Sir Richard O'Brien, Larry O'Donnell, Sir Con O'Neill, Rt Hon. Stanley Orme MP, Professor Paul Ormerod, Herman Ouseley, Rt Hon. Dr David Owen MP, David Owen of Rubery Owen, Bill Page, Bruce Page, John Pardoe, Geoffrey Parker, Reg Parkes, Rt Hon. Cecil Parkinson MP, Sir Anthony Part, Chris Patten MP, Jack Peach, Don Perrygrove, Professor Maurice Peston, Rt Hon. Lord Peyton, Colin Phipps, Sir Leo Pliatzky, Jonathan Porritt, Rt Hon. Enoch Powell MP, Rt Hon. Reg Prentice MP, Rt Hon. James Prior MP, Rt Hon. Francis Pym MP, Reg Race, Jim Rae, Jimmy Reid, Margaret Reid, Professor John Rex, Sir Adam Ridley, Rt Hon. Nicholas Ridley MP, George Rieartie, Ron Rigby, Rt Hon. Geoffrey Rippon QC, MP, Derek Robinson, Sir John Rodgers, Rt Hon. William Rodgers, John Rosamund, Jack Russell, Rt Hon. Norman St John-Stevas MP, Lord Scanlon, Jeremy Seabrook, Lady Seear, Lynne Segal, Madron Seligman MEP, Brendan Sewill, Professor R. K. Shaw, Robert Sheldon MP, William Shelton MP, Ray Sherlock, Sir Aldred Sherman, Rt Hon. Peter Shore MP, Clare Short MP, Margaret Simey, Ex-US Treasury Secretary William Simon, Dennis Skinner MP, Rt Hon. John Smith QC, MP, T. Dan Smith, Ranjit Sondhi, Bernie Steer, Rt Hon. David Steel MP,

A. N. Stephen, Rt Hon. Donald Stewart MP, Rt Hon. Lord Stewart, Jack Straw MP, Dick Taverne QC, Robert Taylor, Mike Thomas, Rt Hon. Jeremy Thorpe, Andy Tyrie, Harry Unwin, Hon. William Waldegrave MP, Rt Hon. Peter Walker MP, Oliver Walston, Professor Sir Alan Walters, John Waring, Sir Douglas Wass, Professor Lord Wedderburn, Sidney Weighell, Ben Whitaker, Mary Whitehouse, Rt Hon. Viscount Whitelaw, Alan Whittome, Clive Wilkinson, Professor Bernard Williams, Rt Hon. Shirley Williams, Rt Hon. Lord Wilson of Rievaulx KG, Johannes Witteveen, Tess Woodcraft, Peter Woodsford, Hugh Wyper, George Young.

INDEX